Working with
dBASE IV and dBASE III PLUS

Working with dBASE IV and dBASE III PLUS

Bruce J. McLaren

Indiana State University

HarperCollins*Publishers*

Sponsoring Editor: Rick Williamson

Development Editor: Liz Lee

Project Coordination: BMR of Corte Madera

Text and Cover Design: Gary Palmatier, Ideas to Images

Cover Photograph: Murray Alcosser

Photo Research: BMR of Corte Madera

Production: Michael Weinstein

Compositor: Ideas to Images

Printer and Binder: Courier Corporation

Cover Printer: The Lehigh Press, Inc.

Working with dBASE IV and dBASE III PLUS

Library of Congress Cataloging-in-Publication Data

McLaren, Bruce J.
Working with dBASE IV and dBASE III PLUS / Bruce J. McLaren.
p. cm.
Includes index.
ISBN 0-06-500529-5
1. dBASE IV (Computer program) 2. dBASE III PLUS (Computer program) I. Title.
QA76.9.D3M3954 1991
005.75'65—dc20 91-34550
CIP

91 92 93 94 9 8 7 6 5 4 3 2 1

Contents

Preface

TEXT'S FOCUS

Virtually all people in the business environment need to know how to use a computer to assist in decision making and—more importantly—to boost their productivity. *Working with dBASE IV and dBASE III PLUS* offers a comprehensive introduction and keystroke tutorials for the best-selling database programs, dBASE IV and dBASE III PLUS.

HARDWARE REQUIREMENTS

This book targets the IBM-compatible microcomputer as the standard hardware. There are many excellent computers that meet this standard. Each machine should be equipped with a hard drive or connected to a local area network that provides the dBASE application software from a file server. While dBASE III PLUS does not require a hard drive, it operates better if a hard drive is present. dBASE IV does require use of a hard drive. Each machine should have at least 512 KB of random access memory, preferably 640 KB. A printer is essential.

FEATURES

In addition to covering the dBASE IV software package, *Working with dBASE IV and dBASE III PLUS* offers these features:

- The book begins with a discussion of the use and expansion of microcomputers, their application in business today, and an overview of products currently on the market. It is supplemented by Appendix A, a Buyer's Guide to evaluating and choosing new software and hardware.
- Detailed, step-by-step keystroke tutorials lead students through the software; they learn by actual hands-on experience.
- The writing style in *Working with dBASE IV and dBASE III PLUS* is clear and friendly.
- The text contains thorough explanations of the various commands, with realistic screen displays that illustrate their use.
- The dBASE III PLUS package is covered in a separate chapter, Chapter 8, complete with examples and a comparison with dBASE IV.
- The last chapter contains numerous examples of integrating data between dBASE, WordPerfect, and Lotus 1-2-3.

ORGANIZATION

The textbook consists of nine chapters:

- Chapter 1 contains an overview of microcomputer applications and a discussion of microcomputer hardware components. Chapter 2 deals with the DOS operating system and utility software programs such as Windows, PC-Tools, and Norton Utilities.

- Chapters 3 to 7 teach dBASE IV. The first dBASE chapter contains a concise QuickStart section, designed to get new users into the software as quickly as possible. Remaining chapters cover organizing the database, preparing reports and labels, building queries and screen forms, dBASE dot commands, SQL operations, and programming with dBASE IV.
- Chapter 8 provides an overview of the features in the dBASE III PLUS version for those instructors who want to cover that product. Chapter 9 is a comprehensive presentation of transferring data between dBASE and two other popular programs, WordPerfect and Lotus 1-2-3.

APPROACH

Working with dBASE IV and dBASE III PLUS presents a thorough and comprehensive view of this application. While the beginning chapter of each module presumes little knowledge by the user, later chapters present commands and techniques that advanced users will find useful in the business environment.

The discussion questions and exercises are designed to thoroughly test the student's knowledge. Exercises are graded by difficulty, and are organized by increasing degree of challenge.

LEARNING AIDS

Each chapter contains a number of learning aids for students:

- **Learning objectives,** five to fifteen per chapter, are placed at the beginning of each chapter.
- **Hands-on examples** and illustrations are used to demonstrate specific computing tasks. These clearly explained examples feature numbered steps and multiple screen illustrations. Most chapters have at least six examples.
- **Content summary,** one to three pages long, concludes each chapter and is organized by main chapter headings.
- **Key terms** list the commands and essential vocabulary covered.
- **Discussion questions** appear at the end of each chapter. These are suitable as short-answer examination questions or for class discussions.
- **Exercises** are challenging hands-on tests of knowledge—six to fifteen per chapter—that are presented in order of increasing difficulty for each chapter topic.
- **Chapter projects** are content-inclusive tasks concluding each chapter. Projects may be assigned for group solution, as extra credit, or as less-structured yet comprehensive exercises.

Appendices include a Buyer's Guide, a DOS command summary, and a summary of dBASE functions.

Chapter Exercises

A critical part of any software tutorial is the opportunity for students to test their skills. *Working with dBASE IV and dBASE III PLUS* includes more than 100 discussion questions and hands-on chapter exercises. Most are designed with business situations in mind, yet require little prior business knowledge. These challenging exercises appear in increasing order of difficulty so that instructors can choose the proper level.

A floppy disk containing data files is available with this textbook. The data disk includes database files, text files, Lotus spreadsheet and graph files, and various other files needed to solve the exercises. Use of the data disk enables students to focus on the assigned software task rather than on data input.

Solutions to all discussion questions and chapter exercises are provided in the Instructor's Manual and its accompanying solutions disk.

Comprehensive Chapter Projects

Each chapter ends with a comprehensive project. The project offers the student an opportunity to use the applications software to solve a realistic business problem. The projects are less structured and are more challenging than other chapter exercises. The project places the student in the role of a consultant retained to solve a particular problem. In this role the consultant must define objectives, consider alternatives, and build the model using the tools within the software package.

Extensive PC Buyer's Guide

Appendix A is included as a supplement for those interested in purchasing a new computer or upgrading existing equipment. It offers advice to the new buyer and goes into more detail about hardware components than Chapter 1 does. The five-step purchasing procedure will be helpful for those who aren't sure where to start. This Buyer's Guide will assist the course instructor who is constantly asked, "What shall I buy?"

SUPPORT PACKAGE

Each adopter of the text will receive an Instructor's Manual. The manual contains sample course outlines and numerous teaching suggestions for using the textbook. Each chapter has learning objectives, a detailed chapter outline, teaching hints, and complete solutions to all discussion questions and chapter exercises. Hints for solving chapter projects are also included. The solutions disk accompanying the manual has over 50 files containing solutions to each chapter exercise and most of the example files used within the text. A set of transparency masters and the data disk are included with the manual. A test bank is also included with the Instructor's Manual.

TO THE STUDENT

The material covered in this textbook is easily grasped if you practice on the computer while reading the chapter. First, read through the hands-on examples and the accompanying explanations. Then, while sitting at the computer, follow the same steps. Review your progress after each step when doing the examples. Compare your screen with the one in the textbook. Write down any differences or print a copy of the screen to discuss with your friends and the instructor.

Like any other learned skill, your computer knowledge will fade away if it is not used. Take every opportunity to practice using the software in other courses, your job, and in other applications. This book will serve as a reference in the future when you need to learn more of the dBASE commands and functions.

ACKNOWLEDGMENTS

Without the help of many people a project of this nature could not be completed. These individuals include colleagues, family, friends, students, reviewers, and publisher staff members.

My appreciation goes to the School of Business at Indiana State University and Dean Herb Ross for their support. In particular, I would like to thank Professors Belva Cooley, Dennis Bialaszewski, Jim Buffington, Kwang Soo Lee, Jennifer Lee, Billy Moates, and Ross Piper of the Systems and Decision Sciences Department at Indiana State University for their cooperation in reviewing the manuscript and using a previous version of this material in the classroom. Professors Sandy Barnard, John Swez, and Chat Chatterji gave valuable assistance. Paul Hightower provided some of the photographs used in the textbook. Emily Varble offered many suggestions for the manuscript.

I am grateful to numerous students at Indiana State University who used various drafts of the manuscript.

I would like to thank Vice President Anne Smith and CIS Editor Rick Williamson of HarperCollins for their support in this project. Business Media Resources and Gary Palmatier of Ideas to Images produced the text. My thanks go also to Liz Lee for her assistance in the development of the manuscript.

Many thanks go to the reviewers of this manuscript and its predecessor version. Reviewers included:

Robert M. Adams, Clarke College

William E. Burkhardt, Carl Sandburg College

Jason Chen, Gonzaga University

Amir Gamshad, Tennessee State University

Franca Giacomelli, Humber College

Douglas A. Goings, University of Southwest Louisiana

James Hanson, Cleveland State University

Ernest Harfst, Kishwaukee College

Ann W. Houck, Pima Community College

Anne M. Knicely, DeVry Institute

Carroll L. Kreider, Elizabethtown College

Patricia Laffoon, Union University

Dennis H. Lundgren, McHenry County College

Gretchen Marx, Saint Joseph College

Jeanne Massingill, Highland Community College

Cathleen C. McGrath, Highland Community College

Carl M. Penzuil, Corning Community College

Marilyn J. Pulchaski, Bucks County Community College

Tom E. Rosengarth, Westminster College

Laura Saret, Oakton Community College

James B. Shannon, New Mexico State University

Steven Silva, DeVry Institute

Richard G. Stearns, Parkland College

Susan V. Wiemers, McHenry County College

Finally, special thanks go to my wife, Professor Connie McLaren, for her steady encouragement and careful reading of everything associated with this manuscript. Without her support this book would not exist.

Bruce J. McLaren

Working with

dBASE IV and dBASE III PLUS

1

Microcomputer Software Applications

Objectives

After completing this chapter, you should be able to:

- Describe the categories of microcomputer applications in business.
- List the components of the system unit and describe their functions.
- Describe the three types of secondary storage devices.
- Discuss the various video options.
- List the types of printers and describe uses for each.
- Discuss connectivity options.
- List the steps in buying a personal computer (covered in Appendix A).

INTRODUCTION

In the few short years since 1982, personal computers (PCs) have changed the way computing is done. No longer are we tied to large, shared-use computers. Inexpensive personal computers have brought affordable computing to the desktops of all organizations. The more than seventeen million personal computers in use have dramatically increased the productivity of students, managers, office workers, and users of all kinds. Low cost and powerful software has enabled us to accomplish tasks directly, without going through the computer department. PCs can save time and make our work more accurate.

Although other types of microcomputers are briefly discussed in the first chapter, this textbook will focus on IBM-compatible personal computers. This first chapter will introduce you to some of the major microcomputer applications and take you on a tour of a microcomputer. Chapter 2 will cover the disk operating system (DOS) and some utility programs. Coverage of the dBASE IV database package begins with the Chapter 3 QuickStart section and proceeds in increasing detail in the following chapters. Chapter 8 provides an overview of other versions of dBASE. Chapter 9 details transfer of information between dBASE IV, Lotus 1-2-3, and WordPerfect 5.1. The Appendix contains a Buyer's Guide for selecting personal computing software and hardware as well as summaries of dBASE commands and functions.

Some chapter material, like that in this chapter, is designed to be read traditionally. At other times you will be reading along as you follow steps at the PC. Each hands-on application section is clearly marked as an **Example:**, with important actions highlighted in color. Of course, you will want to try many of the techniques on your own as you read about them. Remember, the more you experiment with and use an application, in this course and in others, the more skill you will develop!

BUSINESS APPLICATIONS SOFTWARE

Word processing software enables us to create documents—letters, reports, proposals, invoices—electronically (see Figure 1-1). Corrections are easily made, and letter-perfect copies can be quickly produced on a variety of printers and paper. Authors can make changes in page format and content rapidly, resulting in improved documents. Word processing software is able to correct spelling errors or offer suggestions for alternative wording. Personalized form letters can be prepared for a few or hundreds of people. Phrases can be highlighted for emphasis. With a laser or other high-quality printer, near-typeset documents can be produced quickly.

Electronic **spreadsheet software** is used for representing row-and-column worksheets of numbers (values) and words (labels) and has nearly replaced the calculator for many business applications (see Figure 1-2). You can create worksheets that will add columns of values, calculate percentages of a total, and prepare a graph of the values, all from the same program. Spreadsheets can be used to answer "what-if" questions—change a value and the spreadsheet will immediately recalculate the worksheet and display the results. Spreadsheets can be used to prepare budgets, accounting statements, sales forecasts, price lists, and financial ratio analyses. Extensive financial planning can be accomplished with spreadsheets, including loan amortization, present values, and depreciation. Professors use spreadsheets to calculate student grades and statistics. We can store data in spreadsheets and recall values that match certain criteria; for example, we might retrieve real estate listings that match a buyer's criteria. Spreadsheets can be used to quickly create bar and line graphs, and pie charts.

Database management software is used to store large amounts of data and permit us to recall certain records when needed (see Figure 1-3). Databases can be sorted on different data values (called key fields) and reports can be printed

```
Microcomputer Applications in Business

     Word processing software enables us to create documents --
     letters, reports, proposals, invoices -- electronically.
     Corrections are easily made, and letter perfect copies can be
     quickly produced on a variety of printers and paper. Authors can
     make changes in page  format and content rapidly, resulting in
     improved documents. Word processing software is able to correct
     spelling errors or offer suggestions for alternative wording.
     Personalized form letters can be prepared for a few or hundreds
     of people. Phrases can be highlighted for emphasis. With a laser
     or other high-quality printer, near-typeset documents can be
     produced quickly.

     Electronic spreadsheet software is used for representing row and
     column worksheets of numbers (values) and words (labels) and has
     nearly replaced the calculator for many business applications.
     You can create worksheets that will add columns of values,
     calculate percentages of a total, and prepare a graph of the
     values, all from the same program. Spreadsheets can be used to
     answer "what-if" questions -- change a value and the spreadsheet
     will immediately recalculate the worksheet and display the
     results. Spreadsheets can be used to prepare budgets, accounting
     statements, sales forecasts, price lists and financial ratio
D:\WP51\1-01.WP                                   Doc 1 Pg 1 Ln 1.33" Pos 2.5"
```

FIGURE 1-1

Screen Showing WordPerfect 5.1 Word Processing Software

```
A1: [W13] 'SMITHRV -- B. McLaren  6/27/89                                 READY

          A         B         C         D         E         F         G
1   SMITHRV -- B. McLaren  6/27/89
2
3               SMITHTON RECREATIONAL VEHICLE SALES, INC.
4
5                             1987      1988      1989
6                         ----------------------------
7   SALES                     1405      1205      1150
8   EXPENSES
9     Cost of Vehicles       786.8     674.8       644
10    Commissions           47.208    40.488     38.64
11    Salaries                 120     130.8   142.572
12    Administrative           175       175       175
13    Marketing/Adv.           180       220       250
14                        ----------------------------
15      Total Expenses    1309.008  1241.088  1250.212
16
17  GROSS PROFIT            95.992   -36.088  -100.212
18
19
20
01-Nov-90  04:32 PM
```

FIGURE 1-2

Screen Showing Lotus 1-2-3 Spreadsheet Software

in the desired order. You can build forms electronically to enter data directly into the database, without transcribing from paper records. A user can build a query to retrieve records that match specific criteria and output the information in sophisticated reports. Databases are used for storing medical information, lists of textbooks required for college courses, inventories of video tape libraries, student records, and much more. Data can be retrieved from the database and transferred to spreadsheet programs for further analysis. Data for form letters can be retrieved from the database and transferred to the word processor for printing. Some database management programs can be used to create full information systems, such as a cable television rental and billing system.

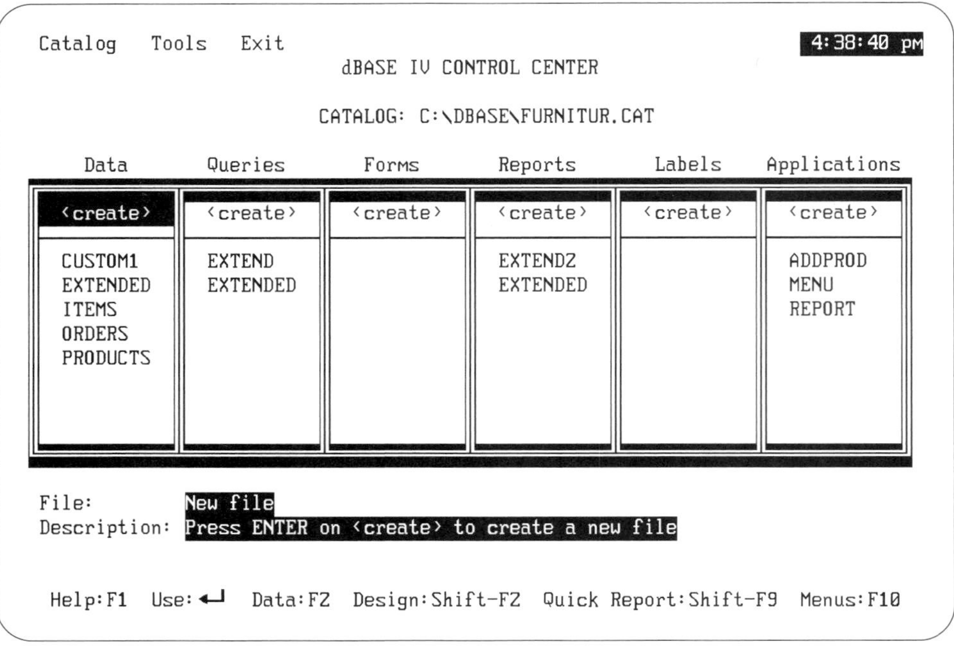

FIGURE 1-3

Screen Showing dBASE IV Database Software

Sophisticated business graphics are possible with **graphing application programs.** You can start with basic data from a spreadsheet program, or add data directly. Existing graphs can be annotated for emphasis. Three-dimensional, shaded, and multiple graphs can be created on the same page. Output can go to high-resolution black-and-white printers, to color printers, or to color slides. **Presentation graphics** are used to create text graphics with large letters for group presentations. Formal documents prepared with a word processor can include imported graphics. **Desktop publishing programs** produce reports and brochures that closely resemble typeset quality. Graphs and artwork can be included within such documents. Freehand artwork can be accomplished with paint packages. **Computer-assisted design (CAD) software** has all but replaced mechanical drawing with pencil and paper. Figure 1-4 shows a sample graph from the Harvard Graphics software package.

Personal computers are frequently used as **terminals,** communicating with remote-host computers over telephone lines. Users are able to check electronic mail and perform other tasks from home, on the road, or from the office. **Accounting applications** are often implemented on personal computers with inventory, accounts receivable and payable, general ledger, order entry, and more modules. Many taxpayers save time by using income tax software applications on a microcomputer. Not only is the process automated, but errors are avoided and you can quickly make changes if another deduction or inventory item is discovered. **Project management software** can assist the manager to oversee projects with long durations. Tasks can be entered into the project database and a critical path calculated. Progress against plan can be plotted, with tasks that have fallen behind schedule highlighted for attention.

Many **recreational applications** for microcomputers have been created. You can fly realistic airplanes and helicopters, skipper submarines, or handle air-traffic-controller duties. You can chase criminals in a world-wide pursuit; search for clues in a "who-dunnit"; play chess, bridge, football, golf, and baseball against the computer; or improve your SAT score. Many **personal improvement programs** are available, including packages that teach children math, language, and other skills. Library-type databases are available for microcomputers,

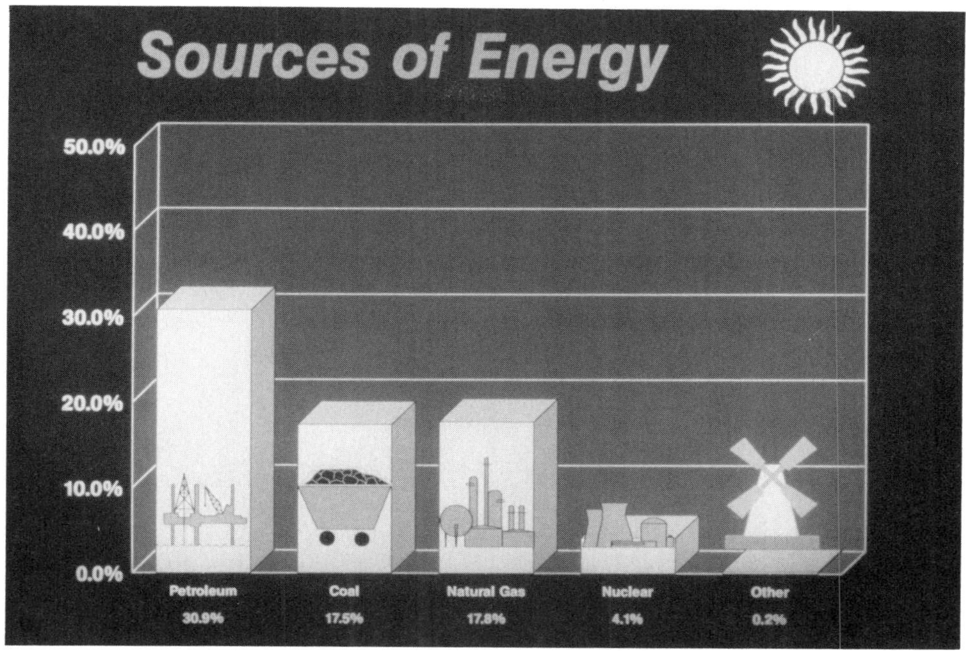

FIGURE 1-4

Sample Graph from the Harvard Graphics Software Package

including annotated and indexed Bible programs, demographic data, financial and stock market data, and industry statistics.

Programmers have access to the entire range of languages on microcomputers. BASIC is often included with the computer, and full-feature versions of all major languages—Pascal, COBOL, FORTRAN, C—are available. The personal computer is especially convenient for writing and debugging (correcting mistakes) programs in that it frees the programmer from relying on a large shared-use computer called a mainframe.

Each application improves the productivity of the user, and enhances the ability to do his job effectively. Many applications did not exist before microcomputers achieved widespread distribution, but are firmly entrenched today. In fact, the ease of use and friendly interface with the computer has affected the way mainframe computing applications are written today.

MICROCOMPUTER EQUIPMENT

Several different families of microcomputers are available today, but each shares a common set of system components. The computer consists of the system unit, some peripheral devices for input, output, and storage, various printing devices, and communications and expansion items. Figure 1-5 shows a schematic diagram of these components.

Figure 1-6 shows a typical IBM personal computer, and Figure 1-7 shows an Apple Macintosh computer. These represent the most popular business microcomputers available today.

Computer System Unit

The main module of the microcomputer is the system unit, consisting of a **microprocessor, primary memory** (RAM and ROM), **I/O ports** (input and output), and **expansion slots.** The components are mounted on a large electrical circuit board (called the **motherboard**) along with the power supply, on/off and reset switches, disk drives, and the video adapter board. The components are connected electrically to the **signal bus,** where the data, address, and control signals travel between parts of the computer. Figure 1-8 (on page 10) shows the inside of the system unit.

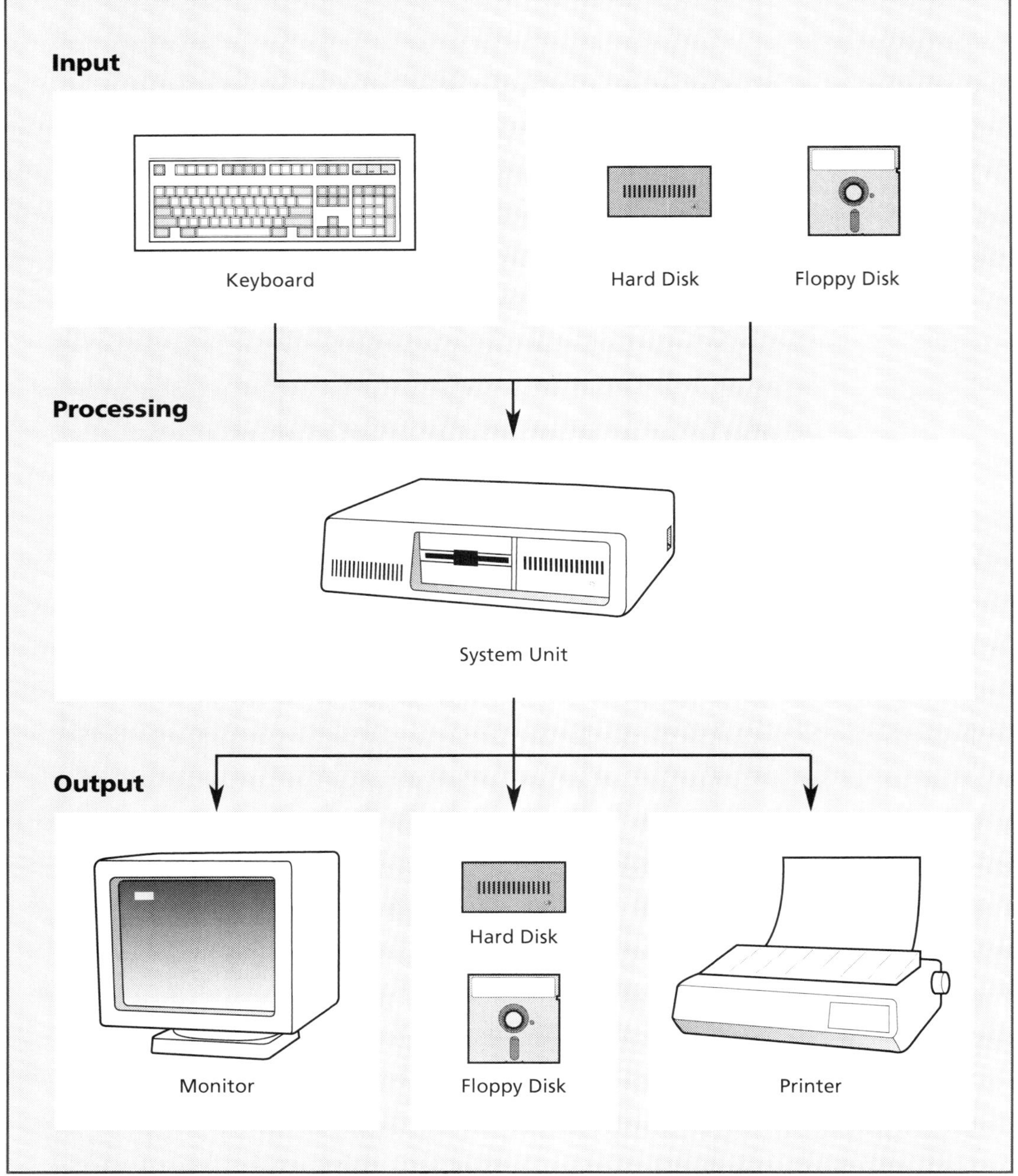

FIGURE 1-5

Microcomputer System Components

The Microprocessor

The microprocessor is a thumbnail-sized integrated circuit (chip) and is responsible for calculations and processing. IBM-compatible computers use the Intel family of microprocessors (8088, 8086, 80286, 80386SX, 80386, 80386SX, and 80486) while Apple Macintosh computers use Motorola microprocessors (68000, 68010, 68020, and 68030). The speed of the microprocessor is expressed in megahertz, or millions of clock cycles per second. Computers with faster processors are able to process more data but also cost more. Figure 1-9 shows an Intel 80486 microprocessor. Most computers have a socket for installing a **numeric coprocessor chip,** useful for speeding up numeric operations such as found in spreadsheet and graphics applications. Further discussion of these components is contained in the Buyer's Guide supplement in the Appendix.

FIGURE 1-6

IBM Personal Computer

FIGURE 1-7

Macintosh Personal Computer

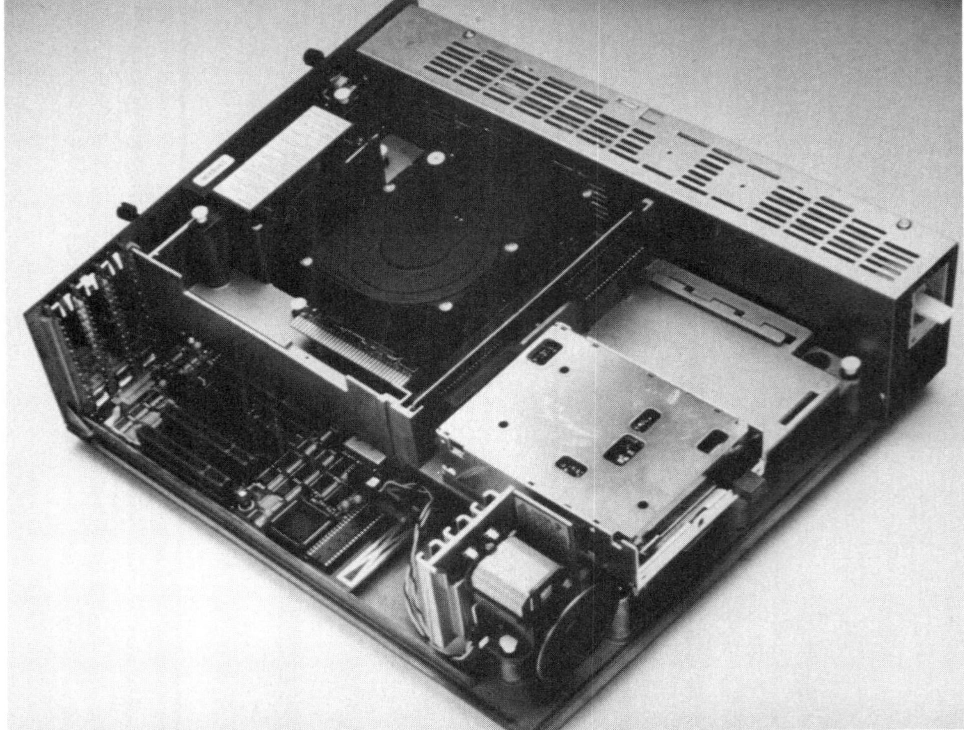

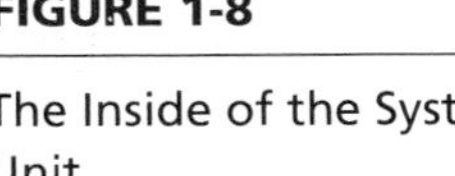

FIGURE 1-8

The Inside of the System Unit

Primary Memory: RAM and ROM

Primary memory is used to temporarily store the application programs and data while the programs execute. **Random access memory (RAM)** chips are volatile—that is, they only "remember" their contents while power is on in the computer. **Read-only memory (ROM)** chips are non-volatile, and programs stored in these chips are permanent. ROM chips are used for controlling the internal functions of the computer, not for applications programs. The BIOS (Basic Input-Output System) is stored on ROM chips.

The amount of RAM is measured in bits and bytes. A **bit** is a single storage point with a value of 0 or 1 and comes from the words "**b**inary dig**it**." A **byte** is a group of 8 bits, and represents one character of storage. The prefix *kilo-* in front of bit or byte means approximately one thousand; the *mega-* prefix means one million. Individual RAM chips are typically sold in 256-kilobit or 1-megabit sizes, but 4- and 16-megabit chips are on the horizon. DRAM stands for dynamic random access memory. Nine DRAM chips are needed for a complete set. A SIMM is a single in-line memory module consisting of nine DRAMs mounted on one carrier. Both types of RAM chips are common today.

The total amount of RAM in IBM-compatible computers is usually 640 kilobytes (640 KB) or more. Computers with more RAM can run larger programs and may execute these programs faster. The newer 80286 and 80386 computers may be ordered with 4 or more megabytes (MB) of RAM.

Input/Output (I/O) Ports: Parallel, Serial, Game

The system unit also contains the Input/Output (I/O) ports for the computer. Parallel interfaces use 8 wires to send all 8 bits (1 character) at the same time. The serial interface uses a single wire and sends the 8 bits one after another.

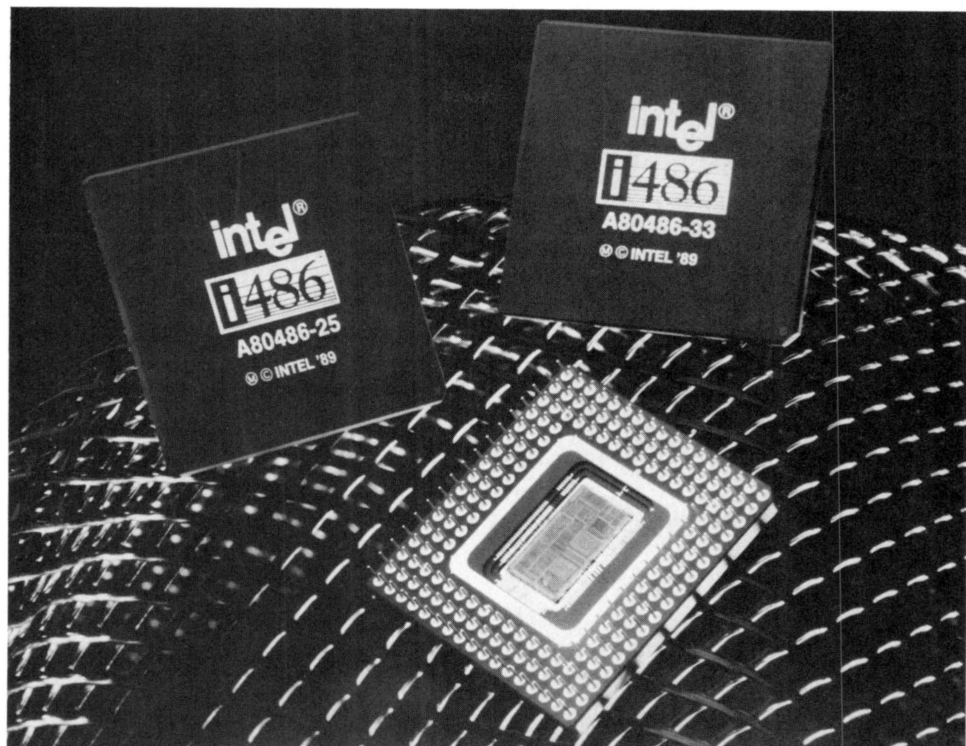

FIGURE 1-9

An Intel 80486 Microprocessor

Parallel interfaces transfer data much quicker than serial. **Parallel ports** are used for most printers. IBM-compatibles may contain up to three parallel ports (named LPT1, LPT2, and LPT3). **Serial ports** may also be used for printers, but are more often used for other peripherals such as an external modem or a mouse. IBM-compatible computers usually come with two serial ports (named COM1 and COM2) but newer computers may have COM3 and COM4 ports. A joystick can be connected to the **game port;** the game port is an extra-cost item in most computers. Many game programs can use a joystick to make inputs easier. Other ports in the system unit include connectors for the keyboard and monitor.

Expansion Slots

The system unit usually contains room for expansion cards that support additional features. These add-on cards are plugged into slots at the left rear of the system unit. The slots are attached directly to the **signal bus** of the computer, and thus can be accessed by the microprocessor and other circuits. The signal bus refers to the connections between various parts of the system unit. The edge of an expansion card protrudes from the rear of the computer and may have a cable connector for attaching a peripheral device. IBM has changed the type of expansion slots with each new personal computer family. The PC/XT models use the most common style that transfers 8 bits at a time. The AT model uses 8 additional data lines to transfer 16 bits at a time. The PS/2 line introduced the micro channel architecture (MCA) where 16 or 32 bits are transferred at a time. While PC/XT cards may be inserted into AT slots, the opposite is not true. And PC/XT/AT cards are not compatible with MCA cards. A typical expansion card is shown in Figure 1-10.

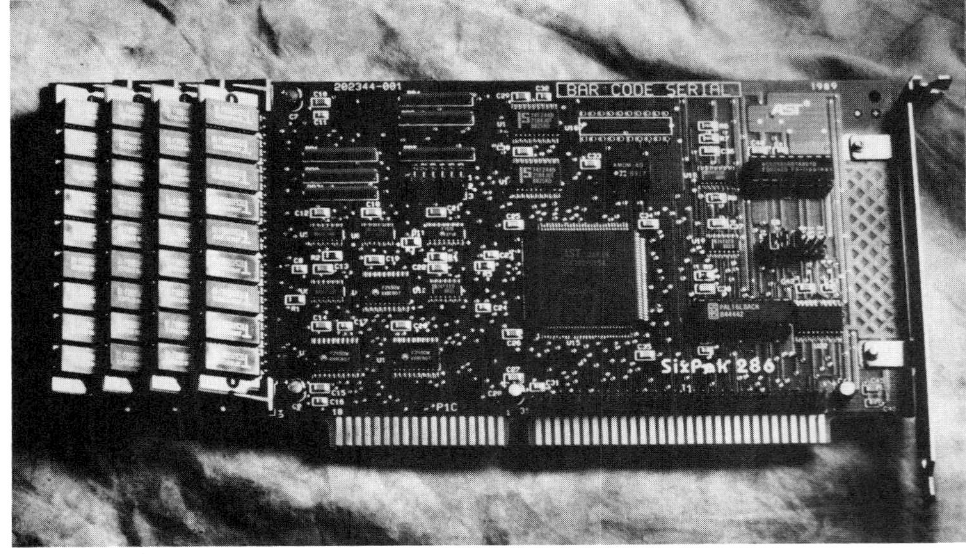

FIGURE 1-10

A Typical Expansion Card

Peripheral Hardware

Usually contained within the system unit are the data storage devices, floppy and hard **disks.** The **video adapter** and **video monitor** are used for visual output of text and graphics. The **keyboard** contains the usual typewriter keys, laid out in QWERTY fashion (top row letter keys begin with QWERTY), plus additional function and control keys used for entering commands. The **mouse** and **joystick** are pointing devices used to facilitate input. **Magnetic tape drives** are increasingly used to back up the contents of a hard disk drive to protect data in the event of a failure of the hard drive.

Disk Storage Devices

Floppy and hard disks are considered non-volatile (permanent) secondary storage units. Hard drives hold more data than RAM, and, because they use a magnetic code for storage, will retain their contents when power is removed from the computer. **Hard disks** are usually fixed within the computer and cannot be removed without disassembly. **Floppy disks** are used to distribute software, and can be moved from computer to computer. Common storage capacities of floppy disks range between 360 KB and 1440 KB (1.44 MB). The two most common floppy disk sizes (given as the diameter of the disk) are 5.25 inches and 3.5 inches. The earlier 8-inch size has been discontinued in favor of smaller disks. Most computers are being sold with the 3.5-inch disk drives. Notebook-size computers use 2-inch disks. Figure 1-11 shows several different floppy disk sizes. Figure 1-12 illustrates the capacities associated with various sizes of floppy disks.

Floppy Disks

Floppy disks are relatively inexpensive, yet provide secure storage of data if handled properly. Data are stored on a circular disk of mylar plastic that is coated with a magnetic material similar to that used in audio tapes. Figure 1-13 shows the construction and features of the two most popular types of floppy disks.

The 3.5-inch disks come with a hard-plastic case and a spring-loaded sliding door covering the area where data is written on the disk. The case is constructed so that the disk can be inserted only in the proper manner (the

FIGURE 1-11

Different Floppy Disk Sizes

Disk Size (diameter)	Type*	Capacity (bytes)**	
2 inches	DD	730,112	(720 KB)
3.5 inches	DD	730,112	(720 KB)
3.5 inches	HD	1,457,664	(1.44 MB)
5.25 inches	DD	362,496	(360 KB)
5.25 inches	HD	1,213,952	(1.2 MB)

* DD is Double Density, HD is High Density

** KB mean kilobytes, MB means megabytes

FIGURE 1-12

Capacities Associated with Various Sizes of Floppy Disks

5.25-inch disk could easily be misinserted in the drive). The disk also contains a write-protect window in the lower left corner. If the slide in the window is closed, the disk may be read from and written on normally. When the slide is moved and the window is open, the disk cannot be written on, a safety feature designed to protect valuable data.

The 5.25-inch disk has a rectangular slot in the upper right side. If the slot is open, the disk may be read and written on normally. When the slot is covered with an opaque metallic tape, the disk is write-protected. Unfortunately, the tape can loosen and fall off, rendering the write-protection inoperative. Because the jacket on a 5.25-inch disk is thin, never write on the disk or on the label attached to the disk except with a felt-tip pen. The pressure from the pen or pencil point could damage the surface of the disk, causing lost data. The hard case of the 3.5-inch disk allows the user to write safely on an attached label.

When carrying floppy disks, especially the 5.25-inch variety, protect them from becoming pinched (as in a three-ring binder) or from other physical

FIGURE 1-13

The Construction and Features of Floppy Disks

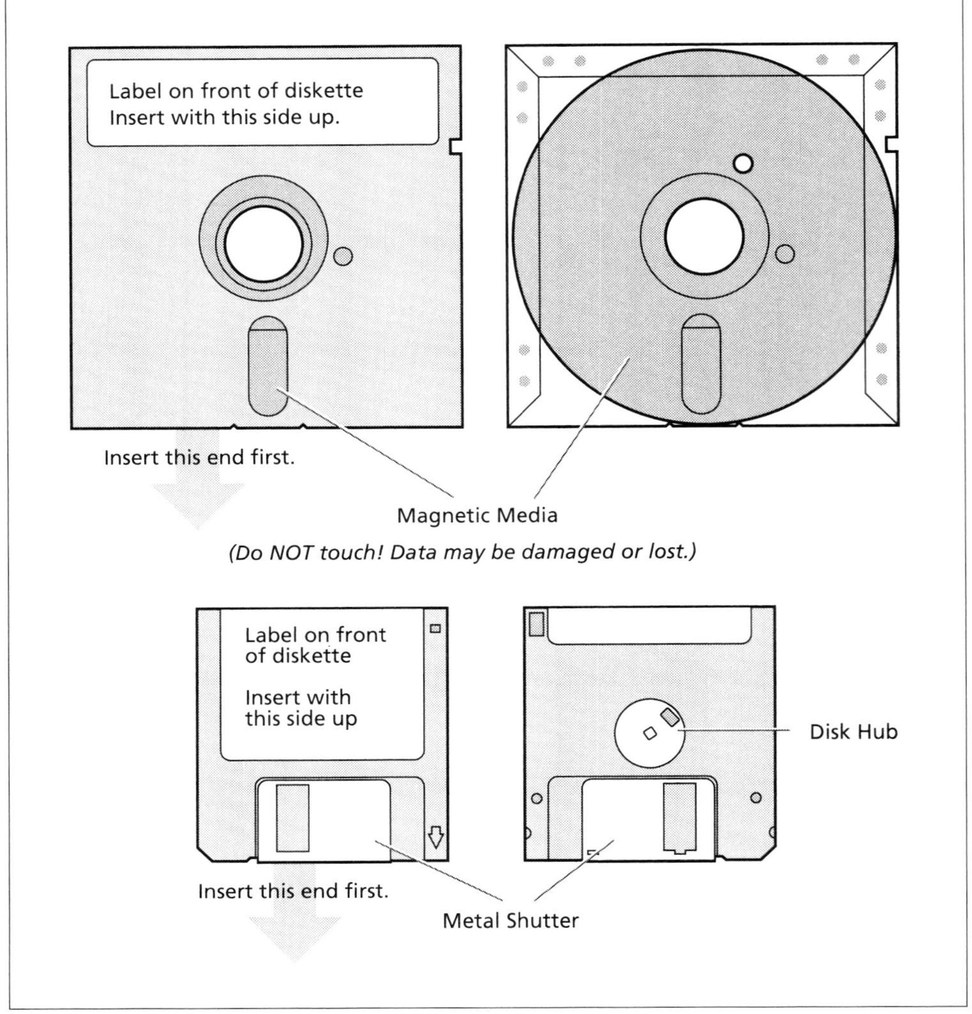

damage. Avoid magnetic fields of all kinds—even a tiny magnetic charge can erase your disk. Magnetic paper clip holders can ruin a disk. Never paper-clip a disk to other items. Avoid leaving disks in hot places, especially automobiles. Heat can damage or destroy the contents of a disk. Extreme cold and liquid spills can also harm a disk.

Hard Disk Drives

Hard disk drives provide spacious storage with very fast retrieval speeds. Storage capacities range from 20 MB to 100 MB or higher, representing the storage of 30 or more floppy disks. New computers designated for local area networks can range to 300 MB or more per drive, providing storage equivalent to many minicomputers. Hard drives use two or more highly polished, coated aluminum disks that spin at 3600 RPM. Hard drives provide access to data at ten times the rate of floppy disks. Most business computers use floppy disks for transferring software onto the hard disk, then programs and data are permanently stored on the hard drive.

Figure 1-14 shows the physical design of a typical hard disk drive. Each disk surface has its own read/write head, and there is a high-speed data link between

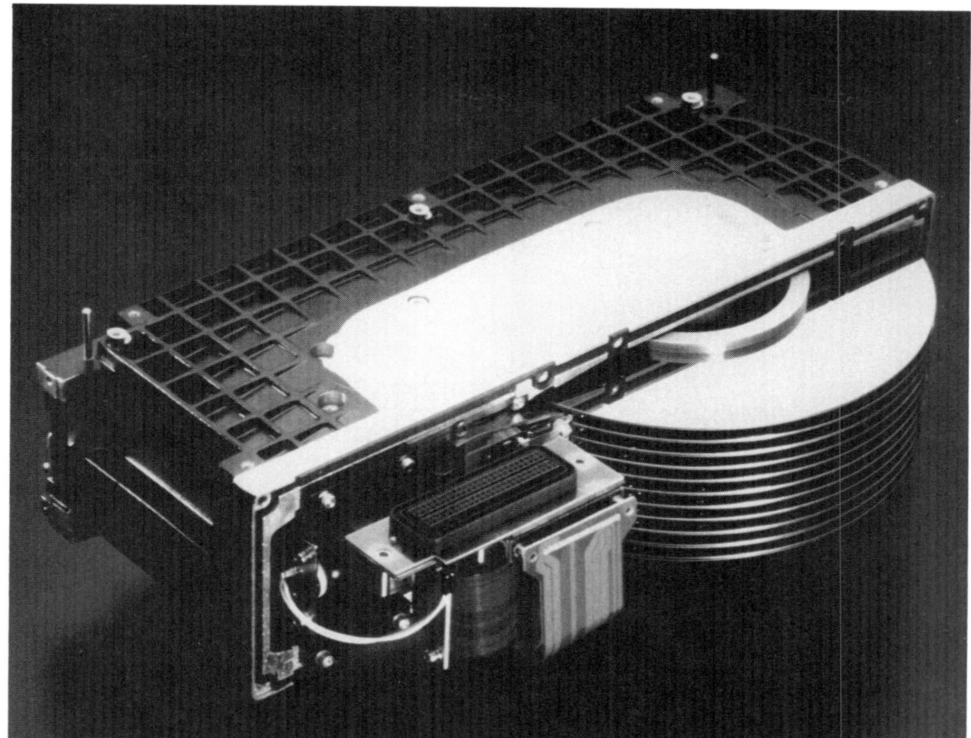

FIGURE 1-14

The Physical Design of a Typical Hard Disk Drive

the hard drive and its controller board, located inside the system unit in an expansion slot or built into the motherboard. The distance between the head and the disk surface is only a few millionths of an inch, allowing dense storage and high capacity on the drive. This small clearance is the reason why damage to the disk's surface may occur if the drive is jostled while spinning. Care must be taken when working with a hard drive. This is one of the most expensive parts of the computer and the one part most likely to fail over the computer's lifetime due to its mechanical complexity and close working tolerances.

Hard Disk Backup Devices

Hard disk drives must be regularly copied onto a **backup device** to protect against lost data in the event that the drive malfunctions. The usual medium for these backups is the floppy disk, but for large hard drives this requires many floppy disks, even if the high-density versions are used. Backing up on floppy disks is time consuming and requires that the user be physically present to exchange floppy disks. For example, a full 30 MB hard disk might require as many as 25 1.2 MB floppy disks and take 30 minutes or more to back up. There is a section in the DOS chapter on backing up and restoring hard drives using floppy disks.

A higher capacity backup scheme uses a **cartridge,** or **cassette tape,** unit for storage, and permits the user to use a single tape for a backup, rather than several boxes of floppy disks. The tape units come with backup software that allows automatic after-hours backups, saving work time. The tape drives are small, usually fitting in the same space as a floppy disk drive. Some units are designed to be moved from computer to computer and come with an external box and external power supply. There must be a separate tape-controller card for each computer used with a portable tape unit. Figure 1-15 shows a tape cartridge holding 60 megabytes of data, equivalent to more than 50 floppy disks.

FIGURE 1-15

A Tape Cartridge Holding 60 MB of Data

Video Adapter

Also located inside the system unit is the **video adapter** for the computer. This circuit board's role is to convert the video instructions of the program into a video signal that the monitor can understand. IBM has introduced several video standards, each one requiring a different video adapter-and-monitor combination. Attaching the monitor into the wrong type of video board can result in permanent damage to the monitor.

The earliest video standard, monochrome text, is obsolete today. It was replaced by the **monochrome graphics (MGA) standard,** also known as the Hercules monochrome standard, and offers 720 x 348 pixels (horizontal x vertical) resolution. A **pixel** is the smallest point of light on the screen that can be turned on or off independently. The first color standard, **color graphics adapter (CGA),** offered low-resolution color (320 x 200 pixels in 4 colors and 640 x 200 in 2 colors).

The next video adapter introduced by IBM was the **enhanced graphics adapter (EGA).** It offered substantially higher resolution at 650 x 350 pixels in 16 colors. The EGA video adapter could also be used with the monochrome and CGA monitors. The newest widely accepted video standard is the **video graphics array (VGA)** offered by IBM when they introduced the PS/2 microcomputer line. At 640 x 480 pixels and up to 256 colors, this video standard offers higher resolution for graphics and CAD (Computer-Assisted Design) applications. Higher video resolution may become standard in the near future: Super VGA is 800 x 600, and the IBM 8514A and XGA video offers 1024 x 768 pixels.

Video Monitor

The monitor is the primary output device of the microcomputer. Figure 1-16 shows a typical monitor. It must match the video adapter (monochrome, CGA, EGA, VGA, Super VGA, 8514A) installed in the computer. **Ergonomics** is the study of how individuals can work more effectively with devices in the workplace. Monitors are designed with ergonomic features such as low glare, tilt and swivel

FIGURE 1-16

A Typical Video Monitor

base, good contrast, and low radiation emissions. Most users place the monitor on top of the system unit, although floor-mounted (tower) computers allow the monitor to sit flat on the desk. Ergonomic studies show that the ideal height of the center of the monitor is 13 inches above the table. Color monitors offer easier viewing than monochrome monitors. Creative use of color makes a program easier to learn and use.

The Keyboard

The keyboard for IBM-compatibles is the primary input device and contains 84 or 101 keys, depending on the layout. Figure 1-17 shows a typical **PC keyboard.** The white keys in the middle represent the typical keys found on a typewriter, while the gray keys are those with special functions. The numeric keypad at the right edge does double duty—those keys can be used as a number keypad, similar to a calculator layout, or for moving the cursor around on the screen. In numeric keypad mode many numbers can be entered quickly. The **function keys** at the left edge of the keyboard have special meaning within each software application, and will be defined in later chapters. The special keys on the keyboard are illustrated in Figures 2-4 and 2-5, and include **Enter, Tab, Ctrl, Shift, Alt, Esc, BkSp, NumLock, ScrollLock, PrtSc, Ins, Del, Home, End, PgUp, PgDn,** and the four arrow keys.

Most keyboards have LEDs (red or green light emitting diodes) to show the status of the **CapsLock, NumLock,** and **ScrollLock** toggle keys. With the toggle keys, the first keypress activates the feature, and the second releases it. In addition, many applications will have on-screen indicators for these. The **Ctrl** and **Alt** keys work in a similar fashion to the **Shift** key. They are used in combination with another key: hold down the **Ctrl** or **Alt** key, then press another key. These keys are used extensively with word processing and database software applications, and in recreational software. The 101-key enhanced keyboard has the function keys across the top of the keyboard instead of at the left, and duplicates the cursor control keys between the regular keyboard and

FIGURE 1-17

A Typical 84-key PC Keyboard

the numeric keypad. The latter allows full-time use of the numeric keypad at the same time as cursor control keys.

Pointing Devices: Mouse, Joystick, Trackball, Light Pen

Pointing devices like the mouse, joystick, trackball, and light pen are designed to make input easier and more natural. Rather than force the users to the keyboard and character input, the users can move the **mouse** as if they were pointing to a menu item on the screen with their fingers. With a little practice, most users find the mouse permits them to pick from menu items with speed and is faster than using the keyboard to type in commands. Figure 1-18 shows a typical mouse, so named because of its shape and the cable which resembles a mouse tail. Mice have 1 to 3 buttons on top for entering commands, and a ball that rolls inside a collar as it is moved across the table. The user moves a pointer on the screen to a predetermined target by moving the mouse on the table in the same direction. The pointer, often called the **cursor,** will stop when the mouse stops moving. Depressing a mouse button (clicking) while the cursor is in a menu box will activate that menu choice. The **joystick** is more difficult to use because the cursor will continue to move as long as the joystick is held in one direction.

The **trackball** is a kind of upside-down mouse mounted so that the ball rotates in a collar. The user can roll the ball with his hand in any direction, causing the cursor to move in that direction on the screen. The trackball saves desk space in that it needs no extra room, unlike the mouse. The **light pen** is a wand that the user touches against the screen to make menu choices. Special software is able to convert the touch into a row-and-column location. A more expensive kind of pointing device is the touch-sensitive screen which requires special hardware. The user can simply touch the screen with a finger and the location is noted for menu choices.

Printing Devices

While the video display is the primary output device, most users will need to print final results at the end of a session. Printers can be classified by print speed and print quality. Cost is usually dependent on these characteristics. Draft quality **dot matrix printers** are the mainstay of the microcomputer world (refer to Figure 1-19). Fast, reliable, and versatile, these printers can produce draft versions of documents and reports, as well as graphics. Most dot matrix printers have a dual-pass mode in which the characters are double-struck, producing

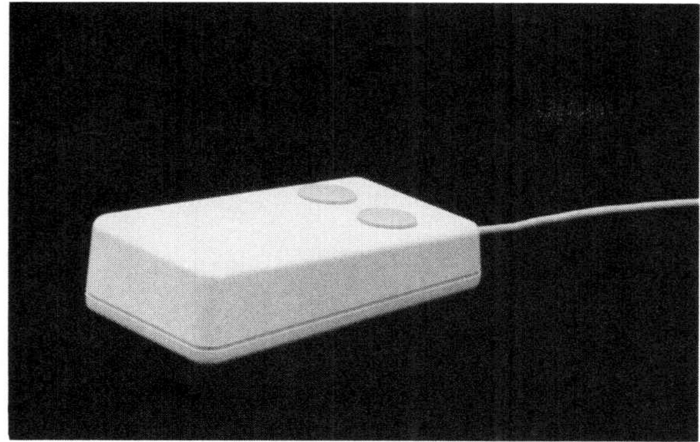

FIGURE 1-18

The Mouse, One Type of Pointing Device

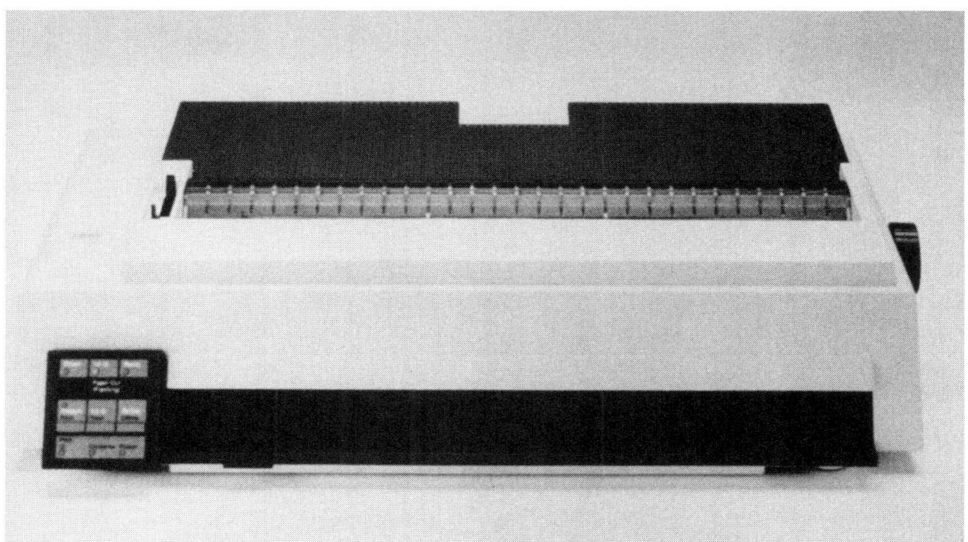

FIGURE 1-19

Dot Matrix Printer

near-letter quality, which is acceptable for most purposes. Dot matrix printers use a print head consisting of 9, 18, or 24 pins which are fired electrically against a ribbon and onto the paper, leaving an image of closely spaced dots. Print heads with more pins produce images with less space between dots, improving print quality. Printers with 24 pins cost $100-$200 more than 9-pin printers. Dot matrix printers can be programmed to produce different print styles or fonts by changing the spacing between characters and the dot pattern. Print speeds range from 100 to 400 characters per second in draft mode, and 20 to 120 characters per second in near-letter-quality mode.

A relatively recent technology offers high print quality and faster print speeds. **Ink jet printers** work by squirting a fine droplet of ink against the paper, making no impact and little noise. New models print up to 300 characters per second and offer high resolution graphics capabilities. These printers are also available in higher-cost color versions, providing full-color output at high speed.

The high end of microcomputer printers is the **laser printer.** Using a low-power laser and technology taken from the copier industry, the laser printer "paints" tiny dots on a light-sensitive drum which picks up black toner particles where it was exposed. Paper is given a small electrical charge, and the toner is transferred from the drum to the paper. The final step is to fuse the toner onto the paper by heating it as it exits the printer. Laser printers offer near-typeset

FIGURE 1-20

Two Models of the Hewlett-Packard Laserjet

quality at high dot resolutions, with 300 or more dots per inch. Because the printer uses the dot approach to forming characters, different print styles and sizes can be easily programmed and printed. Thus the laser printer is very versatile. Its graphics capabilities exceed those of dot matrix printers in quality and speed. Laser printers have enabled many users to do desktop publishing, an application where documents and reports can be composed and printed in final form without going to a typesetter. Two models of the Hewlett Packard Laserjet are shown in Figure 1-20.

For high quality printing, **daisy wheel printers** offer typewriter-like features but print much slower than ink jet or laser printers—15 to 70 characters per second. The name comes from the arrangement of the print wheel, with molded characters at the end of "petals" of a daisy. The printer works by rotating the print wheel until the correct character appears at the top, then striking the petal with a small hammer, pressing the "petal," or print element, against the ribbon and ultimately against the paper. The character is fully formed, not composed of dots, and resembles the output of an electric typewriter. Many electric typewriters now use daisy wheel print technology. Daisy wheel printers are not as versatile as other printers. Each typeface requires that the user change print wheels, and these printers cannot print graphics. Daisy wheel printers have become less popular since ink jet and laser printers were introduced.

Plotters are used to print graphic images; a variety of plotter types are shown in Figure 1-21. Moving a pen against the paper in the horizontal and vertical directions, the flatbed plotter is able to print images directly, much as a human would draw them. A plotter is rather slow at printing characters, but is able to draw arcs and diagonal lines directly and continuously without approximating the line with dots as the dot matrix, ink jet and laser printers would do. Some plotters are able to exchange pens for different line widths or more colors. Large-scale plotters move the pen in the vertical direction, and move the paper in the horizontal direction to create images. Plotters are useful for creating high-quality, colorful images for CAD (computer-assisted design) and for business graphics. Although plotters are relatively expensive, other kinds of printers can produce only single-color images. Plotters are

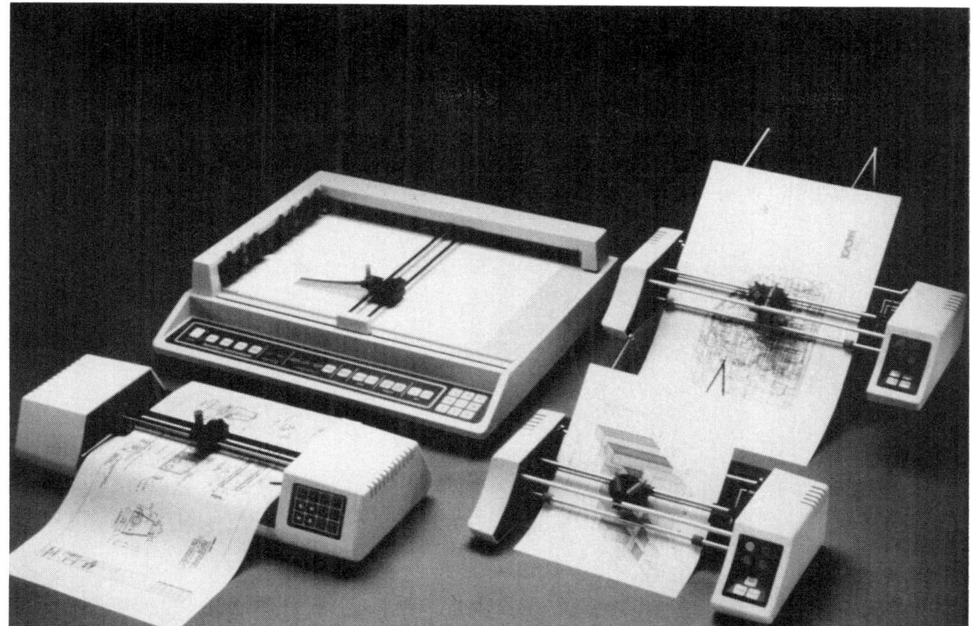

FIGURE 1-21

Four Types of Pen Plotters

sometimes used to create graphics on transparency film for presentations with an overhead projector.

Another kind of output device is the **film recorder.** This device produces high-quality color images on 35 millimeter slide film for presentations with a slide projector. Although expensive, these devices can produce better-quality images at higher resolutions and less distortion than is possible when taking a photograph of the monitor's screen. Some companies will accept print files by disk or via telephone, and can expose, develop, and return the slides by overnight express.

Connecting to Other Computers

Modems connect computers over telephone lines, permitting remote computing and exchange of data. A modem takes digital (0 or 1) signals from the computer and converts them to analog signals for transmission over the telephone. At the other end is a compatible modem which will convert the analog signal back into a digital format for the other computer. If you listen to a modem while it is transmitting, you'll hear a high-pitched whine, the carrier signal, signifying the two modems are communicating, and a series of whistles or tones representing the data being transferred between modems. The most popular speeds today are 1200 and 2400 bits per second, representing about 120–240 characters per second. Faster modems are available for high-volume situations. Voice-grade telephone circuits support speeds up to 9,600 bits per second.

Internal modems are built into an expansion card and are installed in an expansion slot in the system unit. They come with a built-in serial port. **External modems** connect to a serial port, so one must be available. External modems cost more because they need a case, an extra power supply, and a serial cable to connect to the computer (see Figure 1-22). The telephone line plugs directly into the modem, and most modems will automatically dial a number or answer the phone. No telephone is needed, although one can be plugged into the modem for normal use of the phone line. Most modems require that a private, single-line telephone connection be available; party lines are not allowed for

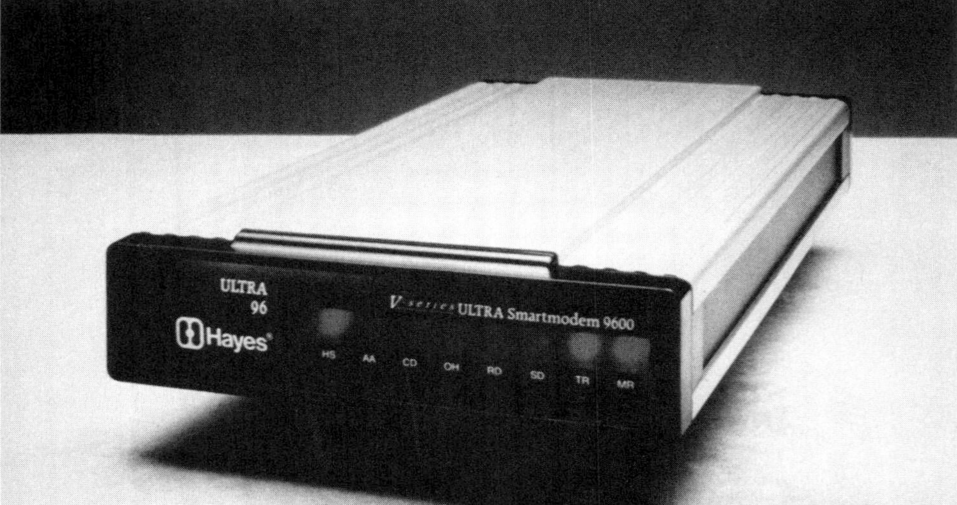

FIGURE 1-22

An External Modem

FIGURE 1-23

An Internal Modem with Communications Software

data communications. To use a modem with a PC, you must use communications software that converts the microcomputer into a terminal. Many modems come with free communications software; Figure 1-23 shows an internal modem package that includes software.

A new kind of modem is the **fax card,** which converts the PC into a facsimile machine. The fax card is able to receive fax messages over the telephone from other fax machines and stores them on the disk in graphics format. You can print them out on a compatible dot matrix or laser printer. You can create a message with a word processor, store it on the disk, then use the fax card to send the message to other fax machines. If the outgoing fax message is already in hard copy form, an **optical scanner** can be used to convert the image into a graphics format which is stored on the disk for transmission. The scanner reads the light and dark areas on a document, converting these areas to a digital (on or off) pattern of dots which can be manipulated by graphics programs.

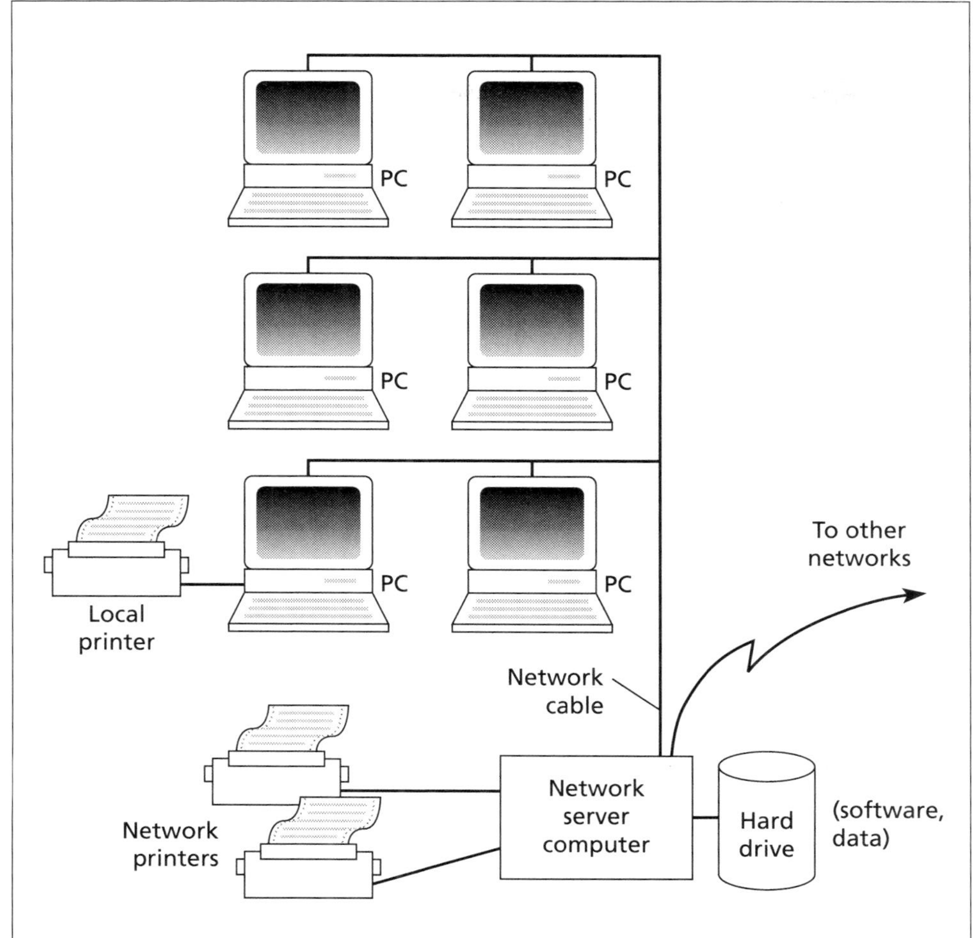

FIGURE 1-24

A Local Area Network (LAN) Used to Link Individual Microcomputers

A **local area network (LAN)** is a group of microcomputers connected to each other and to a **server computer,** sharing the server computer's hard disk and printers. LANs permit each user to access common programs and data. A high-end PC acts as a dedicated network file server and is connected to the shared hardware. Expensive resources such as laser printers, scanners, and tape drives may be used as though they were attached to each user's machine. Less expensive computers may be used as workstations because they can share the more expensive hardware attached to the server. Each station must have a **network interface card** connecting it to the network cable and a network software license. While personal computers are usually thought of as being independent, stand-alone machines, when included in a LAN they have the capability of shared computing power much greater than any individual component and at a fraction of the cost of a multi-user computer. Figure 1-24 shows a local area network used to link microcomputers in a classroom.

Local area networks carry some disadvantages. They can be complex to install and configure, requiring significant technical expertise. Because network users depend on the server and the network cable for access to data and resources, failures in these components can render the entire network inoperative. Stand-alone versions of some software packages will not run properly on a network, requiring either a network version or that the software be installed on each user's hard drive. Because network users have potential connections to data on the server, it is important to safeguard sensitive data with appropriate access privileges.

Expansion Alternatives

All IBM-compatible personal computers are capable of addressing at least 1 MB of memory; 640 KB of this is **conventional read/write RAM,** and the remainder **(high memory)** is used for the BIOS read-only memory (ROM), video memory, and hard disk controller ROM. For applications requiring extra memory, several types of RAM are available. **Expanded memory (EMS)** is used with 8088 processors to provide additional RAM—EMS RAM is "swapped" through a 64 KB-window above 640 KB, with conventional RAM in the first 640 KB. Applications programs like Lotus 1-2-3 that have been programmed to take advantage of expanded memory can handle larger problems. **Extended memory** is used with 80286, 80386, and 80486 processors which are capable of addressing more than 1 MB of RAM. Extended memory addresses begin at 1 MB. Figure 1-25 shows how memory is subdivided. Most memory expansion boards can be set up to handle conventional, expanded, or extended RAM. Some memory management programs can convert extended memory into expanded memory without changing the board's settings. For example, with an 80386 processor all expansion memory (beyond 640 KB) should be configured as extended memory; the memory manager program should be installed in the configuration file to enable the use of EMS memory.

Accelerator boards with a faster microprocessor can be added to older computers to speed up their operations. Rather than replace the entire computer, an 80286 processor can be added at a cost of 20% of the new computer. All the

FIGURE 1-25

Memory Allocation in IBM-Compatible Computers

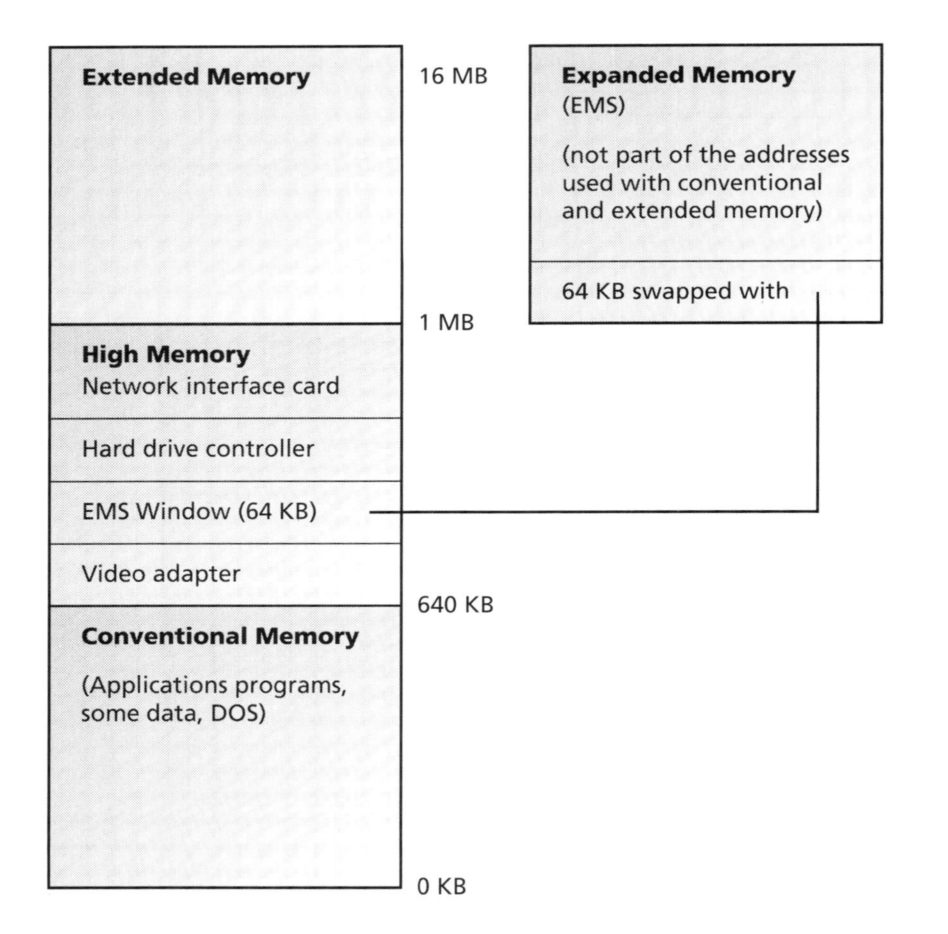

old peripherals can be used with the accelerator board, but there is a speed penalty because the new processor cannot take advantage of newer devices and a faster signal pathway or bus. For 80286 owners, accelerator boards featuring the 80386SX processor provide many advantages of the 386 chip without the full expense of replacing the entire computer. While 286 and 386 processors are able to access more memory than the 8088, most DOS programs are written for the 8088. The 286 and 386 simply run the same applications faster. This is likely to change in the future as more applications are written for the newer processors. The OS/2 operating system, Lotus 1-2-3 Release 3, and Microsoft's Excel spreadsheet are examples of software that will not operate on 8088 machines.

Miscellaneous Supplies and Accessories

Blank disks are required for all computers, even those equipped with hard disks. Diskette storage boxes are useful for keeping floppy disks organized and stored properly. Printers require paper and printer ribbons or ink cartridges. Laser printer toner cartridges must be replaced every 3000–5000 pages. Cables are needed to attach peripherals to the computer. Adapters are often needed to convert cables to fit a specific port. Many users struggle to find enough power outlets for their equipment—power strips with multiple outlets can solve that problem. Some power strips come with a **surge protector** in case there are power surges on the line. Caution is in order—never operate a computer during a thunderstorm. The best surge protection is to unplug the computer from all power outlets *and* unplug the telephone line from the modem. For critical applications, particularly in local area networks, you may install an **uninterruptible power supply (UPS)** to assure uninterrupted operations, even during a power outage.

CHAPTER REVIEW

Microcomputer Applications in Business

Microcomputers have dramatically increased our productivity. Word processing, electronic spreadsheets, database managers, graphics and desktop publishing applications make our work easier, improve accuracy, and save time. Telecommunications software allows us to connect our personal computers to larger computers and share data effectively. Recreational software provides entertainment and can help us learn.

Microcomputer Equipment

The microcomputer's system unit contains the microprocessor, primary memory, input/output ports, video adapter, and expansion slots. Secondary storage devices such as floppy and hard disk drives are used for permanent storage of data and programs. Other standard peripherals include the keyboard and video monitor. Accessories include a mouse and other pointing devices, a tape drive for disk backups, and a printer. Dot matrix printers provide good quality text and graphics at a reasonable price. For better print quality choose an ink jet or laser printer. Plotters produce high-quality graphical output in many colors. Film recorders produce images directly on 35 millimeter slide film for slide presentations.

Modems are used to connect computers over standard telephone lines. Local area networks provide the opportunity to share expensive hardware resources like laser printers and to share programs and data electronically.

When buying a microcomputer, analyze needs and applications before comparing prices. Mail order suppliers can save money but may not provide a suitable level of support. Choose your vendor carefully.

KEY TERMS

accelerator board
accounting applications
backup device
bit (**b**inary dig**it**)
byte
cartridge (cassette tape)
color graphics adapter (CGA)
computer-assisted design (CAD) software
conventional read/write RAM
cursor
daisy wheel printer
database management software
desktop publishing program
dot matrix printer
enhanced graphics adapter (EGA)
ergonomics
expanded memory (EMS)
expansion slots
extended memory
fax card
film recorder
floppy disk
function keys
game port
graphing application programs
hard disk
high memory
I/O ports
ink jet printer
joystick
keyboard
laser printer
light pen
local area network (LAN)
magnetic tape drive
microprocessor
modem (internal, external)
monochrome graphics (MGA) standard
motherboard
mouse
network interface card
numeric coprocessor chip
optical scanner
parallel port
PC keyboard
personal improvement programs
pixel
plotter
presentation graphics
primary memory
programmers
project management software
random access memory (RAM)
read-only memory (ROM)
recreational applications
serial port
server computer
signal bus
spreadsheet software
surge protector
terminals
trackball
uninterruptible power supply (UPS)
video adapter
video graphics array VGA
video monitor (display)
word processing software

DISCUSSION QUESTIONS

1. Contrast word processing, spreadsheet, and database management applications. When is each useful?
2. List at least three graphics applications packages.
3. Define desktop publishing.
4. List and describe the major components of the microcomputer system unit. What is the function of each?
5. Contrast floppy and hard disks. Are there situations in which the floppy disk is preferable? Explain.
6. Compare parallel and serial I/O ports. What peripherals are typically attached to the I/O ports?
7. List the advantages of each of the following printers: dot matrix, ink jet, laser, and plotter. When is each most likely to be used?
8. Describe the purpose of a modem. Can you think of reasons when an external modem is preferred to an internal modem that plugs into an expansion slot?
9. Compare the four kinds of memory: conventional RAM, expanded memory (EMS), extended memory, and ROM.
10. List at least three kinds of pointing devices. When are pointing devices more useful than the keyboard?

11. What is a fax card? How does it differ from an ordinary fax machine?
12. Describe a local area network and discuss the advantages of connecting microcomputers with a LAN.
13. What functions does an accelerator card perform?
14. Why is a numeric coprocessor useful for business computing?
15. Contrast mail order and local vendors for computer hardware and software. What are the advantages of each?
16. Contact a local computer store and find out the prices of blank floppy disks in the four standard sizes: 360 KB, 720 KB, 1.2 MB, and 1.44 MB. Calculate the cost per 1000 characters of storage. Which is most economical?

CHAPTER 1 PROJECT
COMPUTER CONSUMER GUIDE

For this project you should prepare a comprehensive report on at least three different personal computer models. Assume that the buyer is a college sophomore majoring in Business. The three models should be from the following categories:

- Laptop computer
- 8088-based desktop computer
- 80286-based desktop computer
- 80386-based desktop computer
- Macintosh computer

Before gathering data you should compile a list of features for the computer system. The list might include some of these items:

- Floppy disk size, capacity
- Hard disk capacity
- Amount of system RAM
- Speed of the microprocessor
- Type of video (video adapter, monitor)
- Type of keyboard (84 or 101 key)
- I/O ports
- Number and type of expansion slots

Peripheral devices on your list might include some of these items:

- Mouse
- Printer type, speed, print quality
- Modem (internal, external) and speed
- Miscellaneous equipment

Your report should include a comparison of product features, specifications and prices. Local computer stores and your college computer center may have special pricing programs for college students. Don't forget to ask about warranty and service information.

2

The Operating System: DOS and Utility Software

Objectives

After completing this chapter, you should be able to:

- Explain the purposes of an operating system.
- Describe the purpose of the special keys on the keyboard.
- List the steps necessary to boot the computer.
- Format a blank floppy disk.
- Discuss the elementary DOS file commands.
- Discuss hard disk subdirectory commands.
- Describe how to backup and restore a hard disk.
- Explain how to create a DOS command batch file.
- Describe the capabilities of utility programs.
- Discuss DOS shells for multitasking and OS/2.

INTRODUCTION

The **operating system** is a collection of system programs that manage the computer's resources. These programs perform such tasks as scanning the keyboard to see if a key has been pressed, displaying information on the monitor, sending characters to the printer as it is able to print them, handling disk allocation and read/write requests, performing housekeeping duties for applications programs, and communicating with the user through keyboard commands. You must have an operating system and it is usually purchased with the computer. The operating system for IBM compatibles is called **PC-DOS** or **MS-DOS;** only IBM brand computers use PC-DOS but for most purposes they are nearly identical. We will use the single abbreviation **DOS** (Disk Operating System) to describe both. This book will assume DOS version 3.3 or higher.

The operating system is stored in a number of places in a PC. A portion of it is permanently stored in the BIOS read-only memory, instantly available at power-up. **BIOS** stands for **Basic Input/Output System.** The purpose of the BIOS is to interpret the specific hardware configuration for DOS functions, allowing the same DOS to be used on almost any IBM-compatible computer. The BIOS in each IBM-compatible machine is slightly different, corresponding to design differences between machines. The remainder of the operating system is stored on the **boot disk,** the disk which contains DOS and is used to start up the computer; the term "boot" comes from "pull yourself up by your bootstraps."

The boot disk can be a floppy disk or a hard disk, and contains special programs stored in three files. Two of the files are hidden and don't appear in file (directory) listings. These two files must be placed in the boot tracks, the first two tracks of the disk. During boot-up they are automatically loaded into the RAM of the microcomputer by the BIOS program and, when they are successfully loaded, control is passed to these programs contained in the RAM. The third file, COMMAND.COM, is the command interpreter. Together, the two hidden files and COMMAND.COM comprise much of the operating system. Additional utility programs are stored as separate files, not part of the previous built-in set, to save memory space. These external commands are described later in the chapter, and summarized in the command summaries at the end of the chapter.

ELEMENTARY DOS COMMANDS

Getting Started: Booting Up the Computer

To start the computer, the system or boot diskette must be in the boot drive. This drive is the top or left drive in a floppy-disk machine, called the A drive. In a hard disk machine the boot disk is the internal drive, called the C drive. Because hard drive computers will boot automatically without inserting the floppy disk, we will describe the floppy configuration steps that the user must take and point out differences for hard drive machine users where needed. Network users may follow a different procedure, but in most cases it is similar to the hard disk procedure. Figure 2-1 shows the location of the boot drive in a typical floppy-drive PC.

Example: *Booting Up the Computer*

1. If you do not have a hard disk, insert the diskette into the A drive with the label up and the read/write window facing into the machine. 3.5-inch diskettes can be inserted only the proper way; the drive will grab the disk from the user and seat it if the disk is inserted correctly. Push the disk in slowly until it slips into place. The 5.25-inch diskette, however, *can* be inserted incorrectly, so take care to orient the disk properly. Before the diskette can be read, the door on a 5.25-inch drive must be closed after the disk is in place. Most 5.25-inch drives use a lever or door that is moved 90 degrees to close the opening. Practice opening and closing the door.

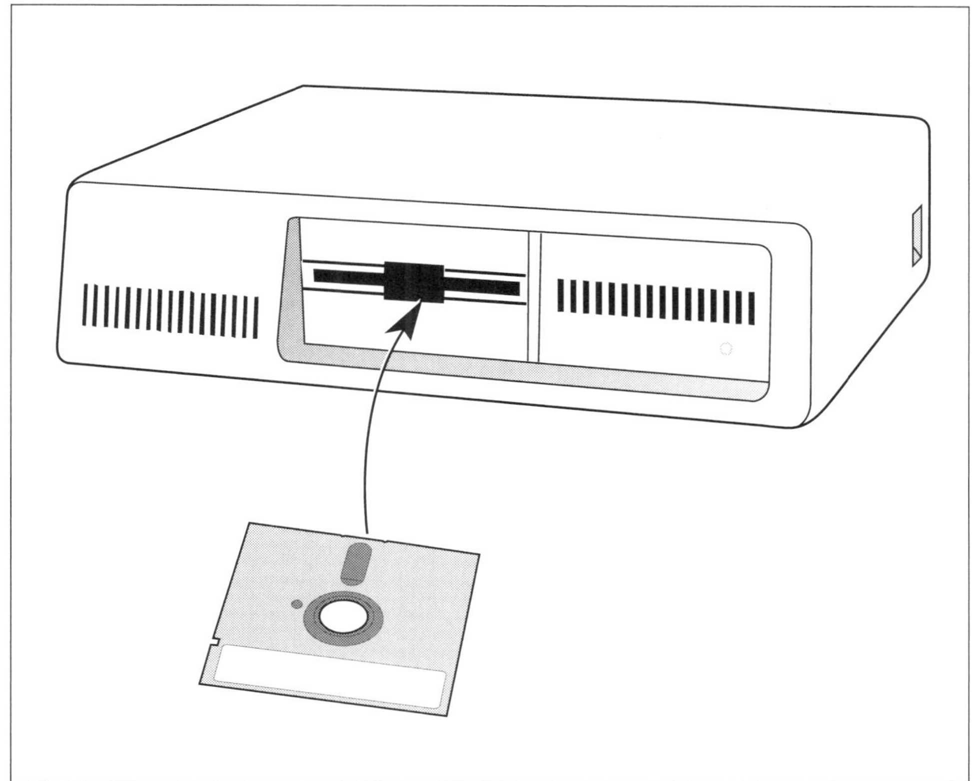

FIGURE 2-1

Location of the Boot Drive in a Typical Floppy-Drive PC

2. With the boot disk in position in the A drive, (not necessary with a hard disk computer—see step 5 below) turn on the power to the computer. The power switch is usually located in the right front or right side. Some computers also require that the monitor power switch be activated.
3. The PC will go through a power-on self-test (POST) procedure, taking several seconds. When it determines internal circuits and memory are functioning properly, the computer will begin to boot, reading the two hidden files from the boot disk. These files, called IO.SYS and MSDOS.SYS on most non-IBM brand machines, and IBMBIO.COM and IBMDOS.COM on IBM machines, contain the bulk of DOS. When the two files have loaded properly from the boot disk, those programs begin to execute.
4. If the wrong disk has been inserted in the boot drive, an error message like "Non-system disk—insert proper disk and press any key to continue" is displayed.
5. With a hard disk machine the boot disk is always in place inside the computer. When starting a hard disk computer, do *not* put any disk in the A drive before turning the power on.
6. The system will display the log-on message shown in Figure 2-2 and may ask the user to set the proper date and time. If the date and time are correct, press the Enter key; otherwise enter the correct values in the format shown on your screen.
7. Figure 2-3 shows the screen after the boot process has been completed. The A> prompt indicates that DOS is ready for you to enter a command or run a program. Hard disk computer users will see the C> prompt. Network users may see a C> prompt or the F> prompt.

```
Current date is Tuesday  5-16-1989
Enter new date (mm-dd-yy):
```

FIGURE 2-2

DOS Initial Log-On Message

```
Current date is Tuesday  5-16-1989
Enter new date (mm-dd-yy):
Current time is  10:21:18.55
Enter new time:

Microsoft(R) MS-DOS(R)  Version 3.3
             (C)Copyright Microsoft Corp 1981-1987

A>
```

FIGURE 2-3

Boot-up Screen for DOS 3.3

Changing the Date and Time

Many personal computers have a built-in battery-operated clock, and the current date and time are displayed during the boot procedure. Because date and time information are maintained for files that are stored on the disk, you should always enter the correct date and time. If the wrong date or time is entered, you can use the DOS **DATE** and **TIME** commands to make changes. These commands display the current date and time, and provide a guide for you to enter correct values. With most computers, these commands do not *permanently* change the date or time, merely the in-memory values. Because it varies from model to model, you should refer to the computer operations manual for the command that will update your computer's internal clock.

At the DOS prompt type **DATE** and you will see the following message from DOS. Input the correct date in the same manner as the current value.

```
Current date is Tue 5-16-1989
Enter new date (mm-dd-yy): _
```

Changing Disk Drives

The DOS prompt indicates the **default disk drive,** and signifies that you may enter commands. Any disk command issued will apply to the default drive, unless the command includes a different drive designator. Disk drives are lettered, starting with A and ending with the last drive. Hard disk users will probably see C> in the prompt line, indicating the default drive is C, the hard drive. Network users will find drive letters beyond A, B, and C, indicating connection to the network server's hard disks. Floppy-disk users see the default drive as A. To change the default drive, simply enter the desired drive letter followed by a colon, then press **Enter.** For example, **B:** will cause the default drive to become B, the second floppy drive. When changing to a new drive, be certain there is a diskette in the drive first or you will get a "Drive not ready" error message. In this case, place the disk in the drive and press **R** to retry the command.

Removing the Diskette

For computers with a 3.5-inch drive, press the small button on the face of the drive to eject the diskette. To release a 5.25-inch disk, open the drive door or lever and pull out the diskette. Some drives have a small spring which will eject the disk when the door is opened.

The Keyboard and Correcting Mistakes

The original IBM PC and XT models came with the standard 84-key keyboard with function keys at the left side, pictured in Figure 2-4. The IBM AT and later models came with the enhanced keyboard, with function keys across the top and an extra set of cursor control keys, allowing simultaneous use of the numeric keypad and arrow keys. An enhanced keyboard is pictured in Figure 2-5. Commands are entered much as you would with an electric typewriter. After you have typed the command, press the **Enter** key to execute that command. The Enter key may be labelled with an L-shaped left arrow instead of the word "Enter."

DOS normally requires that you press the **Enter** key to complete a response or command, providing an opportunity to make changes before the Enter key is pressed. If you make a mistake in typing, erase any incorrect characters with the **Backspace** key, located above the **Enter** key at the upper right side of the keyboard. The Backspace key may be designated by a left-facing arrow, or the abbreviation "BkSp." To make a correction, backspace until you erase the incorrect character, then retype the remainder of the response or command correctly, and press the Enter key.

Some other keys of interest include the **Tab** key, sometimes labelled with two opposite facing arrows. The Tab key works in the same way as on a typewriter, moving the cursor over several spaces (usually five) to the right. Some software provides for a backwards Tab, by pressing **Shift-Tab.** The four arrow keys on the numeric keypad will move the cursor around the screen in the desired direction, although only the left arrow functions in DOS, where it acts as a destructive Backspace, erasing characters as the cursor moves left. In an application like

FIGURE 2-4

The 84-Key PC Keyboard

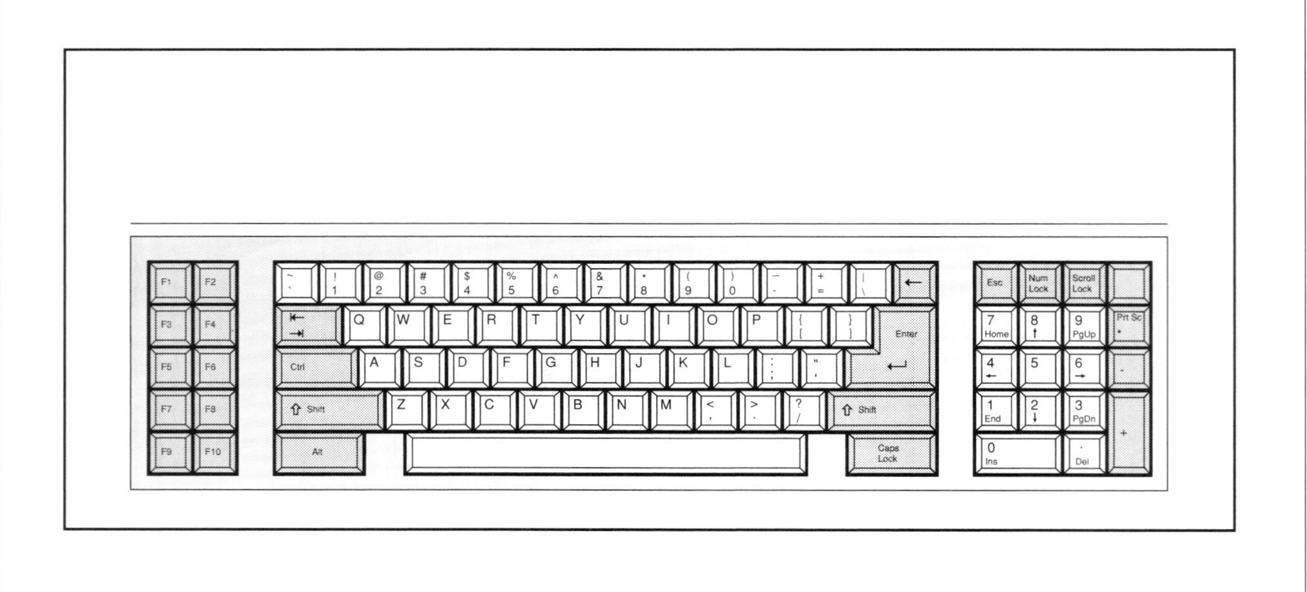

FIGURE 2-5

An Enhanced Keyboard

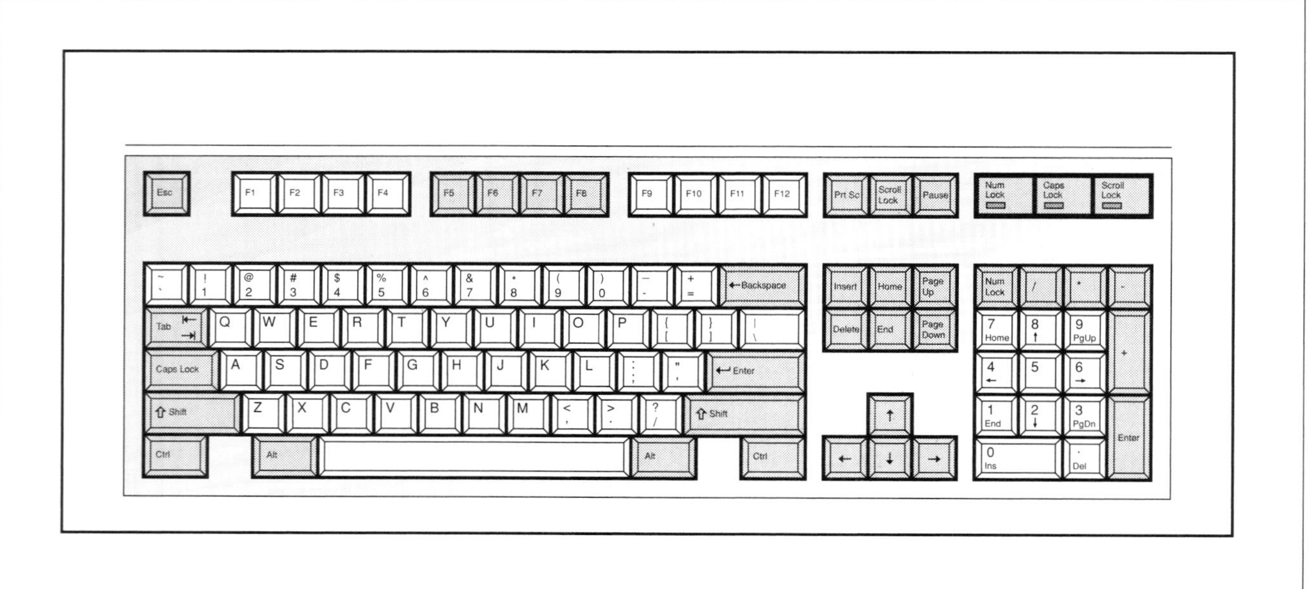

WordPerfect, these keys move the cursor without deleting any characters. In Lotus 1-2-3 the arrow keys move the cursor to new locations, again without erasing any characters.

The numeric keypad normally is set for cursor control, using the lower symbol on each key. However, if the **NumLock** key is pressed once, the keypad functions are shifted to the upper symbol on each key, representing the numbers and decimal point. Most keyboards have a **light-emitting diode (LED)** to indicate whether the keypad is set for numbers or cursor control. **CapsLock** causes a capital letter to be entered when an alphabetic key is pressed. It has no effect on other keys; it is not a Shift Lock key. A second press of CapsLock returns the keyboard to normal lowercase mode.

The other keys on the keypad **(Home, End, PgUp,** and **PgDn)** have different functions depending on which application is running. These keys are used to move the cursor around the screen in larger jumps than the arrow keys provide. The **Del** key is used to delete the character beneath the cursor, but normally has no function in DOS. The **Ins** key is a **toggle** key—one key press switches the setting and the second key press switches it back to the original setting. The **Ins** key switches the PC between overtype and insert modes. In overtype mode, new characters typed in replace characters already in that screen position. In insert mode, new characters typed in "push" existing characters over, making room for the new ones to be inserted. The function of these two keys depends on the specific application package.

Warm Boot: Restarting the Computer with Ctrl-Alt-Del

There are several other useful key combinations available through DOS. The **warm boot** sequence of **Ctrl-Alt-Del** will cause the computer to restart and go through a normal boot process. The warm boot is quick because it does not go through a memory check as is done when the machine is powered up. You may need to perform a warm boot if a program "hangs," or is no longer working. To perform a warm boot, hold down the **Ctrl** and **Alt** keys, then depress the **Del** key. A **cold boot** occurs when the machine's power switch is turned on, or when the Reset button is pressed. If Ctrl-Alt-Del has no effect, press the Reset button. If your machine does not have a Reset button, turn the power off and wait until the disk drives stop spinning (no noise is coming from the system unit). Then turn the power back on and the computer will boot again.

Screen Print Commands

Each of the applications packages has its own printing menus and procedures. However, the PrtSc key has two printing functions within DOS.

- When used in combination with the Ctrl key, **Ctrl-PrtSc** will toggle the printer on so that anything that is subsequently displayed on the screen will also be printed on the printer. This is a useful way to get a printed copy of a disk directory, or to document a sequence of complicated commands. Press **Ctrl-PrtSc** again to disable the print echo.
- **Shift-PrtSc** will cause a "snapshot" of the screen's present contents to be sent to the printer. Only text mode screens can be captured in this fashion unless the DOS GRAPHICS command is used first. Most screens in DOS, WordPerfect, Lotus 1-2-3, and dBASE appear in text mode. On enhanced keyboards you may press **PrtSc** or **Shift-PrtSc**.

Example: *Printing the Screen's Contents*

---

1. Insert your data disk in the A drive, type **DIR A:** and press **Enter.**
2. Make sure the printer is attached and turned on.
3. When the DOS prompt reappears, press **Shift-PrtSc** to copy the contents of the screen to your printer.

Working with Files

File Names and Terminology

DOS **file names** are used when retrieving or saving files on the disk. File names consist of several parts: optional drive letter and optional subdirectory path, the name, and an optional file extension. If present, the drive letter is followed by a colon and gives the drive on which the file is located. Subdirectories are discussed later in this chapter. The **name** is descriptive and can be from one to eight characters long. Allowable characters are A–Z, a–z, 0-9, and $ % ' - @ { } ~ ` ! # ( ) &. The name is chosen by the user and should describe its contents. The **extension** is optional, and contains from one to three characters, preceded by a period. Some programs add an extension to file names while others let the user pick one if desired. Figure 2-6 shows a sample of some standard file extensions and their meaning.

In DOS, files with .COM and .EXE extensions represent executable programs, and can be executed just by typing the file name. Files with a .BAT (batch) extension represent sets of user commands that have been stored in a file for later execution. These may also be executed by giving the file name. Many software packages use .BAT files to install software and start the program with ease. Figure 2-7 shows examples of valid and invalid DOS file names.

FIGURE 2-6

Sample File Extensions

Extension	Program	Meaning
.EXE	DOS	Executable program
.COM	DOS	Executable program
.BAT	DOS	Batch file of DOS commands
.WPM	WordPerfect	Macro file
.BK!	WordPerfect	Backup file
.WK1	Lotus 1-2-3	Spreadsheet file
.PIC	Lotus 1-2-3	Graph image file
.PRN	Lotus 1-2-3	Text file
.DBF	dBASE	Database file
.MDX	dBASE	Multiple index file
.PRG	dBASE	Program file
.CHT	Harvard Graphics	Chart file

FIGURE 2-7

Examples of Valid and Invalid DOS File Names

Valid File Names	Invalid File Names	Reasons
DEMO.BAT	FILE 1.JKL	Space in file name
ACE123.XYZ	INCOMESTMT.FIL	Name > 8 characters
FILENAME.EXT	DESKTOP.FILE	Extension > 3 chars.
A:199.000	BJM.123.456	Two periods in ext.
MCTAVISH	CFILENAME.EXT	No : after C, 9 characters long
BUDGET89.WK1		
1239-16.DBF		
C:WP{WP}.SET		
WP.EXE		

Wildcard File Name Templates

When copying or deleting files, the file names may be spelled out precisely, or an abbreviation for the file name may be created using a DOS **wildcard template.** The * and ? are special wildcard characters which allow matching of any character. The ? represents a single character position, while the * represents any characters which follow. For example, ABC?F.EXT would be matched by ABCDF.EXT, ABC9F.EXT and ABC-F.EXT, but not by ABCDE.EXT or ABCF.EXT. WP*.* would be matched by any file starting with the letters WP. WP{WP}.SET, WP.EXE and WP{WP}US.THS all match. The ? may be used in any position in the name or extension, but the * must always come at the end of the name or the extension. Wildcards are especially useful when referring to an entire group of files with a single command. For example, you could copy all of the WordPerfect program files that begin with WP with the command, **COPY WP*.*.**

Initializing a Blank Disk: FORMAT

Before a blank floppy diskette can be used to store data, it must be **formatted.** The formatting process scans the disk for bad data storage regions and **initializes** the disk's file directory and file allocation table (FAT). The FAT tells the computer where on the disk each file is stored. This command's syntax is

```
FORMAT drive: /switches
```

The switches include formatting a low-density 5.25"-disk in a high-capacity disk drive (/4), adding a volume label of up to 11 characters (/V), and making this a system (boot) disk (/S). The boot switch must appear last in the list, if used. Other FORMAT switches are described in your DOS manual. The volume label is recorded magnetically in the disk's directory. You should also place a sticky label on the disk identifying its content and giving your name. Unless you use a felt-tipped pen, never write directly on this sticky label when it is attached to the disk—write on the label, then peel it off and affix to the diskette. Examples of the FORMAT command include:

FORMAT A: /V Format a blank disk in drive A to its standard capacity. If drive A is a high-capacity drive (1.2 MB or 1.44 MB), high-capacity media must be used. DOS will ask you to provide a volume label (up to 11 characters) which is displayed whenever the disk's directory is listed. DOS 4.01 will automatically use **/V** by default.

FORMAT B: /4 Format a 5.25-inch blank disk in drive B to low-density capacity (360 KB). The **/4** is not necessary if the B drive is a 360 KB drive.

FORMAT A: /N:9 Format a 720 KB diskette (using 9 sectors per track) on a 3.5-inch high-capacity A drive. The **/N:9** is not necessary if drive A is a 720 KB drive.

FORMAT A: /S Prepare a system (boot) disk in drive A using standard drive capacity.

Example: *Formatting a Blank Floppy Disk*

Before trying this example, you will need to obtain a blank disk of the size and capacity appropriate for your computer system. For this example we will assume you are formatting a diskette that matches your drive. (Remember that formatting a disk will erase any information previously stored on it, so if you don't have a blank floppy, be sure to pick a disk that you wish to erase.)

1. Make sure the computer has started up, with the A> or C> prompt displayed on the screen.
2. Next issue the command **FORMAT A:** and press the **Enter** key. We will not place the DOS boot files on this disk, leaving more room to store programs and data.
3. DOS will next instruct you to insert the blank floppy disk into drive A. If you issued the wrong command, pressing **Ctrl-C** will abort the command and return you to the DOS prompt. Make sure the disk is *not* write protected:
   - On 5.25-inch disks, remove the tape covering the slot on the right edge of the diskette.
   - With 3.5-inch diskettes, slide the small plastic cover in the disk's lower-left corner so that the write-protect window is closed.
4. When prompted, properly insert the blank disk in drive A and close the door. [Note: 3.5-inch drive doors do not have to be closed.] For most disk drives, you will place the thumb of your right hand on the diskette's label and insert the sliding window edge (for 3.5-inch disks) or read/write window (for 5.25-inch disks) into the drive, label up. 3.5-inch diskettes have a small arrow in the upper left corner to help you orient the disk.
5. Press **Enter** to begin the formatting process. The disk drive activity light will indicate that the disk in that drive is being accessed. After a few moments, DOS may display the progress of the format.
6. When the formatting is finished, a "Format complete" message will be given, along with the space available on the disk. [Note: if there are fewer bytes available than total disk space, DOS may have found bad spots on the disk and locked them out. DOS 4.01 users will see additional information about the number of allocation units on the disk and the volume serial number.]
7. At the question "Format another (Y/N)?" reply **N** and press **Enter** to return to the DOS prompt. Figure 2-8 shows a similar command.

The Disk Directory

The **disk directory** contains information about the files stored on that disk. File name, file size bytes (characters), and date and time of the file's creation are displayed for the user. The directory also contains information about where on the disk that file is stored, and the status of the **file attributes,** but this information is not displayed to the user. A file directory of the DOS 3.3 boot disk is shown in Figure 2-9. DOS 4.01 adds the volume serial number to the display.

To display the directory for the default drive, enter the **DIR** command. The disk's **volume label,** MS330PP01, is shown at the beginning of the listing. The remainder of the entries are data or program files. The date and time that each file was created or last changed is shown in the last two columns of the directory listing. The final entry displays the amount of free space remaining on the disk, approximately 5,000 characters in this instance.

```
C:\>FORMAT A: /N:9
Insert new diskette for drive A:
and strike ENTER when ready

Format complete

    730112 bytes total disk space
     20480 bytes in bad sectors
    709632 bytes available on disk

Format another (Y/N)?n
C:\>
```

This disk has some bad sectors.

FIGURE 2-8

Formatting a Blank Floppy Disk (720K Format)

```
 Volume in drive A is MS330PP01
 Directory of  A:\

4201     CPI     17089   7-24-87  12:00a
5202     CPI       459   7-24-87  12:00a
ANSI     SYS      1647   7-24-87  12:00a
APPEND   EXE      5794   7-24-87  12:00a
ASSIGN   COM      1530   7-24-87  12:00a
ATTRIB   EXE     10656   7-24-87  12:00a
CHKDSK   COM      9819   7-24-87  12:00a
COMMAND  COM     25276   7-24-87  12:00a
COMP     COM      4183   7-24-87  12:00a
COUNTRY  SYS     11254   7-24-87  12:00a
DISKCOMP COM      5848   7-24-87  12:00a
DISKCOPY COM      6264   7-24-87  12:00a
DISPLAY  SYS     11259   7-24-87  12:00a
DRIVER   SYS      1165   7-24-87  12:00a
EDLIN    COM      7495   7-24-87  12:00a
EXE2BIN  EXE      3050   7-24-87  12:00a
FASTOPEN EXE      3888   7-24-87  12:00a
FDISK    COM     48919   7-24-87  12:00a
FIND     EXE      6403   7-24-87  12:00a
FORMAT   COM     11671   7-24-87  12:00a
GRAFTABL COM      6136   7-24-87  12:00a
GRAPHICS COM     13943   7-24-87  12:00a
JOIN     EXE      9612   7-24-87  12:00a
KEYB     COM      9041   7-24-87  12:00a
LABEL    COM      2346   7-24-87  12:00a
MODE     COM     15440   7-24-87  12:00a
MORE     COM       282   7-24-87  12:00a
NLSFUNC  EXE      3029   7-24-87  12:00a
PRINT    COM      8995   7-24-87  12:00a
RECOVER  COM      4268   7-24-87  12:00a
SELECT   COM      4132   7-24-87  12:00a
SORT     EXE      1946   7-24-87  12:00a
SUBST    EXE     10552   7-24-87  12:00a
SYS      COM      4725   7-24-87  12:00a
        34 File(s)      5120 bytes free
```

FIGURE 2-9

Directory of the DOS 3.3 Boot Disk

```
A>DIR /W

 Volume in drive A is MS330PP01
 Directory of  A:\

4201     CPI    5202     CPI    ANSI     SYS    APPEND   EXE    ASSIGN   COM
ATTRIB   EXE    CHKDSK   COM    COMMAND  COM    COMP     COM    COUNTRY  SYS
DISKCOMP COM    DISKCOPY COM    DISPLAY  SYS    DRIVER   SYS    EDLIN    COM
EXE2BIN  EXE    FASTOPEN EXE    FDISK    COM    FIND     EXE    FORMAT   COM
GRAFTABL COM    GRAPHICS COM    JOIN     EXE    KEYB     COM    LABEL    COM
MODE     COM    MORE     COM    NLSFUNC  EXE    PRINT    COM    RECOVER  COM
SELECT   COM    SORT     EXE    SUBST    EXE    SYS      COM
       34 File(s)      5120 bytes free

A>
```

FIGURE 2-10

Wide Directory of the DOS 3.3 Boot Disk

Listing File Names: DIR

The directory list command **DIR** can be used to list all files, or can show a subset. DIR B: will list only the files stored on the disk in the B drive. DIR WP* will show all files beginning with WP on the default (A) drive. An abbreviated directory listing showing only file name and remaining space is available with the **DIR /W** command, the /W meaning "wide." The same directory from above, but with the wide listing, looks like that of Figure 2-10.

The **DIR /P** command is used to automatically pause the directory listing when the screen is filled. Pressing any key will display the next page of file information.

Copying a File: COPY

The **COPY** command is used to copy a file from one disk to another, or to make a new copy on the same disk with a different name. The format of this command is:

```
COPY [d:]oldfilename [d:]newfilename
```

If you include a new drive letter without a newfilename, the file is copied with the same name onto the new drive. The [d:] parameters are used to optionally provide the drive letter for each file. If no drive letter is specified, DOS assumes the file is located on the default drive. Some examples:

COPY ALPHA B:	Copies a file called ALPHA from the default drive to the B drive using the same name.
COPY B:BUDGET C:TEMP	Copies a file called BUDGET from the B drive onto the C drive as TEMP.
COPY *.* B:	Copies all files from the default drive to the B drive.

```
C>TYPE AUTOEXEC.BAT
PATH C:\DOS;C:\WP;C:\DBASE;C:\PCPLUS;C:\
PROMPT $P$G
MSMOUSE
MIRROR
SETUP HP.PMF
C>
```

FIGURE 2-11

Displaying the Contents of AUTOEXEC.BAT File with TYPE

COPY OLDONE NEWONE Copies a file called OLDONE under the new name NEWONE on the default drive.

COPY P&L8? C: Copies all five-character file names starting with P&L8 onto the C drive. Any character matches the ? in the template.

Displaying the Contents of a File: TYPE

The **TYPE** command is used to display the contents of a text file on the screen. (It gives unpredictable results on other file types such as WordPerfect, Lotus 1-2-3, or dBASE files.) For example, the command **TYPE AUTOEXEC.BAT** will display the contents of the AUTOEXEC.BAT file, as shown in Figure 2-11, although your AUTOEXEC.BAT file will probably not be the same.

Example: *Display the AUTOEXEC.BAT File*

1. If you booted from a floppy, make sure that the boot disk you used is in the A drive. Issue the command **TYPE AUTOEXEC.BAT** and press **Enter.**

   OR

1. If you booted from the hard drive, enter the command **TYPE C:\AUTOEXEC.BAT** and press the **Enter** key.
2. If there is an AUTOEXEC.BAT file on your boot disk, its contents will be displayed on the screen.

Printing the File: PRINT

While the TYPE command displays the contents of a text file on the screen, the **PRINT** command will send the file to the printer for hard copy. PRINT works in the background, sending characters to the printer as it is able to print them, while you can continue working with the PC on another task. The format of this command is

```
PRINT filename /switches
```

Switches include such features as number of copies to print, which printer to send the file to, line length, page length, and more. See your DOS manual for details.

PRINT C:LETTER.TXT	Will send file LETTER.TXT to the default printer.
PRINT BID C:PAYLIST	Will print files BID and PAYLIST on the default printer.

Removing a File: DEL

To delete a file, use the DOS **DEL** or **ERASE** command. DEL permits you to delete a single file, or a group of files by specifying a wildcard template. Every file can be deleted with the *.* template, but care should be given when using this command. It is sometimes possible to "undelete" a file using a utility program such as PC-TOOLS or Norton Utilities, but only if no other files have been created or altered on that disk since the deletion. See the last section of this chapter for details.

Examples of the DEL command are shown below.

DEL SHARKS.TXT	Deletes file SHARKS.TXT from the default drive.
DEL B:*.DBF	Delete all files with a .DBF extension from the B drive.
DEL A:*.*	An extremely dangerous command, this will erase all files in the current directory from the A drive. DOS will ask you to confirm all *.* deletions.

Changing a File's Name: RENAME

The **RENAME** command is used to change a given file's name to something new. The format is

```
RENAME oldfilename newfilename
```

Only one file may be renamed at a time, so wildcards are not used. RENAME may be abbreviated as REN for faster typing.

RENAME FREDDY JOHNNY	Renames FREDDY on the default drive to new name JOHNNY.

DOS Disk Commands

Copying an Entire Disk: DISKCOPY

The **COPY A:*.* B:** command can be used to copy all files from one drive to another, but the **DISKCOPY** command is more efficient. This command copies all information between two compatible (same density, size) disks, track by track. Several files are copied at once, being stored in RAM, to reduce the number of disk swaps. The syntax of this command is

```
DISKCOPY sourcedrive: targetdrive: /switches
```

The sourcedrive is typically A: or B:, and the targetdrive may be the same drive. If you specify only one drive, it is used both as source and destination, and DOS prompts you when to switch disks. This version is most often used when there is only a single floppy drive in the system, or when the two drives are different types. DISKCOPY will automatically format the destination disk if it is not already formatted, saving time. The most often used switch is /V, verify that all files are copied properly. Examples of this command:

DISKCOPY A: B: Copy all information from drive A to drive B. Source disk goes in drive A and target disk in drive B.

DISKCOPY A: A: /V Copy all information from the source disk to the target disk, verifying that the two disks agree. DOS prompts the user to alternately place source or target disk in the A drive.

Comparing Two Disks: DISKCOMP

DISKCOMP is used to compare two disks to see if they contain the same data. An explanatory message is given if the disks are not the same.

```
DISKCOMP sourcedrive: targetdrive:
```

DISKCOMP compares the disks track by track, reporting any differences. It will only compare compatible media, meaning the size and capacity must be the same. Examples:

DISKCOMP A: B: Compare disks in drives A and B.

DISKCOMP A: A: Compare disks using only drive A; DOS will prompt the user to switch disks as needed.

Checking the Disk: CHKDSK

Occasionally the disk's directory may be logically damaged. That is, the directory does not accurately depict the location of files stored on that disk. The most common cause for such errors is removing the disk at the wrong time. Stray magnetic fields may also induce random errors on the disk. The **CHKDSK** command will check the directory and file allocation table (FAT) for consistency, and report any errors found. It will also show statistics about disk usage, space remaining, and RAM usage. The format for this command is:

```
CHKDSK drive: /switch
```

Directory errors are serious and may jeopardize the contents of a disk. It is a good idea to run this command frequently, and fix any errors that are found. In particular, you should not continue to use a disk with directory errors because new files saved on the disk may not be safely stored. It is also a good idea to make more than one copy of important work—keep current copies of your files on two diskettes. Output from the CHKDSK command on a hard drive might look like Figure 2-12. DOS 4.01 displays some additional information.

The /F switch instructs DOS to attempt to correct the errors it encounters. Do not try to use a disk with a damaged directory—seek assistance when your disk has CHKDSK problems. Do not use the CHKDSK command on a computer attached to a local area network because it does not work with network drives. CHKDSK errors generally indicate lost data. Disk repair utility programs such as Mace Utilities and Norton Utilities may help in recovering lost data.

```
C>CHKDSK

Volume HARD_DRIVE  created Sep 17, 1988 4:54p

 33435648 bytes total disk space
    47104 bytes in 4 hidden files
    96256 bytes in 32 directories
 28776448 bytes in 1440 user files
    10240 bytes in bad sectors
  4505600 bytes available on disk

   655360 bytes total memory
   540288 bytes free
```

FIGURE 2-12

Status Report from the CHKDSK Command

Example: *Checking Your Disk*

Make sure your data disk is in the A drive (or whatever is appropriate for your computer).

1. Enter the command **CHKDSK A:** and press **Enter.** DOS will examine the disk's directory and display a report of disk space and RAM usage.

WORKING WITH HARD DISKS

A hard disk offers a large storage space and much quicker retrieval and storage of files without the disk swapping that occurs with floppies. Many software packages require use of a hard disk drive. WordPerfect is distributed on 10 or more floppy disks and works more effectively on a hard drive machine. The procedure to install, or initialize, and implement a hard disk drive is shown in Figure 2-13. See your DOS manual for specific instructions.

Using Subdirectories

Because of the immense storage space of a hard disk, from 50 to hundreds of times more storage than on a floppy disk, the storage space should be well organized. The DOS subdirectory technique is used to subdivide the hard disk (or a floppy disk) into smaller, more manageable sets of files. A **subdirectory** is a grouping of related files and is specified by the user. The **root directory,** designated with a back-slash (\), is the beginning point for subdivision. The root directory contains the system tracks and other start-up files. Each software application is typically given its own subdirectory when the package is installed. Thus to use a particular package you should first change to that subdirectory, then execute the program.

Some packages create further subdirectories within the application subdirectory to store certain files. For example, you might have a WordPerfect subdirectory called WP51 and within it, have subdirectories called LEARN and

Three steps are required to prepare the hard drive for use after it is physically installed in the system unit:

- The DOS **FDISK** command will **partition** the drive for use with DOS, as described in the instructions that accompany the drive. This step involves assigning certain cylinders of the drive as a DOS partition (usually the C drive), and setting up the boot partition. The FDISK program will provide default values which are usually correct.
- After partitioning, **low-level formatting** (sometimes called preformatting) is done. This step may be done automatically, or you may have to go through another utility program, depending on specific hard drive and controller used. This step also permits you to enter any bad cluster numbers — DOS will automatically lock these clusters out and not use them for storage. The CHKDSK command's status report includes a line for "Bad Sectors."
- The third step involves using the FORMAT program to **initialize** the drive. The /S switch is chosen to copy the hidden system files onto the drive and make it ready as a boot drive.

FIGURE 2-13

Steps in Initializing a Hard Disk Drive

```
C:\─┬─ANALYST
    ├─FS
    ├─HG
    ├─KW
    ├─OAKMTN
    ├─PBRUSH
    ├─VPX
    ├─SPJ
    └─WP51────────┬─LETTERS
                  └─LEARN
```

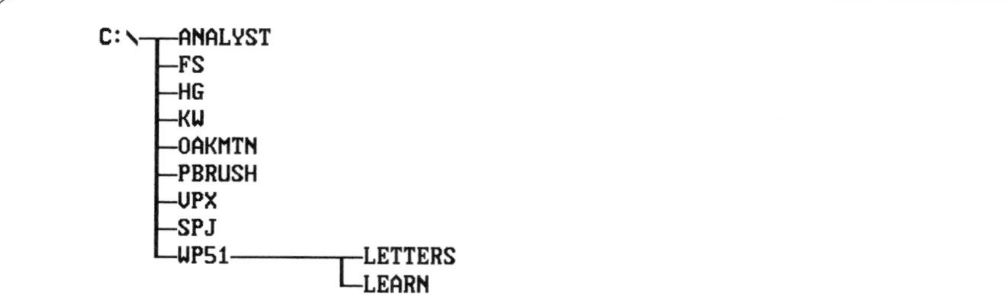

FIGURE 2-14

Graphical View of Subdirectory Structure

LETTERS. When viewed, the subdirectory organization resembles a tree lying on its side. The DOS **TREE** command will display the directory structure in a hard-to-read fashion. There are better utility programs for this, such as Norton Utilities. DOS 4 presents a graphical view of the subdirectory structure, shown in Figure 2-14.

Making a New Subdirectory: MKDIR or MD

To create a new subdirectory, use the DOS **MKDIR** command, abbreviated **MD.** This will create a subdirectory with the specified name within the *current* directory. This command does *not* change to the new subdirectory, however. Use the **CD** command to change to a specified directory. Directory names follow DOS file name rules without extensions. At the C> prompt, type:

MD WORDPROC Create a new subdirectory called WORDPROC within the current directory.

Changing to a Subdirectory: CHDIR or CD

The DOS **CHDIR** command, abbreviated **CD,** is used to change the current or default directory to a specified one. For example, at the C> prompt type:

CD WORDPROC Change the default directory to WORDPROC.

MD REPORTS Create a new REPORTS (child) subdirectory within the WORDPROC (parent) directory.

MD SCHOOL Create the SCHOOL subdirectory, also within the WORDPROC subdirectory.

CD . . DOS uses the special file name ". ." to represent the parent of the current subdirectory. If you are in the SCHOOL subdirectory, this command changes to SCHOOL's parent, WORDPROC. The special file name "." represents the name of the current directory.

The subdirectory structure for the example is shown in Figure 2-15.

Removing a Subdirectory: RMDIR or RD

RMDIR (abbreviated **RD**) will remove an existing subdirectory, provided it is empty or contains no files or subdirectories. To remove a directory, use the CD

```
C:\—WORDPROC—┬—REPORTS
             └—SCHOOL
```

FIGURE 2-15

Example of a Subdirectory Structure

command to change to the *parent* directory of the one you wish to delete. For example, to remove the last directory added above (SCHOOL), first change to the WORDPROC subdirectory, then remove the SCHOOL directory. At the C> prompt type:

CD \WORDPROC	You must specify the *complete* subdirectory path when changing the subdirectory.
RD SCHOOL	Remove the subdirectory SCHOOL. If SCHOOL contains any files or subdirectories DOS will not complete the removal. Delete all files in the SCHOOL subdirectory before issuing the RD command.

Displaying the Subdirectory Name: PROMPT

DOS provides the **PROMPT** command to help you know which subdirectory is the default one. The command

```
PROMPT $P$G
```

will change the DOS prompt from C> to C:\WORDPROC>, indicating that WORDPROC is the current directory. Each time you change directories, the DOS prompt will give your location. The PROMPT PG command can be added to the AUTOEXEC.BAT file; when the computer boots and the AUTOEXEC.BAT file is executed, the PROMPT command will automatically take effect for that session.

Pathname Rules

DOS Pathnames: Drive, Directory, and File Name

The full DOS **pathname** consists of **drive:\path\name.ext.** Drive and path are optional parts of the pathname if you are referring to files within the current default subdirectory. The pathname is used to completely identify a file and its storage location. It is possible for files *in different subdirectories* to have the same file name. But two files cannot share the same pathname. Here are some examples of pathnames that could be used in commands such as COPY, REN, DEL, and TYPE.

C:BOOKS.DBF	Here the path is omitted, so file commands default to the current subdirectory.
C:\DBASE\BOOKS.DBF	The DBASE subdirectory is given first, then the file name itself.
WP\CH2	The drive designator is optional, defaulting to the default drive. In this case WP is the subdirectory name.
C:\WP\LETTERS\OTOOLE	Here the path refers to the file called OTOOLE in the LETTERS subdirectory within the WP subdirectory of the C drive.

Setting a Search Path: PATH

When issuing a file command, DOS will first look in the default subdirectory, then any other subdirectories that appear in the **search path.** The **PATH** command is used to create the search path. In the AUTOEXEC.BAT file illustration given earlier in this chapter, the search path command was:

```
PATH C:\DOS;C:\WP;C:\DBASE;C:\PCPLUS;C:\
```

DOS will first look in the current subdirectory for files to load. If the files are not there, DOS will look in each of the subdirectories shown in the PATH command, in the order listed. If the same file name exists in more than one subdirectory, the first one encountered is loaded. Be cautious when naming more than one file with the same name.

Backing Up A Hard Disk

Hard disks are subject to occasional failure, jeopardizing the disk's contents. Prudent users will conscientiously practice a program of regular backups on floppy disks or a tape backup unit. There are two kinds of DOS backups: you could use the COPY command to copy specific files to formatted diskettes, or use the DOS **BACKUP** command. The COPY technique is useful when working on a particular assignment, and it is simple to copy your file to a floppy disk. This chapter is copied onto a floppy disk at the end of each writing session. However, COPY becomes tedious when there are many files to copy.

Copying the Hard Disk: BACKUP

The BACKUP command copies a file, a group of files, a subdirectory and all its files, or an entire disk's contents onto one or more floppy disks. The syntax of this command is

```
BACKUP fromdrive:[pathname] todrive: /switches
```

The "fromdrive" gives the letter of the drive to be backed up; the "todrive" gives the drive location to which the files are copied. The optional pathname identifies the location (subdirectory name, file name) of the file(s) you wish to save on the floppy disk. Wildcard templates may be used to specify groups of files. The floppy disk in the "todrive" does not have to be formatted unless you are using an older version of DOS that does not offer a built-in formatting option, requiring that a sufficient number of formatted disks be available before the BACKUP is begun. BACKUP will prompt you to insert additional disks as needed until all of the specified files are backed up. The disks should be numbered consecutively on the disk's external label. The most commonly used optional switches are:

/A Add newly backed-up files to other files already on the floppy disk. If not specified, any information previously stored on that diskette is destroyed.

/D Back up those files dated on or after a certain date (/D:date). Date is entered as mm-dd-yy form.

/F Format destination disks without prompting. This could destroy data if the wrong disk is inserted.

/S Back up files in subdirectories of the current directory.

/M Back up only those files modified since previous backup. The DOS archive attribute is used to indicate if the file has been changed since the last backup.

Some examples of the BACKUP command follow.

BACKUP C:WP*.DOC A: /A	Back up all files ending with the .DOC extension from the WP subdirectory of the C drive. Append these files to any already on the backup disk in drive A.
BACKUP C: A: /D:05-17-89	Back up all files dated after 5/17/89 in default subdirectory of the C drive onto the A drive.

Restoring the Hard Disk: RESTORE

The counterpart to the BACKUP command is the DOS **RESTORE** procedure. Files saved with BACKUP must be accessed with RESTORE. You must use the same DOS versions of BACKUP and RESTORE. The syntax for this command resembles that for BACKUP:

```
RESTORE fromdrive: todrive:pathname /switches
```

The "fromdrive" indicates where the floppy disk containing the backed-up files is located; the "todrive" gives the drive where the files are to be restored. Pathname is optional, and indicates which files or groups of files to restore. If pathname is omitted, all files on the backup set are restored to the hard drive. Switches include /B and /A (restore files before/after a given date), /M (restores only those files modified since the last backup), and /S (restores subdirectories also). Your DOS manual has additional details.

RESTORE will re-create subdirectories on the hard disk with the same organization that existed when they were backed up unless overridden by the user. Some examples:

RESTORE A: C:\DBASE	Restore all files from the A drive to the DBASE subdirectory.
RESTORE A: C: /S	Restores all files to the C drive, including those in subdirectories, from the backup disks in the A drive.

Copying Files and Directories: XCOPY

The COPY command is used to copy a file, or a group of files, from a single directory to a single directory. The DOS **XCOPY** command will copy files and the underlying directory structure (including lower-level directories if they exist) from one drive to another. If the directories on the target disk do not already exist, DOS will create them before copying files to them. The format of this command is:

```
XCOPY [d:][path][filename] [d:][path][filename] /switches
```

The /S switch will force XCOPY to copy lower-level subdirectories; otherwise only the current directory and its files are copied. The /D switch copies files that were modified on or after a specified date. The /M switch copies only those files that have been modified since the last time they were backed up or copied with XCOPY. Some examples:

XCOPY A: B: /S	Copies all the files and subdirectories from the A drive to the B drive. Lower-level directories are copied.
XCOPY A:\UTIL B:	Copies the \UTIL directory and its files from the A drive to the B drive.

File Storage and Disk Fragmentation

Files are stored in clusters; a cluster is a unit of disk space amounting to 2048 characters on a hard disk, or 512 characters on a floppy disk. In DOS 4.01 clusters are known as disk allocation units. As old files are deleted from the disk, that space is made available for new files. If a new file is larger than the next set of contiguous clusters in the directory, the file is stored in two or more non-adjoining clusters on the disk. Over time the files on the disk become fragmented and access times slow considerably as the disk heads are moved back and forth to retrieve a file. To remedy this situation, files should be repositioned to contiguous, or adjoining, clusters. Although there are no DOS programs to accomplish this, you can copy the files to a newly-formatted disk and the files will not be fragmented. Both Norton Utilities and PC-TOOLS offer utilities that can "defragment," or compress, an existing disk, improving performance significantly.

ADVANCED DOS CONCEPTS

User-Prepared Startup Files

Part of the boot-up process utilizes two special user-created files, **CONFIG.SYS** and **AUTOEXEC.BAT.** These optional files are placed in the root directory of the boot disk and are processed automatically after the other system files are loaded. These files are used to create special hardware and software configurations that are not a standard part of DOS.

The CONFIG.SYS File

CONFIG.SYS contains special configuration commands that are loaded into memory for the duration of the session. Installation instructions for new application packages frequently mention adding lines to the CONFIG.SYS file. Some installations do this automatically while others ask the user to do so manually. For example, WordPerfect recommends the following in your CONFIG.SYS:

```
FILES=20
BUFFERS=20
```

These commands instruct DOS to handle up to 20 open files simultaneously; 6 is the default number with no FILES= command in the CONFIG.SYS file. The BUFFERS command reserves a certain amount of RAM to speed up disk accesses. DOS will transfer several consecutive clusters at the same time, placing them in the **disk buffer** in memory. Fewer disk accesses are usually needed with more buffers, improving efficiency. The installation program that comes with some software packages may automatically modify your CONFIG.SYS file. Knowledge of *how* the CONFIG.SYS commands work is not critical to successful use of the application, but be sure your CONFIG.SYS matches the requirements of your software.

Example: *Creating a CONFIG.SYS File with COPY CON*

If the CONFIG.SYS file does not exist, you can create one with the COPY CON command. CON is a special DOS reserved word that refers to the system console, or keyboard. The COPY CON command will copy the keyboard keystrokes to the designated file. Its usage is:

```
COPY CON filename
```

The entries to create the CONFIG.SYS file are shown in Figure 2-16.

1. Type the three lines shown in the figure, then press **Enter.** The **^Z** (Ctrl-Z) at the end of the last line tells DOS to terminate the copy operation and create the new file.

```
A:\>COPY CON CONFIG.SYS
    FILES=20
    BUFFERS=20^Z
       1 File(s) copied

A:\>
```

FIGURE 2-16

Results of COPY CON CONFIG.SYS Command

2. If there was an existing CONFIG.SYS file on the default drive, its contents have been replaced by the lines that you entered with this command.

The AUTOEXEC.BAT File and TSR Programs

The AUTOEXEC.BAT file contains DOS commands and other programs that should be run every time the computer is booted up. Some typical AUTOEXEC commands set up the search path, change the DOS prompt, initialize certain print utilities such as a print spooler, load the **driver software** that controls the mouse, and load other **terminate-and-stay-resident (TSR) programs.**

Also called memory resident programs, TSR programs reside in RAM and can be called into action from within other programs with a special keystroke, called the **hot key sequence.** PC-TOOLS has a set of desktop utilities that can be used at any time, even while another program is running. TSR programs provide useful functions but occasionally can interfere with each other or with applications software. Many technicians suggest removing some or all of the TSR programs if a newly purchased package doesn't work properly.

A **print spooler** uses a portion of RAM to hold output characters for the printer. Because the computer can generate output much faster than the printer can accept it, the spooler allows the software to work ahead of the printer. Most printers can be equipped with an internal or external buffer, but the print spooler offers more features and typically more capacity. Expanded or extended memory can be used for the print spooler, conserving conventional RAM for regular applications.

A **RAM disk** can be established to emulate a speedy disk drive in RAM. By copying an application to the RAM disk, then executing it from that drive, it may execute much faster than from a floppy drive or hard drive. Of course, RAM disks do occupy memory that might be better used for ordinary storage. DOS provides a means of creating a RAM disk in extended memory, saving conventional RAM for applications programs and data.

DOS Command Keys

The Command Line Template

The previous DOS command line is automatically saved in a portion of memory. You can re-run the same command, or modify parts of it, without having to retype the entire command. The function keys at the left side or top edge of the keyboard and the numeric keypad keys have special meanings in DOS. The function keys are identified as F1–F10. These keys can save time by repeating or making changes to the previous command. Use of the keys in DOS is explained below. [Note: the meanings of these DOS function keys change when a specific application program is loaded.]

F1 Copies the characters from the previous command, one at a time. You can copy a few characters, make a change, and then copy the remaining characters.

F2 char Copies all characters up to the specified character, and places them on the command line.

F3 Copies the entire previous command to the command line.

F4 char Skips over the characters from the previous command to the character specified.

F6 Places an end-of-file character (Ctrl-Z) in the command line. This is useful when creating a file with the **COPY CON filename** command.

Esc Voids the current command line and lets you start over again.

Ins Enter insert mode with the first keypress; return to normal mode with second keypress. Allows insertion of characters into previous command line template.

Del This key passes over characters from the previous command line, one at a time. It "removes" characters from the previous template.

You can enter repetitive commands using the **F3** key without retyping them, or make slight changes to commands that are similar. For example, you might be looking through a stack of diskettes for a certain file called CRIB.TXT. Put the first disk in the A drive, and type **DIR CRIB.TXT**. The DIR command will search the disk and indicate whether the file resides on that disk. If the file is not on that diskette, insert the next one and press **F3** instead of typing in the whole DIR command. Press **Enter** to execute the command.

Other DOS Commands

The MS-DOS 3.3 manual lists over 50 commands, most of which are not used by the typical user. Some of the commands are used for creating DOS batch files as described in the next section. A few of the more useful commands are briefly described below. Some versions of DOS may contain additional commands, or more options within existing commands. For more details, see the command summaries at the end of this chapter or your DOS manual.

ATTRIB Display file attributes or change attributes such as **read-only** or **hidden** file. See section below.

CLS Clears the screen. This is useful when finishing an application and leaving the computer's power on. Avoid leaving the same image on the screen—it can become "burned in" on the inside of the screen, causing permanent damage.

FC Display differences between two files.

GRAPHICS Allows printer to print certain graphical images from the screen.

LABEL Allows a disk's volume label to be changed.

MODE This is a multi-purpose command that enables you to configure the equipment attached to your computer. The MODE command can divert printer output from one port to another, configure the screen mode, and on some Zenith computers can turn the modem on or off, adjust the clock speed, and set the time until the screen goes blank (for battery operated computers).

RECOVER Upon a CHKDSK or other disk read error, this command can be used in an attempt to recover readable portions of a damaged file.

VER This will display the DOS version number on the screen.

VOL Display the disk's volume label. The label is also displayed when the directory of that disk is retrieved.

File Attributes

DOS maintains four file attributes which normally are not displayed with the directory listing. The attributes can be changed with the DOS ATTRIB command, but this is more handily done with a utility program such as PC-TOOLS or Norton Utilities, described later in this chapter.

- The **hidden** attribute will cause the file to not appear in a directory listing.
- The **read-only** attribute permits normal file access but prohibits the file from being changed or deleted.
- The third attribute, **system** status, describes a file as being a special system file, used in the boot process.
- The final attribute, **archive,** is used to indicate that the file has been modified since the last time it was backed up. This attribute is used when a partial backup of only changed files is desired; the normal backup procedure is to copy all files to backup media.

CREATING AND EXECUTING DOS BATCH FILES

Batch Command Files

Batch files contain DOS commands and calls to other programs that you might type from the prompt line. Putting frequently-used commands together in a batch file permits them to be executed with one command, instead of keying in the individual lines. AUTOEXEC.BAT is the most commonly used batch file. It was described earlier. AUTOEXEC.BAT is automatically executed by DOS if it is stored on the boot disk in the root directory. Any DOS command can be placed in a batch file with appropriate options specified.

Batch files can accept parameters and can execute different sections depending on the values of these inputs. These parameters are entered after the name of the batch file, and are numbered by DOS. The name of the batch file is %0, the first parameter is %1, and so on. Some commonly used batch file DOS commands include:

ECHO text This command will display the words found in "text" on the screen as the batch file executes.

ECHO OFF This will suspend the normal display output from most DOS commands so the user does not view each command as it is executed. **ECHO ON** will resume output from commands.

REM [text] This is a remark statement, useful for describing the batch file. They are optionally displayed on the screen as the batch file executes unless ECHO OFF is entered before the REM line.

PAUSE [text] PAUSE will cause the batch file to stop executing and prompt the user to press a key to continue. If text is included after PAUSE, that text will also display unless ECHO OFF appeared first.

CLS CLS will clear the screen and place the cursor in the upper left corner.

:label Indicates the start of a particular section in the batch file. The IF and GOTO statements will send execution to the section of the macro that has a matching label.

GOTO label Transfer execution to the named label.

IF .. GOTO .. The IF command compares two character strings; if they are identical, control in the batch file is passed to a specific line. For example,

```
IF "%1"=="B" GOTO BACK
```

compares the first parameter entered in the batch file command line to "B". If it is B, control goes to a line in the batch file containing :BACK; if not, it goes to the next line of the file.

Creating a Batch File with COPY CON

Batch files can be created in several ways. The simplest is to use the **COPY CON filename.BAT** command. This command provides for any characters entered on the console device (the keyboard) to be placed in the named file. Care should be taken in entering each line of the batch file because once a line is entered, it cannot be changed without a word processor or creating the entire file again. The last line of the batch file must end with the **F6** or **Ctrl-Z** character, the standard DOS end-of-file character.

Example: *Creating a Batch File with COPY CON Filename*

In this example we will create a small batch file called SHOW.BAT which will display all of the files on the default drive whose names begin with A, B, or C.

1. At the DOS prompt type **COPY CON SHOW.BAT** and press **Enter**. You will not see any prompt after pressing the **Enter** key.

   ```
   C:\>COPY CON SHOW.BAT
   ```

2. Next type in the following three lines:

   ```
   DIR A*
   DIR B*
   DIR C*
   ```

3. After you have typed in the last line above, press the **F6** key and **Enter.** You will see the characters "^Z" appear at the end of the last line. DOS will issue a message, "1 File(s) Copied," indicating that the new file has been created.
4. Issue the command **TYPE SHOW.BAT** to see if the file displays properly.
5. To execute the batch file, at the DOS prompt type **SHOW** and press **Enter.**

   ```
   C:\>SHOW
   ```

Using EDLIN to Create a Batch File

DOS includes a rudimentary line editor called EDLIN. This program allows you to create a file line by line, and to make corrections to existing files. EDLIN is described in the DOS manual.

Creating a Batch File with Your Word Processor

One common way to create a batch file is with the ASCII text or non-document file feature of your word processor. WordPerfect uses the Text In/Out command **(Ctrl-F5)** to create text files. Don't use the regular document editing portion of WordPerfect—DOS cannot recognize the special file format used by the word processor. WordStar uses the **Non-document mode** for creating text files; its **Document mode** creates a special file format that DOS cannot read. See your word processor manual, or the WordPerfect section of this textbook, for instructions on creating a text file.

Example Batch Files

Simple batch files can be great time savers. Suppose you have two printers attached to your computer, one a dot matrix and the other a daisy wheel printer. The MODE command can be used to divert normal output from the dot matrix printer, usually attached to parallel port 1 (LPT1), to the daisy wheel on serial port 1 (COM1). Figure 2-17 shows two simple batch files that activate the proper printer port within DOS. To turn on the parallel port, simply type **DOT** at the DOS prompt. To use the daisy wheel printer on the serial port, type **DAISY** at the DOS prompt.

A more complicated batch file, shown in Figure 2-18, uses a single batch file to do both jobs depending on the parameter added to the end of the command. Specify DOT (uppercase) and the batch file will select the dot matrix printer; otherwise the daisy wheel printer will be chosen.

To make installing software packages easier, many publishers include complex batch files. The user is asked questions about his computer configuration, and the batch file copies the appropriate files from the distribution disks to the user's own disks. For a simple installation batch file see Figure 2-19. What does each line accomplish?

```
REM ** DOT.BAT ** Divert printer output to LPT1
MODE LPT1

REM ** DAISY.BAT ** Divert printer output to COM1
MODE LPT1=COM1
```

FIGURE 2-17

Sample Batch Files

```
REM ** PR.BAT ** Divert printer output to proper port
IF "%1"=="DOT" GOTO DOT
:DAISY
MODE LPT1=COM1
GOTO END
:DOT
MODE LPT1
:END
```

FIGURE 2-18

Printer Setup Batch File

```
C:
CD\
COPY A:KWMAIN.BAT
MD KWTRACK
CD KWTRACK
COPY A:*.* C:
CD\
```

FIGURE 2-19

Software Installation Batch File

```
DEL C:\DTEMP\*.*
CD DTEMP
PAUSE  Insert the source disk in A:
COPY A:*.* C:
PAUSE  Now insert the destination disk in A:
COPY *.* A:
CD \
REM  Finished ... returning to root directory
```

FIGURE 2-20

Floppy Copy Batch File

Another batch file example (Figure 2-20) is a set of commands to copy one floppy disk to another by temporarily storing the files in a special subdirectory on the hard drive. What does each line accomplish?

NON-DOS UTILITY PROGRAMS

DOS has its roots in the microcomputer operating system called CP/M, popular more than 10 years ago. While internal DOS operations have continually changed, the user interface has remained consistent, and many think it to be rather "unfriendly." To solve this problem, and to provide additional functions not previously available with DOS, several vendors have developed excellent companion utility products. These utility programs offer a better user interface and additional functions, provide much-improved disk backup and restore, and permit multiple programs to be loaded in memory at the same time for rapid switching, also known as **multitasking.**

File Management and DOS Shell Programs

A **DOS shell** is a program that presents menus for managing files and entering DOS commands. Because the normal DOS commands may be difficult for new users to learn and use, DOS shells were designed to replace the usual DOS interface. The two best-known packages are Norton Utilities and PC-TOOLS. Originally sold as tools to undelete files that were erased accidentally, these utilities have grown into much larger, more comprehensive products. In fact, DOS 4.0 was developed, in part, to provide some of the ease of use and additional functions provided by these packages.

The Norton Utilities

Norton Utilities provide more than 20 utility programs to do such things as sort directories, test the disk, find a file by matching text within the file or by file name, maintain and display a graphical directory tree, give disk and file statis-

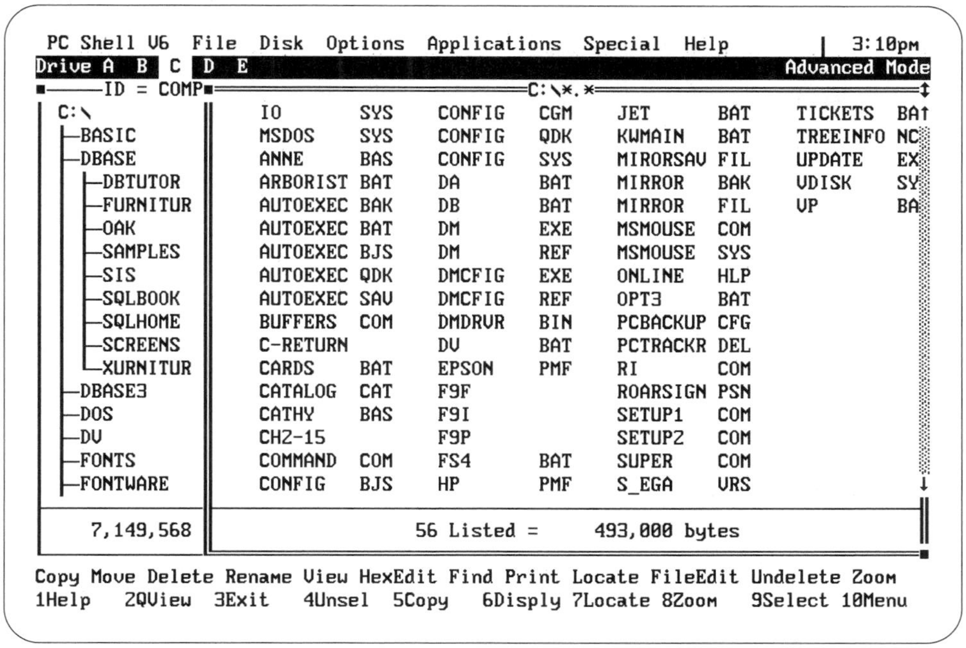

```
 PC Shell V6  File  Disk  Options  Applications  Special  Help        |  3:10pm
Drive A  B  C  D  E                                                Advanced Mode
 ——ID = COMP======================C:\*.*=========================================
 C:\            IO        SYS   CONFIG   CGM   JET       BAT   TICKETS  BAT
 ├BASIC         MSDOS     SYS   CONFIG   QDK   KWMAIN    BAT   TREEINFO NC
 ├DBASE         ANNE      BAS   CONFIG   SYS   MIRORSAV  FIL   UPDATE   EX
 │├DBTUTOR      ARBORIST  BAT   DA       BAT   MIRROR    BAK   VDISK    SY
 │├FURNITUR     AUTOEXEC  BAK   DB       BAT   MIRROR    FIL   VP       BA
 │├OAK          AUTOEXEC  BAT   DM       EXE   MSMOUSE   COM
 │├SAMPLES      AUTOEXEC  BJS   DM       REF   MSMOUSE   SYS
 │├SIS          AUTOEXEC  QDK   DMCFIG   EXE   ONLINE    HLP
 │├SQLBOOK      AUTOEXEC  SAV   DMCFIG   REF   OPT3      BAT
 │├SQLHOME      BUFFERS   COM   DMDRVR   BIN   PCBACKUP  CFG
 │├SCREENS      C-RETURN        DV       BAT   PCTRACKR  DEL
 │└XURNITUR     CARDS     BAT   EPSON    PMF   RI        COM
 ├DBASE3        CATALOG   CAT   F9F            ROARSIGN  PSN
 ├DOS           CATHY     BAS   F9I            SETUP1    COM
 ├DV            CH2-15          F9P            SETUP2    COM
 ├FONTS         COMMAND   COM   FS4      BAT   SUPER     COM
 ├FONTWARE      CONFIG    BJS   HP       PMF   S_EGA     VRS

   7,149,568               56 Listed =      493,000 bytes

Copy Move Delete Rename View HexEdit Find Print Locate FileEdit Undelete Zoom
1Help  2QView  3Exit   4Unsel  5Copy  6Disply 7Locate 8Zoom   9Select 10Menu
```

FIGURE 2-21

PC TOOLS V6 Shell

tics, attach comments to files, and defragment a hard disk, as well as the well-known Norton Unerase facility. The Norton Commander shell acts as an easy-to-use substitute for the DOS command interpreter. You can select subdirectories and files by choosing from menus rather than typing in a sometimes hard-to-remember command. DOS 4.0 offers a similar shell.

PC-TOOLS

PC-TOOLS (version 5 or higher) has evolved into a full-function package offering most of the same features as Norton Utilities, plus a set of desktop tools. The desktop contains notepads and an outline facility, an appointment scheduler and a telecommunications package for accessing remote computers using a modem, a simple editor for creating batch and other text files, three calculators (algebraic, financial using a Hewlett-Packard 12C keyboard, and hexadecimal for programmers), and a database function that will read and write dBASE formatted data files. The PC-TOOLS shell offers menus for various file and DOS functions, as well as offering additional functions. Included in this package are a high-speed backup/restore program to replace the sluggish DOS equivalent, a replacement formatting program that permits reversal of an accidentally-formatted hard disk, a file undelete function, and a program which copies the directory and FAT to a safe spot on the disk, permitting the disk to be rebuilt in case of damage to the directory. The shell is shown in Figure 2-21.

The PC-TOOLS shell allows you to **tag** groups of files that will undergo the same file operation. Using a mouse or the cursor control keys, you can move the cursor to each file desired in the group. Then using the pull-down menu at the top of the screen, perform such file operations as copy, move, delete, change attributes, and more. Most DOS features are available through the shell, and some users rarely use DOS commands. One useful capability is directory maintenance—the ability to change the subdirectory structure quickly. The prune-and-graft option permits you to move a subdirectory from its original location to another parent. PC-TOOLS provides mapping functions to visually depict the disk's physical layout and show where individual files are stored.

Mace Utilities

Mace Utilities is another useful add-on utility package. It offers assistance in rebuilding damaged files and disk directories. This package is also useful at recovering lost data from dBASE data files. The cost of this kind of software is easily justified if lost data is retrieved.

Hard Disk Backup and Restore Utilities

With larger hard drives and heavy reliance upon them for vital business data, systematic backups are mandatory. The DOS BACKUP/RESTORE programs do work, but are cumbersome to use, relatively slow, and require a large number of floppy disks. Even with the higher-capacity 1.2 or 1.44 MB diskettes, many are needed to do a full backup. Fortunately, there are alternative backup programs that make this task somewhat easier. It is likely that backups will be done more often if they are less taxing!

The better backup programs are able to fit 30% more data on the same diskette than usual, so fewer disks are needed. They use a proprietary data compression algorithm and special file format for storing data, and the backup disks can only be read by the accompanying restore utility. These programs maintain a file log, similar to a disk directory. Backups and restorations are done visually, using a menu and graphical display of subdirectories and files. You can select files to be backed up or restored from the screen instead of having to list them on the DOS BACKUP command line. These packages offer multiple options for backups, and are highly recommended. PC-TOOLS contains an advanced backup program. Fastback-Plus is another popular backup package.

For large hard drives, backups on floppy disks take an excessive amount of time. For these users, a cartridge tape drive is recommended both to save time and reduce the effort spent in doing backups. The tape cartridge can be loaded into the computer and the backup can be timed to occur overnight; the user need not be present if the tape will hold the entire disk's contents. Otherwise the user must continually insert and remove a seemingly endless number of floppy disks.

Multitasking Environments: Windows and DESQview

With the popularity of the Macintosh graphical operating system and users' requests for running more than one program at a time, Windows and DESQview provide an alternative **environment** to DOS. These programs load into RAM when the computer boots up, and provide a graphical shell for the user. But their real advantage comes when running programs. With a few keystrokes, you can switch from one program to another, exchange data between programs, and even run two programs at the same time. These environments require additional RAM be installed in the computer beyond 640 KB to hold the programs.

For example, someone running a database application may need to retrieve data from another computer over a telephone line. He could open a second window from the database for the telecommunications program, initiate the communications session, then retrieve the data. Then he can quickly switch back to the database, where nothing has changed since he left. In another case a user might be preparing a report using a word processor, and need to go into the spreadsheet program to do additional analysis, then import the spreadsheet into the report. Windows and DESQview offer similar capabilities but require a fast computer with plenty of RAM to work effectively. If the RAM is not large enough to hold all the desired programs, the hard disk is used to temporarily hold portions of memory, called **pages.** Thus a fast-access-time hard disk speeds up the switching process. Figure 2-22 shows a Windows 3 session with several applications running concurrently.

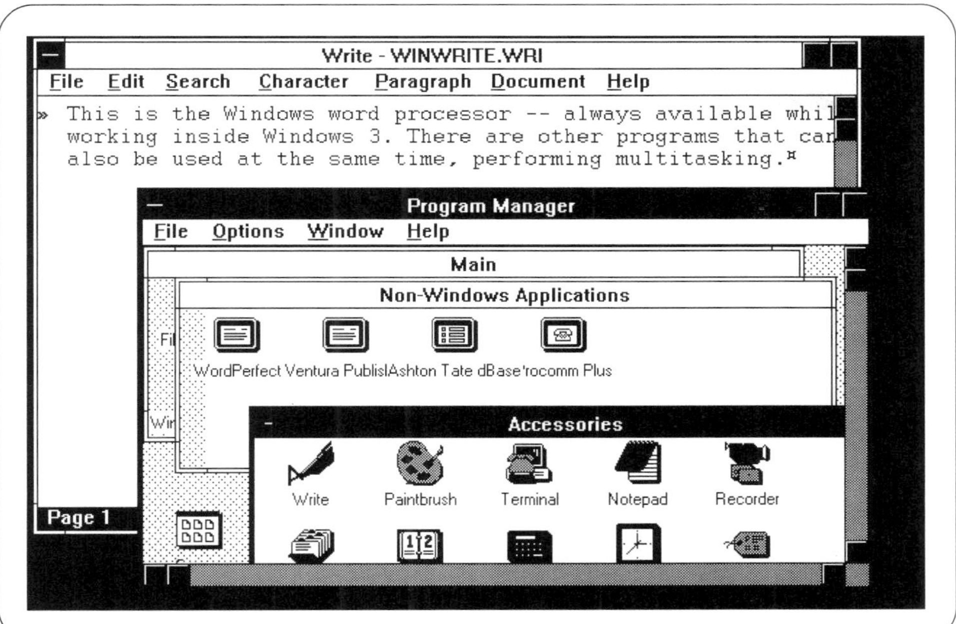

FIGURE 2-22

Sample Windows 3 Screen Display

DOS, OS/2, AND OTHER OPERATING SYSTEMS

Other DOS Versions

When the IBM PC was developed, the prevailing microcomputer operating system was called CP/M. Running on 8080 microprocessor computers, CP/M had to fit into a small amount of RAM. The earliest version of DOS (version 1.0) was introduced in 1981 with the IBM PC. Version 1.0 assumed a minimal memory and secondary storage configuration. Version 1.1 added support for double-sided floppy disks. Later versions of DOS grew larger and more capable. Version 2.0 accompanied the hard disk-based IBM XT. This version supported hard disks and additional file manipulation commands.

DOS 3.0 appeared in 1985 with the introduction of the 80286-based IBM AT personal computer. This version supported the high-density 1.2 MB floppy diskette, and used the setup configuration stored within the computer to determine the type of disk drives attached. DOS 3.1 was introduced shortly after with support for local area networks through the NetBIOS commands.

Support for 3.5-inch drives appeared in DOS 3.2. In 1987 DOS 3.3 extended that support to 1.44 MB 3.5-inch drives, along with the ability to handle different national languages through the use of country codes. Display, keyboard, and printer codes can be modified for certain special language characters.

In 1989 DOS 4.0 was released with improvements in several areas. This version permitted hard disk drives to be larger than 32 MB without special software drivers. DOS 4.0 also came with an optional graphical shell, shown in Figure 2-23, that replaced the DOS prompt and keyboard-entered commands. DOS 4.0 also supports higher-resolution video modes, including the ability to print high-resolution graphics screen images. DOS version 4.01 was released to fix some errors. DOS 5.0 was released in 1991. This version provides more free conventional memory by loading itself in extended memory (286 or higher). Faster than previous versions, it also provides online help.

OS/2—The Multitasking Software

When IBM introduced the PS/2 microcomputer family in 1987, they also announced a new operating system that would solve many problems inherent with DOS and the 8088 microprocessor family. **OS/2** leaps past the 1 MB RAM limitation but requires an 80286 or 80386 microprocessor; 8088/8086 computers

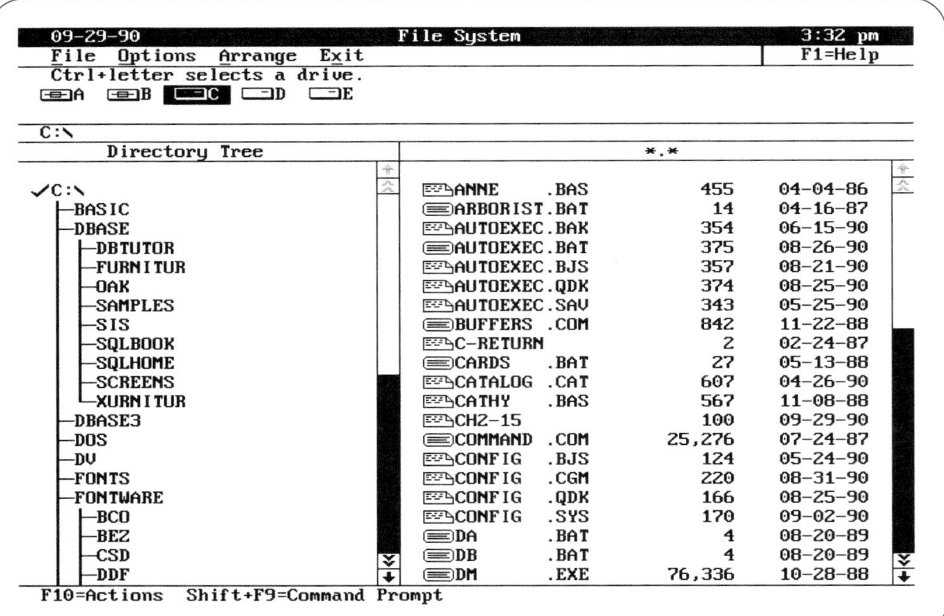

FIGURE 2-23

DOS 4 Graphical Shell

cannot run OS/2 without an accelerator card which replaces the original processor.

With OS/2 software developers can design much larger programs, and accomplish multitasking in a sophisticated manner. OS/2 requires significantly more memory and disk space, generally twice as much as DOS. Thus a computer needs 2+ MB of RAM and a 40 MB or greater disk drive to effectively use OS/2. The complexity of this advanced operating system delayed its introduction for many months, and as of this writing only a portion of software publishers have shipped OS/2 compatible software. While OS/2 will run regular DOS programs, only those programs especially written for OS/2 can be run in the larger memory space and with multitasking.

The OS/2 Presentation Manager is a graphics-oriented environment similar to Windows and to the Macintosh user interface. Users running this version of OS/2 would initiate commands by using a mouse to move the pointer to the screen icon (picture) representing that function. Graphical user interfaces may be easier for new users to master. Users would be able to move between different programs more readily if they shared the same basic user interface.

Some experts predict that both DOS and OS/2 will exist in the future. Users with less demanding needs would use DOS on a smaller computer, while those with sophisticated applications would have OS/2 running on powerful computers. Software publishers may support applications in both environments, or there may be less-powerful versions (or even different programs) for DOS users.

Unix

The **Unix** operating system is widely used in multiple-user minicomputer applications. Because there is a great deal of general Unix software in the public domain, Unix is an attractive environment for those who wish to use that software. Several Unix versions have been created for micro-computers, including SCO Unix and Microsoft Xenix. These versions share the same rich set of programmer tools with the larger Unix implementations, and can also be used for multi-user applications with the 80286 or 80386 microcomputer as host CPU.

Some DOS packages are able to run under Unix. Software written expressly for Unix can be run in a multitasking mode. The user is able to switch quickly from one program to another while the switched-out program continues to run (albeit more slowly) in the background.

DOS COMMAND SUMMARY

Internal DOS commands are always available at the DOS prompt, and are the most commonly used commands. **External commands** are stored as separate files on the DOS disk, and are executed by typing their name. However, DOS must be able to locate the file containing the instructions for that command or you will get the error message, **Bad command or file name,** indicating the file could not be located. For hard disk users, be sure to include in a PATH command the name of the subdirectory where the external DOS commands are located. While this text assumes you are using DOS 3.3, these commands are nearly identical on most versions of DOS. Figures 2-24 and 2-25 contain a summary of the most useful commands.

CHAPTER REVIEW

Elementary DOS Commands

The operating system is a set of utility programs that manage the computer's resources. When the computer is powered up, DOS is loaded from the boot disk into RAM. The AUTOEXEC.BAT and CONFIG.SYS files contain important start-up commands for the computer. DOS file names consist of a name of up to

Command	**Purpose**
BREAK	Allows or disables Ctrl-C interrupt of program
CHDIR (CD)	Change default directory
CLS	Clear the display screen
COPY	Copy specified file(s)
d:	Change default drive to specified letter
DATE	Display and set the current date
DEL (ERASE)	Delete specified file(s)
DIR	List files in a directory
EXIT	Exit the command processor
MKDIR (MD)	Create a new subdirectory
PATH	Set command file search path
PROMPT	Change DOS command prompt
RENAME (REN)	Rename a file
RMDIR (RD)	Remove a subdirectory
SET	Set environment variable
TIME	Display and set the current time
TYPE	Display contents of a file on the screen
VER	Show the DOS version number
VOL	Display the disk's volume label

FIGURE 2-24

Internal DOS Command Summary

FIGURE 2-25

External DOS Command Summary

Command	Purpose
APPEND	Set a search path for data files
ASSIGN	Assign a drive letter to a different drive
ATTRIB	Set or display file attributes
BACKUP	Back up files from one disk to another
CHKDSK	Check directory for errors, also display free RAM and disk space remaining
COMMAND	Start the DOS command processor
COMP	Compare the contents of two files
DISKCOMP	Compare the contents of two disks
DISKCOPY	Copy contents of one disk
EXE2BIN	Convert .EXE files to binary format
FC	Compare files, display differences
FDISK	Configure and initialize hard disk
FIND	Locate a specific text string
FORMAT	Prepare a new disk for storing data
GRAFTABL	Load a table of graphics characters
GRAPHICS	Prepare DOS to print graphics screens
JOIN	Join a disk drive to a path
LABEL	Display and change disk volume label
MODE	Set operating characteristics for devices such as monitor and I/O ports
MORE	Display screen of output at a time
PRINT	Print contents of file
RECOVER	Recover from errors in file
REPLACE	Replace previous version of file with new version of same name
RESTORE	Restores files that were previously backed up
SORT	Sorts data in ascending or descending order
SUBST	Substitute a string for a path
TREE	Display subdirectory structure and file names
XCOPY	Copies files and subdirectories

8 characters and an optional 3-character extension preceded by a period. The * and ? wildcard characters let you refer to groups of files sharing common name elements.

Working with Files

The directory of a disk contains information about the files stored on that disk, including the date that each file was last changed. Files can be copied, renamed, printed, or deleted from the disk. Blank disks must be formatted prior to being used. Data disks are used to store programs and data, while system disks can boot the computer.

Working with Hard Disks

Hard disks offer large storage capability and fast storage and retrieval of information. They should be organized into separate subdirectories for each application. Disk backups are necessary in case the disk drive should fail. DOS offers built-in programs to back up and restore hard drives, but improved packages are available from other vendors for this important task.

Creating and Executing DOS Batch Files

DOS batch files are used to automatically execute sequences of commands. Virtually any DOS command can be placed in a batch file, and additional batch file commands are available to accomplish various programming tasks.

Non-DOS Utility Programs

Several utility programs that augment DOS functions are available from other vendors. For instance, a deleted file can be undeleted if certain conditions are met. DOS shells offer an alternative user interface to the DOS command interpreter. Some utility programs can offer multitasking capabilities, running two or more programs in memory at the same time.

DOS, OS/2, and Other Operating Systems

OS/2 was announced at the time the IBM PS/2 line of personal computers was introduced. OS/2 offers multitasking capabilities, along with a graphical user interface similar to that of the Macintosh computer. However, OS/2 requires an 80286 or higher microprocessor and much more RAM than does DOS. Programs must be written especially for OS/2, and software producers have been slow to produce new OS/2 programs. At this writing it appears that DOS applications will exist alongside OS/2.

KEY TERMS

archive
AUTOEXEC.BAT
Backspace key
BACKUP
Basic Input/Output System (BIOS)
boot disk
CapsLock key
CHDIR (or **CD**)
CHKDSK
cold boot
CONFIG.SYS
COPY
DATE
default disk drive
Del key
DEL (or **ERASE**)
DIR
disk buffer
disk directory
Disk Operating System (DOS) (MS-DOS, PC-DOS)
DISKCOMP
DISKCOPY
DOS shell
driver software
End key
Enter key
environment
Esc key
extension
external commands
F1 key
F2 key
F3 key
F4 key
F6 key
FDISK
file attributes
file names
FORMAT
formatted disk
hidden file
Home key
hot key sequence
initialize
Ins key
internal commands
light-emitting diode (LED)
low-level formatting
MKDIR (or **MD**)
multitasking
name
NumLock key
operating system
OS/2
pages
partition
PATH
pathname
PgDn
PgUp
PRINT
print spooler
PROMPT
PrtSc key

RAM disk
read-only file
RENAME
RESTORE
RMDIR (or **RD**)
root directory
search path
Shift-PrtSc
subdirectory
switches
Tab key
tag
terminate-and-stay-resident (TSR) programs
TIME
toggle
TREE
TYPE
Unix
volume label
warm boot
wildcard template
XCOPY

DISCUSSION QUESTIONS

1. Explain the purpose of an operating system. What is the operating system used with IBM-compatible microcomputers?
2. What are the differences between a system (boot) disk and a data disk?
3. Why do we format blank disks before they are used? Explain how to format a data disk.
4. Explain the use of the following keys: Backspace, left arrow, Esc, NumLock, CapsLock, Shift, F3, Shift-PrtSc, Control-PrtSc.
5. Which of the following DOS file names and pathnames are not valid?

```
HECTOR.123       FILENAME        B:SPECIAL.FILE
ACCOUNTING       ACTG.A          C:\WP\FILE99.CHK
123.BILL         BILL.123        A:DATADISK
BUDGET89.WK1     DOCUMENT. 45    C:/LOTUS/LOTUS.COM
```

6. Which command is used to erase a file permanently?
7. Which command is used to display the contents of a file on the screen? On the printer?
8. Which command can be used to display the disk's file directory? Explain the information contained in the disk directory. Which command can be used to verify that the directory is logically correct?
9. Discuss the usefulness of organizing hard disks into subdirectories. Which commands are needed when working with subdirectories?
10. Explain the purpose of the DOS search path. How can one be set up?
11. Discuss the special files AUTOEXEC.BAT and CONFIG.SYS. What role do they play with the microcomputer?
12. Give at least two ways to copy all the files from one disk to another.
13. Define disk fragmentation and discuss how to resolve this problem.
14. What is a DOS batch file? Why are they useful?
15. Why do we need to do hard disk backups? How are they accomplished in DOS?
16. What is meant by the term *multitasking?* What tools are available to do multitasking on a personal computer?
17. Why are programs such as PC-TOOLS and Norton Utilities useful? Discuss their features that are absent from DOS.
18. What is OS/2? Discuss its future use. Will it replace DOS?

EXERCISES

1. Format a blank floppy disk as a data disk. Then obtain a directory of that disk. You'll get a "File not found" message. A printed copy of your screen may be obtained by using the **Shift-PrtSc** command after the directory is displayed on the screen.

2. Use the DOS DATE and TIME commands to change the date and time on your PC, then change them back to the correct values.

3. Using the wildcard technique, obtain a directory of only the .COM files on the boot disk.

4. Change the default drive to the drive where your data disk resides. Then copy all of the .COM files from the boot disk to your floppy disk using the wildcard template procedure.

5. Create the following file on your data disk by using the **COPY CON TEST** command. The last thing to enter is the F6 command which will produce a ^Z on the screen. ^Z is the representation for **Ctrl-Z,** and is *not* created by typing the ^ key and Z.

```
This is a sample file created from the console.
It consists of three lines.
This is the last line
[F6]
```

6. Copy the TEST file to another file, SECOND. Are their directory entries identical?

7. Rename the TEST file as FIRST.

8. Delete the SECOND file from the disk.

9. Apply a write-protect tab over the notch of the data disk if it is a 5.25-inch diskette. For 3.5-inch disks open the small sliding window in the lower-left corner. Reinsert the disk in the drive. Then attempt to delete the FIRST file. What does the message mean? [Be sure to remove the write protect tab or close the slider window on your data disk before attempting to save anything else.]

10. Use the CHKDSK program to verify that the directory of your data disk is correct. What other information is displayed?

11. On your data disk, create a directory called PAPERS. Within the PAPERS subdirectory, create two more subdirectories called MIS and ENGLISH. Copy the FIRST file from the root subdirectory into the MIS subdirectory.

12. Use the DOS PRINT command to obtain a printed copy of the FIRST file on the printer.

13. Use the DOS VER command to display the version of your operating system.

14. If you have a hard disk on your computer and a sufficient supply of floppy disks, use the BACKUP command to make a backup copy of the root subdirectory of the hard disk. Use the /D switch to backup only those files created or changed during the current year (after January 1 of this year).

```
ECHO OFF
REM  ** Menu Program for Exercise 15
ECHO 1. WordPerfect Subdirectory
ECHO 2. Lotus Subdirectory
ECHO 3. dBASE Subdirectory
ECHO Enter the number of the desired choice and press Enter

ECHO OFF
REM ** 1.BAT  To switch to the WP Subdirectory
CD \WP

ECHO OFF
REM ** 2.BAT  To switch to the LO Subdirectory
CD \LO

ECHO OFF
REM ** 3.BAT  To switch to the DB Subdirectory
CD \DB
```

FIGURE 2-26

Sample Batch Files for Exercise 15

15. Use the COPY CON command to prepare batch files for the following menu exercise. The menu file, MENU.BAT, should display the following menu:

```
1. WordPerfect directory
2. Lotus directory
3. dBASE directory
```

The user then will press **1, 2, or 3** (and press **Enter**) to switch to the appropriate directory.

Enter the MENU.BAT file and the three batch files 1.BAT, 2.BAT, and 3.BAT as shown in Figure 2-26. Before running these files, be sure to create the WP, LO, and DB subdirectories on the default drive.

CHAPTER 2 PROJECT
GRAPHICAL USER INTERFACES

There has been considerable discussion of the differences between the DOS command-line interface and graphical interfaces such as the icon-driven Macintosh operating system. This project is intended to highlight many of the differences between DOS and other operating system environments. You will need to do additional research on some of the products discussed in the chapter. Your report should focus on the following issues:

- Other user interfaces (DOS 3.x shells, DOS 4, Windows, OS/2 PM, Unix, Macintosh)
- Ease of learning with graphical user interfaces (GUI)
- Ease of use with GUI
- Comparison of common DOS commands with Macintosh equivalents
- Future directions for IBM-compatible operating system and user environment.

3

Introduction to Database Management with dBASE IV

Objectives

After completing this chapter, you should be able to:

- Define these database terms: field, record, file, database.
- Contrast list manager and database management software.
- Discuss the four user modes with dBASE.
- Discuss the uses of the six main field types.
- Explain how to use the Control Center menus.
- Discuss the use of the dBASE file catalog.
- Create a database file structure and append data to the database.
- Demonstrate how to move the record pointer through the database.
- Use the Edit and Browse commands to examine and make changes to data records.
- Delete specified records from the database.
- Know how to use the dBASE Help system.
- Describe some of the file types used in dBASE IV.

INTRODUCTION

This chapter introduces database concepts and terminology. Fields, records, files, and databases are defined, along with the dBASE implementation of each. Basic database operations are presented, along with typical applications of database software. The four types of dBASE user modes are given. The chapter provides examples of each user mode.

The QuickStart section provides instructions for starting dBASE IV version 1.1. The Control Center menu system is introduced, with an explanation of the Menu Bar, work surface, file panel, Status Bar, navigation line, and message line sections of the display.

The Control Center commands for creating a database file and appending data are explained. The chapter includes a discussion of the dBASE file structure and types of database fields available. Methods of moving the record pointer through the file are discussed, along with commands for editing, deleting, and listing records.

The chapter concludes with an explanation of the dBASE IV on-line Help System and a discussion of various types of files used with the dBASE IV system.

DATABASE MANAGEMENT CONCEPTS

Simply stated, a **database** is a set of data values organized for easy user access. The database management software can help us create a database structure to hold the data and perform such operations as add data, display and sort values, edit or change the data values and create reports. We will begin with basic definitions.

Database Terminology

A **field** is the smallest identifiable piece of data in the data hierarchy. A field represents an attribute or measurement of some object or event. For example, in the veterinary spreadsheet database we store the treatment date, customer's last name, pet type, treatment type, invoice amount, and payment status fields. Each of these measurements is a separate field.

The collection of related fields regarding one object or event in a database is known as a **record**. The collection of fields about one treatment could be considered a record in our example. A group of similar records is called a **file**. Thus the complete set of treatment records is a file.

A database is a set of related files. The definition for a **database** is more difficult to represent with our veterinarian example. We might consider an expanded set of data, including a file of information about owners, a file of standard treatments and associated charges, and a file containing accounting records of the veterinary practice. The illustration in Figure 3-1 describes the relationship among data in our hierarchy.

List, File, and Database Managers

We can distinguish between databases and list managers by the capabilities of the software package. A **list manager** is capable of storing data fields in record format for a single file at a time. The list manager lets you edit data records manually. You can sort the records in the file into different orders and make reports from that file. A list manager is generally simple to use and has fewer commands to master than a file manager or database manager.

The **file manager** offers more sophisticated features, plus all of the list manager features. You can build custom data entry screens, index files, create simple reports, import and export data from/to other software packages, and create complicated queries. Lotus 1-2-3 offers many of these file management features.

FIGURE 3-1

Data Hierarchy: Character, Field, Record, File, Database

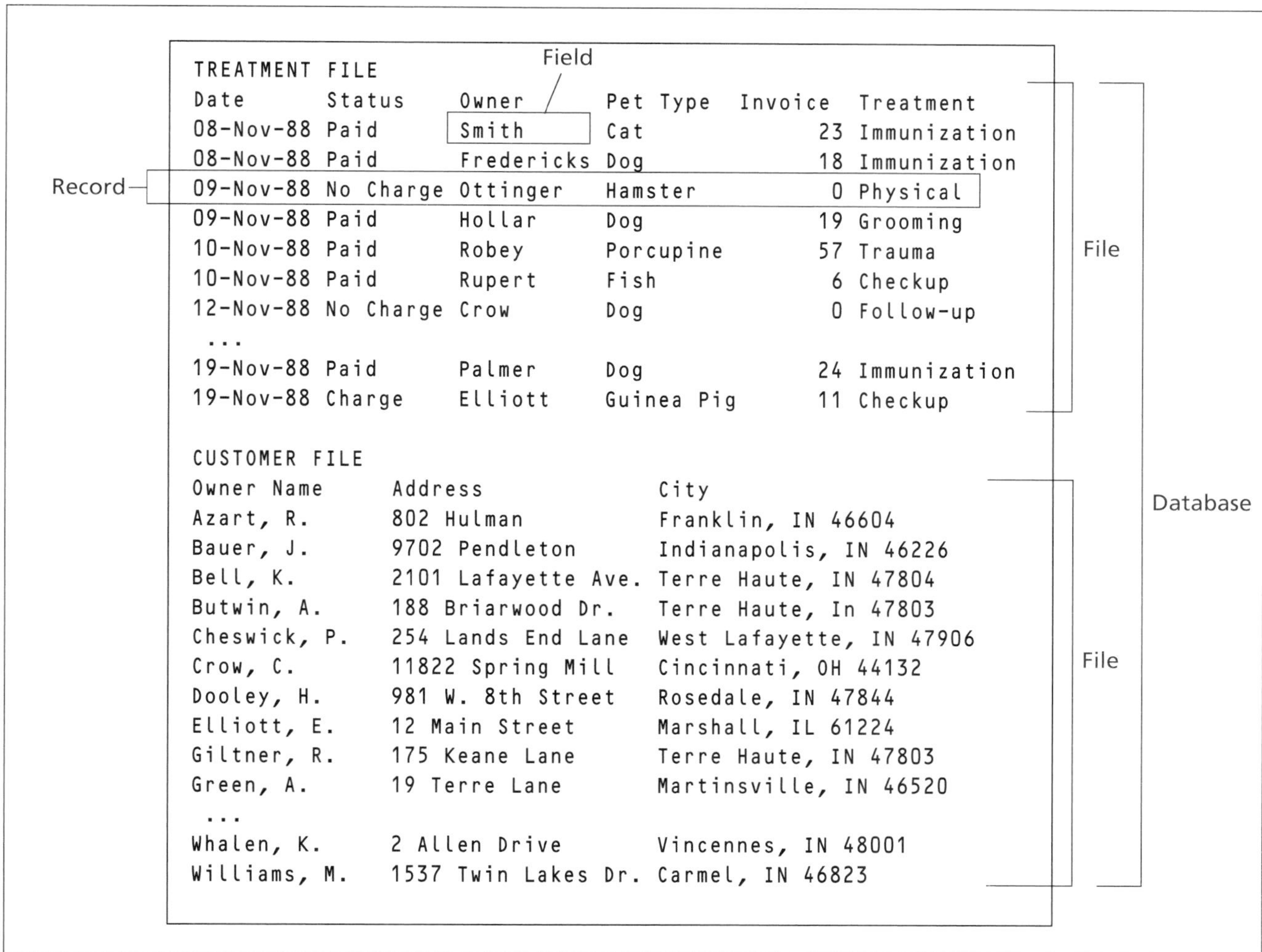

TREATMENT FILE

Date	Status	Owner	Pet Type	Invoice	Treatment
08-Nov-88	Paid	Smith	Cat	23	Immunization
08-Nov-88	Paid	Fredericks	Dog	18	Immunization
09-Nov-88	No Charge	Ottinger	Hamster	0	Physical
09-Nov-88	Paid	Hollar	Dog	19	Grooming
10-Nov-88	Paid	Robey	Porcupine	57	Trauma
10-Nov-88	Paid	Rupert	Fish	6	Checkup
12-Nov-88	No Charge	Crow	Dog	0	Follow-up
...					
19-Nov-88	Paid	Palmer	Dog	24	Immunization
19-Nov-88	Charge	Elliott	Guinea Pig	11	Checkup

CUSTOMER FILE

Owner Name	Address	City
Azart, R.	802 Hulman	Franklin, IN 46604
Bauer, J.	9702 Pendleton	Indianapolis, IN 46226
Bell, K.	2101 Lafayette Ave.	Terre Haute, IN 47804
Butwin, A.	188 Briarwood Dr.	Terre Haute, In 47803
Cheswick, P.	254 Lands End Lane	West Lafayette, IN 47906
Crow, C.	11822 Spring Mill	Cincinnati, OH 44132
Dooley, H.	981 W. 8th Street	Rosedale, IN 47844
Elliott, E.	12 Main Street	Marshall, IL 61224
Giltner, R.	175 Keane Lane	Terre Haute, IN 47803
Green, A.	19 Terre Lane	Martinsville, IN 46520
...		
Whalen, K.	2 Allen Drive	Vincennes, IN 48001
Williams, M.	1537 Twin Lakes Dr.	Carmel, IN 46823

The full **database manager** adds multi-file capability, sophisticated report-writing, and programmability via a macro-like language. Some less capable packages are billed as database management software, even though they do not offer full features.

Basic Database Operations

Most database programs support the basic set of database operations.

- The **create** operation builds the record structure, or the names, types, and width of fields in each record. dBASE supports six field types: character, numeric, float, date, logical, and memo.
- The **append** operation adds data values to the database, either manually entered from the keyboard or imported from another file.
- Once the database is built and populated with data, you can **edit** the data to correct mistakes or update field values.

- The **sort** operation changes the order of the records according to specified fields.
- The **retrieve** operation will search and display records that match certain criteria.
- **Reporting** operations are used to make printed or screen reports.

dBASE User Modes

dBASE IV is a full-featured database management software package. It can be used in several ways by users with varying degrees of experience and computer expertise. They are listed in order of increasing user sophistication.

Turnkey Custom Database System

Applications in this mode are first developed by experienced programmers. Users do not interact directly with dBASE. Rather, they see custom menus and follow instructions that are specific to the application itself. Other than invoking the system, users enter no dBASE commands. For example, a metal-working shop might use dBASE to develop a custom job tracking system that monitors the status of customer orders.

Control Center Menus

In this mode users will enter instructions through the dBASE Control Center, an elaborate menu system. Some prior training is necessary, although most choices are made from a limited set of menus. Some relatively sophisticated activities, such as building a report or custom screen form, can also be accomplished through the same set of menus. Most users will begin with this level, as does this textbook.

Direct Commands at Dot Prompt

Experienced dBASE users may wish to bypass the menu system and enter commands directly at the dBASE **dot prompt** character. This mode requires that at least the first four characters of the desired command be entered from the keyboard, along with any qualifiers and command options. This mode may be faster than going through the Control Center, but will be more difficult for new users. Those familiar with previous versions of dBASE will have little trouble entering the familiar dot prompt commands.

Developing dBASE Programs

The programs developed in this dBASE mode consist of dot prompt commands and other programming instructions. While similar to Lotus macros, these programs are stored as separate disk files. dBASE programs allow repetitive applications to run more quickly and with fewer errors than by entering the commands manually each time the application is run. A section of Chapter 7 will introduce dBASE programming.

dBASE IV QUICKSTART

This section assumes that you will be using the dBASE IV **Control Center** to enter commands. Previous versions of dBASE III used a simpler menu system called

ASSIST. Beginning users will want to use the Control Center rather than enter commands directly. dBASE III PLUS is covered in Chapter 8.

Starting dBASE IV

Although dBASE III PLUS can be used from a two-floppy drive personal computer, dBASE IV requires a hard disk unit with at least 3 megabytes of free space on the drive. You may store your data files on a floppy disk or on the hard drive. Before dBASE IV can be used, it must be installed on the hard drive with the supplied INSTALL program. We will assume that your computer center has already accomplished the installation steps. If not, follow the instructions given in the Getting Started manual packaged with dBASE IV.

Floppy Disk Users (Data Files Only)

Assuming that your computer has been set up with a DOS Path to the DBASE subdirectory, change to the disk drive (typically A) where you have placed your data disk. At the A> prompt, type **DBASE** and press the Enter key. dBASE will load from the hard drive but all *data files* will be placed on the floppy disk.

Hard Disk and Network Users

At the C> prompt (or whatever prompt your local area network provides), type **DBASE** and press the **Enter** key. Your data files will be placed in whatever subdirectory you started dBASE IV from.

After a few seconds, you will see a startup screen that asks you to confirm that you have read the license agreement. Press **Enter** to go to the next screen. Unless your version of dBASE has been configured in a different manner, the next screen will be the Control Center menu.

Using the Control Center Menus

Figure 3-2 shows the Control Center when dBASE starts up. Your screen may vary somewhat, depending on the initial catalog and whether any databases have already been created. To activate the Control Center from the dot prompt, type **ASSIST** and press the **Enter** key. The Control Center consists of several elements common to most dBASE screens.

- The top row at the left of every screen holds the **Menu Bar**, accessed by pressing the **F10** function key.
- System time is displayed in the top right corner.
- Different screens will have various displays in the **work surface** area, just below the Menu Bar.
- At the bottom, beneath the work surface is the **status area** which gives name and description of the highlighted file. In other screens you will get a **Status Bar** which provides information about the current screen, database file in use, record pointer location, and toggle settings.
- Immediately below the status line is the **navigation line** which explains how to accomplish activities relevant to the current screen.
- The **message line,** below the navigation line in other screens, provides information about the command currently selected or the area of the work surface that is highlighted.

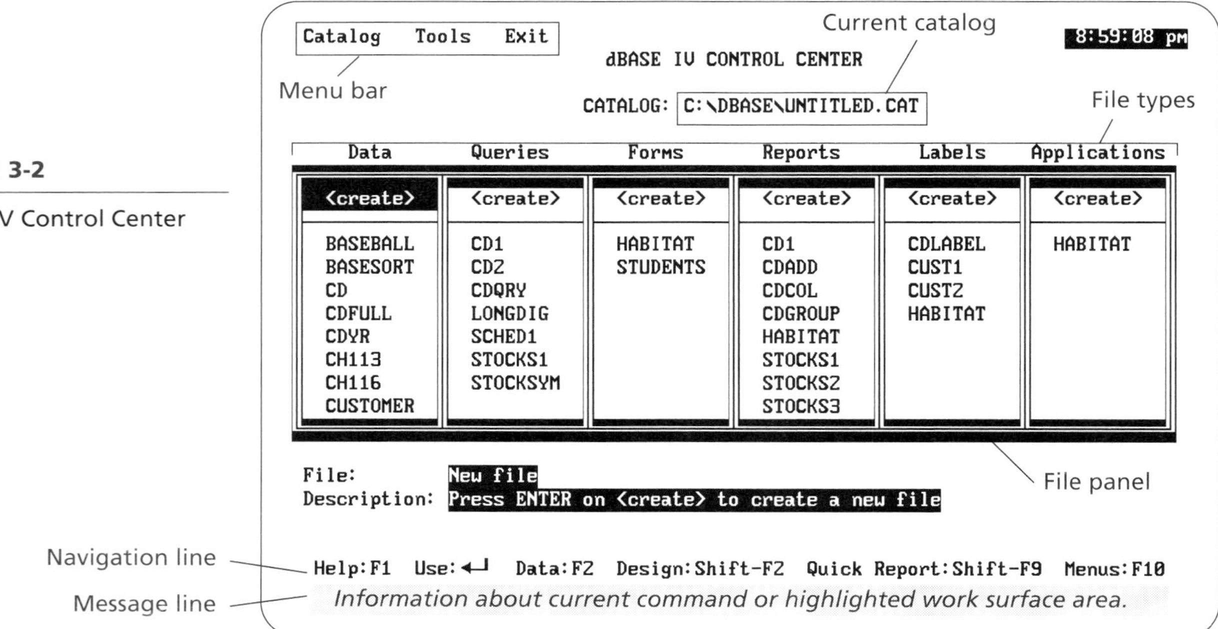

FIGURE 3-2

dBASE IV Control Center

Menu Bar

The Menu Bar is shown in the upper left corner. In this particular screen there are three menu choices:

```
Catalog   Tools   Exit
```

Each work surface screen will have Menu Bar selections that are appropriate to that screen. To activate the Menu Bar, press the **F10** function key (equivalent to the slash key from Lotus 1-2-3). You may also select a specific Menu Bar choice by holding down the **Alt** key and tapping the first letter of the desired choice. A **pull-down menu** will appear, as shown in Figure 3-3.

Available choices from that pull-down menu appear in bright text. Dim or gray text menu choices are not currently available. The message line at the bottom of the screen provides a brief explanation of the highlighted choice. If a different Menu Bar choice with its pull-down menu is desired, use the left or right arrow keys to select it. To select an item from a pull-down menu, move the cursor with the up or down arrow keys to that choice and press **Enter**. To leave the Menu Bar and return to the work surface, press the **Esc** key.

Files Panel and the dBASE Catalog

Below the Menu Bar in the Control Center is the name of the current catalog. A dBASE **catalog** contains information about files belonging to an application. The default catalog is called UNTITLED, but your computer's default may be different than the examples shown in this chapter. You may use the *Use a different catalog* Menu Bar choice to select a different catalog.

The **File Panel** shows the dBASE files in the selected file catalog. Files are displayed in each panel by their **type**.

- **Data** files contain data records.

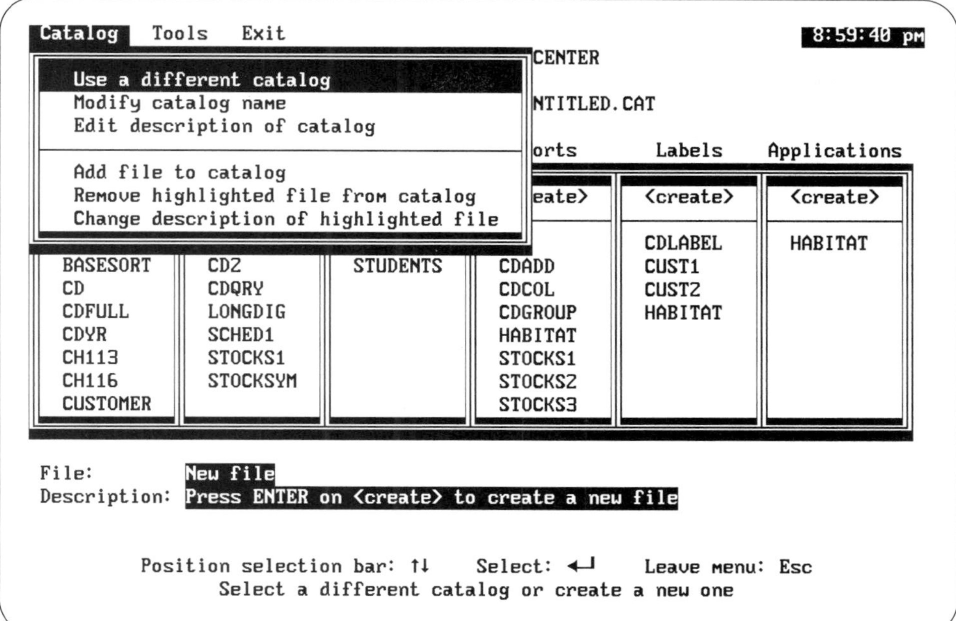

FIGURE 3-3

Catalog Pull-Down Menu Bar

- **Queries** are conditions that specify which records are to be retrieved, similar to Lotus queries.
- **Forms** are custom screen input formats.
- **Reports** are specifications for printed outputs.
- **Label** files give specifications for printing mailing labels.
- The **Applications** panel provides a means of creating and executing user-written dBASE programs.

Each panel is divided into two sections. The top section permits you to create a new file in that panel. The bottom section lists files that have already been created for that panel. The default panel is the <create> Data mode, highlighted in the left center of the screen. To create a new data file, press the **Enter** key. To open an existing file, use the arrow keys to move the cursor to that file's name in the lower panel area and press **Enter**.

Status Areas

Below the panel area is the name of the current file and its description. If you have moved the cursor to a <create> block, the file name will indicate **New file**, with instructions on the description line below on how to create such a file.

In other dBASE screens you will see the **Status Bar**, followed by the **navigation line** and **message line**. An example of the Status Bar is shown in Figure 3-4. The Status Bar is split into several boxes by double vertical lines. The name of the display screen is in the first box, followed by the name of the file being displayed or created. The DEL, NUM, CAPS, and INS toggle indicators are shown in the last box in the Status Bar. Information in the other boxes will vary with the particular screen displayed. The navigation line explains possible keystrokes that might be entered at this screen. The message line clarifies the currently selected option, if any.

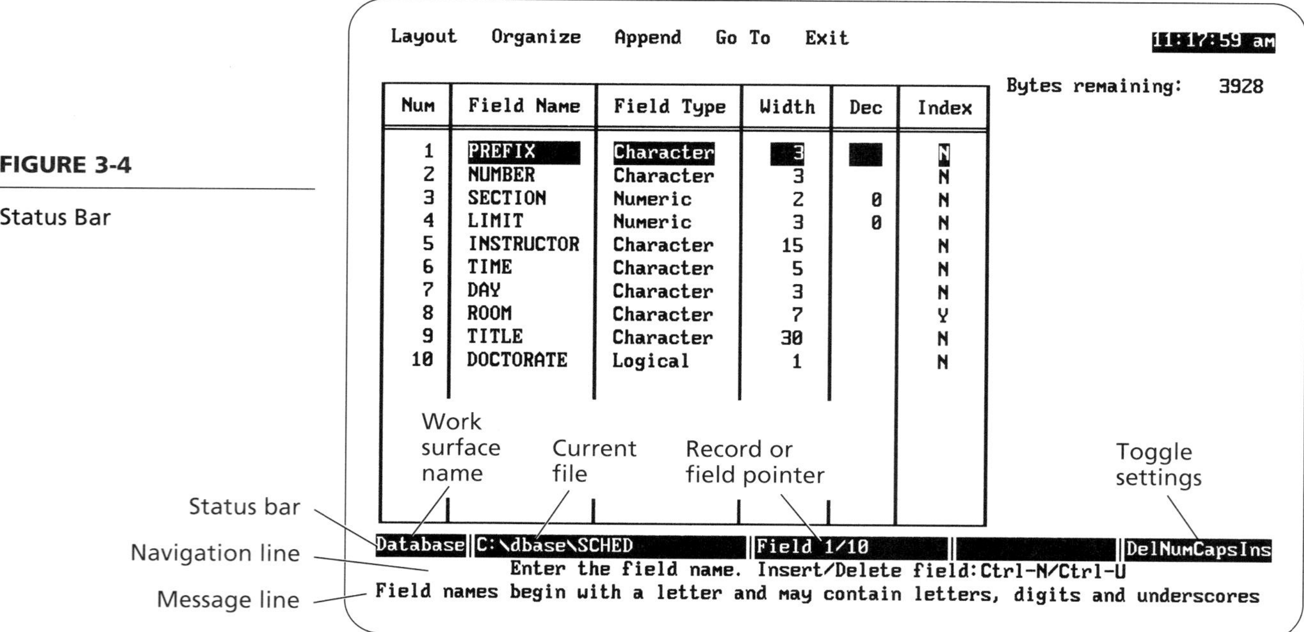

FIGURE 3-4

Status Bar

FIGURE 3-5

General dBASE IV Function Key Assignments

Key	**Function**	**Meaning**
F1	Help	Activate dBASE Help System
F2	Data	Display data values in Edit or Browse screen
F3	Previous	Moves to previous field or page
F4	Next	Moves to next field or page
F5	Field	Add or modify field on current layout surface
F6	Select	Select field or text on current layout surface
F7	Move	Move selected field or text
F8	Copy	Copy selected field or text
F9	Zoom	Open/close memo field or other object
F10	Menus	Activate Menu Bar
Shift-F1	Pick	Display list of choices for current operation
Shift-F2	Design	Activate the design screen of current file type (data, query, form, report, label)
Shift-F8	Ditto	Fills in current field with data from same field of previous record
Shift-F9	Quick Report	Print quick report of data

Function Key Assignments

dBASE IV provides a shortcut method for selecting certain commands or menu options by use of the function keys. The most useful function keys and their effects are shown in Figure 3-5. Some work surfaces utilize additional function keys; these are described where appropriate.

Creating a New Database File

There are two steps in creating a database file. First you must **design the structure** of the record. That is, determine the appropriate data fields, then choose a

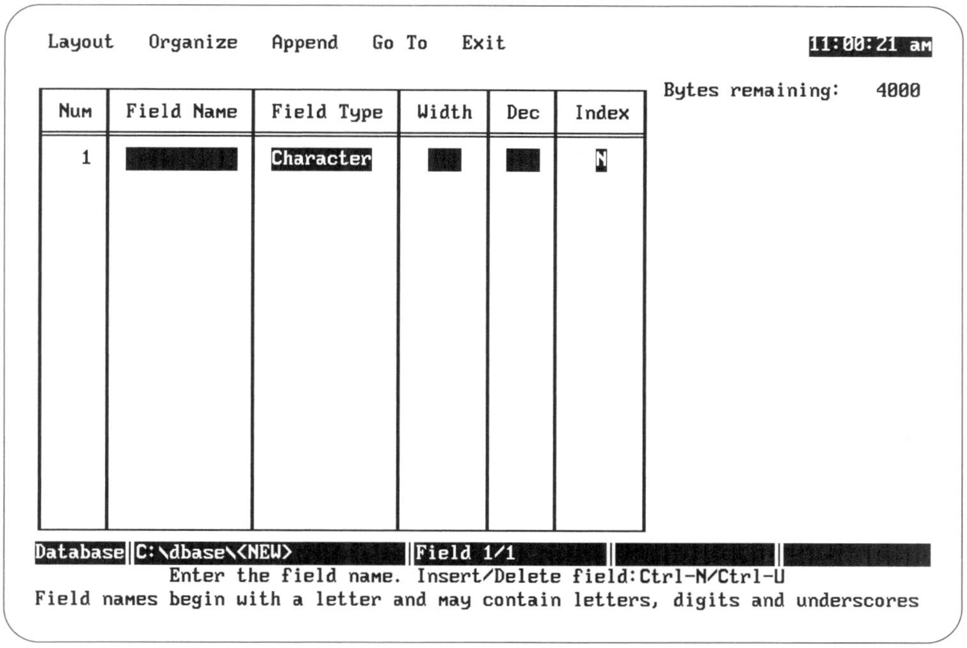

```
Layout   Organize   Append   Go To   Exit                  11:00:21 am

                                                  Bytes remaining:   4000
 Num | Field Name | Field Type | Width | Dec | Index
   1 |            | Character  |       |     |   N

Database  C:\dbase\<NEW>          Field 1/1
        Enter the field name.  Insert/Delete field:Ctrl-N/Ctrl-U
Field names begin with a letter and may contain letters, digits and underscores
```

FIGURE 3-6

Database Screen for Creating Data Structure

meaningful name, a type, and the proper width for each field. Any relationships between records, such as ordering the records in an index, may be established at this point. The second step involves populating the database file by **appending data** to it.

Create the Structure

The **Database screen** in Figure 3-6 results from the **Create** choice from the Data panel in the Control Center. See Figure 3-2.

The table in the screen will be filled with field specifications for the current database. dBASE field names must begin with a letter, and may be up to ten characters (letters, digits, and underscores) long. The underscore is the only special character allowed in field names. dBASE IV allows 255 fields per record, doubling the limit of previous dBASE versions. You can define up to 4000 characters total in all fields in a record; dBASE displays the number of bytes (characters) still remaining as you add each new field.

Types of Database Fields

dBASE IV supports six different field types.

- **Character fields** contain text characters and digits in a fixed width.
- **Numeric fields** hold numbers that are used in mathematical operations.
- **Float fields** are used for very large or very small numbers, and are new with dBASE IV.
- **Date fields** contain dates in a special format.
- Results of conditions—true or false—are stored in **logical fields.**
- **Memo fields** hold large amounts of textual data and can vary in width.

Character fields hold names, addresses, titles, zip codes, social security numbers, and most types of data that are not intended for use in mathematical calculations. Character fields are analogous to Lotus labels. These are fixed width fields—you must choose the number of characters for this field before storing data in the field. Unused space in a character field is wasted. Character fields may hold up to 254 characters.

Numeric fields are used for storing numbers such as SAT scores, grade point averages, hourly wages, annual sales, and property tax assessments. You must specify the overall width in characters, and the number of places to the right of the decimal point. The width must be at least two characters larger than the number of decimal places to accommodate a minus sign and decimal point. For example, a field width of 6 with two decimal places would permit numbers up to 999.99 to be held in that field. In negative numbers the minus sign occupies one place in the field. Numeric fields may hold up to 20 digits.

dBASE IV adds the **Float** field type, for holding very large or very small floating point numbers, similar to numbers we represent with scientific notation. Avogadro's number, 6.02×10^{23}, is such a number. Float fields represent numbers but are represented differently than numeric type by dBASE. Float fields hold up to 20 digits.

Dates in dBASE are stored in a special field, unlike Lotus where they are stored as numbers. Date fields are always 8 characters long, and use the default format MM/DD/YY. Dates can be displayed in alternate formats, and functions can be used to extract the month, day, year, or day of the week.

It is helpful to store true or false (or yes or no) responses in a **logical** field, rather than in a character field. Logical fields always take one character. Examples include logical fields that answer questions similar to the following:

- Are you a member?
- Is this backed up?
- Is a hard disk required?
- Are you an hourly worker?
- Taxable purchase?

Memo fields let you record large amounts of data such as comments. These fields are stored in a different file than the other fields, but are used just as the other fields are. You don't need to specify the width of a memo field—dBASE will automatically allocate as much additional space as is necessary (up to 512KB characters) for the field. Unused space is not wasted with memo fields. Memo fields hold the same type of information as character fields, but are generally used for unstructured responses such as explanations or comments.

Building the CD Example Database

We will use a compact disk library to explain the data terminology. This example will be used to illustrate dBASE IV techniques. For each compact disk there will be several fields:

- Artist — Name of the performer or group
- Title — Title of the performance
- Publisher — Name of the disk publisher
- Catalog — The catalog number
- Year — Year of issue

- Class Music category (jazz, rock, classical)
- Length Total recording time in minutes
- Digital Whether this is a digital recording.

Example: *Entering the Structure*

1. First start dBASE and wait until the Control Center screen appears.
2. Move the cursor to the <create> choice in the Data panel and press **Enter**. You'll see the Database work surface screen of Figure 3-6.
3. You must enter the name, type and width of the eight fields in the current file, using the Database table. Type the name of the first field **ARTIST**. Press the **Enter** key to go to the Field Type box.
4. The field type defaults to Character, but the other choices are available by pressing the first letter of that choice. In this case press **Enter** to select Character type.
5. You'll next be asked to supply the width of the field, in characters. Width refers to the overall width of the field, including decimal places for numeric fields. The Dec box indicates the number of decimal places. Type the ARTIST field's width, **18**, and press **Enter**. dBASE will skip over Dec for non-numeric fields.
6. The Index box is used to indicate whether the file should appear in sorted order according to the field. You may have more than one index. For now, leave this as N by pressing **Enter**. A blank template for field 2 will appear.
7. Fill in the rest of the Database work surface for the remaining fields. Figure 3-7 shows the table filled in with a description of the fields. All of these specifications form what is known as the structure of the database file.

Layout   Organize   Append   Go To   Exit   11:02:22 am

Bytes remaining: 3924

Num	Field Name	Field Type	Width	Dec	Index
1	ARTIST	Character	18		N
2	TITLE	Character	26		N
3	PUBLISHER	Character	12		N
4	CATALOG_NO	Character	9		N
5	YEAR	Character	4		N
6	CLASS	Character	3		N
7	LENGTH	Numeric	3	0	N
8	DIGITAL	Logical	1		N
9		Character			N

Database ‖C:\dbase\<NEW> ‖Field 9/9

Enter the field name. Insert/Delete field:Ctrl-N/Ctrl-U

Field names begin with a letter and may contain letters, digits and underscores

FIGURE 3-7

Complete Data Structure for CD Example Database

Making Changes to the Structure

If you have made a mistake or wish to make changes to the structure, use the cursor keys to move the cursor to the proper box and enter the correction. (If you have exited the Database Design (structure) screen you may return by pressing **Shift-F2** from the Control Center.) Pressing the **Ins** key once will put you into Insert mode, indicated in the toggle settings of the Status Bar. Pressing **Ins** again will turn off insert mode. If you need to insert a field between two others, move the cursor to the second field and press **Ctrl-N** to open a new field line. To delete a field move the cursor to that field and press **Ctrl-U**.

Saving the Structure

When you have finished creating the record structure, press **F10** to activate the Menu Bar. Choose the **Exit** command, and select the *Save changes and exit* bar. [Note: You may also exit from most work surfaces by pressing the **Ctrl-End** command.] dBASE will ask you to supply a file name for the structure to be saved. Regular DOS filename rules are in order—the file name may have up to eight characters and should not contain spaces. Don't enter a file extension—dBASE will use .DBF as the default extension for all database files.

Example: *Saving the Structure*

---

1. Press **F10** to activate the Menu Bar, then select **Exit**. Press **Enter** to select the *Save changes and exit* line.
2. When prompted for the file name, type **CD** and press **Enter**.
3. If you're asked if you wish to "Input Data Records Now Y/N?" Answer **N**.
4. After a few seconds the main Control Center screen will appear. Our new file will appear in the Data panel above the horizontal line, signifying this is the file currently in use. You'll also see the file name below the file panel, next to the FILE: heading.

Printing the Structure

dBASE will print the file structure on your printer if the file structure has been saved. From the Control Center, move the cursor to highlight the desired filename. Press **Shift-F2** to bring up the Database work surface. Press the **F10** key to activate the Menu Bar, and move the cursor to the **Layout** menu. Move the cursor to *Print database structure* and press **Enter**. See Figure 3-8. Normally you will press **Enter** again when the next menu appears to *Begin printing*.

Adding Data to the File

To view the existing data or to add new data, press the **F2** key. You will see a screen similar to Figure 3-9. The status line shows the **Edit screen** name, the path and filename currently in use, and the Record pointer showing which record number we're viewing, in this case **None** because the database file is empty. The shaded area next to each field name represents the width available for storing data for that field.

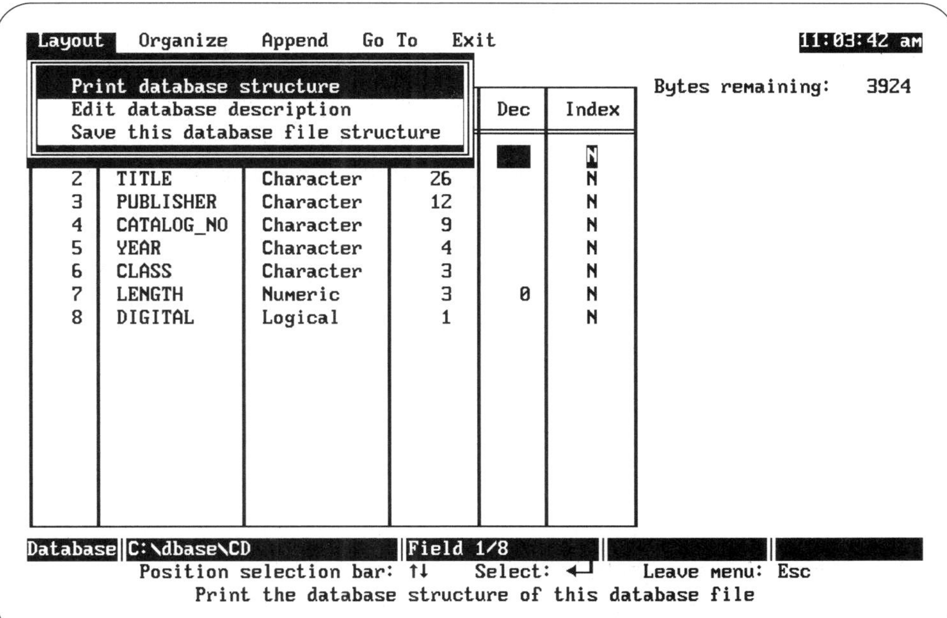

FIGURE 3-8

Layout Menu Bar for Printing Data Structure

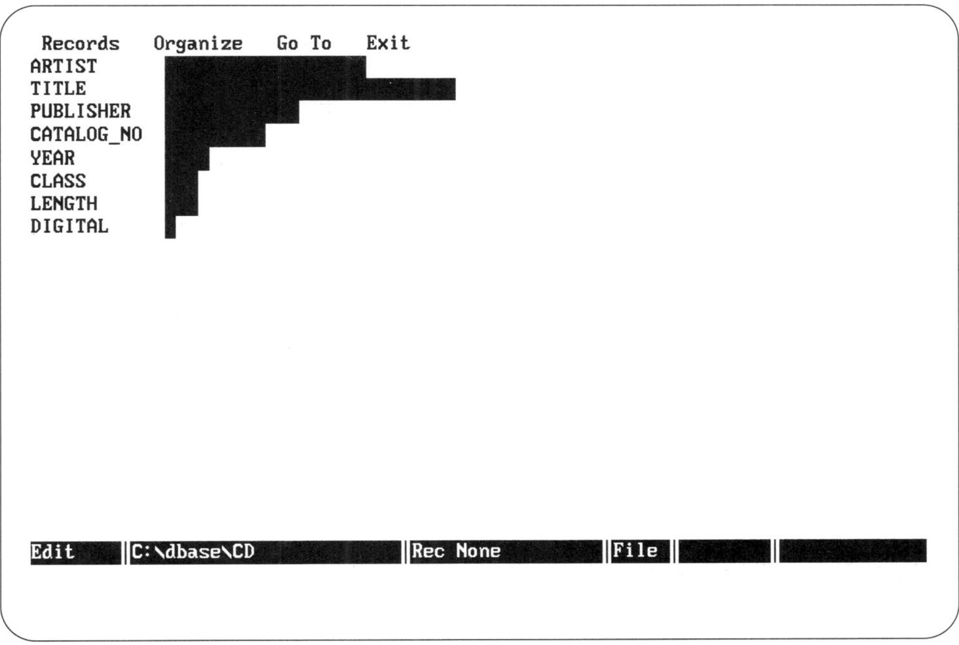

FIGURE 3-9

Edit Work Surface for Adding Data to the CD Database

If the file is empty, dBASE will display a blank template for entering field values. To enter the first record's data into the fields, simply begin typing in the ARTIST field shaded area. Use the **Del** and **BkSp** keys as needed to correct mistakes. Remember that dBASE is in overtype mode unless the Ins indicator is lit in the Status Bar. If you fill a field with characters dBASE will automatically move to the next field. If you don't fill the field entirely, press **Enter** to move to the next field. When the last field is filled at the end of the record, dBASE will automatically save this record and skip to the next record. Press **Enter** to go to the next record if the last field is not filled.

Example: *Adding the First Record*

1. If the CD file is not in use, from the Control Center move the cursor to the **CD** filename in the Data file panel and press **Enter**.
2. At the next dialog box select **Display data** and press **Enter**. You should see the blank Edit screen of Figure 3-9.
3. In the first field type **The Canadian Brass**. When you have filled the field dBASE will automatically move to the next field. [Note: It is also possible to configure dBASE to require the user to press **Enter** to move on to the next field. Check with your lab assistant for your particular installation.]
4. In the second field type **High, Bright, Light and Clear**. Because the field width is only 26 characters, the final three characters in the title may go into the next field and will need to be deleted to enter RCA.
5. In the PUBLISHER field type **RCA** and press **Enter** to move on to the next field.
6. In the CATALOG_NO field type **RCD14574**.
7. In the YEAR field type **1983**.
8. In the CLASS field type **CL**, the code for classical, and press **Enter** to go to the next field.
9. In the LENGTH field type **51** and press **Enter**. Notice that numbers are right-justified in the numeric field.
10. The DIGITAL field shows whether this CD is a digital recording. Press **Y** and indicate a true value. Figure 3-10 shows the completed first record, just before the screen changes to the second record.
11. dBASE will store the completed record and display a blank Edit screen for record 2. The record pointer in the Status Bar shows Rec EOF/1, meaning we're at the end of the file with a total of 1 record.

FIGURE 3-10

Completed First Record for Example Database

FIGURE 3-11

First Six Records in the CD Example Database

ARTIST	DISK TITLE	PUBLISHER	CATALOG_NO	YEAR	CLASS	LENGTH	DIGITAL
The Canadian Brass	High, Bright, Light and Cl	RCA	RCD14574	1983	CL	51	Y
Wiener Philharmoni	Beethoven: Symphony No. 9	Deutsche Gr.	419598-2	1987	CL	72	Y
Wynton Marsalis	Trumpet Concertos	CBS Master	MK37846	1983	CL	40	Y
Stern, Rampal	Play Vivaldi & Telemann	CBS Master	MK35133	1978	CL	44	N
Glenn Gould	Bach Goldberg Variations	CBS Master	MK3777	1982	CL	51	Y
Festival Strings L	Adagio Albioni, Pachelbel, B	Deutsche Gr.	4132248-2	1972	CL	62	N

12. To add data for the next record, enter the data shown below:

```
Wiener Philharmonic
Beethoven: Symphony No. 9
Deutsche Gr.
419598-2
1987
CL
72
Y
```

13. When the blank input screen for the third record appears, you can signal that you have finished entering the data records for now: instead of typing something into the first field, press **Alt-E,** then **Enter** to Exit to the Control Center screen.
14. From the Control Center press **F2** to move to the Edit screen. You may use the PgUp and PgDn keys to examine the two records in the file.
15. You may add more records from Edit screen. Press **Alt-R** to activate the Records Menu Bar. With the cursor on the *Add new records* line, press **Enter**. dBASE will display a blank record 3. Fill in the values according to Figure 3-11.
16. Add the remaining records in the same way. The six records for the CD example are shown in Figure 3-11. Then press **Alt-E**, **Enter** to save.

Moving the Record Pointer

dBASE keeps track of the current record in the database with the **record pointer**, shown in the Status Bar at the bottom of the Edit screen. For instance, the value 1/6 indicates the record pointer is set at record 1 and that there are a total of 6 records in the database. To move to the previous record press the **PgUp** key; **PgDn** will take you to the following record.

To move to a specific record, first press the **F10** key to activate the Menu Bar. Then move the cursor to the **Go To** menu, as shown in Figure 3-12. You can select Top record, Last record, choose a specific record number, or skip forward or backward a fixed number of records.

To activate one of these choices, use the arrow keys to move the cursor to the desired action and press **Enter**. Or you may press the first letter of the desired command to execute it directly. For example, to move to the third record, activate the *Record Number* option, then enter **3** as the record number.

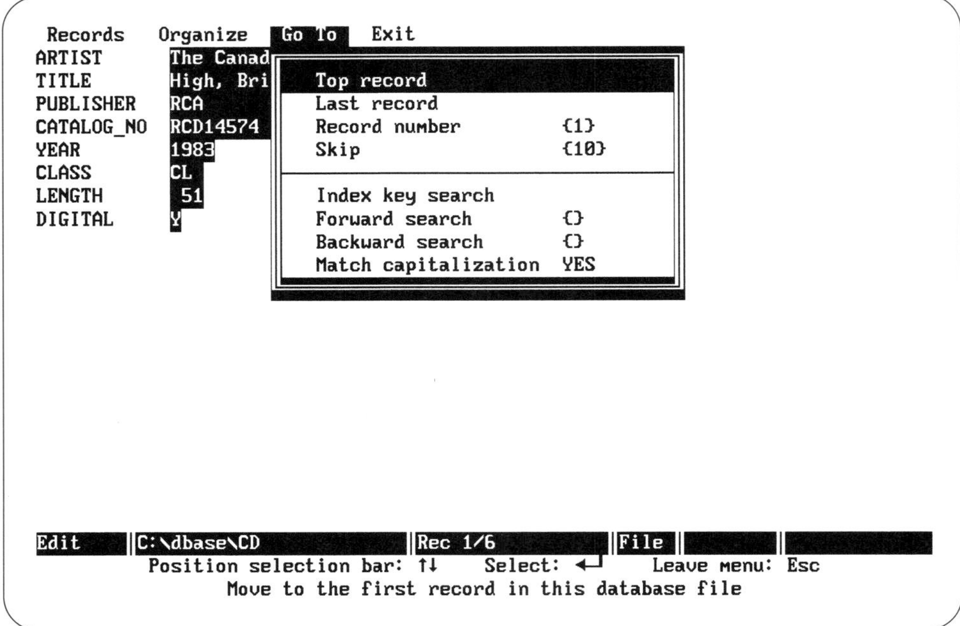

FIGURE 3-12

Go To Record Positioning Screen

The lower options in the Go To menu are used with indexed files to search for records containing certain values. Indexed database files will appear in order according to the key field used in that index. Indexed files are discussed in Chapter 4.

Manipulating the Data

dBASE provides a way to perform basic data operations. The Edit and Browse screens allow you to view the data and optionally make changes. From these screens you can also delete undesired records using control-key commands or with the Menu Bars.

Making Changes with Edit

The **Edit screen** displays the fields of the current record vertically, one per line. You see only as many fields of the current record as fit on one screen, currently 17. Additional fields from the same record will be displayed on the next screen. The Status Bar indicates the record pointer's location.

To make a change to an existing field, first use the arrow keys to move the cursor to that field. Then make corrections as needed by typing over existing characters or inserting new ones. Remember that the Status Bar shows the status of the Insert indicator in the lower right corner. If you want to edit another record, use **PgUp** and **PgDn** to position the record pointer on the desired record. The changes to a record are saved when you move the cursor to another record. When you have completed making changes, press **Ctrl-End** to save the changes to the current record, or press the **Esc** key to abort these changes and return to the Control Center.

Some of the other keystroke commands available for making changes are shown in the table of Figure 3-13. These commands generally work with Edit, Browse, and other editing screens.

Making Changes with Browse

The **Browse screen** transposes rows and columns from the Edit screen, showing one record per row. Fields extend across the screen, with as many showing as

Command	Meaning
↑	Move up one row on screen
↓	Move down one row on screen
←	Move left one character in current field
→	Move right one character in current field
PgUp	Display previous screen
PgDn	Display next screen
Home	Move to beginning of current field
End	Move to end of current field
Tab	Move to next field
Shift-Tab	Move to previous field
Enter	Move to next field
Esc	Leave Edit screen without saving changes to current record
Ctrl-←	Move to beginning of previous word in field
Ctrl-→	Move to beginning of next word in field
Del	Delete character beneath cursor
Backspace	Delete character to left of cursor
Ins	Toggle between overtype and insert modes
Ctrl-T	Delete from cursor position to beginning of next word
Ctrl-Y	Delete from cursor position to end of current field
Ctrl-End	Save changes and leave Edit screen

FIGURE 3-13

dBASE Edit Screen Commands

will fit onto one screen. Browse permits you to see more records at a time than Edit mode does. The six records of the CD database are shown in the Browse screen of Figure 3-14.

Many of the editing commands used in the Edit screen also work in the Browse screen. The arrow keys move the cursor in a similar fashion, although the meanings of rows and columns are exchanged. Pressing the ↓ key moves to the next record in Browse, and pressing the **Tab** key or **Enter** moves toward the next field. You can switch between the two views (Edit and Browse) of your database file by pressing the **F2** function key.

Deleting Records

dBASE uses a two-step procedure for **deleting records** from the database. Records are first marked for deletion, and then, in a later step, those marked records are actually deleted. Marking records for deletion is accomplished with the **Records** choice in the Menu Bar of the Edit and Browse screens. Move the record pointer to the record you wish to delete, then press the **F10** key to activate the Menu Bar. Move the cursor to the *Mark record for deletion* choice and press **Enter**. The word **Del** will appear in the Status Bar whenever that record is displayed. (You can also mark a record for deletion by using the shortcut **Ctrl-U** command, without going through the Menu Bar. As Ctrl-U is a toggle, another press will clear the deletion mark.) If you wish to "undelete" a record marked for deletion, use the same procedure to access the record and select the **Records** choice from the Menu Bar. This time the Record menu choice will say *Clear Deletion Mark* instead of *Mark record for deletion.* The Del indicator will disappear when you clear the mark.

Records that have been marked for deletion ordinarily appear in printed reports marked with an asterisk (*) before the record number, and will appear

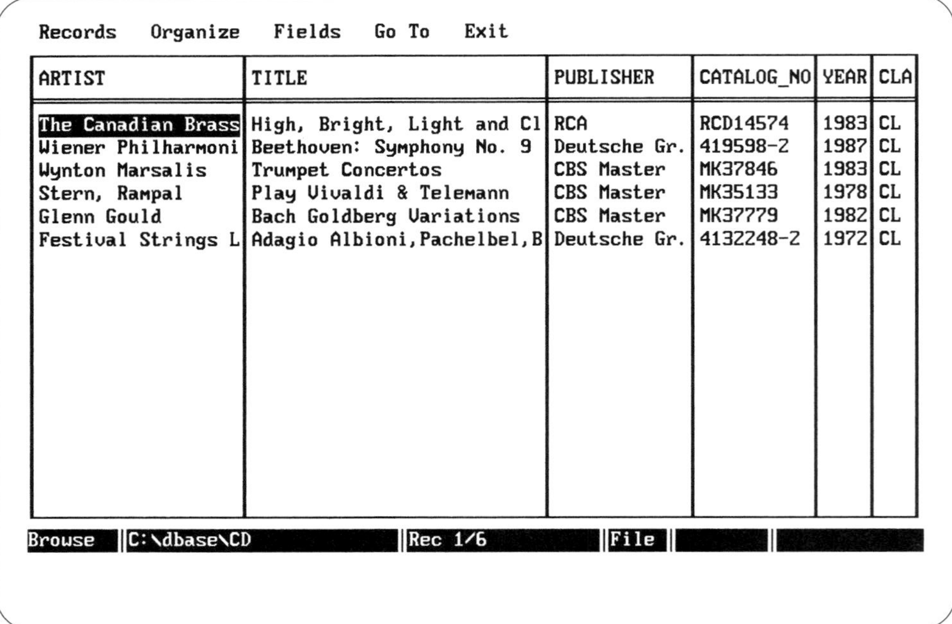

Records Organize Fields Go To Exit

ARTIST	TITLE	PUBLISHER	CATALOG_NO	YEAR	CLA
The Canadian Brass	High, Bright, Light and Cl	RCA	RCD14574	1983	CL
Wiener Philharmoni	Beethoven: Symphony No. 9	Deutsche Gr.	419598-2	1987	CL
Wynton Marsalis	Trumpet Concertos	CBS Master	MK37846	1983	CL
Stern, Rampal	Play Vivaldi & Telemann	CBS Master	MK35133	1978	CL
Glenn Gould	Bach Goldberg Variations	CBS Master	MK37779	1982	CL
Festival Strings L	Adagio Albioni,Pachelbel,B	Deutsche Gr.	4132248-2	1972	CL

Browse ║C:\dbase\CD ║Rec 1/6 ║File ║

FIGURE 3-14

Browse Screen Showing CD Records

(with DEL in the Status Bar) on the screen as you browse through the records. You can change the setting that will cause deleted records to not appear in printed or screen displays. (In the main Control Center menu use the **Tools** choice, go to *Settings*, select *Deleted* and change the response from Off to **On**.)

To permanently erase records marked for deletion, use the *Erase Marked Records* option in the **Organize** menu in the Edit or Browse screens.

Listing Records on the Printer: Quick Report

dBASE has a **Quick Report** feature, activated from most menus with the **Shift-F9** command. This command will print the fields across the page, one record per line, similar to the Browse display screen. If the record is too wide to fit on one line, it will wrap around to the next line, producing a printout that is somewhat difficult to read. The Quick Report screen appears in Figure 3-15.

The default choices with this menu are usually correct and you can press **Enter** when dBASE shows you the *Begin printing* command. dBASE places a blank page before your report and may place one after, depending on how it was installed at your computer center. Chapter 5 covers preparing custom reports with dBASE.

Example: *Creating a Quick Report*

This example shows how to create a Quick Report for the CD example database file.

1. From the Control Center be certain the **CD** database file is in use. If so, it will appear in the top section of the Data file panel. If not, move the cursor to the CD filename and press **Enter** two times to place it in use.
2. To invoke the Quick Report menu, press **Shift-F9**. We will assume that the default values are sufficient. See Figure 3-15.

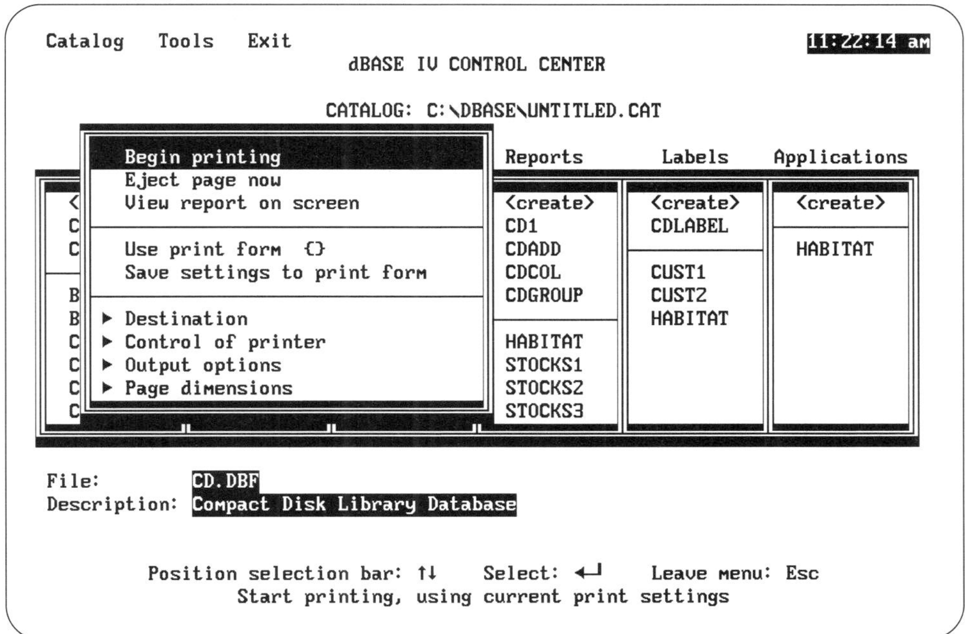

FIGURE 3-15

Quick Report Menu

3. Make sure the printer is attached to your computer and that it is powered up and ready to print. Move the cursor to *Begin printing* and press **Enter** to begin printing.
4. dBASE will print the report, then return to the Control Center automatically. The report is shown in Figure 3-16.

Obtaining Help in dBASE IV

Like Lotus 1-2-3 and many other business applications, dBASE IV provides context-specific on-line help whenever **F1** is pressed. Thus you may receive help at any menu, and the help screen will be pertinent to that menu. For example, suppose we are at the Control Center and wish help on selecting files. Pressing the F1 key produces the screen in Figure 3-17.

Many help screens are more than a single page. Pressing **F4** will bring up the next screen, while **F3** will bring up the previous screen. You can see help on Related Topics by moving the cursor to the Related Topics box and pressing **Enter**. The dBASE Help Contents Index is also available by moving the cursor to the Contents box and pressing **Enter**. At this screen is a list of help topics, including the screen you just viewed. Pressing the **F3** key at this menu will bring up a list of more general topics, while **F4** will display a list of more specific topics. You may print the Help screen at any display by moving the cursor to the Print box and pressing **Enter**. To leave the Help system press the **Esc** key.

Suppose you had entered the Database screen and were attempting to index the CD database, with the cursor on the *Create new index* Menu Bar option. Pressing **F1** will produce the Help display in Figure 3-18.

Closing the Database

Because dBASE automatically saves changes to the database file on your disk it doesn't need to be saved manually as with other software packages. However, you may wish to close the database file and use another. From the Control Center screen, move the cursor to the open database file in the Data

FIGURE 3-16

Quick Report from Example CD Database

```
Page No.    1
10/31/90

ARTIST               TITLE                        PUBLISHER      CATALOG_NO  YEAR  CLASS  LENGTH  DIGITAL

The Canadian Brass   High, Bright, Light and Cl   RCA            RCD14574    1983  CL         51  Y
Wiener Philharmoni   Beethoven: Symphony No. 9    Deutsche Gr.   419598-2    1987  CL         72  Y
Wynton Marsalis      Trumpet Concertos            CBS Master     MK37846     1983  CL         40  Y
Stern, Rampal        Play Vivaldi & Telemann      CBS Master     MK35133     1978  CL         44  N
Glenn Gould          Bach Goldberg Variations     CBS Master     MK37779     1982  CL         51  Y
Festival Strings L   Adagio Albioni,Pachelbel,B   Deutsche Gr.   4132248-2   1972  CL         62  N
                                                                                             320
```

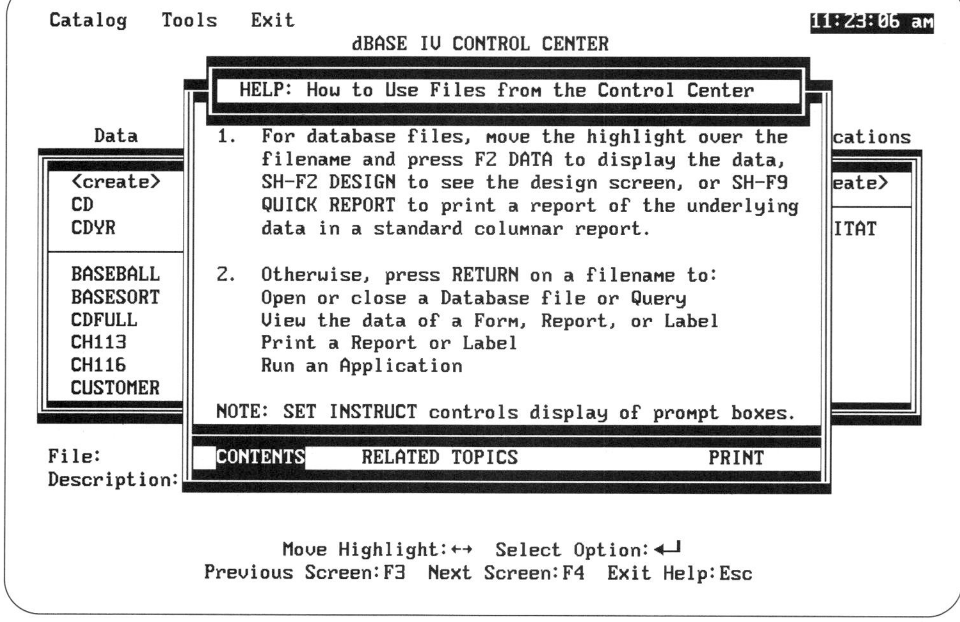

FIGURE 3-17

dBASE Help Menu

panel, above the horizontal bar, and press **Enter**. You will see the screen in Figure 3-19.

The **Close File** option is highlighted. Pressing **Enter** will close the database file and move its name below the horizontal bar, with other database files. If you open a second database file while a file is in use, the first file is automatically closed before the second is opened, without loss of data. Caution: If you are storing your database files on a removable (floppy) disk, **be certain to close the file before removing your disk.** All files are automatically closed when you leave dBASE.

Opening an Existing Database File

To use the data from an existing file, move the cursor to the file panel in the Control Center. Then move the cursor to a named file in the lower section and press **Enter.** You will see the box in Figure 3-20 in the center of your screen.

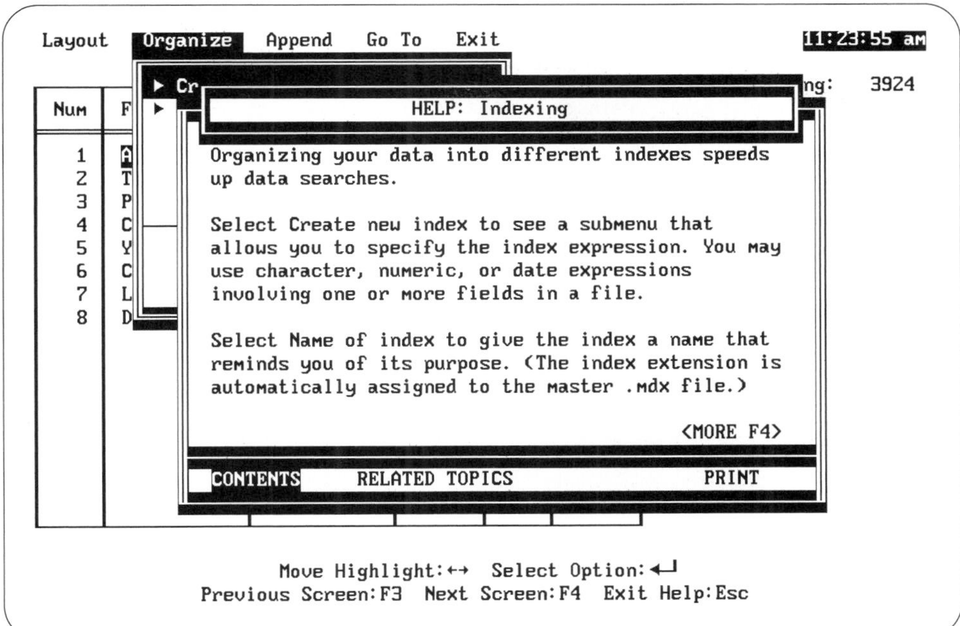

FIGURE 3-18

Index Command Help Screen (Context-Specific)

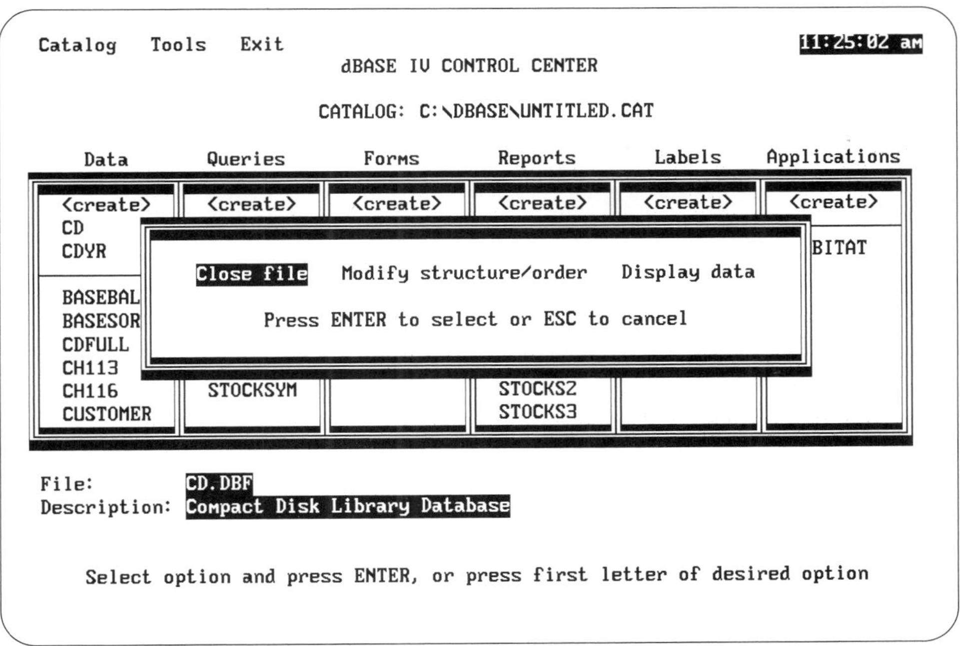

FIGURE 3-19

Close File Dialog Box

The **Use File** selection leaves you in the Control Center. At this point you may use any of the regular dBASE features. The **Modify Structure/Order** takes you to the Database screen, equivalent to pressing **Shift-F2**. The **Display Data** choice takes you to the Edit or Browse screens, equivalent to pressing **F2**.

Leaving dBASE IV

You must return to the Control Center screen in order to Exit from dBASE. Press the **F10** key to activate the Menu Bar, and select **Exit.** Then move the cursor to the *Quit to DOS* choice and press **Enter**. dBASE will close all open files,

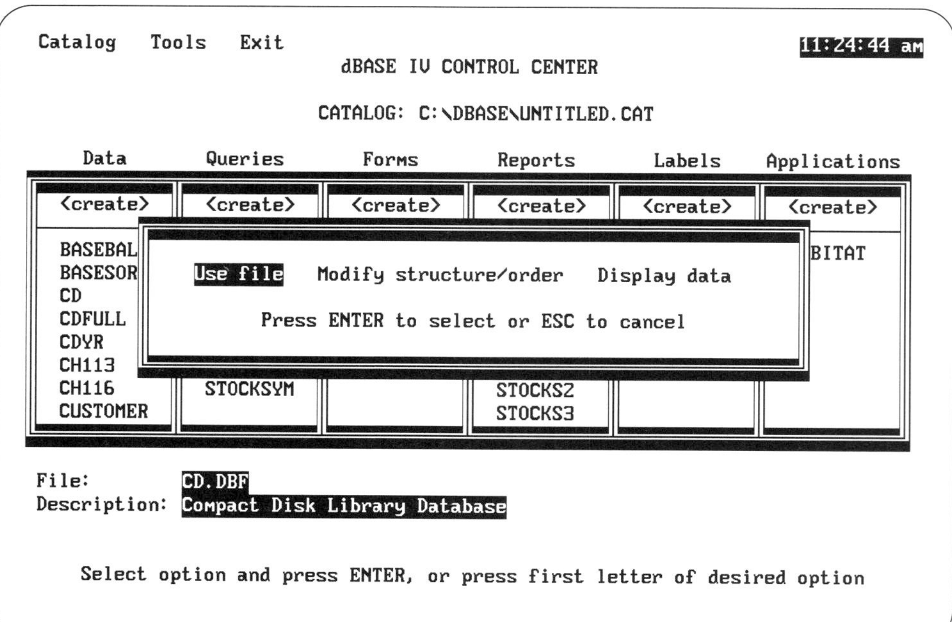

FIGURE 3-20

Open an Existing File Dialog Box

and return to the DOS prompt. If you are using a floppy disk, at this point you can safely remove your diskette.

dBASE IV File Types

dBASE IV uses more than sixty **file types** as database, index, report forms, label forms, queries, and screen forms are created. dBASE uses the three-character file extension to indicate the type of file. To speed execution of reports, labels, forms, and queries, dBASE translates them into object files whose file type ends in O. The most common file types are described below.

Extension	*Meaning*
.DBF	Database file containing the structure of the file and the field values (except for memo fields).
.DBT	Memo field values database file.
.MDX	dBASE IV multiple-tag index file; contains up to 47 different expressions.
.NDX	Index file for pre-dBASE IV versions; contains a single index expression and pointers to match .DBF record.
.FRM	Report form design file.
.FRO	Compiled (executable) report form file.
.LBL	Label form design file.
.LBO	Compiled (executable) label form file.
.PRG	Program file containing commands.
.DBO	Compiled (executable) program file.
.QRY	Standard query design file containing conditions for finding and displaying information.

.QBE	Query-by-example design file.
.QBO	Compiled (executable) query file.
.SCR	Custom data entry screen form design file.
.TXT	ASCII text output file.
.VUE	View file storing selected fields from selected records as generated through a query.
.CAT	Catalog file containing database, query, form, report, and label files that relate to an application.

CHAPTER REVIEW

Database Terminology

A database is a set of data values organized for easy user access. A field represents an attribute or measurement of some object or event. A record is a collection of related fields about that object or event. A file is a group of records about similar objects. A database is a group of related files. In dBASE IV the term "database file" is used as a synonym for file. The dBASE "Catalog" roughly describes the generic term for database. We use the dBASE nomenclature in this textbook.

List, File, and Database Managers

List and file management software packages are able to store data fields in record formats for a single file at a time. List managers are generally simpler to use and easier to learn. They typically offer sorting and limited reporting capability. File managers allow the user to build custom data entry screens and build queries for retrieving records according to specified conditions. Database management software such as dBASE IV adds multi-file capability, linking records together by common field values. Sophisticated query and report building are found in this type of software. Database management software also provides a programming language so that programs of stored commands (similar to Lotus 1-2-3 macros) can be created.

dBASE User Modes

dBASE IV provides four user modes, ranging from custom turnkey applications to an extensive menu system known as the Control Center. Nearly all of the dBASE IV commands are available from the Control Center, departing from earlier versions of dBASE. dBASE IV also has a mode where commands can be entered directly at the dot prompt, providing a consistent interface for users of previous dBASE versions.

Starting dBASE

Type **DBASE** at the DOS prompt to begin dBASE. Data files will be saved and retrieved from whatever drive or subdirectory you began in when you started dBASE. The initial menu is the Control Center, which provides access to data files, queries, and reports. The Control Center consists of the Menu Bar in the upper left corner, the File Panels in the center, and Status Area in the bottom.

The Menu Bar

The Menu Bar provides access to commands that are appropriate to the current display screen. The Menu Bar is activated by pressing the F10 key, then using the arrow keys to move the cursor to the appropriate selection in the pull-down menu. Selections that are dimly lit are not available at the current time. Pressing the Esc key will erase the Menu Bar and return to the underlying display screen.

File Panels and dBASE Catalog

The File Panels in the Control Center provide access to various files created in dBASE. The six panels list existing databases, queries, screen forms, reports, label forms, and applications, and permit you to create new files of these types. A dBASE Catalog lists all the files associated with a particular set of applications. The Status Area at the bottom of the screen includes a list of function key commands for that screen.

Creating a New Database File

The first step in creating a new database file is to design the file structure. You need to determine the appropriate data fields, enter names for those fields, and select the type and specify the width of each field in number of characters. There are six field types in dBASE IV: character fields hold text characters (letters and digits), numeric fields are used for numbers, float fields hold very large or very small numbers, date fields are used for dates, logical fields take true or false values, and memo fields are used for holding longer comments. You may have up to 255 fields in a single record, which may be up to 4000 characters long.

Building the Database

To enter the file structure, press the Shift-F2 command from the Control Center. At the Database screen, you can enter the field name, field type, and field width in the appropriate boxes. Field names can be up to 10 characters long and may contain digits and the underscore character. Field widths for date, logical and memo fields are automatically set. To insert an omitted field before an existing field, move the cursor to the existing field and press Ctrl-N. You can then fill in the boxes for the new field. Ctrl-U can be used to delete a field from the structure. To save the file structure, press Ctrl-End. When you return to the Control Center, the new file name will appear in the Data file panel.

Adding Data to the File

To add data to your new file, from the Control Center press F2. You will see the Edit screen in which the field names appear at the left side of the screen. A box indicates where data is to be placed for each field. The width of the box corresponds to the width of the field in the file structure. The Status Line at the bottom of the screen gives the name of the file in use and the record pointer location in the file. Use the arrow keys to move between fields. Corrections can be made before going on to the next record. When you are finished entering new data, press the Ctrl-End key. The records are automatically saved in the file and you will return to the Control Center.

Manipulating the Data

To view the data press F2 from the Control Center. The Edit screen shows the fields from a single record down the screen in the same fashion as you entered them. Pressing PgDn or PgUp will display the next or previous record in the Edit screen. Pressing the F2 key again will take you to the Browse screen, where the fields are displayed across the screen, and several records appear at the same time. You can also make changes while viewing the data. You can use the Ctrl-U command to mark (or unmark) records for deletion, or go through the Records menu in the Menu Bar and select the *Mark record for deletion* (or *Clear deletion mark)* choice. dBASE does not permanently erase deleted records until you give a separate command. To return to the Control Center activate the Menu Bar and select the *Save changes and exit* bar.

Creating a Quick Report

Quick reports are accessed from the Control Center by pressing Shift-F9. dBASE prepares a printed report in which the fields are placed across the page, side by side. If the fields and/or records are wider than the page width, they will wrap around to the next line of the page. dBASE will print as many records as will fit on each page until all records are printed.

Obtaining Help in dBASE IV

There is an extensive help system in dBASE that is context-specific. Pressing the F1 key will bring up one or more help screens pertinent to the command or screen in use at the time. The F4 and F3 keys can be used to move between help screens. Help for related topics is available as a menu choice and from that screen you can request more general or more specific topics.

Closing the Database

To close the database file you should move the cursor to the file name in the Data panel and press the Enter key, then select the *Close File* option. Files are also closed when you exit out of dBASE. For floppy disk users, never remove your diskette that holds the data files until all files are closed. To leave dBASE from the Control Center, select the *Exit to DOS* Menu Bar option.

dBASE File Types

dBASE IV uses more than sixty different file types to represent different kinds of information. File types include database files, memo files, single and multiple indexes, and command line program files. Others include report forms, label forms, query files, and data entry screens. The three-character file extension conveys the file's type.

KEY TERMS

append records
Applications panel
ASSIST
Browse screen **(F2)**
catalog
character field
Control Center
create structure
data file
database
database manager
Database screen **(Shift-F2)**
database structure
date field
deleted records
Display data **(F2)**
dot prompt
Edit screen **(F2)**
field
file
file manager
File Panels
file types
float field
forms
Help screen **(F1)**
label

list manager
logical field
memo field
Menu Bar
message line
Modify structure/Order **(Shift-F2)**
navigation line
numeric field
pull-down menu
queries
Quick Report **(Shift-F9)**
record
record pointer
report
retrieve
sort
Status Bar
work surface

DISCUSSION QUESTIONS

1. Define the following database terms:
   a. file
   b. field
   c. database
   d. record.
2. Describe the basic database operations: create, append, edit, sort, retrieve, report.
3. List the four dBASE user modes and describe the kind of user most likely to work in that mode.
4. Sketch the opening Control Center display and discuss the use of each of its components: Menu Bar, File Panels, Status Area.
5. Describe the use of the six file types that are cataloged in the File Panel area: Data, Queries, Forms, Reports, Labels, and Applications.
6. Explain how one can activate selections from the Menu Bar. How can you "cancel" a Menu Bar that was activated by mistake?
7. Discuss the steps in building a new database file in dBASE IV.
8. What are the six types of fields supported by dBASE IV? Give sample entries for each field type.
9. List the limitations in the file structure for a single database file:
   a. Number of fields per record
   b. Maximum width of a field name
   c. Total record length, in characters
   d. Maximum width of each field type
   e. Number of records per file
   f. Maximum length of the database file name.
10. Describe the use of the following commands when issued from the Control Center.
    a. **F1**
    b. **F2**
    c. **Shift-F2**
    d. **Shift-F9**
    e. **F10**
11. Discuss the similarities and differences between the Edit and Browse display screens in dBASE IV. When should each be used?

12. Suppose you have finished entering the first record on the Edit screen, and wish to clear the screen and edit data for the second record. How is this accomplished?
13. Discuss the information that normally appears on the Status Bar at the bottom of the Edit or Browse screens. If necessary, go to the computer and activate the Edit screen and experiment with various keys.
14. How can the record pointer be moved to a specific record? Explain the options in the **Go To** Menu Bar selection.
15. Explain how you can make changes to the data stored in an open dBASE file.
16. Discuss how records are deleted in dBASE. What can you do if a record was accidentally marked for deletion?
17. Explain how to access the dBASE Help system. After an initial help screen appears, discuss options for obtaining more help. How do you leave the Help system?
18. Explain how to close an open database file. Why don't you have to go through a separate step to "save" a database file on your disk?
19. How do you leave dBASE IV? Explain the caution about removing a data diskette before closing all files.

EXERCISES

1. Go to your computer lab and practice starting dBASE IV. Bring up the main Control Center screen and use the Help command (**F1**) for various sections. Activate the Menu Bar with the **F10** command, and move the cursor to different selections. Make sure you know how to Exit from dBASE IV.
2. Using the Create option from the Control Center, build a structure for the following database file. Call the file **CUSTOMER** when you save it. Don't enter any data yet. Use the *Layout* Menu Bar selection while at the Database screen to print the file structure on the printer.

Fieldname	**Type**	**Width**
CNAME	Char	15
ADDRESS	Char	20
CITY	Char	14
STATE	Char	2
ZIPCODE	Char	5
LASTORDER	Date	8
TAXABLE	Logical	1

3. If you have not already created the file structure for the previous problem, do so now. Otherwise use the Control Center to open the **CUSTOMER** data file. Use the **F2** Data command to display the first record, and append the Figure 3-21 records to the file. Remember that you can correct errors in previous fields before entering the TAXABLE field value. After you have finished entering the records, obtain a Quick Report printout. The lines on the report will wrap around to the next line.

FIGURE 3-21

Sample Data for Exercise 3

CNAME	ADDRESS	CITY	STATE	ZIPCODE	LASTORDER	TAXABLE
Jones, Bill	244 19th St.	Wabash	IN	47521	06/21/89	Y
Hollar, W.	1804 Thames	Richmond	IN	47154	10/15/89	N
Anderson, M.	Box 28	Vincennes	IN	48231	02/01/88	Y
Snow, B.	605 Ohio St.	Terre Haute	IN	47807	09/13/89	Y
O'Reilly, W.	1332 Western	Cory	IN	47823	09/30/89	N

4. Use the Edit facility to make the following changes to your CUSTOMER database file.
   a. Replace the first name of record 1 with the initial **B.**
   b. The third record ADDRESS should be **Box 128**.
   c. Change the date of record 5 to **09/31/89**. Did dBASE accept it? Leave the date as originally entered.
   d. Add the following record's data as record 6.

      Mains, W.

      2199 West Lawrin Princeton, IN 47233

      06/12/72 Y
   e. Obtain a Quick Report of the revised database file.

5. Copy the **SCHED.DBF** and **SCHED.MDX** files from the textbook data disk to your own work area. Then start dBASE IV and add that file to your catalog:
   a. Activate the Menu Bar from the Control Center, then choose the **Catalog** menu. Select the *Add file to catalog* line and select the SCHED.DBF file from your work area.
   b. Use the Browse screen to display the data in this file.
   c. Delete record 14 and record 23 from the file.
   d. Using Browse, change the records taught by Olson to be taught by **Oaks**.
   e. Change the time of the MIS 320 class to **3:30** in room **SB 106**.
   f. Insert the following new course at the end of the file:

      MIS 430 1 30 Jefferson 11:00 TTH SB 806

      Distributed Data Processing F
   g. Obtain a Quick Report printout of the file with changes.

6. Create the structure for the following database. You may choose appropriate data names for your fields, along with the field types. Print the structure on the printer. We will add data for this file in a later chapter.

   The Lost River School PTA has assembled a database of parent volunteers that help with the school's programs. You have been asked to help by putting this database on the office computer. The following information is maintained for each volunteer: First name, last name, telephone number, specialty area (e.g., office, field trips, computer, reading, miscellaneous), years of previous volunteer experience, time preference (morning or afternoon), day preference (M,T,W,Th,F), and children's names.

CHAPTER 3 PROJECT
REGISTRAR'S OFFICE

This project will have you prepare a database file containing all of the courses you have taken at the college including any transfer courses. The fields should include the following:

Chapter 2 will cover the disk operating system (DOS) and some utility programs. Coverage of the dBASE IV database package begins with the Chapter 3 QuickStart section and proceeds in increasing detail in the following chapters. Chapter 8 provides an overview of other versions of dBASE. Chapter 9 details transfer of information between dBASE IV, Lotus 1-2-3, and WordPerfect 5.1. The Appendix contains a Buyer's Guide for selecting personal computing software and hardware as well as summaries of dBASE commands and functions.

Course number (e.g., MIS 376)

- Course title
- Date the course was started (e.g., 08/26/90)
- Instructor's name
- Credit hours
- Course grade (e.g., B+).

After entering the courses you have completed, add the courses you are now taking, but leave the grade field empty. Prepare a Quick Report showing all of the information in your personal database. If you read ahead in Chapter 4, your database can be sorted or indexed and reports created showing records in different order.

4

Intermediate Database Management with dBASE IV

Objectives

After completing this chapter, you should be able to:

- Modify the database structure.
- Organize the records in a specific order with the Sort and Index operations.
- Work with dBASE memo fields.
- Build a custom data entry form.
- Create queries with the query-by-example facility.

INTRODUCTION

The Control Center is explored in more detail, including the ability to make changes in the structure of a database file and in the sequence of records. Sorting and indexing are compared, with several examples to illustrate their use. The use of memo fields is illustrated.

Much of the power of database management systems comes from their ability to manipulate the data and create customized reports, labels, queries, and data entry forms without having to write traditional programs. The chapter includes the preparation of custom data-entry screen forms. The dBASE Query-by-Example (QBE) facility is covered in the latter part of the chapter. Filter conditions are described, along with the preparation of a view skeleton. The use of queries for viewing certain records is demonstrated.

ORGANIZING THE DATABASE

The first section explains how to make changes to the database structure such as changing a field's width and adding a new field. The next section presents ways to change the order of the records in the database file.

Changing the Database Structure

One advantage in working with a database program is the ease with which you can make changes to the structure of the database file. You can add new fields or change the length of fields easily, and dBASE will automatically copy the old records into the new format. You can even change the name of existing fields, but you must follow a certain procedure in order to not lose the data in the existing field.

We start with the Control Center screen and select the database file whose structure is to be changed. Use the **Shift-F2** command to examine the design of the database file. dBASE will display the Organize menu when you get to the Database screen. Pressing **Esc** will leave the menu bar and show the underlying screen. To change the length of a field, use the arrow keys to move the cursor to the proper field and type in the correct value. To insert a new field at the end of the existing fields, move the cursor below the last field and a new blank field will open up. To insert a new field between two existing fields, move the cursor to the lower field and press **Ctrl-N**. A new blank field will appear. Fill in the rest of the information for that field.

When you have finished making changes to the structure, press **Ctrl-End**. dBASE will make changes to the structure and automatically fill in the values from the old database file. You will then return to the Control Center screen. To view the results of the changes, press the **F2** key and the Data screen will appear.

Changing the Record Order

There are three ways to organize the order of the records in a database file. The first requires no additional action, while the other two involve further work.

- You can leave them in their data entry or **natural order**, which is the default choice. Records appear in record number order.
- You can **sort** the database file on one or more key fields, saving the sorted results in a new database file. The original file remains in natural order. Because sorting creates an additional database file whose records are in the desired order, you must have additional disk space for storing those records.
- The final method involves **indexing** the database file on one or more database fields. The index determines the order in which the records are to appear, and provides a means of ordering the records in multiple ways. The index method allows rapid retrieval of a record based upon

looking up a value in the index. The index file takes up some additional space on the disk, but much less than the sorted file would.

Sorting Database Records

To sort records, select the desired database file from the Data file panel of the Control Center. Issue the **Shift-F2** command to access the Database screen. On the menu bar the **Organize** choice is highlighted as shown in Figure 4-1. Select *Sort database on field list* in the lower half of the menu and you will see the Figure 4-2 screen.

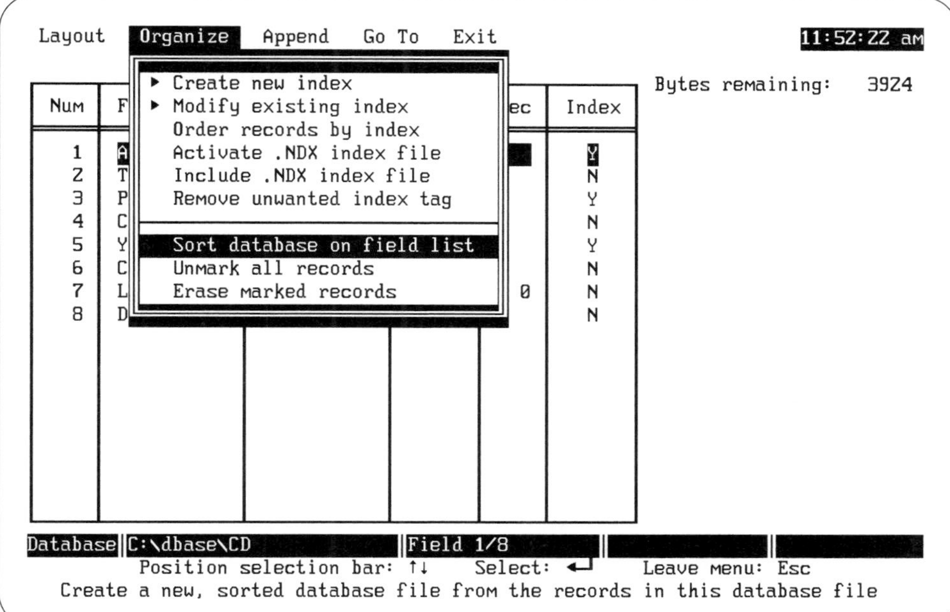

FIGURE 4-1

Organize Menu: Sorting Database Records

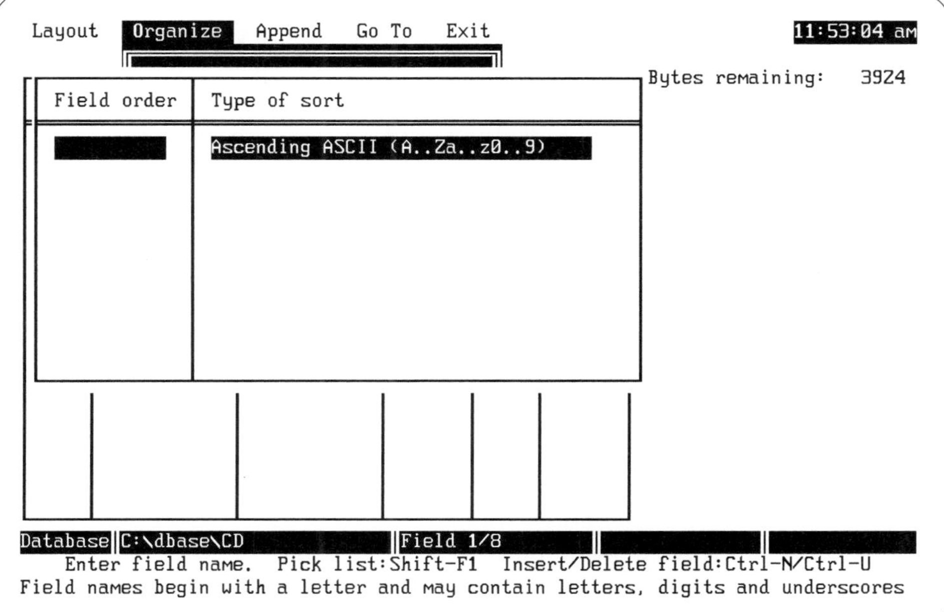

FIGURE 4-2

Database Sort Screen (Before Specifying Key Fields)

To sort the database you must provide the **key fields** on which you want to sort the data. The first field you list is the **primary key**, or the field that is most important in sorting. Any other fields are **secondary keys**, used to determine the order for records that have the same primary key value. For instance, a primary key might be last name, and a secondary key could be the first name. The Field Order column will hold the names of the key fields.

You must specify the Type of sort for each key field. There are four choices:

- Ascending ASCII
- Descending ASCII
- Ascending Dictionary
- Descending Dictionary.

Ascending sorts go from lowest to highest, in increasing order. **Descending** sorts are in decreasing order, from highest to lowest. The ASCII sorts use the **ASCII code** for characters in which the capital letters come before the lowercase letters. The **Dictionary sort** will consider capital and lowercase letters as the same letters. You can press the spacebar to move between the four sort types.

The last input necessary for the sort operation is to select the name of the database file that will hold the sorted records.

Example: *Sorting by Year*

Suppose we want to sort our CD database by the Year, in ascending (increasing) order. Make sure you have the **CD** database file in use from the Control Center.

1. Activate the Database screen by pressing **Shift-F2**.
2. The **Organize** menu bar should be selected when you enter the Database work surface. If it is not activated, press **Alt-O** to activate it. [Note: Version 1.1 also permits use of the Organize menu bar from the Edit and Browse work surfaces.]
3. Press **S** to select *Sort database on field list* line. You should see the Sort screen of Figure 4-2 next.
4. In the first column (Field order) enter the primary key field name, **Year**. [Hint: If you cannot remember the exact spelling of the fields in the database, press **Shift-F1** for a list from which you can pick the field; move the cursor to the desired field and press **Enter** to place it in the box.]
5. Press **Enter** after the field name to go to the Type of sort column. Press the space bar until Ascending ASCII sort type appears, then press **Enter** to select that choice.
6. At the next line press **Enter** on an empty field order box, signifying you have specified all sort keys. [Note: You can also press **Ctrl-End** to indicate you have completed this step.]
7. dBASE will next ask for the name of the new Sort file. Fill in **CDYR** and press **Enter**. dBASE will do the sort, creating the new CDYR database file.
8. Type in an appropriate file description and press **Enter.** When that is complete, you will return to the Database screen.

```
Records   Organize   Fields   Go To   Exit
```

ARTIST	TITLE	PUBLISHER	CATALOG_NO	YEAR	CLA
Festival Strings L	Adagio Albioni,Pachelbel,B	Deutsche Gr.	4132248-2	1972	CL
Stern, Rampal	Play Vivaldi & Telemann	CBS Master	MK35133	1978	CL
Glenn Gould	Bach Goldberg Variations	CBS Master	MK37779	1982	CL
The Canadian Brass	High, Bright, Light and Cl	RCA	RCD14574	1983	CL
Wynton Marsalis	Trumpet Concertos	CBS Master	MK37846	1983	CL
Wiener Philharmoni	Beethoven: Symphony No. 9	Deutsche Gr.	419598-2	1987	CL

```
Browse  C:\dbase\CDYR          Rec 1/6          File
```

FIGURE 4-3

Browse Screen Showing Sorted Records

9. Press **Alt-E** to **Exit** to the Control Center, choosing the *Abandon* line because we have made no changes to the original CD file.

10. You will see the new file, CDYR, in the Data panel of the Control Center. Move the cursor down to that file and Press **F2** to view the data in the CDYR file, shown in Figure 4-3. (You may have to press **PgUp** to move the pointer to the top record.) You'll notice that the records appear in ascending order by the Year, from 1972 to 1987.

Indexing the Records

dBASE **indexes** provide a means of accessing data records very rapidly without requiring significantly more storage space. An index creates a set of pointers that allow you to directly access the database file in a certain order.

Two kinds of indexes are available in dBASE IV. The original **.NDX index file** was used in previous dBASE versions and contains the index for a single field expression. If you wished to access the file in more than one order, a separate index file had to be created for each expression. For example, in the CD file we might wish to create indexes for the ARTIST field and for the YEAR field. In order for the indexes to be properly updated, you must always specify each .NDX index file name when opening a database file. It is recommended that you *not* use the .NDX index procedure with dBASE IV.

dBASE IV introduced the simpler **multiple-index .MDX file** where up to 47 different field expressions can be used for indexes. The multiple index expressions are represented by **tags**. Thus only one file is needed to contain all of the indexes. Multiple-index filenames default to the same name as the database file, but with the .MDX extension. We will only demonstrate examples of the multiple index technique in this textbook.

Example: *Creating a New Index Tag*

If the **CD** database file is not already in use, go to the Control Center and open it from the Data panel.

1. To review the data structure, press the **Shift-F2** command to go to the Database screen. The Menu Bar will highlight the *Create new index* line in the **Organize** menu. If you wish to review the field names, press the **Esc** key and the Menu Bar will disappear. You can reactivate the **Organize** menu bar by pressing the **F10** key or entering **Alt-O**. [Note: This can also be done in the Edit and Browse screens in version 1.1.]
2. Press **Enter** while the cursor points to the *Create new index* line, then press **Enter** on the *Name of Index* line.
3. The first index tag will provide for an alphabetical listing by the ARTIST field. In this case, we will enter **ARTIST** and then press **Enter** as the name of the first index tag. You will then see the screen in Figure 4-4.
4. After supplying the index tag name, move the cursor to the *Index expression* line and press **Enter** to open the {} symbols.
5. You can enter only valid field names (or expressions involving those fields) from the current file in use. Type the name of the index field, **ARTIST** and press **Enter** to complete the entry. If you enter an incorrect expression, dBASE will display the *Variable Not Found* error message in a box. If you need help in entering the field name, press the **Shift-F1** expression builder command. You'll see a list of valid field names and operators, and can move the cursor to the desired line and press Enter to use that field or operator.
6. You may select the index order, Ascending or Descending; the default is ascending, or from lowest to highest. (Dictionary order is ***not*** available in the index.) Press **Ctrl-End** to save the results. [Note: If you don't wish to

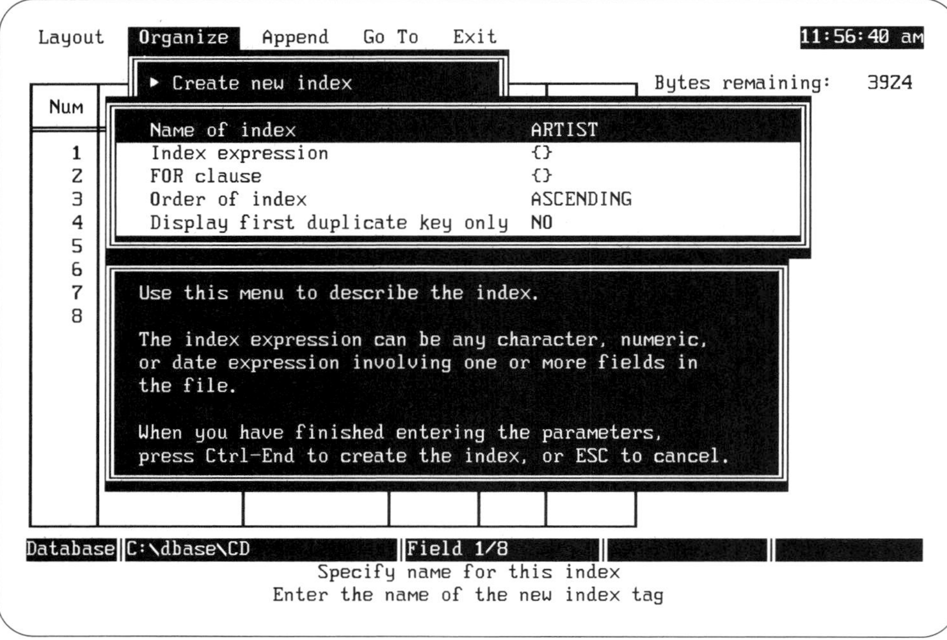

FIGURE 4-4

Organize Menu—Create New Index

execute the index command, press the **Esc** key instead of Ctrl-End and dBASE will discard the index command.]

7. dBASE will build the index table and the records will be displayed in the new order. (CD.MDX is the name of the index file itself, combining the name of the data file, CD, with the .MDX multiple index extension.)
8. Press **F2** to go to the Browse or Edit screens to view the rearranged records.

When a database file is first opened, no index is active. The records remain in natural order. The next example will demonstrate how to activate an index tag that was previously created.

Example: *Activating an Index Tag*

We'll begin with the **CD** database file from the previous example. Open this file from the Data panel of the Control Center.

1. Select the Database screen with the **Shift-F2** command.
2. Move the cursor to the *Order records by index* line in the **Organize** menu bar. Press **Enter** to activate that selection, and your screen should look like Figure 4-5.
3. To activate the ARTIST tag in the CD index, move the cursor with the ↑ and ↓ keys to that entry and press **Enter**. [Note: At this point ARTIST is the only entry in the list of tags, so the arrow keys select that tag or natural order.]
4. You can view the records in the desired order by going to the Browse screen (press **F2**). The screen should look like Figure 4-6, in order by the ARTIST field.

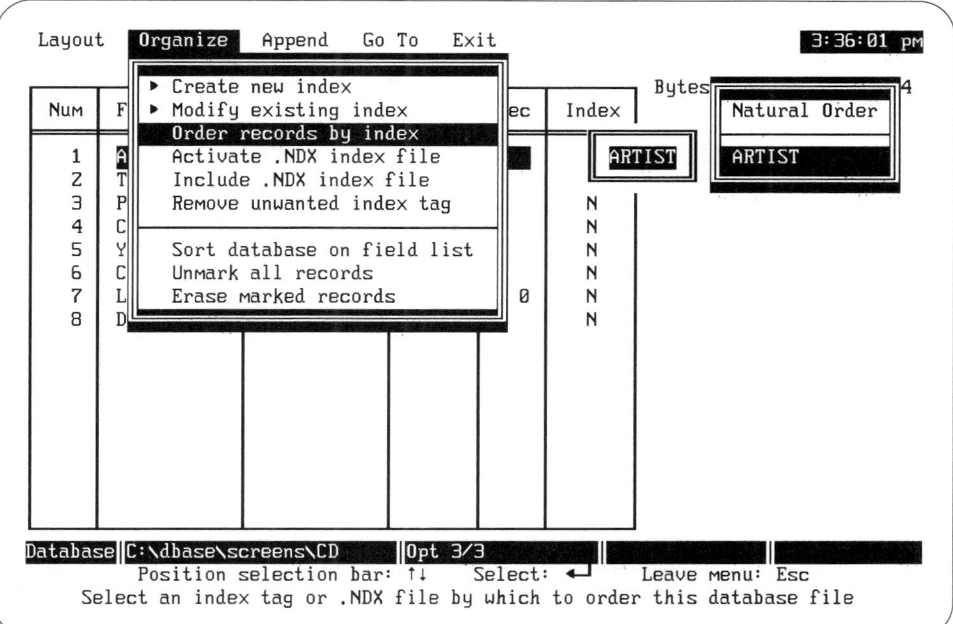

FIGURE 4-5

Organize Menu—Activate Index Tag

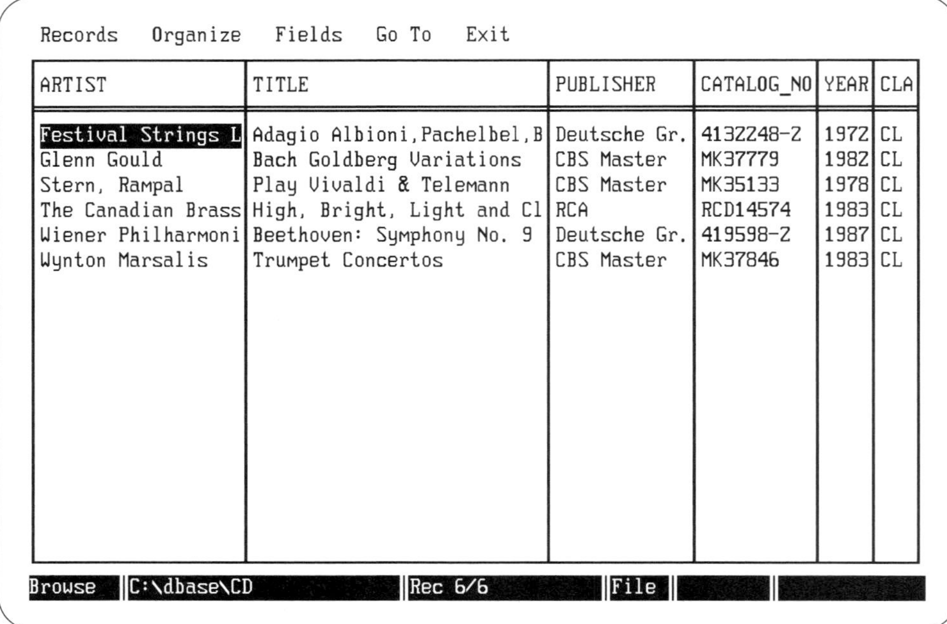

Records Organize Fields Go To Exit

ARTIST	TITLE	PUBLISHER	CATALOG_NO	YEAR	CLA
Festival Strings L	Adagio Albioni,Pachelbel,B	Deutsche Gr.	4132248-2	1972	CL
Glenn Gould	Bach Goldberg Variations	CBS Master	MK37779	1982	CL
Stern, Rampal	Play Vivaldi & Telemann	CBS Master	MK35133	1978	CL
The Canadian Brass	High, Bright, Light and Cl	RCA	RCD14574	1983	CL
Wiener Philharmoni	Beethoven: Symphony No. 9	Deutsche Gr.	419598-2	1987	CL
Wynton Marsalis	Trumpet Concertos	CBS Master	MK37846	1983	CL

Browse ‖C:\dbase\CD ‖Rec 6/6 ‖File ‖

FIGURE 4-6

Browse Screen Showing Records in Order by ARTIST Index Tag

It is possible to have multiple index tags in the CD.MDX index file, and switch between them to change the order of the records. The **master tag** will determine the order of the database file. The following example will demonstrate this procedure.

Example: *Adding Another Index Tag*

We'll assume you have opened the **CD** database file and have activated the **ARTIST** tag. In this example we'll create another index tag for the YEAR field, with recent compact disks listed first (descending order).

1. From the Control Center enter **Shift-F2** to get to the Database screen, and pull down the **Organize** menu bar by pressing **Alt-O**.
2. Move the cursor to the *Create new index* line and press **Enter**.
3. Fill in lines 1, 2, and 4 of the index box with the tag name (**YEAR**), index expression (**YEAR**) and order of index (**Descending**). Figure 4-7 shows the Organize screen for the second index. Then press **Ctrl-End.**
4. To display the records in the new order, press **F2**. See Figure 4-8.

Index tags can also be declared when you build the database file structure. The right-most box in the Database screen for each field line is used to indicate whether that field is to serve as an index. You could change the **N** to **Y** for fields that are to be indexed. Check this column to find the two fields (ARTIST and YEAR) used as indexes in the previous examples.

Searching for Specific Values

dBASE supports two kinds of search commands—one for indexed fields and another for non-indexed fields. Either command can be used from the Edit or Browse screens to locate a record whose field matches a specified value. The indexed search is much faster than the non-indexed search but requires that the field be indexed.

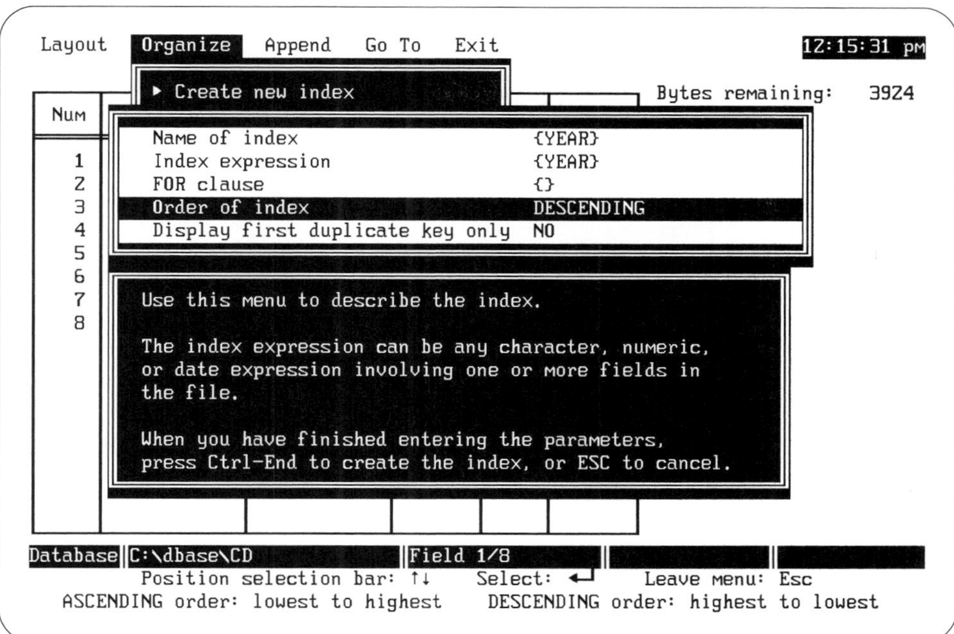

FIGURE 4-7

Organize Screen—Create a Second Index Tag

Records Organize Fields Go To Exit

ARTIST	TITLE	PUBLISHER	CATALOG_NO	YEAR	CLA
Wiener Philharmoni	Beethoven: Symphony No. 9	Deutsche Gr.	419598-2	1987	CL
Wynton Marsalis	Trumpet Concertos	CBS Master	MK37846	1983	CL
The Canadian Brass	High, Bright, Light and Cl	RCA	RCD14574	1983	CL
Glenn Gould	Bach Goldberg Variations	CBS Master	MK37779	1982	CL
Stern, Rampal	Play Vivaldi & Telemann	CBS Master	MK35133	1978	CL
Festival Strings L	Adagio Albioni,Pachelbel,B	Deutsche Gr.	4132248-2	1972	CL

Browse C:\dbase\CD Rec 2/6 File

FIGURE 4-8

Browse Screen Showing Records in Order by YEAR Index Tag

From the Control Center, change to the Browse (or Edit) screen by typing **F2**. Then press **F10** to activate the **Go To** menu bar, shown in Figure 4-9. The top portion of the **Go To** choices moves the record pointer to a fixed location, either top or bottom, or a certain number of records. The bottom **Go To** selections include the *Index key search* choice for indexed fields, and the *Forward search/Backward search* choices for other non-indexed fields.

Index searches are very fast, usually taking less than one second, even for large database files. dBASE will look for the first occurrence of the desired key value and moves the record pointer directly to that record. Searching on non-indexed fields may take a long time, depending upon the number of records

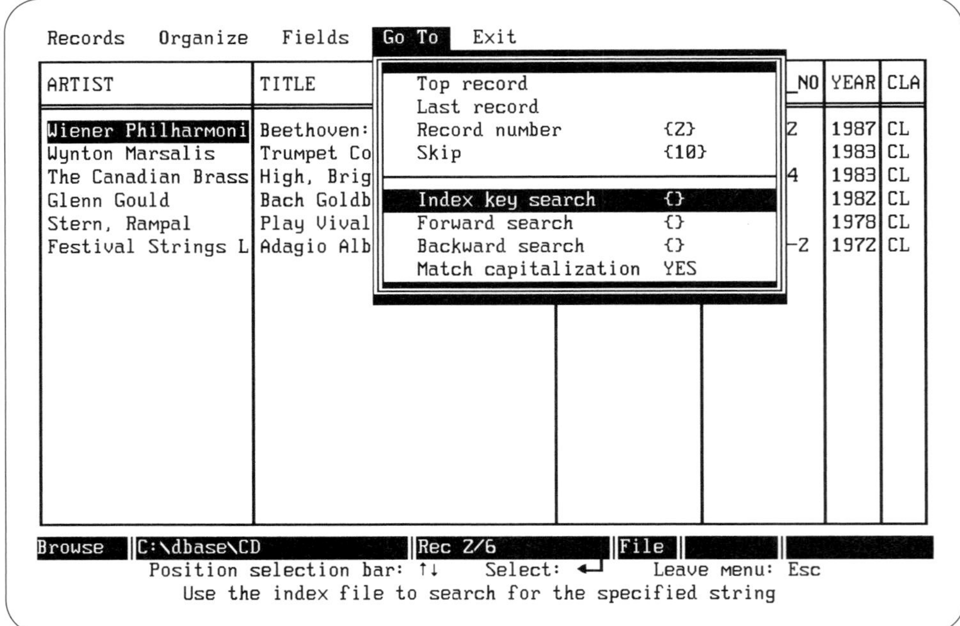

FIGURE 4-9

Go To Menu for Moving Record Pointer

that must be searched sequentially before finding the desired key value. The next example will describe searching with an index key.

Example: *Index Key Search*

1. Make sure that the **CD** file is open, and enter the **Shift-F2** command at the Control Center to move to the Database screen.

2. The previous example left the YEAR tag as the controlling index, and we wish to replace it with the ARTIST tag. Press **F10** to activate the **Organize** bar, and select the *Order records by index* line.

3. The screen will show the two tags we have created for the CD file, as shown in Figure 4-10, with YEAR as the controlling index. Move the cursor from YEAR to ARTIST in the box on the right to select the new tag.

4. Next press **F2** to display the data in the Browse screen. Press **PgUp** to move the record pointer to the top of the screen (and the top of the file in this case because there aren't many records). Use the ↑ and ↓ keys to move the cursor between records, noting that the top record is not record number 1.

5. Suppose we wish to locate the record beginning with **The Can**, referring to The Canadian Brass. Press **F10** to activate the Menu Bar, and select the **Go To** menu bar.

6. Move the cursor to the *Index key search* line and press **Enter**. When prompted for the search string for ARTIST, type **The Can** and press **Enter**. Figure 4-11 shows the **Go To** menu for this search.

7. The record pointer will immediately move to the desired record that begins with the search string. [Note that the last line in the Figure 4-9 **Go To** bar specifies that capitalization in the search string and the data must match. So if you entered **THE CAN** in the search string box, dBASE

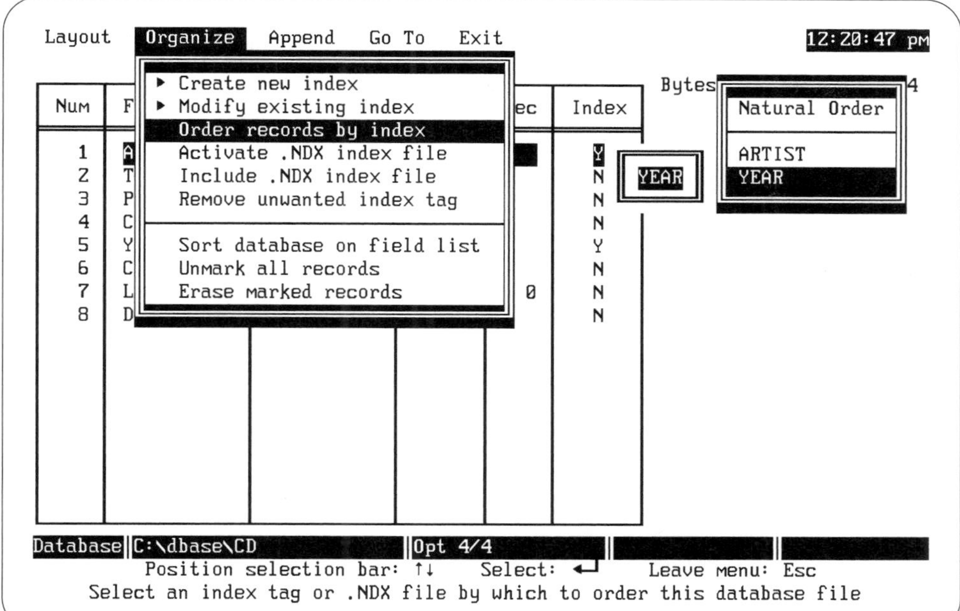

FIGURE 4-10

Organize Menu—Selecting the Index Tag

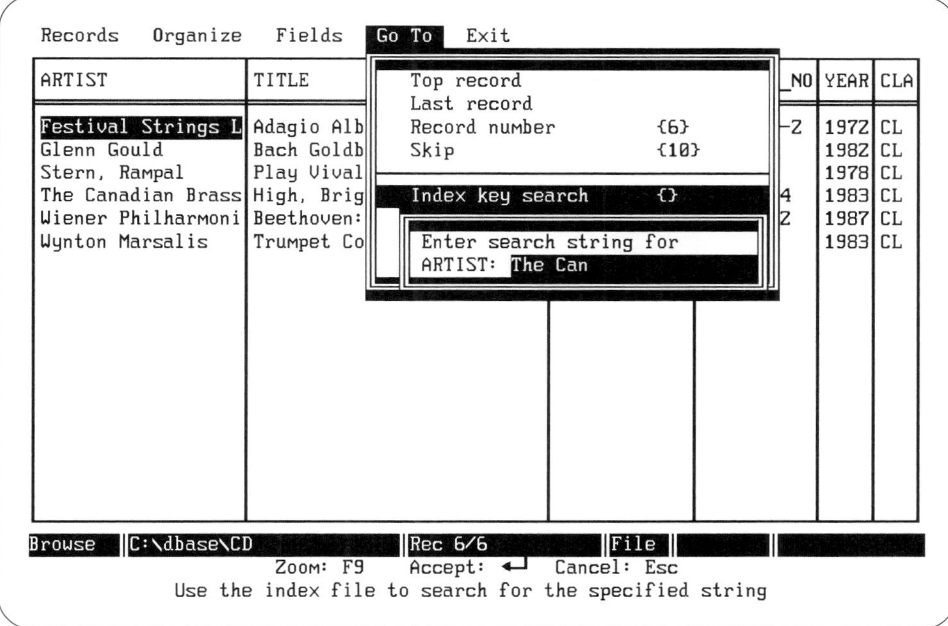

FIGURE 4-11

Go To Menu for Index Key Search

wouldn't find a matching record. If you select the *Match capitalization* line and change it to **NO**, dBASE will ignore differences in capitalization.]

Example: *Searching Without an Index*

1. Open the **CD** database and change to the Browse screen by pressing **F2**. (If the Edit screen appears, press **F2** once more to go to the Browse screen.)
2. Use the ↑ or **PgUp** key to move the record pointer to the first record in the file. Move the cursor to the field that you wish to match a value against;

the **Tab** key moves one field to the right and **Shift-Tab** moves one field to the left. In this case we'll search for a record that has RCA in the Publisher field, so move the cursor to the PUBLISHER field.

3. Next activate the **Go To** menu bar and select the *Forward search* line. Press **Enter** to open the search string box, and fill in **RCA** as the search string. Figure 4-12 illustrates this search screen.
4. When you press **Enter** dBASE will search from the current location through the remaining records until a match is found or the end of the file is encountered. The Browse screen will look like Figure 4-13.

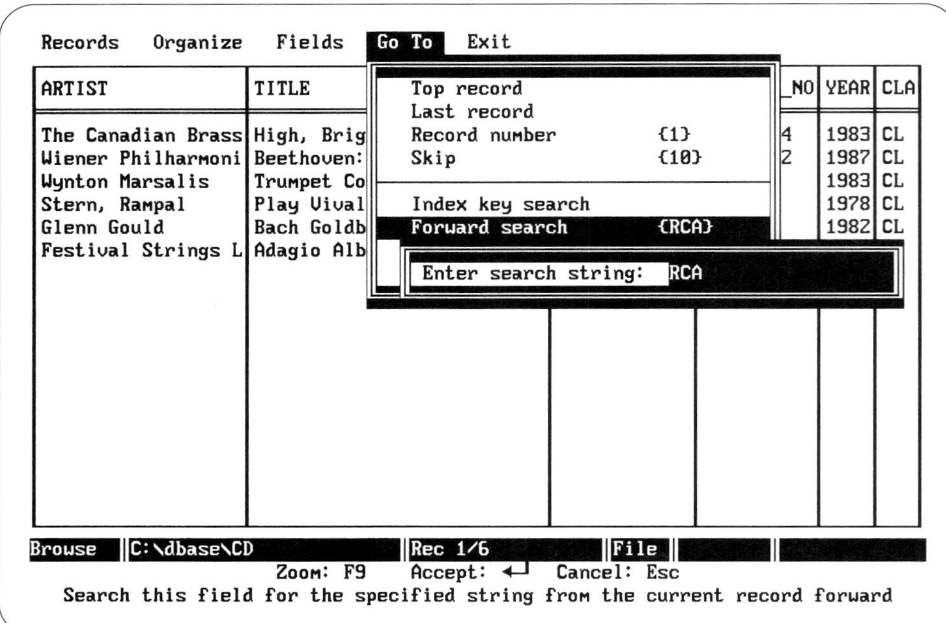

FIGURE 4-12

Go To Menu Showing Forward Search Without Index

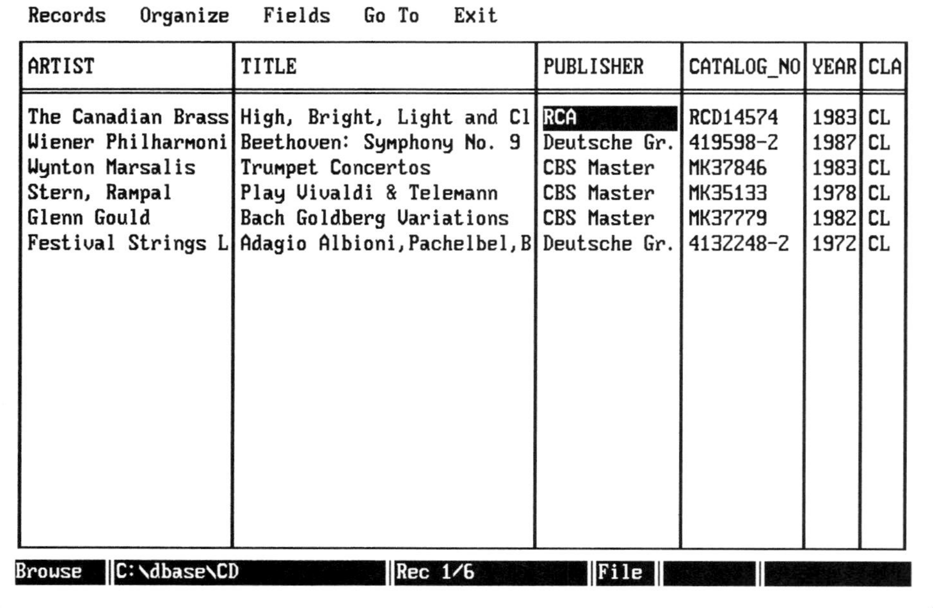

FIGURE 4-13

Browse Screen Showing Forward Search Matching Record

Working with Memo Fields

We introduced the six dBASE field types in the previous chapter. Character and memo fields are used to hold text information; **character fields** have fixed widths up to 254 characters while memo fields have variable widths up to 512 KB characters. **Memo fields** are used to hold comments, descriptions, and other text whose width is not standard from record to record.

Memo fields are stored in a separate file with a .DBT file extension. Whenever you create a database file with a memo field, the .DBT file is automatically created. dBASE fills in the standard width of 10 characters for each memo field in the database file structure, but displays the word memo in the field. To enter or edit data contained in the memo field, move the cursor to the memo field enter box in the Edit or Browse screen, then press **F9**. You will enter the dBASE full-screen edit display, with the ruler line at the top showing column position of the cursor and the left and right margins. Default width for each line in the memo field is 65 characters. dBASE does automatic word wrap if you type beyond the right margin. The full-screen edit display is shown in Figure 4-14.

The contents of memo fields are *not* automatically displayed when you examine the database. At the Edit or Browse screen you can use the **F9** key to view the memo field. To return to the Edit or Browse screen use the **Ctrl-End** command; pressing **Esc** will exit without saving changes. You can print contents of memo fields like any other field using the various Report options described later in this chapter. The memo field will display in the width of the template given in the report file, not the original width with which it was entered in the full-screen edit display.

Example: *Creating a Database File with a Memo Field*

In this example we will build a new database file that will describe the volunteer skills of workers in the Habitat for Humanity project. The fields will include the volunteer's first name, last name, address, city, state, zipcode, and skill.

1. From the Control Center **<create>** a new database file in the Data panel. Enter the structure shown in the Database screen in Figure 4-15. Notice

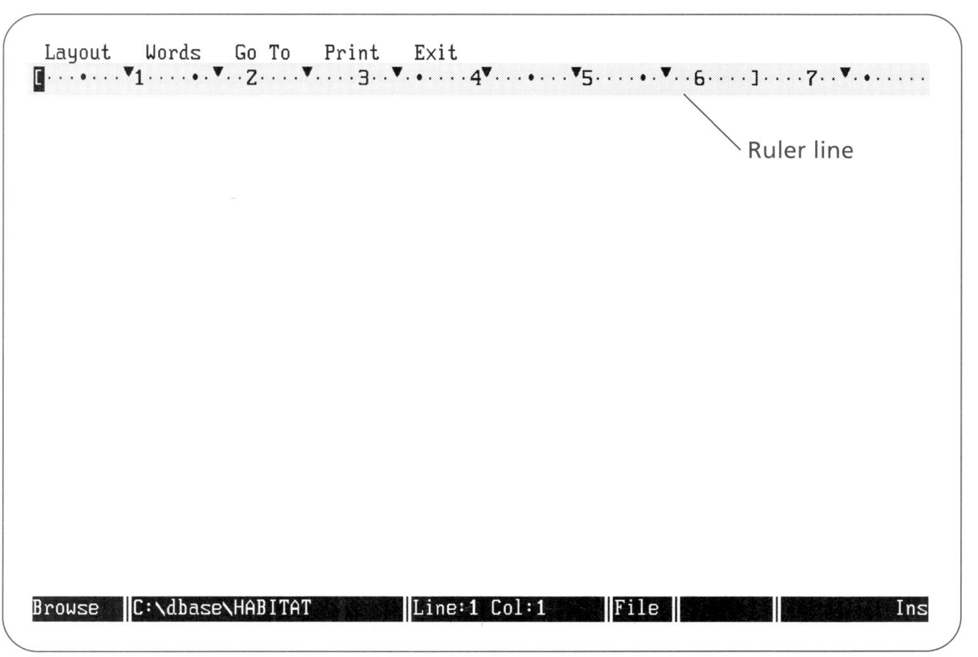

FIGURE 4-14

Edit Screen for Creating or Editing a Memo Field

that we have chosen LNAME and ZIPCODE to be index tags by answering **Y** in the last column.

2. Save the structure by pressing **Ctrl-End**. We will call this file **HABITAT**.
3. When dBASE asks if you wish to append data now, reply **Y**. Enter the data shown in Figure 4-16 for the first record. Remember that when you move the cursor to the memo field, you should press the **F9** key to go to the full-screen edit display. After entering the skill information for that volunteer, press **Ctrl-End** to save that value. Enter the rest of the data.

FIGURE 4-15

Database Structure for Habitat Example Database

```
Layout   Organize   Append   Go To   Exit                          1:29:55 pm

                                                     Bytes remaining:   3929
 Num | Field Name | Field Type | Width | Dec | Index
   1 | FNAME      | Character  |  10   |     |  N
   2 | LNAME      | Character  |  12   |     |  Y
   3 | ADDRESS    | Character  |  18   |     |  N
   4 | CITY       | Character  |  14   |     |  N
   5 | STATE      | Character  |   2   |     |  N
   6 | ZIPCODE    | Character  |   5   |     |  Y
   7 | SKILL      | Memo       |  10   |     |  N

Database ║C:\dbase\HABITAT        ║Field 1/7     ║
             Enter the field name. Insert/Delete field:Ctrl-N/Ctrl-U
Field names begin with a letter and may contain letters, digits and underscores
```

FIGURE 4-16

Field Values for Habitat Database

FNAME	LNAME	ADDRESS	CITY	ST	ZIP	SKILLS FROM APPLICATION FORM
Harold	Garland	1944 South Wentt	Riley	IN	47811	General carpentry; can also use a transit. Has participated in three Habitat projects in the last five years.
Eileen	Pickering	422 Highland Dr.	Terre Haute	IN	47802	Beginner in Habitat. Can organize work groups and do accounting.
Anne	Conrad	1713 Glenview	Bloomington	IN	47432	Wallpapering, painting, interior design
William	Butler	615 Walnut St.	Terre Haute	IN	47807	Concrete work, carpentry and roofing.I am willing to do almost anything that's needed, including electrical, but need some supervision in that area.

4. To terminate the editing, press **Alt-E** and select *Exit*. The values will be stored in the HABITAT file. A later example will show how to prepare a report that displays the volunteer information.

CREATING A CUSTOM SCREEN FORM

dBASE normally uses the Edit or Browse screens for entering data values into records. The Edit screen displays fields vertically down the screen, while the Browse screen places fields horizontally across the screen. Field names are used for input prompts and can sometimes be cryptic. Fields that don't "fit" on the same screen will appear on the next screen, but you can't see them all at the same time. Fields display in the order of their appearance in the database structure. Only a single database file can be used at a time with the Edit and Browse screens.

A dBASE **Form** is a customized data entry screen that makes it easier for the user to enter or edit data. The screen may resemble a manual entry form used to gather data, and can sequence the fields in any order. You can place lines and single- or double-walled boxes in certain sections of the screen. Advanced users may wish to combine entries for two or more database files on the same form.

Creating the Form

The dBASE Forms facility allows you to quickly create customized data entry screens up to 80 characters wide by **painting the form** onto the screen. Changes are made easily and the final result is saved for future use. Creating the form involves these steps:

- Design the form on paper.
- Open the Forms panel in Create mode.
- Place fields on the Layout screen.
- Move fields on the screen as necessary.
- Add titles, input prompts, and boxes.
- Generate the form program (only done once).
- Use the form for entering or modifying records.

Design the Form

The first step is to design the form on paper, using graph paper or a grid to lay out the screen. The typical display has 25 rows and 80 columns available for the form, although some rows at the bottom may be used for the Status Line. Examine the paper forms used within the organization for design ideas. The screen form should resemble the paper form that was used for manual data collection. Fields should appear logically in the order they are normally collected, with suitable prompting lines. The field **template** provides a guide for the field entry—width of the field, location of decimal point, and pre-placement of helpful characters such as parentheses and hyphen in telephone numbers or part numbers. The template can also be designed to permit only certain kinds of data to be placed in a given field, or to require that the data value be within a range.

The screen form should not be too crowded, yet the space should be used efficiently when much data is to be gathered. Dividing the entry form into

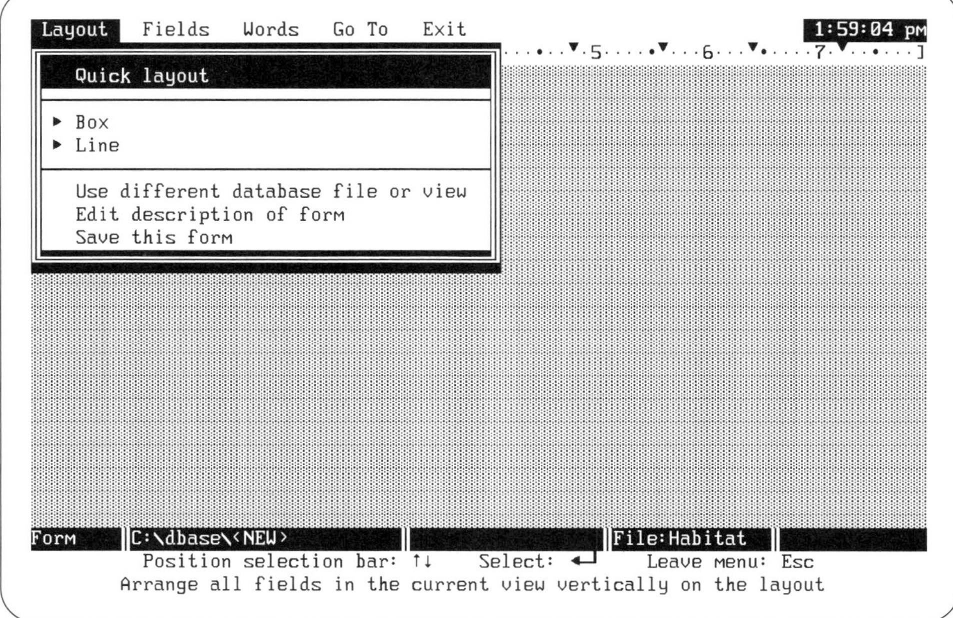

FIGURE 4-17

Form Screen Layout Bar

sections with a line or a box may help the user locate important sections of the form. Avoid using line 0 of the form—that line overwrites the Menu Bar in the Edit screen. Because the form designer may not be the regular user of the form, it is most helpful to design the form together with a regular user.

Example: *Create a Form with Quick Layout*

Before building a screen form, you should open a database file in the Control Center. We will use the **HABITAT** database for this example, and show how to access its memo field through a form.

1. To create a new form, move the cursor in the Control Center to the **<create>** box in the Forms panel and press **Enter**. You'll see the Form screen in Figure 4-17.
2. Press **Enter** to activate the *Quick Layout* selection, shown in Figure 4-18. dBASE will place the fields at the left side of the screen, going down, similar to the standard Edit screen. Field names are provided as prompts and the width of each field is taken from the structure. At this point you can move the fields around the screen as desired.

Moving the Form Elements

The next step is to move the form elements (a field, a text label, a box, or an entire section of the screen)around the screen to their desired location. The status bar shows the location of the cursor. You can type text at any point on the form, using the arrow keys to move the cursor around. **Ins** will toggle between Insert and Overtype modes, as noted in the Status Bar. Avoid typing on top of a database field—move it first, then insert text where that field used to be.

To move a section of the form, use the arrow keys to move the cursor to one of the corners of the section you wish to move. Next press **F6** to begin the

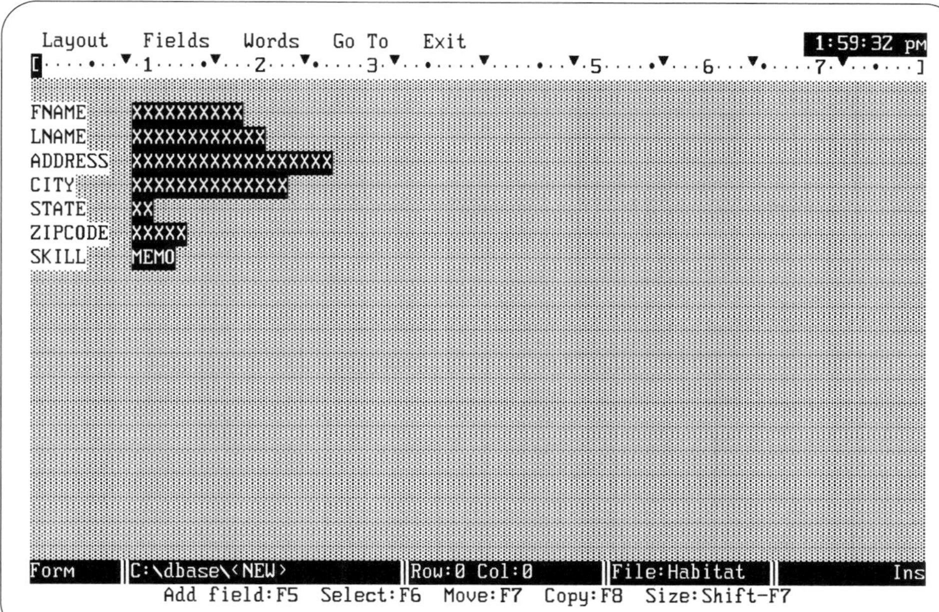

FIGURE 4-18

Quick Layout Placement of Fields on Form

selection of that element; dBASE will prompt you to *Complete selection with Enter*. Move the cursor with the arrow keys until the entire section is highlighted and press **Enter**. For database fields or boxes, moving the cursor to any point on the element, pressing **F6** and then the **Enter** key will select the field. For text labels, move to one end of the label first. Press **F6**, move to the other end of the label with the arrow keys, and then press **Enter**. The element as you have selected it will be highlighted. [Note: If you have not selected all of the element, press **Esc** to abandon the selection. Then repeat the process to select the entire element.] Then you can press **F7** to move that element to a new location, or **F8** to copy it to a new location.

As you use the arrow keys to move to the new location, the highlighted element will appear to travel (as a ghost image) with the cursor. When it is placed in the desired new location, press **Enter** again. If the element overlaps any existing text or fields, dBASE will ask if you wish to *Delete covered text and fields?* If you reply negatively, the move or copy will be abandoned; otherwise the covered portion will be deleted. If you move a field to a position that partially overlaps its old position, the *Delete* prompt will not affect the field you are moving.

The screen in Figure 4-19 shows the goal in our screen design, before any boxes or lines have been added. The participant's full name now appears on a single line, as do the city, state, and zipcode. The field prompts have been rewritten for greater clarification.

Example: *Moving the Fields on the Form and Adding Text*

In this example we will move the fields to their desired locations and add suitable text prompts for the user. We will have to accomplish the following field moves:

- Move LNAME to begin at row 4, column 48.
- Move FNAME to begin at row 4, column 35.

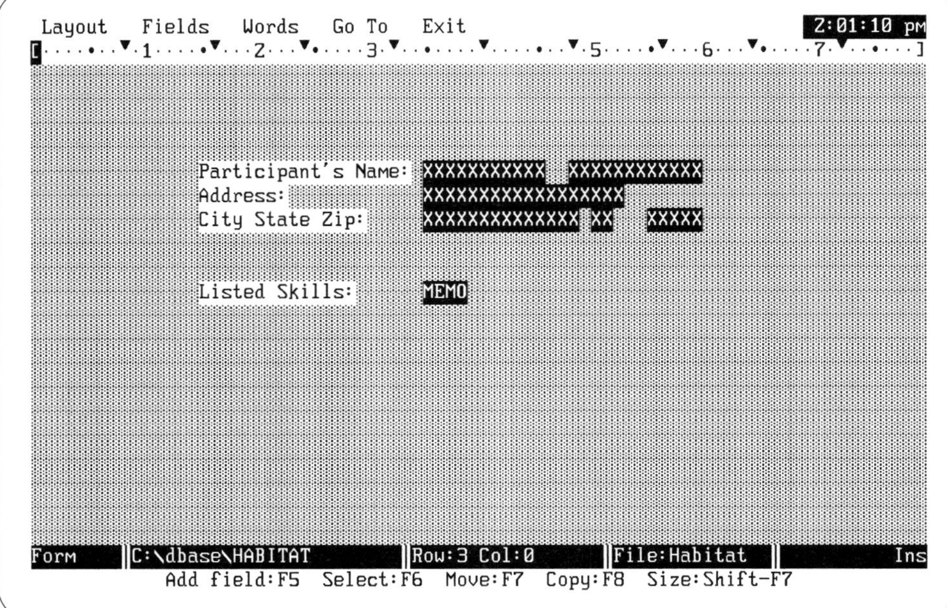
Layout Fields Words Go To Exit 2:01:10 pm
Participant's Name: XXXXXXXXXXX XXXXXXXXXXXX
Address: XXXXXXXXXXXXXXXXXX
City State Zip: XXXXXXXXXXXXXX XX XXXXX
Listed Skills: MEMO
Form C:\dbase\HABITAT Row:3 Col:0 File:Habitat Ins
Add field:F5 Select:F6 Move:F7 Copy:F8 Size:Shift-F7

FIGURE 4-19

Form Design for Habitat Example

- Move ADDRESS to begin at row 5, column 35.
- Move ZIPCODE to begin at row 6, column 55.
- Move STATE to begin at row 6, column 50.
- Move CITY to begin at row 6, column 35.
- Move SKILLS to row 9, column 35.

1. To move LNAME, first place the cursor anywhere within the LNAME field box (shown by the Xs), and press **F6** to select that element. Finish the selection by pressing **Enter**. Press **F7** to move the field. Then move the cursor to row 4, column 48 and press **Enter** to lock in the move to that location.

2. Do the same thing with the other fields according to the table above. Although the field name prompts still look like Figure 4-18, the fields will now look like Figure 4-19.

3. Next we want to rewrite the input prompts. Move the cursor to the first of the original field name prompts, and use successive presses of the **Del** key to delete the characters. [Note: You could also select the field input prompt with the **F6** key, highlight the entire fieldname, and press **Del** once to delete the highlighted field.] Repeat this with all of the existing fieldnames at the left side of the screen.

4. Then enter the following new prompt lines at the indicated locations. Check the results of your screen with Figure 4-19.

Participant's Name:	at row 4, column 15
Address:	at row 5, column 15
City State Zip:	at row 6, column 15
Listed Skills:	at row 9, column 15

5. Next let's add a box around the top portion of the input form. Press **Alt-L** to activate the **Layout** menu bar.

6. Move the cursor to the *Box* line and press **Enter**. Next select *Single line* box. Move the cursor to the desired location for the upper left corner of the box (row 3, column 13 if your form is identical to the example) and press **Enter** to lock it in. Then use the arrow keys to stretch the box to the lower right corner, at row 7, column 61. Press **Enter** to complete the box at that location. Be careful to not cover a part of the form with the box.

7. Add the title below beginning at row 1, column 10:

```
HABITAT FOR HUMANITY - PARTICIPANT'S ENTRY SCREEN FORM
```

8. As with other dBASE generator displays, press **Ctrl-End** (or Alt-E) to save your form design. dBASE will generate a program with the proper statements to reproduce the form whenever you need to edit or display the database. When dBASE prompts for a name for your form, just enter **HABITAT** and press **Enter**. A file called HABITAT.FMT will be created.

Using the Screen Form

When you open a database file for which there is a **screen form** already created in the file catalog, dBASE will not automatically use that form.

You must select the desired entry form *before* you Edit, Append, or Insert records into that database file. (If you haven't opened the database file yet, selecting an entry form does so automatically.) Then, when you select *Display Data* to go to the Edit screen, instead of the usual Edit display, dBASE will use the customized data entry form.

Example: *Using the Entry Form*

1. First move the cursor to the Forms panel and select the **HABITAT** form.

2. Select *Display Data.*

3. Press **F10** to activate the MENU Bar, and select *Add new record* from the **Records** menu bar.

4. Add the following record:

   Michael Witte 1844 W. 46th St. Cayuga, IN 46831

   Electrician, can work with heating/cooling systems.

5. Your screen should look like Figure 4-20. To add data in the memo field, move the cursor to that field, press the **F9** key, and enter the data. To save the memo field data, press **Ctrl-End.**

6. To save the entire record, press **Ctrl-End** again.

Changing the Screen Form

You can make changes to the screen form at any time. From the Control Center, select the desired form from the Forms panel. At the next prompt box, select *Modify layout* instead of *Display data.* dBASE will display the Form screen with the most recent version of the desired form. You can move fields around, add or change text fields, change the size of a field, or add new fields. You may also wish to modify the template and picture for fields. See Chapter 5 for a discussion of dBASE field templates.

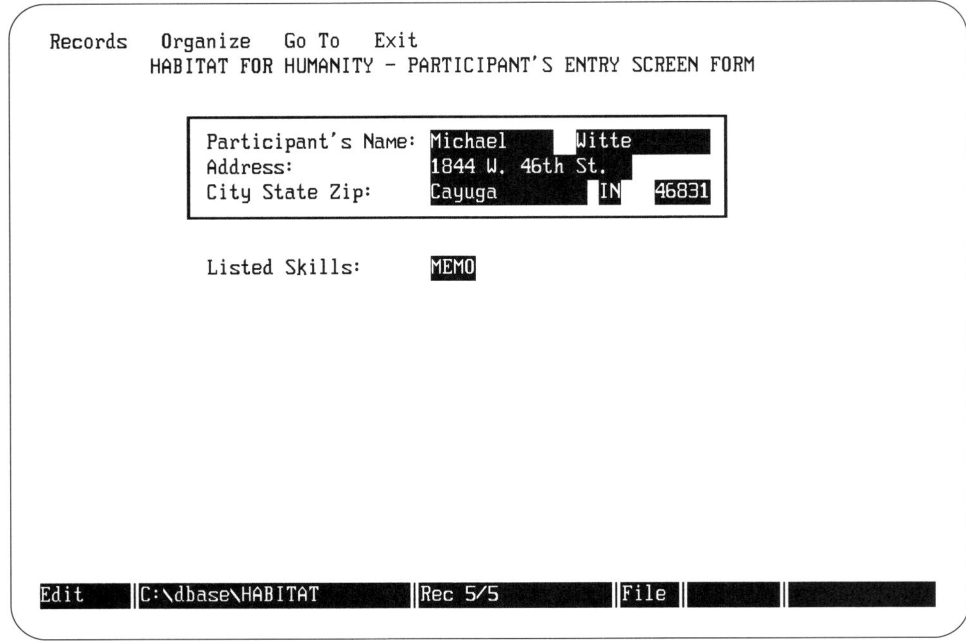

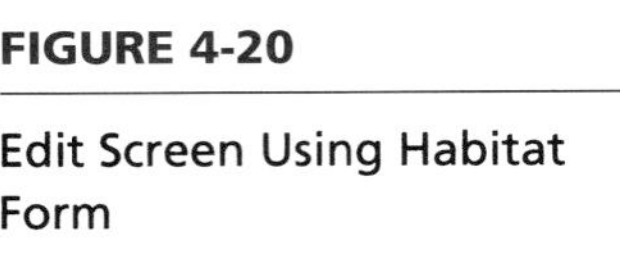

FIGURE 4-20

Edit Screen Using Habitat Form

PREPARING dBASE QUERIES

The capability to display records through the Edit and Browse menus is limited to simple index searches or single-field lookups. The dBASE **Query-by-Example (QBE)** function provides a means of building complex criterion conditions and displaying only desired fields. The QBE functions are accessed through the **Queries panel** in the Control Center.

Creating the Query

Creating a **query** from the Control Center involves three steps:

- First you must select the database file or files containing the desired data. dBASE IV queries support multiple database files.
- Next you build the **condition box** containing the filter conditions (criteria) for selecting data records.
- The third step is the creation of the **view skeleton**, or the set of fields you would like to display for the selected records.
- An optional fourth step involves creating calculated fields of dBASE expressions.

Each step is explained below in a general example. A specific keystroke example appears at the end of the Query section.

Selecting the Database File

From the Control Center, select the compact disk database file (**CD**) and press **Enter**. Choose *Use file* from the next prompt box. If you have previously created queries for use with this file, they will appear above the line in the Queries panel. To build a new query, move the cursor to the **<create>** line in the Queries panel and press **Enter**. You'll see the screen in Figure 4-21.

The name of the database file, CD.DBF, is displayed in the **file skeleton area** just below the menu bar, with the names of all its fields. You can access those fields by successively pressing the **Tab** key and moving to the right; **Shift-Tab** will move the cursor to the left a field at a time. The **End** key will move

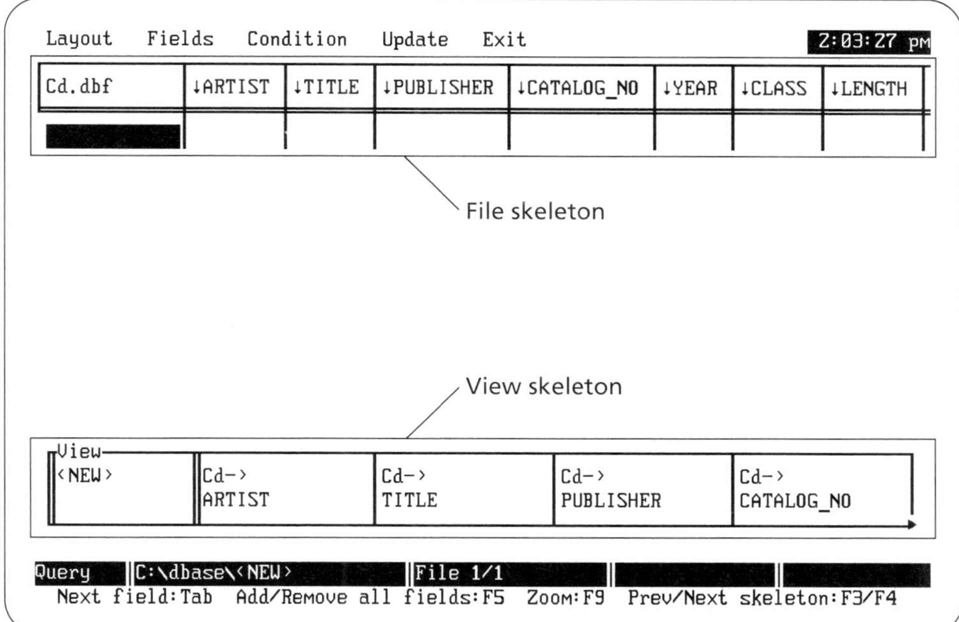

FIGURE 4-21

Query Work Surface for CD Example

directly to the right-most field, while the **Home** key moves to the left-most field. The down arrow before each field name means that field appears in the view skeleton below.

The bottom of the Query screen shows the default **view skeleton** in which all of the CD fields are listed. The view skeleton indicates which fields are to be displayed and their order. It may include calculated fields and fields from other database files. The **Cd->** prefix shown above the field names is the **alias** for the CD database file and indicates the database to which a particular field belongs. All of the fields in this example belong to the CD database file. The last field shown, CATALOG_NO, ends with a right arrow to indicate there are more fields in the record that are not currently displayed on the screen.

Creating the Filter Conditions

The **filter conditions** specify which records are to be displayed. Similar to the criterion range in Lotus worksheets, these conditions are entered beneath the field name in the file skeleton at the top of the Query screen. For example, we may wish to view all of the CBS disks in our database. We can write **"CBS Master"** on the first line beneath the PUBLISHER field name. The quotations are necessary because PUBLISHER is a character field. To view the records that match this condition, press **F2**. The next screen will be Edit or Browse, depending upon which was last used. Press **F2** again to switch to the Browse screen if you do not already have that on your display. There are three records that match this filter condition—three disks in the library are from CBS Masterworks.

Building an "AND" Compound Filter Condition

As in Lotus, you can enter several filter conditions at the same time. Conditions entered on the *same line* (**AND**) must all be true for the record to qualify for retrieval. Press **Shift-F2** to return to the Query screen. Move the cursor to the YEAR field on the same line as the first condition and enter **1983** without

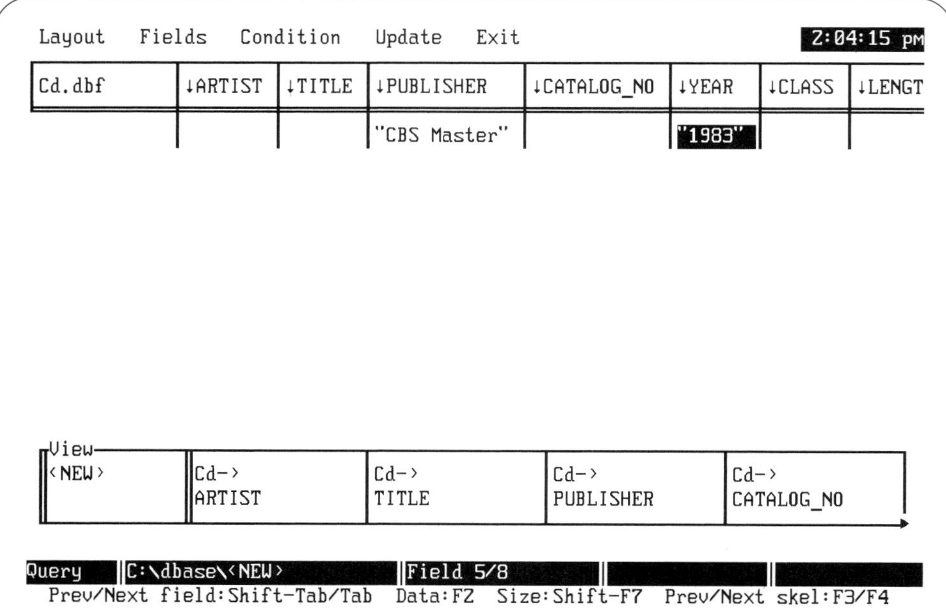

FIGURE 4-22

Filter Condition for "AND" Criteria

quotes. dBASE will beep and prompt you that that is an incorrect expression. YEAR is another character field so you must place quotes around the condition: **"1983"**. The filter condition is shown in Figure 4-22. Press **F2** to display the data records meeting the two conditions. There will be only a single record in this set—the Wynton Marsalis disk meets *both* conditions, a 1983 release date AND from CBS Masterworks.

Building an "OR" Compound Filter Condition

Conditions entered on *separate lines* (**OR**) imply that if any one of the conditions is true a true result will qualify that record for retrieval. Next we'll change the YEAR condition to be on a different line. Press **Shift-F2** to return to the Query screen. Move the cursor to the YEAR field where you entered "1983" and press **Ctrl-Y**, the command to erase the field condition. Then move the cursor to one line *below* the PUBLISHER condition, and re-enter the **"1983"** condition in the YEAR column. The file skeleton should look like Figure 4-23.

Viewing the Data

Now press **F2** to view the data records matching this filter. You should find that four records are displayed—the three that are from CBS Masterworks and an additional one with a 1983 date. Figure 4-24 shows the Browse screen matching this query. You can press **Shift-F2** to return to the Query design screen.

Saving the Query

As is customary with dBASE, pressing **Ctrl-End** while in the Query screen will save the query as a file, placing its name in the Queries panel. Press **Ctrl-End** now, and call the query **CD1**. dBASE will add the .QBE extension to the file when it saves it. You can use this query whenever desired by selecting it from the Queries file panel in the Control Center.

Building a Custom View Skeleton

Suppose you didn't want to see all of the CD fields for the records matching the filter condition. We can change the view skeleton within the query. From the Control Center, move to the Queries panel and select the **CD1** query. It

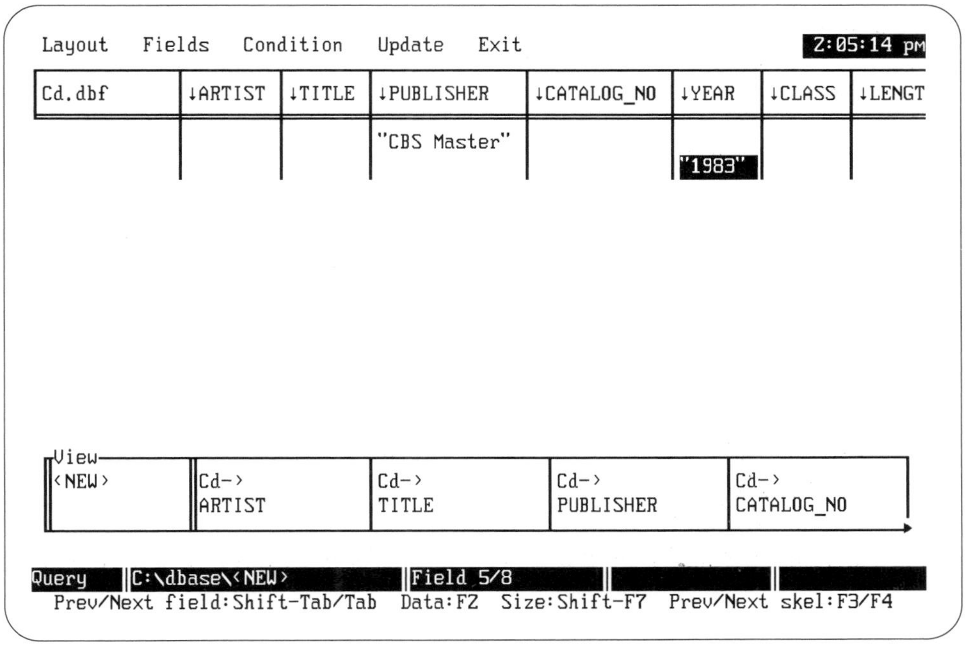

```
Layout   Fields   Condition   Update   Exit                                   2:05:14 pm

| Cd.dbf | ↓ARTIST | ↓TITLE | ↓PUBLISHER    | ↓CATALOG_NO | ↓YEAR  | ↓CLASS | ↓LENGT
|        |         |        | "CBS Master"  |             |        |        |
|        |         |        |               |             | "1983" |        |

View
<NEW>  | Cd->    | Cd->   | Cd->      | Cd->
       | ARTIST  | TITLE  | PUBLISHER | CATALOG_NO

Query  |C:\dbase\<NEW>        |Field 5/8     |      |
 Prev/Next field:Shift-Tab/Tab  Data:F2  Size:Shift-F7  Prev/Next skel:F3/F4
```

FIGURE 4-23

Filter Condition for "OR" Criteria

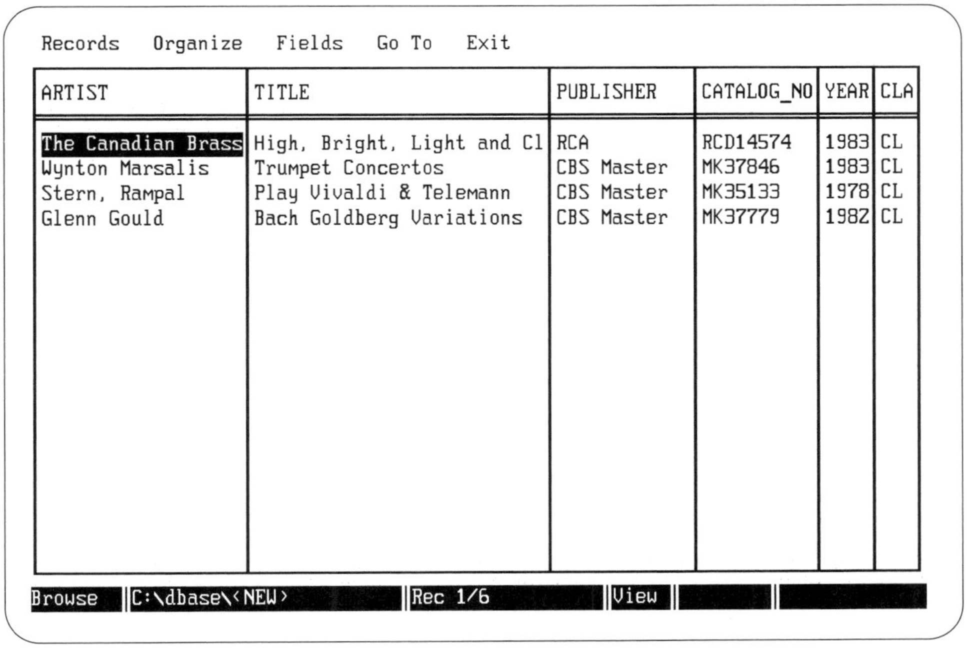

Records   Organize   Fields   Go To   Exit

ARTIST	TITLE	PUBLISHER	CATALOG_NO	YEAR	CLA
The Canadian Brass	High, Bright, Light and Cl	RCA	RCD14574	1983	CL
Wynton Marsalis	Trumpet Concertos	CBS Master	MK37846	1983	CL
Stern, Rampal	Play Vivaldi & Telemann	CBS Master	MK35133	1978	CL
Glenn Gould	Bach Goldberg Variations	CBS Master	MK37779	1982	CL

Browse |C:\dbase\<NEW> |Rec 1/6 |View |

FIGURE 4-24

Data Records that Match "OR" Filter Condition

automatically opens the associated database file. Choose *Modify query* from the next prompt box. To move the cursor from the file skeleton to the view skeleton, press **F4.** (Pressing **F3** will move the cursor back to the file skeleton.) See Figure 4-25. Let's make the following changes to the view:

- Remove the TITLE field.
- Remove the CLASS field.
- Move the DIGITAL field to appear after YEAR.

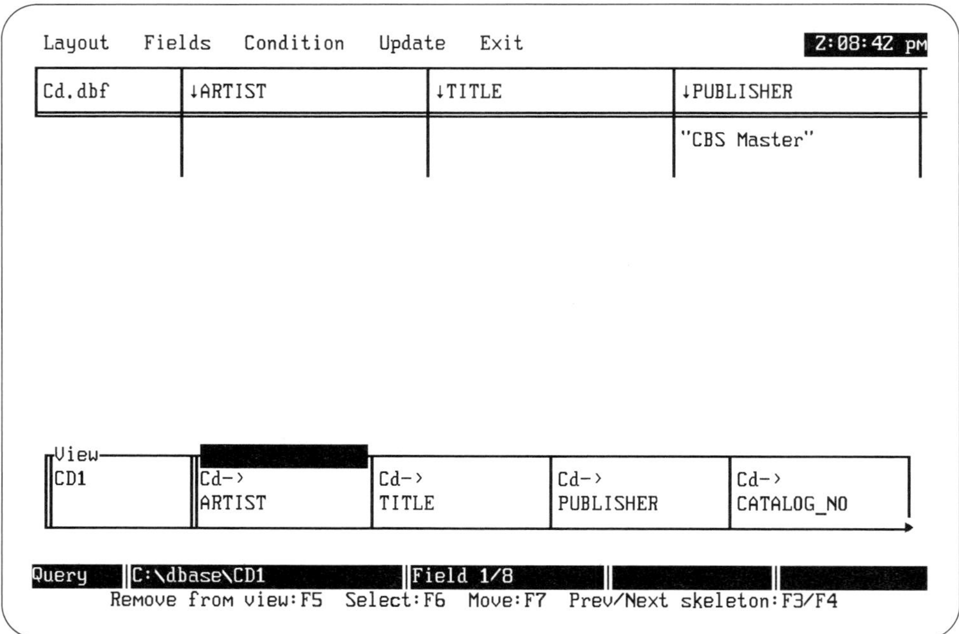

FIGURE 4-25

View Skeleton for the CD1 Query

The function key commands for this screen are shown at the bottom in the Help area.

- **F5** will remove (from the view) the field the cursor is pointing to.
- **F6** allows you to select a field.
- **F7** allows you to move that field to another location.

Move the cursor to the TITLE field using the **Tab** key, then press **F5** to delete that field from our view. Do the same thing to the CLASS field. Be sure to delete the proper fields! Then move the cursor to the DIGITAL field and press the **F6** key to select it. Press **Enter** to lock the selection. Press **F7** to move the field. Then use the **Shift-Tab** (dBASE calls this BACKTAB) key to move the cursor highlighting the DIGITAL field between the YEAR and LENGTH fields. Press **Enter** to lock it in its new place. Next press **F2** to display the records matching the filter condition in the new view. [Hint: You can print the records shown from this query by pressing the **Shift-F9** command and preparing a Quick Report.] The Browse screen for this query is shown in Figure 4-26.

Notice that all of the fields now display on one Browse screen, and the order matches our changes. Press **Shift-F2** to return to the Query screen. To save the new query, press **Ctrl-End**. dBASE will replace the previous CD1 query with this one. If you wish to save it under a new name, press **F10** to activate the Menu Bar, then select *Save this query* from the **Layout** bar. When prompted for a name, enter **CD2** and dBASE will maintain both queries in the File panel. You may need to erase the existing name shown in the prompt box.

Writing the View as a Database File

Ordinarily you will save the query as described above. Whenever the query is activated, the matching records are shown. By using the **Layout** bar you can optionally tell dBASE to save the records selected by the query in a separate database file. The records are written according to the view skeleton you prepared in the query. The original database file is not changed. This option allows

Records Organize Fields Go To Exit

ARTIST	PUBLISHER	CATALOG_NO	YEAR	DIGITAL	LENGTH
The Canadian Brass	RCA	RCD14574	1983	Y	51
Wynton Marsalis	CBS Master	MK37846	1983	T	40
Stern, Rampal	CBS Master	MK35133	1978	F	44
Glenn Gould	CBS Master	MK37779	1982	T	51

Browse ‖C:\dbase\CD1 ‖Rec 1/6 ‖View ‖

FIGURE 4-26

Records that Match Filter Condition (Reduced View Skeleton)

you to work with just the desired subset of records and fields. Remember that if the original database file changes after the records selected with the view are saved as a database file, the database created with the view file will *not* reflect those changes. You would have to view the altered original database file with the same Query file and save the records again to capture those changes. The Query file always reflects the current status of the database files used in the query.

Example: *Creating a Query*

We wish to display all the records from the CD database file that are digital and whose length is at least 50 minutes. We will display the following fields: ARTIST, LENGTH, and DIGITAL.

1. Go to the Control Center and select the **CD** database in the Data panel. Then move to the Queries panel and select **<create>** to build a new QBE file.
2. At the Query screen, move the cursor to the LENGTH field with the **Tab** key and type the condition **>=50** and press **Enter**.
3. Using the **Tab** key, move the cursor to the DIGITAL field. Then enter **.T.** in the condition box on the same file skeleton line, indicating the true value for this field. What would dBASE do if you entered the **.T.** value on the line *beneath* the **>=50** line? (Assumes either condition will qualify the record for inclusion.) The file skeleton will look like the example in Figure 4-27.
4. Next press **F4** to move to the view skeleton area. Use the **Tab** key to move the cursor to the following fields, pressing **F5** to remove them from the view: TITLE, PUBLISHER, CATALOG_NO, YEAR, and CLASS. Double check before deleting each field. [Note: You can *Add field to view* from the **Fields** menu bar if you delete the wrong field.] After removing the fields, the view skeleton should appear as Figure 4-28.

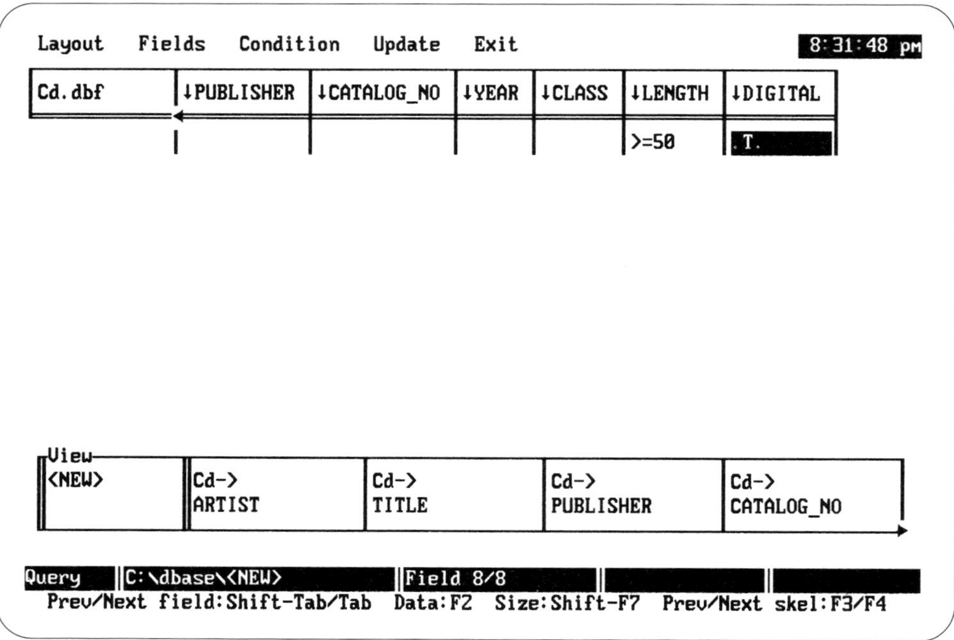

FIGURE 4-27

"AND" Filter Condition File Skeleton

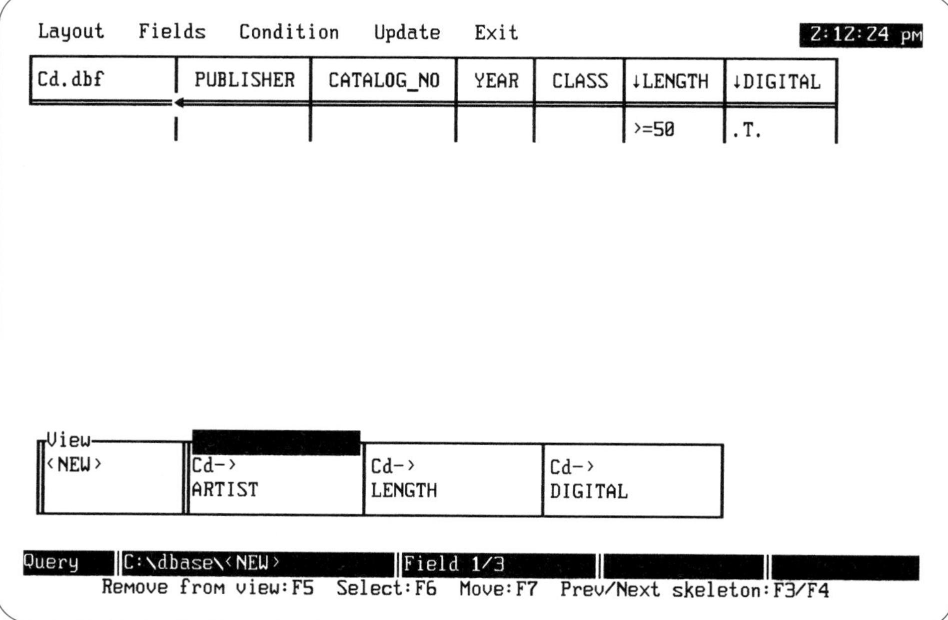

FIGURE 4-28

View Skeleton for Example

5. Next we can press **F2** to view the data records matching our query. Only three records qualify. The Browse screen showing the records that qualify is shown in Figure 4-29.
6. Before returning to the Query screen, let's get a Quick Report of the qualifying records. Press **Shift-F9** to activate the printing process. When prompted, press **Enter** to *Begin printing*.
7. The Quick Report is shown in Figure 4-30 with three qualifying records. dBASE has also totalled the LENGTH field, shown as 174 in the report.

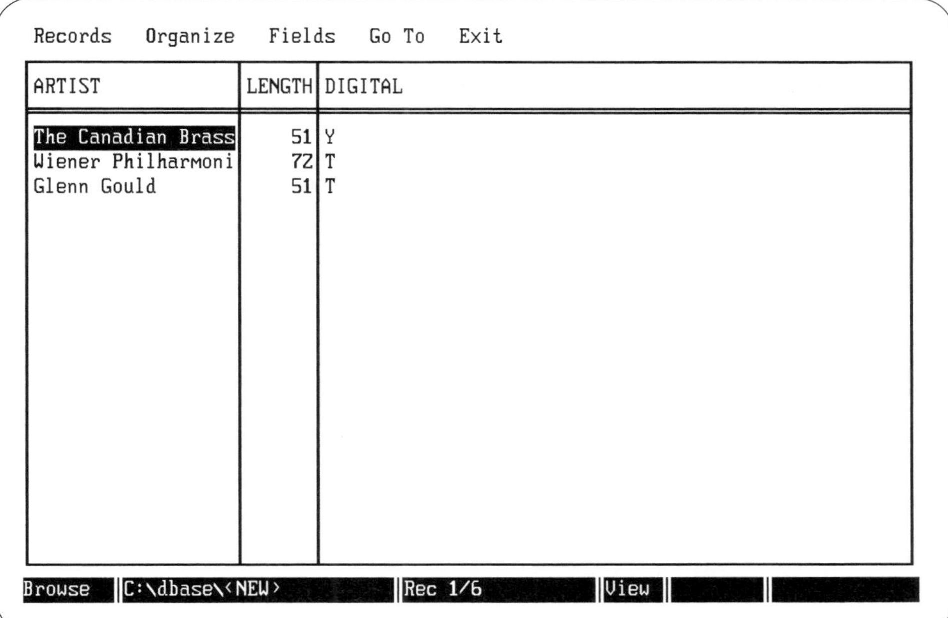

FIGURE 4-29

Browse Screen for Example

```
Page No.    1
10/25/89

ARTIST                  LENGTH  DIGITAL

The Canadian Brass          51  Y
Wiener Philharmoni          72  Y
Glenn Gould                 51  Y
                           174
```

FIGURE 4-30

Quick Report Based on Query Example

8. Finally, we'll save the query. Press **Shift-F2** to return to the Query screen. Then press **Ctrl-End** to save the Query. When prompted, enter the name **LONGDIG** as the query name. This name may remind you that we looked for long disks that were recorded digitally.

Chapter 7 contains an extended example on preparing a query that links two database files together by matching common field values.

The Update Query

dBASE IV also offers the query capability of updating records that match the filter conditions. The four update operations include Replace, Mark, Unmark, and Append.

- The **Replace** operation would allow you to replace the contents of a database field with an expression. The **with** phrase, followed by an expression, appears under the field you wish to change.
- The **Mark** operation would mark for deletion those records that match the filter conditions expressed in the query.

- **Unmark** would remove the deletion mark from selected records.
- The **Append** operation lets you append to another database the records that match the selection criteria. This requires that you have at least two files in the file skeleton.

To prepare an Update query choose the *<create>* line in the Queries panel. Use the **Layout** menu bar and select the *Add file to query* line, specifying the file name when prompted. When the file skeleton appears, move the cursor to the box beneath the file name and enter the name of the operation (Replace, Mark, Unmark, Append). dBASE will remove the View skeleton. Then you should specify the filter conditions for including the record. Finally, activate the **Update** menu bar and select the *Perform the update* line. After dBASE does the update operation you may view the results by pressing **F2**.

The Replace update would permit you to replace the contents of a database field with another field or an expression. For instance, you may want to replace the contents of a character field with the uppercase version of that field. Suppose you inadvertently entered state abbreviations in lowercase. Place **Replace** beneath the filename box. Beneath the State field box in the file skeleton use the expression **with UPPER(State)**. When the update is performed, dBASE will convert the State abbreviation to all capital letters.

Example: Preparing an Update Query to Delete Records

In this example you will mark for deletion records that match specified condition, then unmark them. We will use the CD database for this example.

1. Begin dBASE IV and select **<create>** in the Queries file panel.
2. At the Query screen, press **Alt-L** to activate the **Layout** menu bar. Select the *Add file to query* line and choose the **CD** database file from the pick list shown on the screen.
3. Move the cursor to the block beneath Cd.dbf in the file skeleton, type the word **Mark** and press **Enter**.
4. Next use the Tab key to move the cursor to the Digital field. Type **.T.** in the box beneath the field to indicate that the digital disks are to be marked for deletion. Your screen should look like Figure 4-31.
5. Press **Alt-U** to activate the **Update** menu bar and select the *Perform the update* line. After a few seconds dBASE will ask permission to mark four records for deletion. Reply **Y** and press any key to return to the Query screen.
6. Press **F2** to go to the Browse or Edit screens. Use the **PgUp** and **PgDn** keys to examine each of the records in the CD.DBF file. You will see that four of them are marked for deletion. Figure 4-32 shows the Digital fields for the six records.
7. Now we will remove the deletion marks. Press **Shift-F2** to return to the Query design screen. Use the **Tab** key to move the cursor to the Cd.dbf block and replace **Mark** with **Unmark**. While leaving the .T. in the Digital field, press **Alt-U** to activate the **Update** bar and select *Perform the update.* dBASE will remove the deletion mark from the four digital disks.
8. Finally, save the query under the name **CDUPDATE** with the **Alt-E** command. It will be saved with the .UPD file extension to indicate it is an update query.

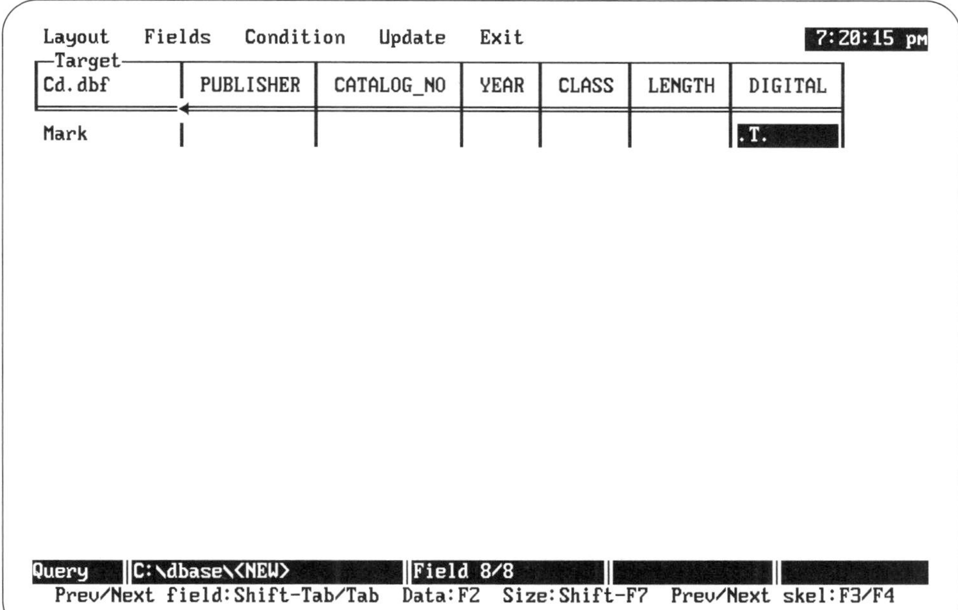

FIGURE 4-31

Query Screen for Update Example

Records Organize Fields Go To Exit

TITLE	PUBLISHER	CATALOG_NO	YEAR	CLASS	LENGTH	DIGITAL
High, Bright, Light and Cl	RCA	RCD14574	1983	CL	51	Y
Beethoven: Symphony No. 9	Deutsche Gr.	419598-2	1987	CL	72	Y
Trumpet Concertos	CBS Master	MK37846	1983	CL	40	Y
Play Vivaldi & Telemann	CBS Master	MK35133	1978	CL	44	N
Bach Goldberg Variations	CBS Master	MK37779	1982	CL	51	Y
Adagio Albioni,Pachelbel,B	Deutsche Gr.	4132248-2	1972	CL	62	N

Browse C:\dbase\CD Rec 1/6 File Del

FIGURE 4-32

Browse Screen Showing Deleted Records for Update Query Example

Ordering Records in a Query

The records in a query will ordinarily appear in the same order as they do in the file used for the query. There are two ways to change the order. You may use an index tag or may direct dBASE to sort the records on one or more fields.

Using an Index Tag in a Query

Because indexes already exist and are much faster than sorting, this is the preferred method for ordering records in a query. To activate an index tag, move the cursor in the File Skeleton to the desired field and press **Alt-F** to activate the **Fields** menu bar. Select the *Include indexes* line and press **Enter** to change the value from *No* to *Yes.* dBASE will place a pound sign (#) in front of the field name in the File Skeleton to signify that field's index tag is activated.

If the file has complex index tags based on field expressions, these will be placed at the end of the File Skeleton and are shown with their tag name instead of a field name. Select these indexes in the same manner as a simple index with the **Alt-F** command.

Sorting the Records

dBASE is able to sort the records in a query in ascending or descending order. To sort on a particular field in the File Skeleton, move the cursor to that field and enter one of the following sort operators:

Asc Ascending ASCII sort where all capital letters will come before lowercase letters.

Dsc Descending ASCII sort from highest values to lowest values. This sort would begin at the end of the alphabet for character fields.

AscDict Ascending dictionary sort where upper and lowercase letters are treated as the same character.

DscDict Descending dictionary sort from highest values to lowest values.

These operators may be entered as a field expression directly beneath the field name in the File Skeleton or you may use the **Alt-F Fields** menu bar and select the *Sort on the field* line, picking the desired sort type from the menu. If you wish to sort on more than one field, add a digit to the end of the sort operator: 1 is the primary key, 2 is the first secondary key, and so on.

As with other sort operations, dBASE will create another database file containing the sorted records so be sure to have enough space available on the default disk drive to hold the sort file. You cannot use a sort operator for a calculated field or a condition box.

CHAPTER REVIEW

Changing the Database Structure

The database structure contains the database file name, the field names, type, and width. The structure can be easily modified to allow insertion of new fields, changing the name or width of fields, or deleting fields. Changing field types is not recommended because data values may be lost. The structure can be copied to another database file without copying data values.

Changing the Record Order—Sorting

dBASE IV database files may be reordered by sorting and indexing. Sorting produces a new database file, requiring the same storage space as the original file. Sorts may be done on any field in the database, in ascending or descending order, and in ASCII or in dictionary order. The latter treats upper and lowercase characters as the same, whereas ASCII order places all the capital letters before all of the lowercase letters.

Indexing the Records

Indexing is much more efficient than sorting. Not only is less space required, but multiple indexes can be activated to maintain the database file in different orders. Two kinds of indexes exist: single-expression index files with the .NDX extension were used in all previous versions of dBASE. dBASE IV introduced the multiple-index file with the .MDX extension. It is recommended that only the latter index type be used with dBASE IV.

Index Tags

You can describe up to 47 different index expressions, called index tags, with a multiple-index file. It is activated along with the database file, thus reducing the possibility that the index file does not match the database file.

Searching for Specific Values

Index searches can very rapidly position the record pointer to the desired record, provided there is a match between the search target and the index. Non-index searches proceed much slower than those with indexes.

Working with Memo Fields

Memo fields are used to store large, unstructured character data. Up to 512KB characters may be placed in a single memo field. Memo values do not appear in the normal Edit or Browse screens: the memo field appears as a shaded box with the word "memo" in it. To enter, view or modify the data in a memo field, move the cursor to the shaded memo box and press the F9 Zoom key. When finished, exit the memo screen by pressing Ctrl-End.

Creating a Custom Screen Form

dBASE forms are custom data entry screens that replace the default screens used for editing and appending data. These forms permit the user to specify the order for data fields, the field input prompt message, and the location on the screen for each field. You can draw boxes around elements on the screen, and draw horizontal or vertical lines on the form. Like the report and label screens, dBASE allows the user to paint the fields onto the screen and to move fields until a satisfactory design is achieved.

Preparing dBASE Queries

Query-by-example (QBE) applications can be constructed that will retrieve desired data according to certain criteria. The QBE query is similar to the Lotus /Data Query application in that the user builds a picture, or example, of the kind of data that matches the criteria or filter condition. You can specify which fields are to be retrieved, and can save the resulting data as a new database file. Update queries can replace fields, mark records for deletion, unmark deleted records, and append records to a database file that match specified conditions.

KEY TERMS

AND filter condition
ascending sort
ASCII sort
character field
condition box
descending sort
dictionary sort
file skeleton area
filter condition
form
index
index search
index tag
master tag
.MDX multiple-index file
memo fields
natural order
.NDX index file
OR filter condition
paint the form
primary key field
Queries panel
Query
Query-by-Example (QBE)
Quick Layout
screen form
secondary key field
sort
sort operators
tag
template
update query
view skeleton

DISCUSSION QUESTIONS

1. Explain the similarities and differences between sorting a database file and indexing that file. Which is generally preferred, and why?
2. Explain the procedure for creating an index tag in the CD database for the ARTIST field. List each step and explain its purpose.
3. Contrast ASCII and dictionary sorts. Which would be preferred for sorting student records by the student's name?
4. Suppose you had a very large file containing all the Business majors at your college. List at least three ways of searching for the occurrence of a student named **LEWIS, Meriwether**. Make any assumptions necessary for your methods.
5. Explain how an index tag can be created at the same time as the file structure is built. Be explicit.
6. Give at least four ways to move the record pointer in a database file to a desired record.
7. Explain the situation in which a memo field is preferred to a character field. Are there any limitations in using memo fields? Explain carefully.
8. Discuss the method that dBASE uses to delete records from a database file. Although the process seems complicated, are there any advantages for doing it this way? Explain.
9. List the steps in creating a custom data entry screen form. How do you activate the form for entering or modifying data?
10. Suppose the form includes a memo field. How do you access that field when using a form to enter data?
11. Explain what the term "QBE" means in dBASE IV. Give an example.
12. Define the following sections of a Query screen.
    a. view skeleton area
    b. condition box
    c. file skeleton area.
13. Discuss the "AND" and "OR" filter conditions that can be built in the Query screen. Explain the meaning of placing conditions on the same or separate lines.
14. Explain how you can create another database file containing the records that match the view skeleton. You may need to explore some of the pull-down menus in the Query screen to answer this question.
15. Discuss the uses of the Update Query. Give examples of how the Replace and Mark operations would be used.
16. How can records be ordered in a query?

EXERCISES

1. Create the EMPLOYEE database with the database structure shown in Figure 4-33 and print a copy of the structure.

   Modify its structure as shown below.

   a. Change the length of the DEPT field to 12 characters.
   b. Add another character field of 10 characters for TITLE.

Field Name	Type	Width
NAME	Char	18
DEPT	Char	10
HIRE_DATE	Date	8
SALARY	Numeric	8 (2 decimal places)
COMMENTS	Memo	

FIGURE 4-33

Database Structure for Exercise 1

c. Add a new field called EMP_NAME of 18 characters.

d. Save the new structure, and print the structure.

e. Modify the new structure, and remove the old NAME field altogether. Can we, in step (c), just rename the old NAME field as EMP_NAME?

2. Open the SCHED database from your data disk, and look at the natural order. Courses are listed by PREFIX, NUMBER, and SECTION.

   a. Sort the database by INSTRUCTOR in ascending order as the primary key, using a dictionary sort; the secondary keys will be PREFIX, NUMBER, and SECTION, all in ascending order. The new database file will be called SCHEDINS.

   b. Prepare a Quick Report of the SCHEDINS database in its natural order.

   c. Why would the new order be helpful? Explain.

3. Open the SCHED database. Using the Organize menu bar in the Modify Structure screen, create several index expressions as described below.

   a. Index on the INSTRUCTOR field; call the tag **INSTR.**

   b. Order the records by the INSTR index tag.

   c. Obtain a Quick Report showing the records in order by Instructor.

   d. Next create an index for the ROOM field; call this tag **ROOM.** Order the records by this index tag and obtain a Quick Report showing the records ordered by the ROOM tag.

4. Open the SCHED file and create a single query for the following conditions. Name the query **SCHED1** after creating the filter and view skeletons. All three conditions must be met.

   a. Limit the view to those classes whose departmental PREFIX is MIS, and

   b. Only courses being taught by a doctorally-qualified person are to be listed, and

   c. Only classes taught on MWF are to be included.

   d. The following fields are to appear in the view: PREFIX, NUMBER, INSTRUCTOR, TITLE, DAY, TIME, DOCTORATE.

   e. Print a Quick Report showing the records that qualify for this query.

5. Use the STOCKS database file and create queries that meet each of the following conditions. Go to the Browse screen to verify that your query is correct. At the Browse screen press **Shift-PrtSc** to print a screen copy of the resulting records or use the Quick Report command to obtain a printed copy.

a. Display all fields for records that are from the NYSE.

b. Display all fields for stocks that have more than 300 shares and that are from the NASDAQ exchange.

c. Create a calculated field by activating the *Create calculated field* line of the **Fields** bar. The calculated field will contain **RECENT*NO_SHARES** and should be called EQUITY. Display all fields for stocks whose EQUITY exceeds $10,000 by entering the condition **>10000** below the calculated field box.

d. Display the records from the NYSE that have an equity of at least $7,500. Use the *Add field to view* line of the **Fields** bar to move the EQUITY field to the view skeleton. Display only these fields: STOCK_NAME, EXCHANGE, RECENT, and EQUITY.

e. While in the Query screen for part (d), save the View as a database file called **NYSE7500** using the *Write view as database file* line of the **Layout** bar. Print the structure of this new database file.

6. Open the empty STUDENTS database file from the data disk. Its structure includes fields for NAME, STUDENT_ID, MAJOR, HRS_EARNED, and GRAD_DATE, and a memo field called COMMENTS. Next build a custom data entry form with the following specifications. Row and column numbers refer to the status bar values. Remember that dBASE starts numbering rows and columns at 0, not 1.

   a. Use the Quick Layout method to place fields on the screen, then move them to the desired place.

   b. Place fields in the following locations.

      NAME field belongs at row 3, column 29

      STUDENT_ID field belongs at row 5, column 29

      MAJOR field belongs at row 5, column 50

      HRS_EARNED field belongs at row 7, column 29

      GRAD_DATE field belongs at row 7, column 50

      COMMENTS field belongs at row 11, column 29.

   c. Add the titles in Figure 4-34 so that there is one blank column before the field that they describe.

   d. Move the cursor to the STUDENT_ID field. Use the *Modify field* line of the **Fields** bar to add two hyphens to the template of the STUDENT_ID field. The template should look like **XXX-XX-XXXX**.

   e. Draw a single-line box around the top portion of the data entry form, beginning at row 2, column 8 and extending to row 8, column 61.

FIGURE 4-34

Sample Titles for Exercise 6

```
STUDENT NAME:
STUDENT ID NUMBER:
MAJOR:
HOURS EARNED:
EXP GRAD DATE:
COMMENTS:
```

```
WILLIAMSON, JEAN  234-50-9834  ACCOUNTING  78  05/01/92
     Transferred to this school from Kaskia College on 1/1/89

HAWTHORNE, STEVE  314-59-9000  MANAGEMENT 104  05/01/90
     Did coop position with Equity Oil Company in 1989

BYNUM, JACOB      632-44-9135  MIS        124 05/01/89
     Is working for IBM in North Carolina as systems engineer
```

FIGURE 4-35

Sample Data for Exercise 7

f. If possible, obtain a printed copy of your form with the **Shift-PrtSc** screen print command.

g. Save the form under the name **STUDENTS**.

7. Use the STUDENTS data entry form created in the previous problem to append data to the STUDENTS database file. Use your name and student data as the first record in the database file, then enter the records in Figure 4-35.

   Print a Quick Report showing the values of the records.

CHAPTER 4 PROJECT
MULTIPLE LISTING SERVICE

You are to prepare a database for homes that are listed for sale by members of the Multiple Listing Service (MLS). The database should include such fields as home listing number, location code, price, style, square feet, number of bedrooms, number of bathrooms, total number of rooms, fireplace (Y/N), air conditioning (Y/N), listing agent's name, date went on market, and a memo field for comments that don't fit into any of the above categories. Add additional fields that seem appropriate.

Data may be obtained from the local newspaper real estate section and from real estate booklets often prepared by the local realtors. Obtain data for at least 20 homes and enter that into your database. Prepare the following items for your database:

- Complete report showing all data in a useful format.
- Sorted listing in descending order by price.
- Group report showing all homes with the same number of bedrooms together; e.g., 5 bedrooms, 4 bedrooms, 3 bedrooms. Use an index tag for this purpose.
- Report for homes less than $100,000.

Next prepare queries for each of the following conditions:

- Homes with 3 or more bedrooms
- Homes with a fireplace and under $150,000
- Homes with 4 bedrooms and at least 3 bathrooms
- Homes with air conditioning or fireplace.

5

dBASE IV Reports and Labels

Objectives

After completing this chapter, you should be able to:

- Describe the steps in building a dBASE IV report.
- Build a dBASE custom layout report.
- Build a control-break (group) report.
- Add a calculated field to a report.
- Discuss use of field template and picture formats.
- Print mailing labels.

INTRODUCTION

Much of the power of database management systems comes from their ability to manipulate the data and create customized reports, labels, and data entry forms without having to write traditional programs. dBASE IV provides the ability to create customized reports and labels in a variety of formats.

This chapter presents a detailed discussion of preparing dBASE IV custom reports and labels. Examples illustrate how to build reports beginning with standard layouts or by placing fields at desired locations. Group reports with subtotals are also shown.

PREPARING dBASE REPORTS

dBASE IV offers a powerful report-writing facility for printing columnar information or mailing labels. We demonstrated the Quick Report (**Shift-F9**) feature in an earlier chapter, but with patience you can design almost any kind of printed report without resorting to writing a program to do so. You can place fields at almost any place on the page, add descriptive headings and titles, and change widths and format output fields as needed. You can design reports up to 255 characters wide in the Reports work surface.

dBASE Reports and Labels

Reports can be generated within dBASE IV in three layout types, or in combinations of the three types. The report generator can be used to modify any of these layout types into a customized report.

- **Column layouts** spread fields horizontally across the page, similar to the Browse screen.
- **Form layouts** arrange fields vertically, one per line, in a similar fashion to the Edit screen.
- **Mailmerge layouts** provide for merge printing where variable information from dBASE fields is substituted into documents, similar to the procedure used with word processing.

Labels are special kinds of reports that resemble the form layout, with fields placed vertically to fit on a mailing label. dBASE provides for **side-by-side labels,** up to a maximum of 255 characters across. This format is also useful for printed reports, not just for printing onto gummed labels. An example is shown in Figure 5-1.

Building the Report Layout

There are several steps in building a custom report:

- Design the report on paper.
- Open the Report panel in Create mode.
- Usually start with a quick layout to place fields.
- Move fields on the page as necessary.
- Add titles and column headings.
- Generate the report program (only done once).
- Print the report.

Design the Report: Report Bands

Most **report designs** contain a centered title of one or more lines at the top of the page, usually repeated on each page of the report. The columns of the report represent different fields or expressions. Each column is headed by a

```
Harold Garland
1944 South Wentt
Riley, IN   47811

Eileen Pickering
422 Highland Dr.
Terre Haute, IN   47802

Anne Conrad
1713 Glenview
Bloomington, IN   47432

William Butler
615 Walnut St.
Terre Haute, IN   47807
```

FIGURE 5-1

Label Format Report

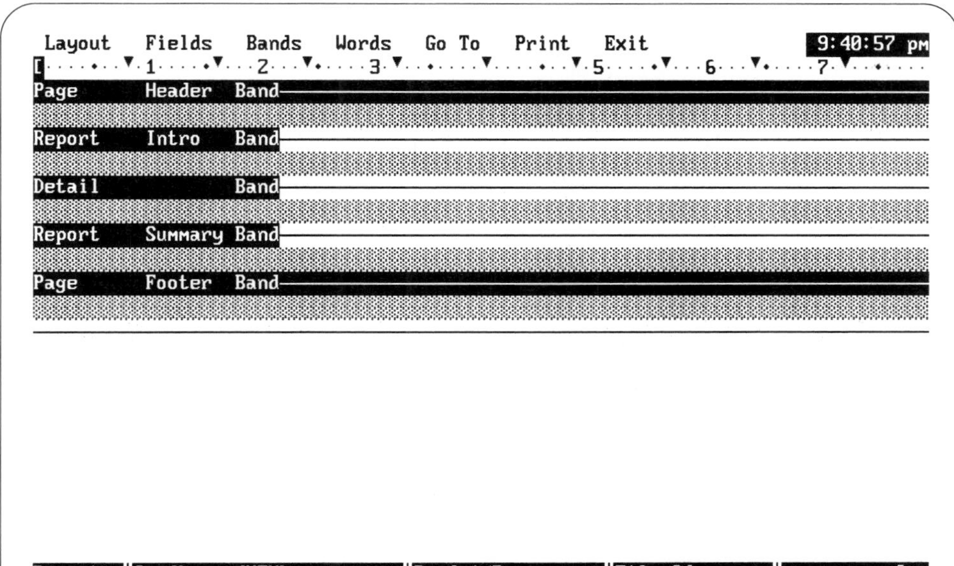

FIGURE 5-2

Opening Report Screen Showing Report Bands

descriptive heading of one or more lines; text field headings are usually left-justified above the column, while numeric field headings are right-justified. Detail lines appear beneath the column headings. **Control-break reports** group data together according to a common field, with subtotals or other summaries appearing before and after these groups of records.

The dBASE IV report generator provides five standard areas—called **report bands** and shown in Figure 5-2—for placing information on a page.

- The **Page Header band** is used for the report title and column headings that will be repeated on each page. The information is printed on each page of the report. dBASE also adds the page number and print date to this band, if desired.

- The **Report Intro band** contains information that appears only at the beginning of the report. This might be used for a cover page, title, or other explanatory information.
- The **Detail band** contains a template showing how individual record values are to appear, laid out by field. The template shows the width for each field and its precise location on the line, including any formatting instructions. The Detail band template is repeated for each record in the file that is printed.
- The **Report Summary band** includes information that appears at the end of the report, after all the detail records have been printed. End of run totals may be placed here, along with other concluding remarks.
- The **Page Footer band** is similar to the Page Header band, providing a place for comments and other footer information. The page footer material is printed at the bottom of each page of the report.

You can add **Group bands** to the report layout that provide special headers summaries for groups of data. These summaries are printed at the end of each group or subgroup, based upon a shared field value. We'll cover group bands in a later example.

Example: *Starting with a Quick Layout*

You must have a database file in use before using the Report generator. For this example we will use the CD database file.

1. From the Control Center, select the CD file in the Data panel. Then move the cursor to the Reports panel and press **Enter** on the **<create>** box. You will see the Report screen shown in Figure 5-2 with empty bands.
2. If it is not already displayed, press the **F10** key to activate the **Layout** menu bar shown in Figure 5-3. The *Quick Layouts* line will be highlighted. Press **Enter** to see the layout type menu. The default layout is *Column layout.* Press **Enter** to make this selection.

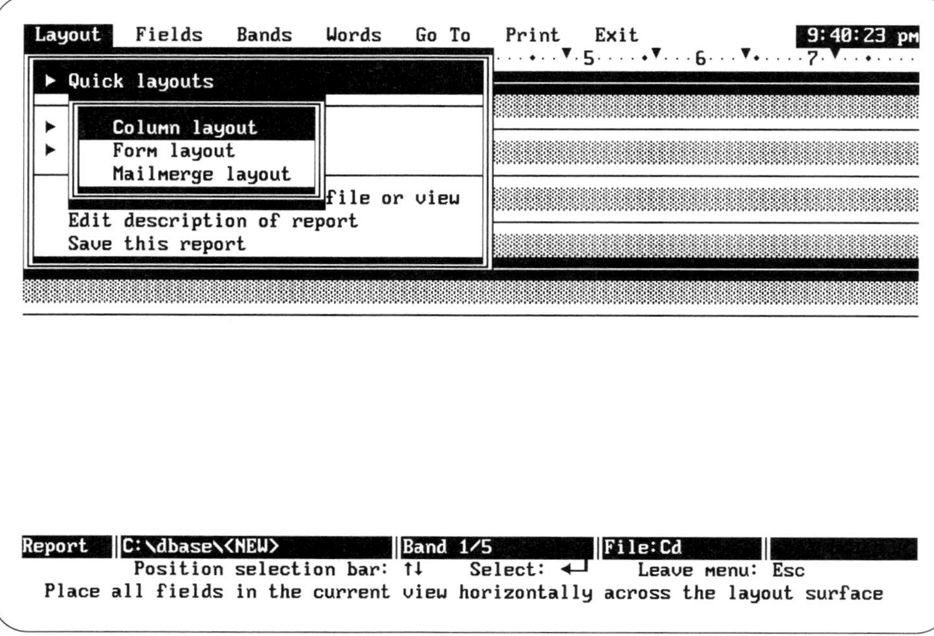

FIGURE 5-3

Quick Layout Menu of the Report Work Surface

3. In choosing the Quick Layout approach, all the fields will be laid out across the page in the same manner as the Quick Report technique introduced in a previous chapter. But now you can make changes, add titles, and customize the report to the way you want it. In Figure 5-4, dBASE has filled in the Page Header and Detail bands with fields from the CD file. Field names are used for column headings and the Detail band templates match the field widths from the database structure.
4. Let's add a title to the report. Move the cursor to line 3, just below the MM/DD/YY template. Remember that dBASE begins numbering at line 0. Line references are given in the same way. You can locate the cursor position box in the status bar. Notice the shape of the cursor: the blinking square indicates you are in Insert mode, while the blinking underscore indicates overtype mode. Let's add two blank lines by pressing **Enter** twice. Notice that the remainder of the report below the Page Header band moves down on the screen.
5. At line 4, column 40 type this title: **COMPACT DISK COLLECTION**. Also replace the column heading "TITLE" with **DISK TITLE**. One way to accomplish this is to switch from Insert to Overtype mode (press the **Ins** key) and simply overtype the correct heading over the old one.
6. Press **Ctrl-End** to save the report specification. When prompted, enter **CDCOL** as the name of the report. When you return to the Control Center, you'll find that dBASE has placed this report in the Reports panel.
7. Finally, let's see what the report will look like when printed. To view the report on the screen, before printing, move the cursor to highlight the name of the report in the Reports panel and press **Enter**. You'll see the dialog box shown in Figure 5-5.
8. Press **Enter** to go to the **Print report** menu in Figure 5-6. The top choice, *Begin printing,* will divert the report to the default printer. The third choice, *View report on screen,* would preview the report on the screen. Because the screen may be narrower than the printer paper being used to

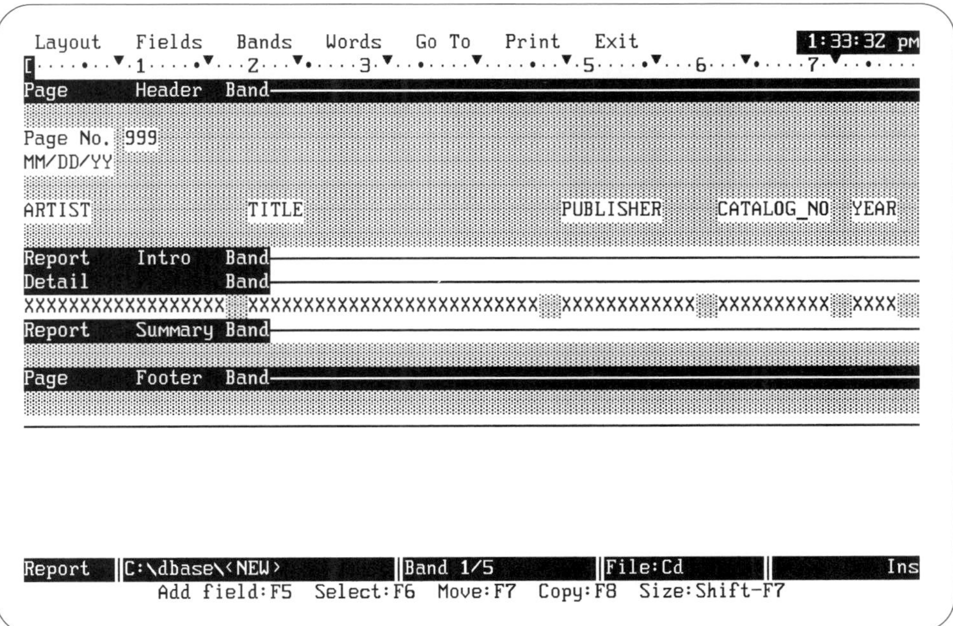

FIGURE 5-4

Report Bands After Using Column Quick Layout Format

FIGURE 5-5

Report Dialog Box

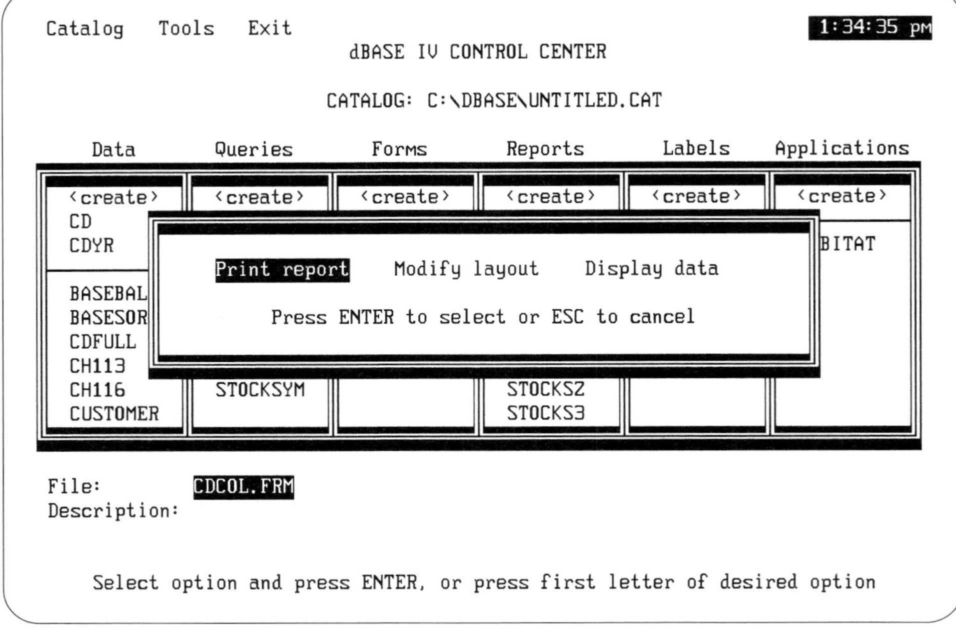

FIGURE 5-6

Print Report Menu

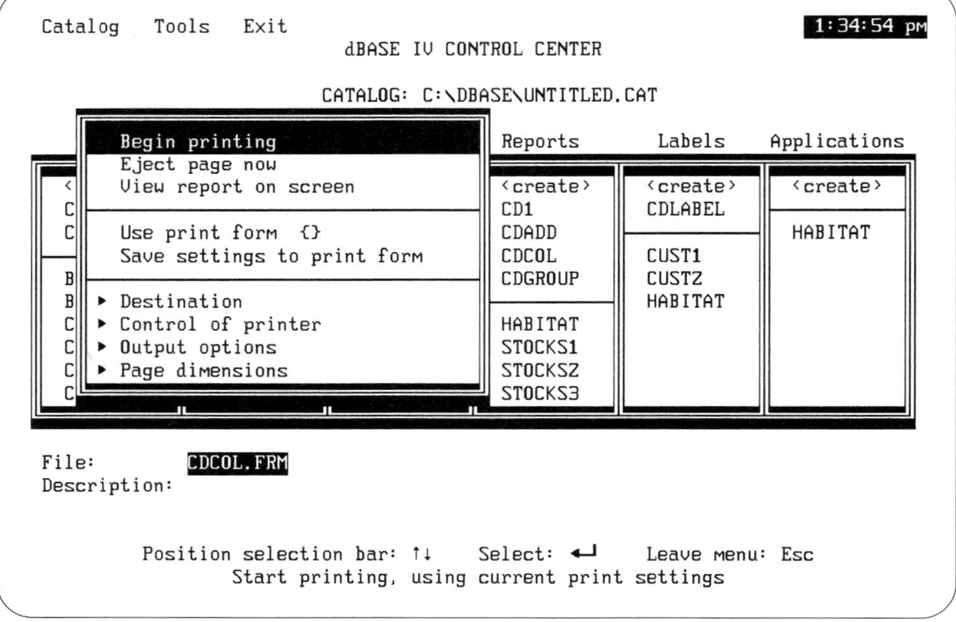

print the report form on, the latter option may not clearly represent how the report will actually appear when printed. In this instance, let's go ahead and print the report. Press **Enter** on the top selection.

9. When the report is finished, dBASE will return to the Control Center. A replica of the report is shown in Figure 5-7. Because the report is wider than 80 columns, it might not display this way unless your printer supports compressed print.

FIGURE 5-7

Finished CDCOL Report Shown in Compressed Print Style

```
Page No.     1
08/22/90

                                 COMPACT DISK COLLECTION

ARTIST               DISK TITLE                  PUBLISHER      CATALOG_NO   YEAR  CLASS  LENGTH  DIGITAL

The Canadian Brass   High, Bright, Light and Cl  RCA            RCD14574     1983  CL         51  Y
Wiener Philharmoni   Beethoven: Symphony No. 9   Deutsche Gr.   419598-2     1987  CL         72  Y
Wynton Marsalis      Trumpet Concertos           CBS Master     MK37846      1983  CL         40  Y
Stern, Rampal        Play Vivaldi & Telemann     CBS Master     MK35133      1978  CL         44  N
Glenn Gould          Bach Goldberg Variations    CBS Master     MK37779      1982  CL         51  Y
Festival Strings L   Adagio Albioni,Pachelbel,B  Deutsche Gr.   4132248-2    1972  CL         62  N
                                                                                             320
```

Example: *Building the Report Using Add Field*

The previous example used the Quick Layout to pre-place fields on the report template. In this example we will create a custom report by adding only the desired fields to the empty template.

1. Begin by opening the **CD** database file from the Control Center. Then move the cursor to the Reports panel and press **Enter** on the **<create>** box. Press **Esc** and a blank template will appear on the Report screen.

2. Our report will include the ARTIST field on the first detail line, along with the PUBLISHER, YEAR, and CLASS. The second detail line will include the TITLE, CATALOG_NO, and LENGTH. We will also want to place one blank line in the Detail band after the field template. The title of the report will be COMPACT DISK LIBRARY on the first line, followed by ARTIST REPORT centered beneath it on the second line. We'll add these later.

3. Move the cursor to the first column of the Detail band, and press **F10** to activate the Menu Bar. Move the cursor to the **Fields** bar and select *Add field.* (To save time, you can press **Alt-F** to directly execute the **Fields** bar.)

4. The next screen in Figure 5-8 shows four columns of fields to choose from: CD, CALCULATED, PREDEFINED, and SUMMARY.

   - The **CD** column includes fields from the current database in use.
   - The **CALCULATED** column allows you to build expressions of field values.
   - The **PREDEFINED** column includes access to such functions as the date, time, record number and page number.
   - The **SUMMARY** column includes statistical functions, such as average, max, min, count and sum.

5. Move the cursor to the ARTIST field in the CD column and press **Enter** to

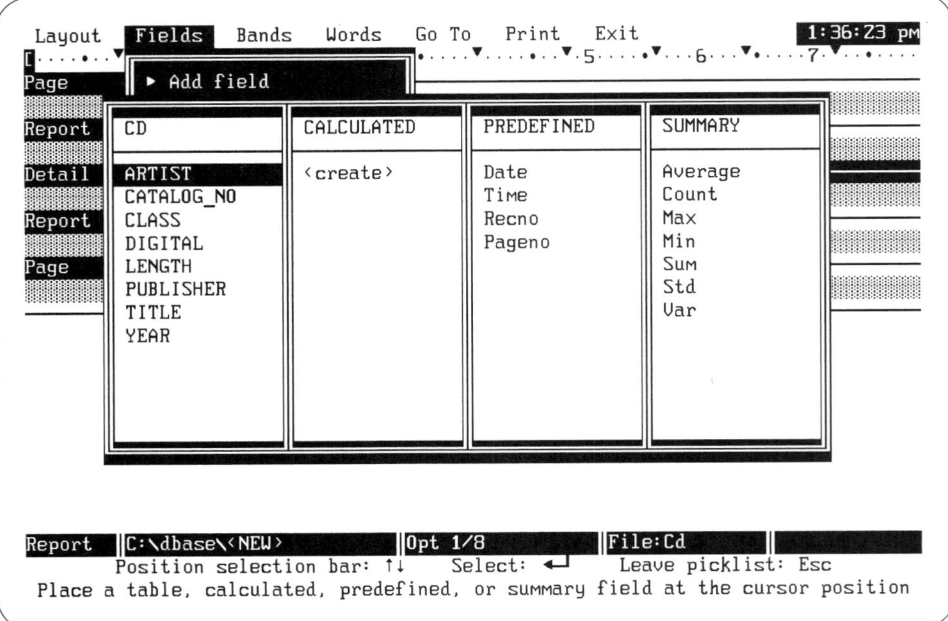

FIGURE 5-8

Report Work Surface with Add Field Option

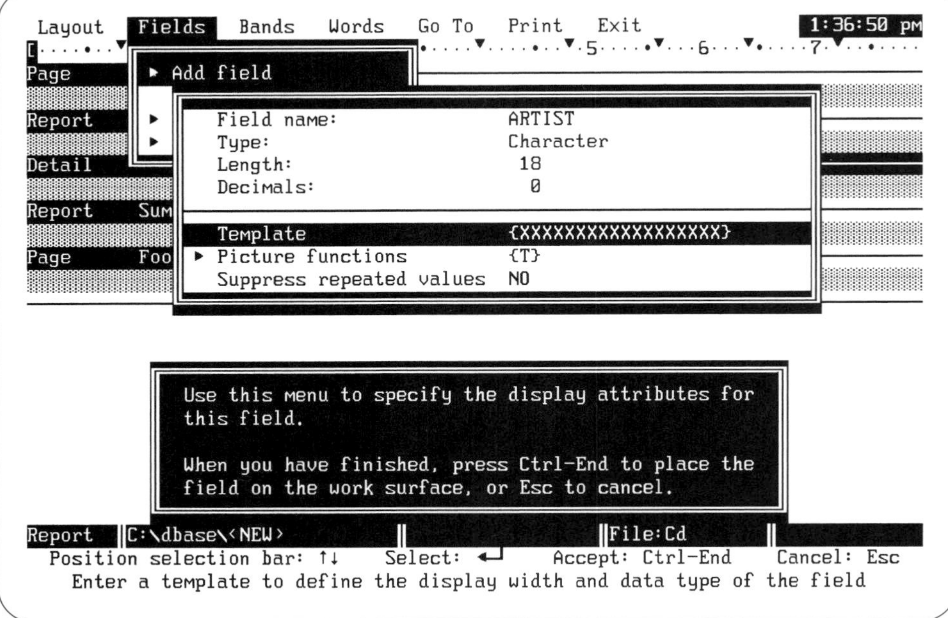

FIGURE 5-9

Add Field Menu

select that field for the Detail band. You will then see a box (Figure 5-9) that displays the structure information about the selected field and additional information about the field as it will appear in the Detail band. The *Template* shows the width of the field represented by the Xs. Numeric fields are displayed as 9s, with the decimal point included if any decimal places are defined. The *Picture functions* line lets you select special formatting characters for that field. The **T** on that line is used to ask dBASE to trim leading and trailing blanks from the field. For now, just press **Ctrl-End** to save the field in the Detail band. We'll discuss field templates and pictures in more detail in the next section.

```
Layout   Fields   Bands   Words   Go To   Print   Exit                7:45:13 pm
[····▼·1····▼···2···▼····3·▼·········▼·······▼·5·····▼···6···▼·····7·▼······
Page      Header  Band
Report    Intro   Band
Detail            Band
XXXXXXXXXXXXXXXXXX              XXXXXXXXXXXX  XXXX      XXX   999
 XXXXXXXXXXXXXXXXXXXXXXXXX      XXXXXXXXX
Report    Summary Band
Page      Footer  Band

Report  ||C:\dbase\CDADD          ||Line:2 Col:0     ||File:Cd         ||          Ins
               Add field:F5  Select:F6  Move:F7  Copy:F8  Size:Shift-F7
```

FIGURE 5-10

Report Design Screen

6. Move the cursor to column 30 with the right arrow key, and give the *Add field* command again. This time select the PUBLISHER field. Press **Ctrl-End** to save that field in the report form.
7. Move the cursor to column 45 and press **F5,** another way to issue the *Add field* command. This time select the YEAR field.
8. In column 55 issue the *Add field* command and choose the CLASS field.
9. In column 62 give the *Add field* command and select the LENGTH field.
10. With the cursor at the end of the first detail line and the INS indicator on, press the **Enter** key to make a new blank detail line *after* the first line. If you make a mistake, a blank line can be erased with the **Ctrl-Y** command, but be careful to not delete a line you wish to save.
11. Now we will prepare the Detail band for the second detail line. Move the cursor to column 1 (locate the cursor position in the status bar) in the second detail line and issue the *Add field* command. This time select the TITLE field. It should be offset from the ARTIST field by one column.
12. Move the cursor to column 30 and give the *Add field* command; select the CATALOG_NO field.
13. With the cursor on the second detail line but after the CATALOG_NO field, press **Enter** to add a blank line beneath the two detail lines. The report design form should look like Figure 5-10.
14. Finally, let's add the Page Header band information. We will place the date at the top left corner, then the title lines. Move the cursor up to that band and press the **Home** key to move the cursor to the left corner. Issue the *Add field* command, this time selecting *Date* from the PREDEFINED column. The template MM/DD/YY will appear in the Page Header band.
15. Press the **Enter** key *five times* to make new blank page header lines. Enter **COMPACT DISK LIBRARY** in column 0 of the second line (line 1)of the Page Header band.

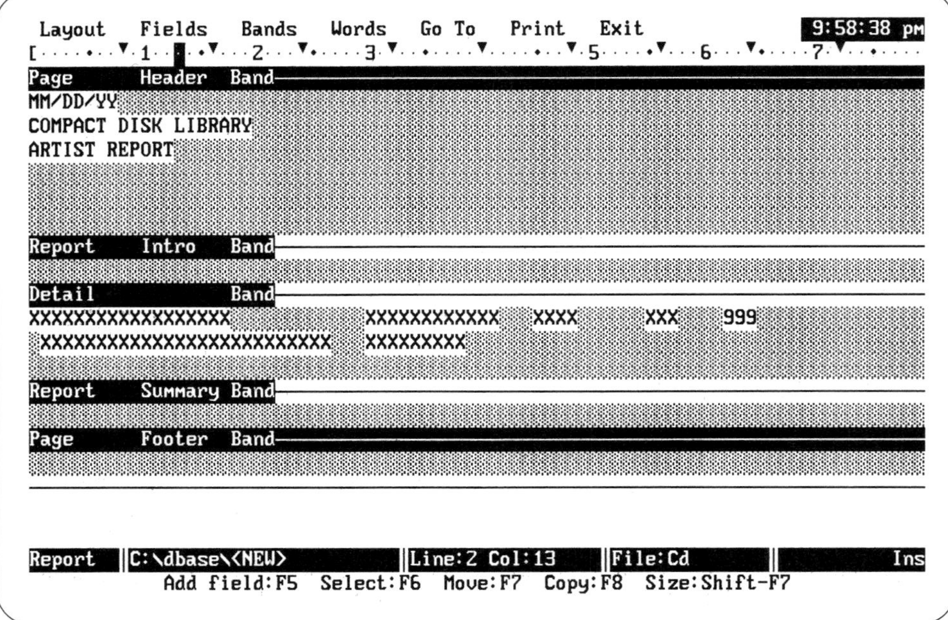

FIGURE 5-11

Page Header Band

16. Then move the cursor to the third Page Header band line (line 2) and enter this title starting in column 0: **ARTIST REPORT**. The band should look like Figure 5-11.
17. We will manually center the two titles above the detail lines in the report. Move the cursor to the first character in COMPACT DISK LIBRARY and press the **F6** function key; move the cursor to the last character of that title and press **Enter** to finish making the selection of the title. Then press **F7** to move the title block. Use the arrow keys to center it above the Detail band fields, around column 21. Press **Enter** to lock it in place. Do the same thing with the second line, centering it beneath the first title line.
18. Then on line 4 of the Page Header band, enter appropriate column headings. Suggested headings are shown in Figure 5-12. Leave line 5 blank—it will act as a border between the column headings and the detail lines. Move the cursor to the Report Intro band and press **Ctrl-Y** to remove the blank line there.
19. Save your report by pressing **Ctrl-End**. When prompted for a name, type **CDADD** and press **Enter** to complete the entry.
20. To print this report from the Control Center, move the cursor to the CDADD entry in the Reports panel and press **Enter** two times. If your printer is ready, press **Enter** one more time on the *Begin printing now* line. A sample of the report is shown in Figure 5-13.

Specifying Template and Picture for Data Fields

Unless you specify differently, dBASE will use the default field width for the field's **template** in reports and labels. The template gives a replica of the field using special characters.

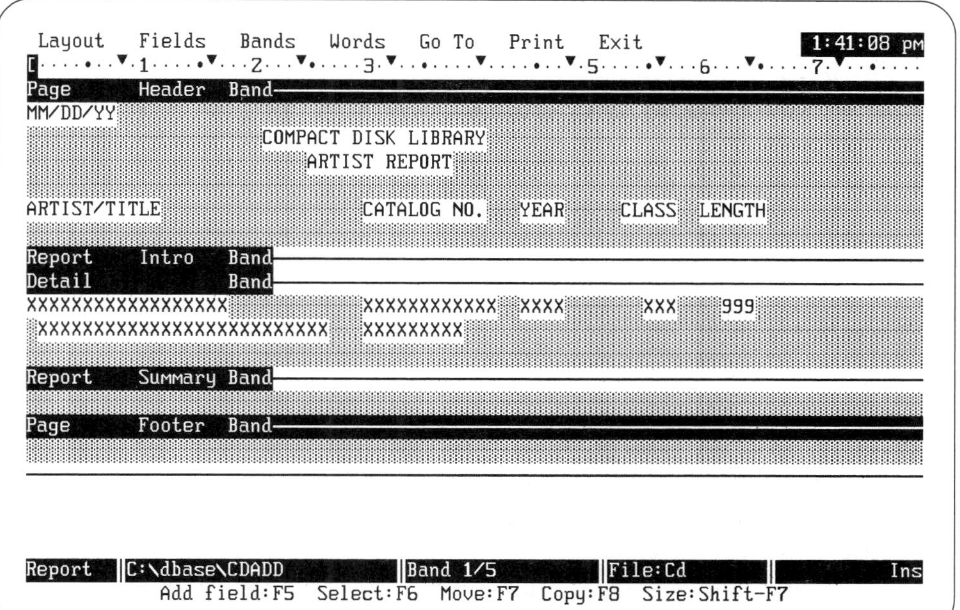

FIGURE 5-12

Completed Report Screen Layout

FIGURE 5-13

Sample Output from CDADD Report

08/22/90

COMPACT DISK LIBRARY
ARTIST REPORT

ARTIST/TITLE	CATALOG NO.	YEAR	CLASS	LENGTH
The Canadian Brass High, Bright, Light and Cl	RCA RCD14574	1983	CL	51
Wiener Philharmoni Beethoven: Symphony No. 9	Deutsche Gr. 419598-2	1987	CL	72
Wynton Marsalis Trumpet Concertos	CBS Master MK37846	1983	CL	40
Stern, Rampal Play Vivaldi & Telemann	CBS Master MK35133	1978	CL	44
Glenn Gould Bach Goldberg Variations	CBS Master MK37779	1982	CL	51
Festival Strings L Adagio Albioni,Pachelbel,B	Deutsche Gr. 4132248-2	1972	CL	62

Character	Meaning
9	Allows only digits and sign
#	Allows digits, spaces and sign
.	Insert decimal point
,	Display comma if number is large enough
*	Display leading zeros as asterisks
$	Display leading zeros as dollar signs
any other	Insert that character into template

FIGURE 5-14

Special Numeric Field Template Characters

Character	Meaning
9	Allows only digits and sign
#	Allows only digits, spaces and sign
A	Allows only alphabetic characters
N	Allows alphabetic, digits and underscore
!	Converts character to uppercase
X	Any character
any other	Any other character is inserted into the template
Y	Only Y or N allowed for logical fields
L	T, F, Y or N allowed for logical fields

FIGURE 5-15

Special Character Field Template Characters

The usual template characters are shown below:

- Numeric fields are shown with a string of 9s; the decimal point is shown if there are any decimal places defined.
- Character fields are shown with a string of Xs.
- Logical fields appear as a single letter L.
- Date fields appear as MM/DD/YY.
- Memo fields appear as MEMO.

Templates may also use other characters for special formatting considerations. Figure 5-14 shows some common template characters for numeric fields and their effects. Figure 5-15 shows common template characters for character and logical fields.

The field's **picture** provides additional means of further display formatting. Figure 5-16 shows possible picture functions for numeric fields. Figure 5-17 shows possible picture functions for character fields. The default value for all of these picture functions is OFF except for trim.

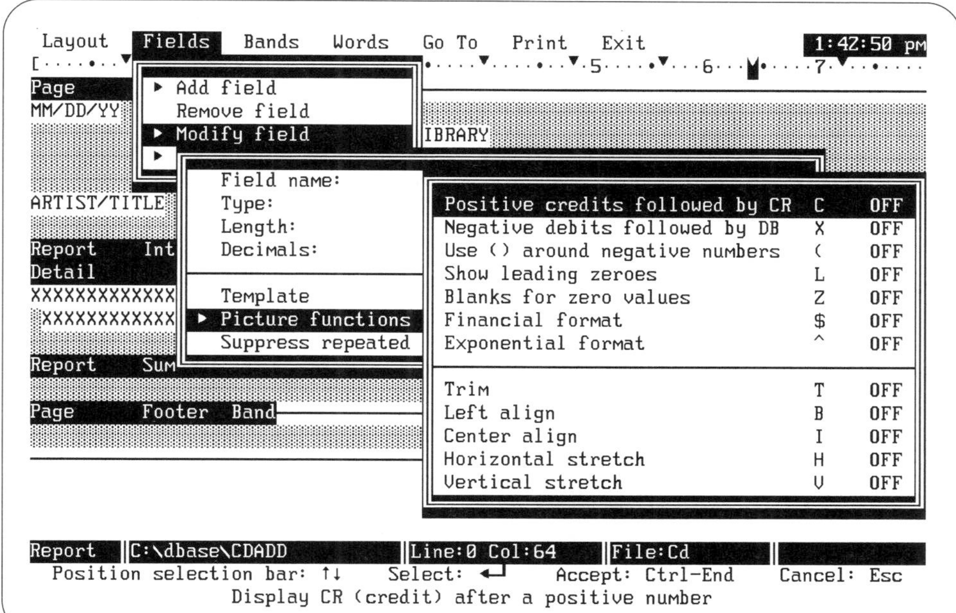

FIGURE 5-16

Picture Functions for Numeric Fields

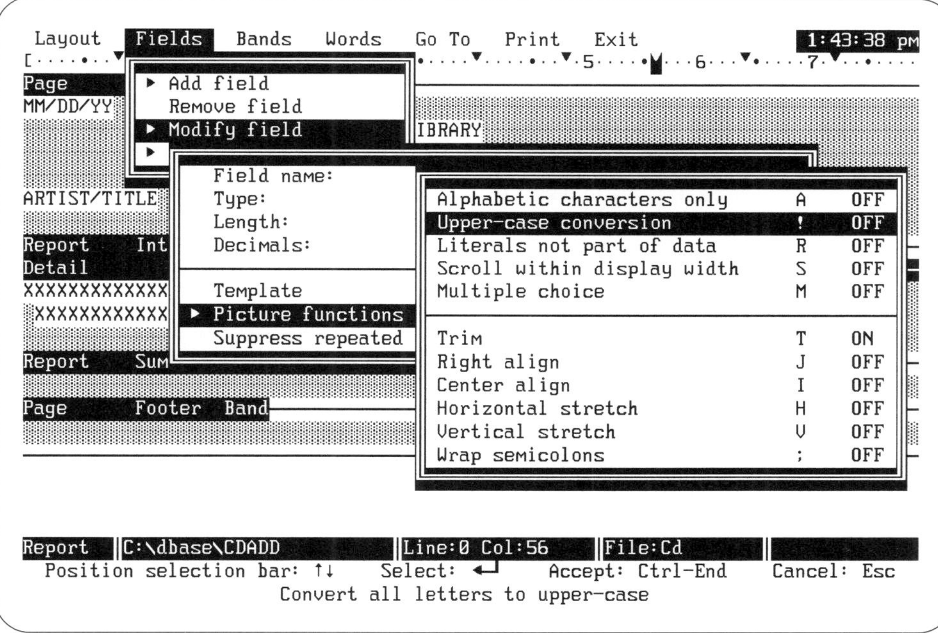

FIGURE 5-17

Picture Functions for Character Fields

Example: *Creating a Formatted Report with Calculated Fields*

In this example we'll use a new database file called PRODUCTS.DBF to build a custom report that features a calculated field and a financial formatted output.

1. Copy the PRODUCTS.DBF and PRODUCTS.MDX files from the data disk. The structure of this database file is shown in Figure 5-18. The index tag for the PROD_NO field is called by the same name, PROD_NO.

FIGURE 5-18

Database Structure for Report Example

```
Structure for database: C:\DBASE\PRODUCTS.DBF
Number of data records:      10
Date of last update   : 09/15/90
Field  Field Name  Type       Width    Dec    Index
    1  PROD_NO     Character      5               Y
    2  PROD_NAME   Character     20               N
    3  PRICE       Numeric        7      2        N
    4  ON_HAND     Numeric        4               N
    5  REORDER     Numeric        4               N
** Total **                      41
```

2. Begin dBASE as usual and select **PRODUCTS** from the Data panel of the Control Center. Press **Enter** to Use file.

3. Move the cursor to the **<create>** line in the Reports panel and press **Enter**. At the Reports work surface press **Esc** to remove the Quick Layout menu. Because the current page width is 132 characters, press **Alt-W** to select the **Words** band, then select the *Modify ruler* line. The cursor will be in the ruler line at top. Move it to column 39 and press] to place the right margin in that column. Now if we use the center command the line will be an appropriate length.

4. Use the arrow keys to move the cursor to column 1 of the Detail band. Refer to the status bar for the cursor's location. Press **F5** to add a field, selecting the PROD_NO field. At the next screen press **Ctrl-End** to complete the field entry. Likewise, place the PROD_NAME field in column 8 of the Detail band.

5. Next we'll add a calculated field in column 30 of the Detail band. Let's assume that there has been a 10% increase in the PRICE field. Move the cursor to column 30 and press **F5** to add a field. You'll see the pick list screen shown in Figure 5-19.

6. Move the cursor to **<create>** in the Calculated column and press **Enter**. Press **Enter** to open the Name line and type **NEW_PRICE** as the name for this calculated field. Press **Enter** complete the entry.

7. Move the cursor to the Expression line and press **Enter** to open that line. Type **PRICE*1.1** and press **Enter**. Move the cursor to the Template and press **Enter** to open that line. The new template will be **999999.99**. Move the cursor to the Picture functions line and press **Enter**; select the *Financial format* line and press the **Space** key to change from No to **Yes.** To finish this entry, press **Ctrl-End** twice and dBASE will place the field into the detail line. See Figure 5-20 for the field information.

8. Move the cursor to column 31 in the Report Summary band and press **F5** to add another summary field that will give the average price of the our furniture. Select the **Average** line from the SUMMARY column in the pick list. Make these entries in the dialog window:

Name	{AVG_PRICE}
Field to summarize on	{NEW_PRICE}
Template	{999999.99}
Picture functions	{$}

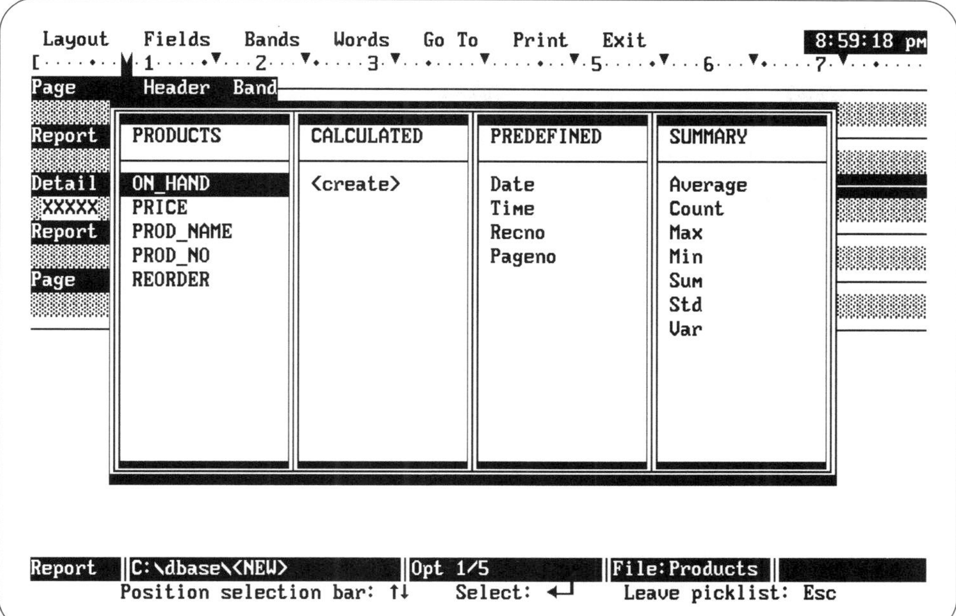

FIGURE 5-19

Pick List Screen for Calculated Field

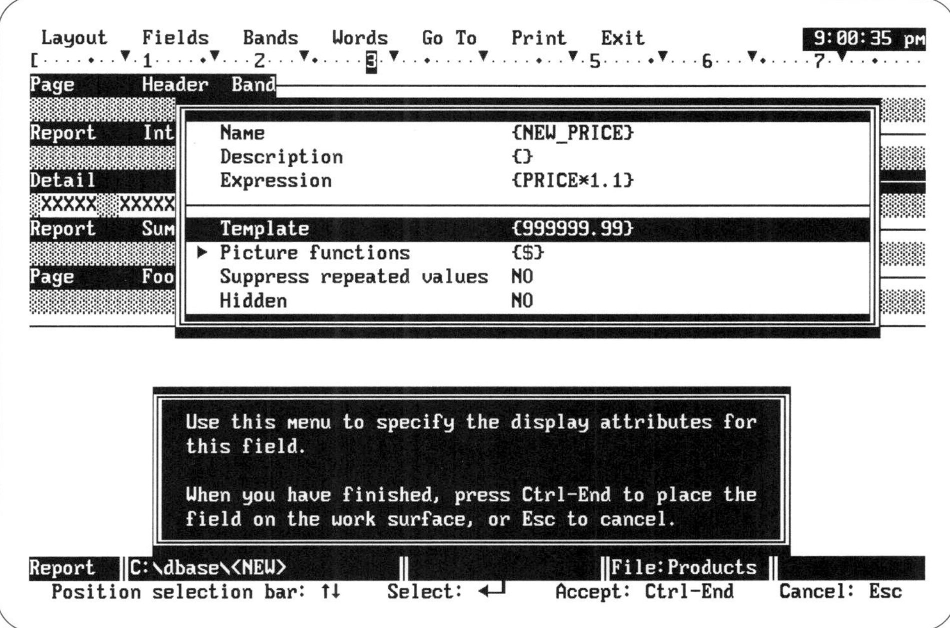

FIGURE 5-20

Template for Calculated Field

9. Because we will not have a Report Intro page, move the cursor to that band line and press **Enter**. The blank line will disappear.

10. Next move the cursor to the Page Header band and place the page title in that band. We'll use the Center command to center the title, so just type **NEW PRICE REPORT** starting at column 0. Then press **Home** to move the cursor back to the beginning of that line.

11. Press **F6** to select the title, move the cursor to the last letter in the title and press **Enter** to complete the selection. Press **Alt-W** to select the **Words** band, then press **P** to choose the *Position* line. In the next box press **C** to

select *Center*. The title will be centered automatically in the current line width, between column 0 and column 39.

12. Press the **End** key to move the cursor to the end of the title, then press **Enter** twice to make a new blank row in the Page Header band. Place these column headings where indicated, shown in Figure 5-21.

PROD	in column 1
DESCRIPTION	in column 8
NEW PRICE	in column 30

    Press **Enter** to add one more blank line after the headings.

13. To save the report press **Ctrl-End**. Give the name **PROD1**.

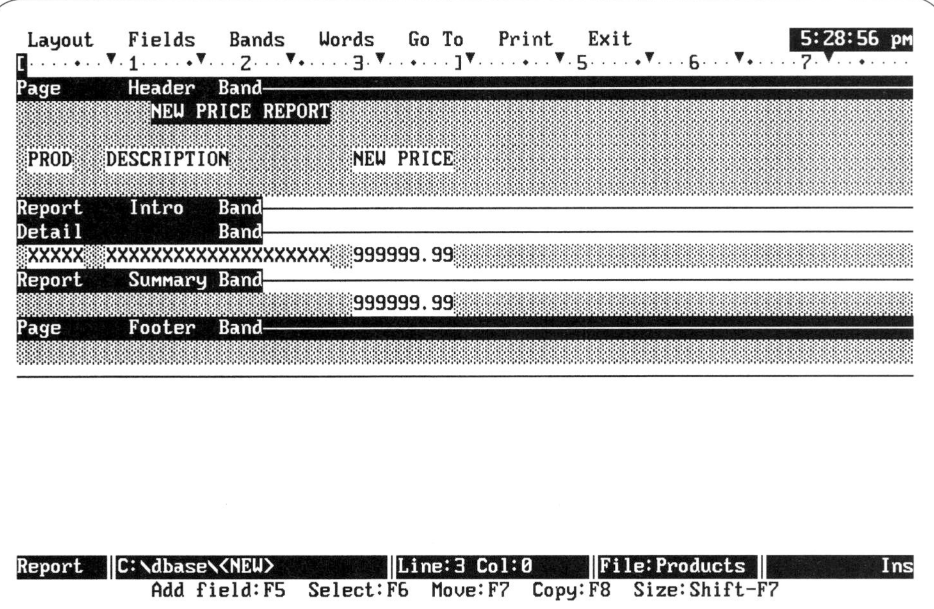

FIGURE 5-21

Final Report Screen

FIGURE 5-22

Sample Report for Example

```
            NEW PRICE REPORT

PROD   DESCRIPTION            NEW PRICE

14253  60" Bookcase             $247.45
14352  48" Bookcase             $219.95
14453  30" Bookcase             $158.40
14552  24" Bookcase             $134.59
16253  Student Desk             $197.95
17352  Sm Kitchen Chair          $83.05
17552  Kitchen Chair            $105.05
21152  End Table                $131.40
22148  Computer Cabinet         $135.78
22768  Printer stand - oak       $54.95
                                $146.85
```

14. At the Control Center move the cursor to the **PROD1** line in the Reports panel and press **Enter**. At the next prompt select *Begin printing* and dBASE will print the report. It appears in Figure 5-22.

Printing the Report

In the previous examples you printed the report on the printer. There are numerous options available in the Print menu. This section describes the most common options. Figure 5-23 shows the **Print** menu bar. This menu appears whether you print from within the Report generator or from the Control Center. The options are described below. Options preceded by a ▶ have submenus that are described but not illustrated.

- *Begin printing*—initiates printing after other options have been established.
- *Eject page now*—causes the current page in the printer to be ejected (it may be blank or have print on it from a previous print cycle); can be done before or after the report has been printed.
- *View report on screen*—causes report to be seen only on the screen, not on the printer; useful for testing new report designs; default value is NO.
- *Use print form {}*—uses print settings previously created and stored under the name specified within the braces.
- *Save settings to print form*—allows you to save the current print settings to a settings file.
- *Destination*—this option allows you to send the report to the printer or to a disk file for inclusion in a word processor; it also allows you to select which printer to use if more than one is installed.
- *Control of printer*—you can use this option to select different print fonts for the report and to specify whether a page feed is to be sent to the printer before or after the report.

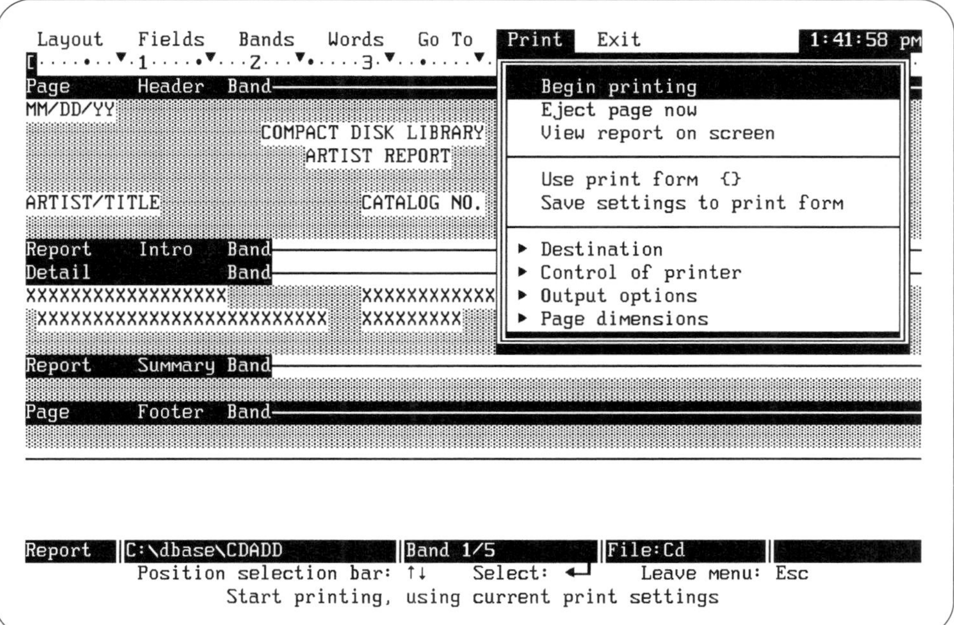

FIGURE 5-23

Print Menu Bar

- *Output options*—this option allows you to specify which pages are to be printed and the number of copies; the default is printing a single copy of all pages.
- *Page dimensions*—this option is used to set the lines per page, the left page offset, and the vertical line spacing (single, double) for the report.

Groups for Subtotals

dBASE IV provides a means of grouping common records in reports. These reports are often called **control-break reports.** For example, you might wish to list the CD library in groups by the publisher. To accomplish this you can open a group band in the Reports work surface and specify the PUBLISHER field as the group field. dBASE will print the information shown in the group bands whenever the publisher field *changes.* You must first order the records so that all of the records that belong to one group appear in consecutive order. Do this either with an index tag or sort the database file on the proper field.

You can also prepare a dBASE expression as the group value, or specify a certain number of records to be included in each group. The following example will illustrate adding a group band to the CDCOL report.

Example: *Adding a Group Band to the Report*

This example will create a new report, then add a group band. The group band will print the compact disks from each publisher in a group. You will also build an index tag for the PUBLISHER field in the CD.DBF file.

1. From the Control Center, with the **CD** data file open, place the cursor on the **<create>** file in the Reports file panel. Press **Enter** to build a new report.
2. Figure 5-24 shows the four fields placed in the report, along with the headings for these fields. Use the **F5** *Add field* command to place the fields at the following locations in the Detail band:

   ```
   Col 5    ARTIST
   Col 26   TITLE
   Col 55   LENGTH
   Col 60   YEAR
   ```

   Refer to the previous example on creating a report with *Add field* if you do not remember the procedure.
3. Next place the cursor in the band directly above the Detail Band header. Press **Alt-B** to activate the **Bands** pull-down menu. Press **A** to choose *Add a group band.* If it is dimly lit, you have probably placed the cursor in the wrong band of the report template.
4. You will see a submenu for describing how a group is formed. Press **Enter** to specify the *Field value* to group on. (The other two menu choices are used to enter a field expression or a fixed record count.) Then move the cursor to the PUBLISHER field and press **Enter**. Figure 5-25 shows the submenu after selecting this field.
5. dBASE will add two new bands to the report. The Group 1 Intro band appears above the Detail band and the Group 1 Summary band appears below the Detail band.
6. Move the cursor to row 0 of the Group 1 Intro band and type **PUBLISHER:** beginning in column 1.

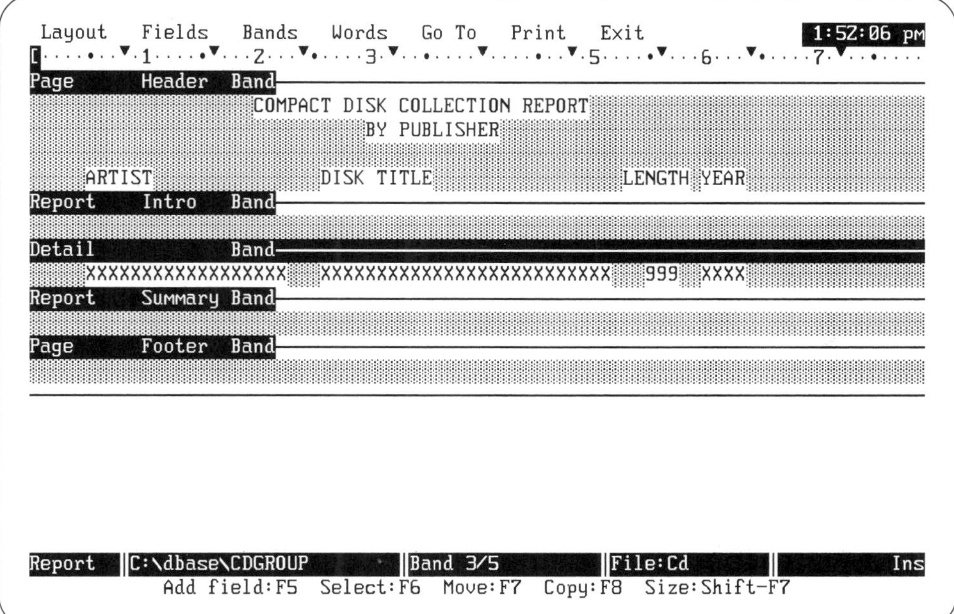

FIGURE 5-24

Sample Report Work Surface for CDGROUP Report

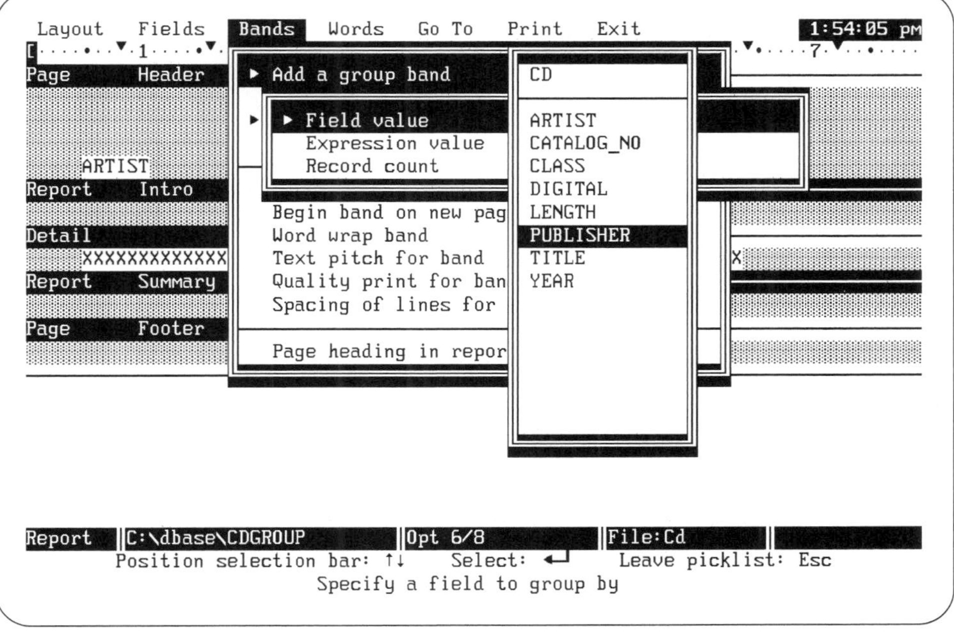

FIGURE 5-25

Specifying the Group Submenu

7. Move the cursor to column 15 and press **F5** to add a field. When prompted, move the cursor to the PUBLISHER field and press **Enter**. Then press **Ctrl-End** to complete the field entry.

8. Press **Alt-E** to exit and select the *Save changes and exit* line. When prompted for the report name, reply **CDGROUP** and press **Enter**.

9. Before you can print the groups report, you must create the PUBLISHER index tag. Move the cursor to the CD file in the Data panel and press **Shift-F2**.

10. At the Database screen select *Create new index* from the **Organize** menu bar. Press **Enter** to provide the tag name for the index and type **PUBLISHER**. Complete the name by pressing **Enter**.
11. Move the cursor to the *Index expression* line and press **Enter**. Type **PUBLISHER** on this line and press **Enter**. Select ascending order.
12. Press **Ctrl-End** to execute the index command.
13. Press **Alt-O** to activate the **Organize** menu bar, then type **O** to select the *Order records by index* line.
14. Select PUBLISHER from the list of index tags. Then press **Ctrl-End** to leave the Database screen.
15. Move the cursor to the CDGROUP file in the Reports panel and press **Enter** three times to run the group report. The output from the CDGROUP group program is shown in Figure 5-26.

---

dBASE IV allows six or more levels of group bands. You may modify or delete existing group bands from the **Bands** menu bar. You can also specify that new groups are to begin on a new page.

Other Print Features in dBASE IV

dBASE IV supports numerous other print features in the Report work surface. You can draw lines or boxes in the report, change print font size and type, adjust line spacing, and set format characteristics for individual fields or headings. Each is discussed below.

Lines and Boxes

These options are available in the **Layout** menu bar. You can specify a single or double line or use your own character. dBASE will instruct you to place the

FIGURE 5-26

Output from CDGROUP Example Report

```
                 COMPACT DISK COLLECTION REPORT
                          BY PUBLISHER

    ARTIST                DISK TITLE                  LENGTH YEAR

PUBLISHER:    CBS Master
    Wynton Marsalis       Trumpet Concertos              40   1983
    Stern, Rampal         Play Vivaldi & Telemann        44   1978
    Glenn Gould           Bach Goldberg Variations       51   1982

PUBLISHER:    Deutsche Gr.
    Wiener Philharmoni    Beethoven: Symphony No. 9      72   1987
    Festival Strings L    Adagio Albioni,Pachelbel,B     62   1972

PUBLISHER:    RCA
    The Canadian Brass    High, Bright, Light and Cl     51   1983
```

cursor where the line is to begin, press **Enter**, then move the cursor to the ending place and press **Enter**. The line appears on the screen as you move the cursor. The box is handled in a similar fashion: position the cursor at the upper left corner and press **Enter** to lock in that corner. Move the cursor to the lower right corner of the box and press **Enter**.

Text Font Size and Line Spacing for a Band

The **Bands** menu bar contains the line, *Text pitch for band*, that lets you determine the horizontal text spacing for all lines within the current band. Choices are:

- Default (whatever setting the printer is using)
- Pica (10 characters per inch)
- Elite (12 characters per inch)
- Condensed (17 characters per inch).

The *Spacing of lines for band* line permits the user to adjust vertical spacing between the lines in that band. Choices are:

- Default (whatever setting the printer is using)
- Single
- Double
- Triple.

Selecting Format Characteristics

You may wish to change the print style of a word or group of words. The *Style* line settings of the **Words** menu bar enable use of six standard formats and five user settings. The standard settings have values of On or OFF and include:

- Normal
- Bold
- Underline
- Italic
- Superscript
- Subscript.

The five user fonts must be configured for the specific printer being used and involve sending control characters to the printer that will enable the desired feature. Your computer lab assistant may be able to help you if you need additional fonts.

Positioning Fields and Text

The *Position* line of the **Words** menu bar is used to place fields at the left edge, centered, or right edge of the existing line. You may need to adjust the left and right line margins in the rule line. This is accomplished via the *Modify ruler* line of the **Words** menu bar.

DESIGNING A LABEL FORM

The label generator within dBASE IV works in a similar manner to the report generator just covered. The steps in preparing a label form are the same as for designing a report. We will use the HABITAT database as an example for creating one-across labels, the most common type.

The first step is to open the desired database file (HABITAT) from the Control Center. Then move the cursor to the **<create>** box in the Labels panel and press **Enter**. You will see a blank Label design screen for the default label size of 15/16 by 3-1/2 inches by one label across the page as shown in Figure 5-27.

To create the label design, use the *Add field* option from the Menu Bar to place the fields, one by one, on the label form. The typical mailing label format will be used:

```
FNAME LNAME
ADDRESS
CITY, STATE ZIPCODE
```

Example: *Building a Label Design*

1. Open the **HABITAT** database file from the Control Center and move to the **<create>** box in the Labels panel and **Enter**.
2. When the label design form appears, move the cursor to the upper left corner of the box. Then press the **Alt-F** key to activate the **Fields** menu bar. Move the cursor to the *Add field* line and press **Enter**. (You can also use the **F5** key to add a field.)
3. You will see a **pick list box** with three columns. The first column presents all the fields from the current database file. The middle column allows you to build a calculated field using dBASE expressions and functions. The third column contains predefined functions such as date, time, and record number. See Figure 5-28.
4. In the first column of the pick list box, move the cursor to the **FNAME** field and press **Enter**. When the attribute box appears, press **Ctrl-End** to save the field on the label form.

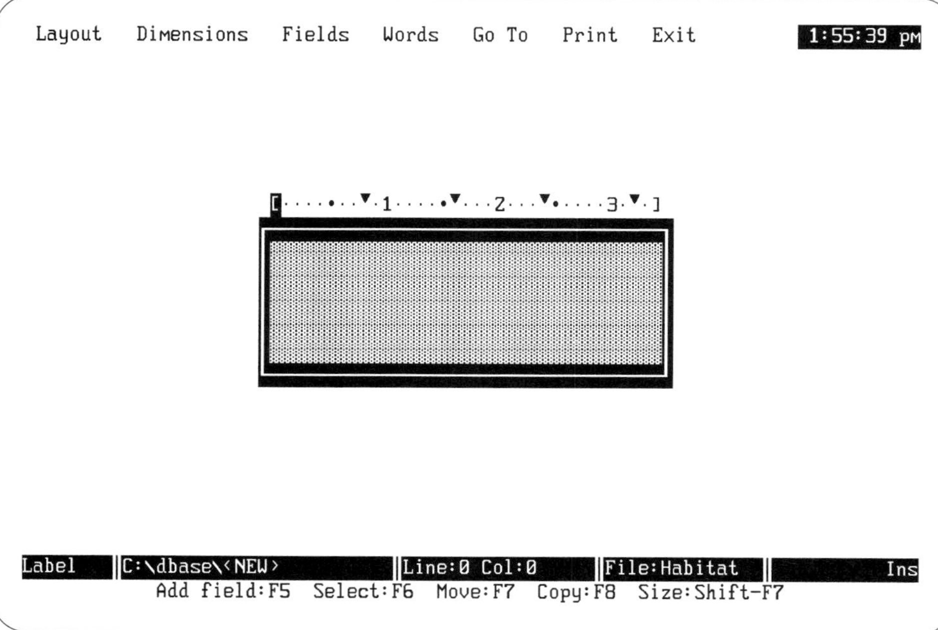

FIGURE 5-27

Label Layout Work Surface

5. Next, move the cursor one column to the right with the → key and repeat the *Add field* selection process for the **LNAME** field.
6. When finished, move to the second line and add the **ADDRESS** field.
7. Then move to the third line and insert the **CITY** field. Rather than move the cursor to the right, place a comma immediately after the CITY field. After one more space, add the **STATE** field, then after two spaces add the **ZIPCODE** field. The final label form should look like Figure 5-29.
8. To save the label form as a file, press **Ctrl-End**. When prompted for a file name, respond with **HABITAT**. A file called HABITAT.LBL is created.

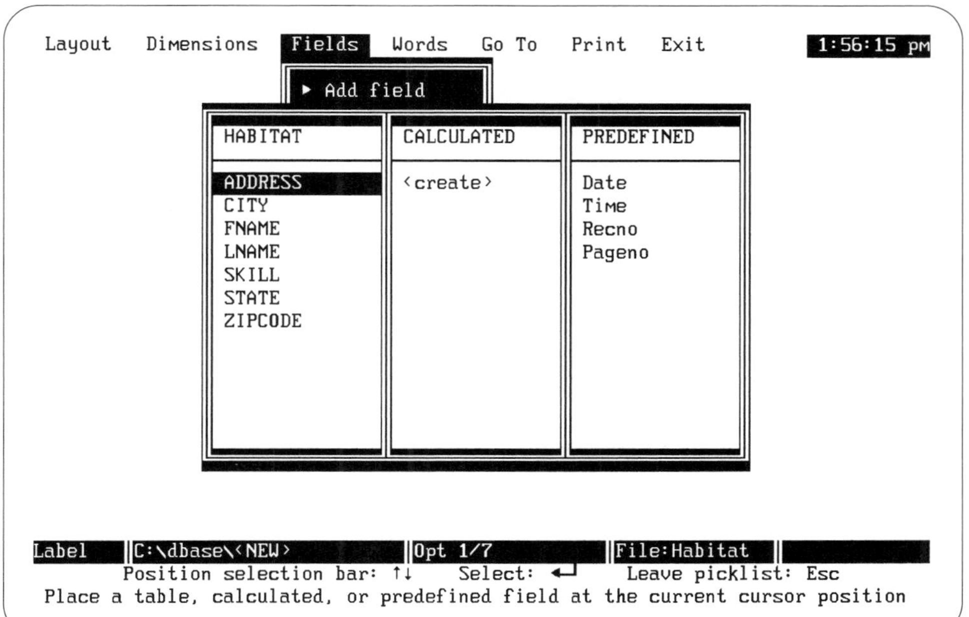

FIGURE 5-28

Label Add Field Menu

```
Layout   Dimensions   Fields   Words   Go To   Print   Exit        1:57:23 pm

[····•··▼·1····•▼···2···▼····3·▼·]
XXXXXXXXXX XXXXXXXXXXX
XXXXXXXXXXXXXXXXXX
XXXXXXXXXXXXXX, XX  XXXXX

Label  C:\dbase\<NEW>  Line:2 Col:25  File:Habitat                  Ins
    Add field:F5  Select:F6  Move:F7  Copy:F8  Size:Shift-F7
```

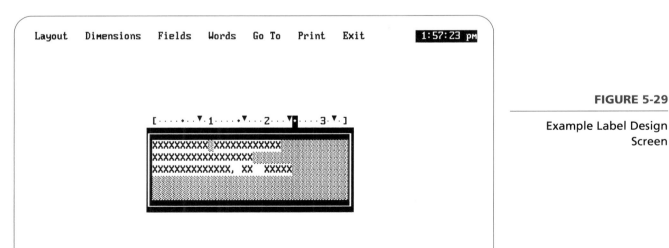

FIGURE 5-29

Example Label Design Screen

9. To print the label with your new design, from the Control Center move the cursor to the Labels panel. Then highlight the desired label form (**HABITAT,** in this case) and press **Enter**. The prompt box shown in Figure 5-30 will appear. Press **Enter** to *Begin printing*. Figure 5-31 shows the printed labels.

Other Types of Labels

You can create custom labels with the **Dimensions option** from the Label work surface menu, shown in Figure 15-32. The default size permits up to five lines of 35 characters each on the label. This menu allows you to change the basic label

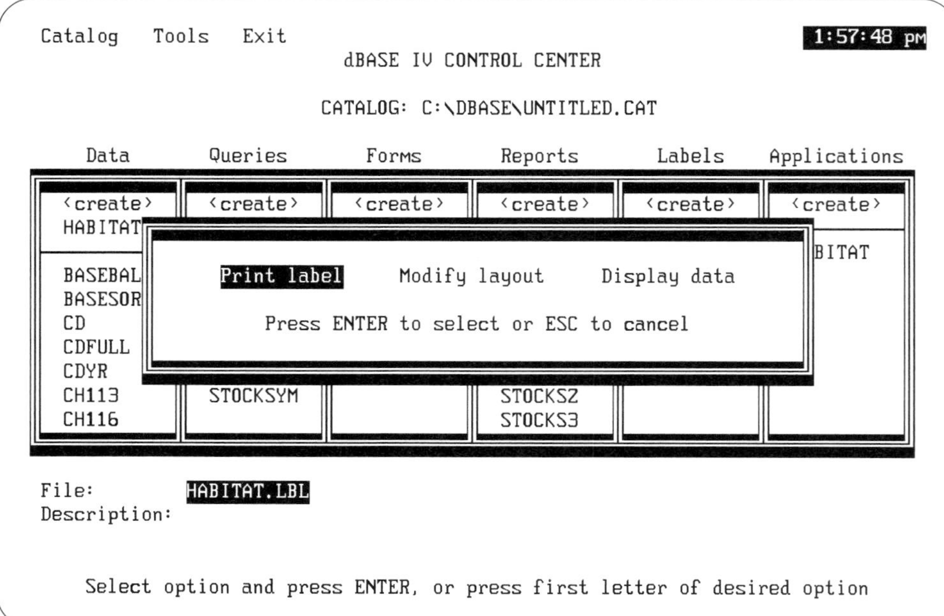

FIGURE 5-30

Print Label Prompt Box

FIGURE 5-31

Sample Label Output from HABITAT Label Design

```
Harold Garland
1944 South Wentt
Riley, IN   47811


Eileen Pickering
422 Highland Dr.
Terre Haute, IN   47802


Anne Conrad
1713 Glenview
Bloomington, IN   47432


William Butler
615 Walnut St.
Terre Haute, IN   47807
```

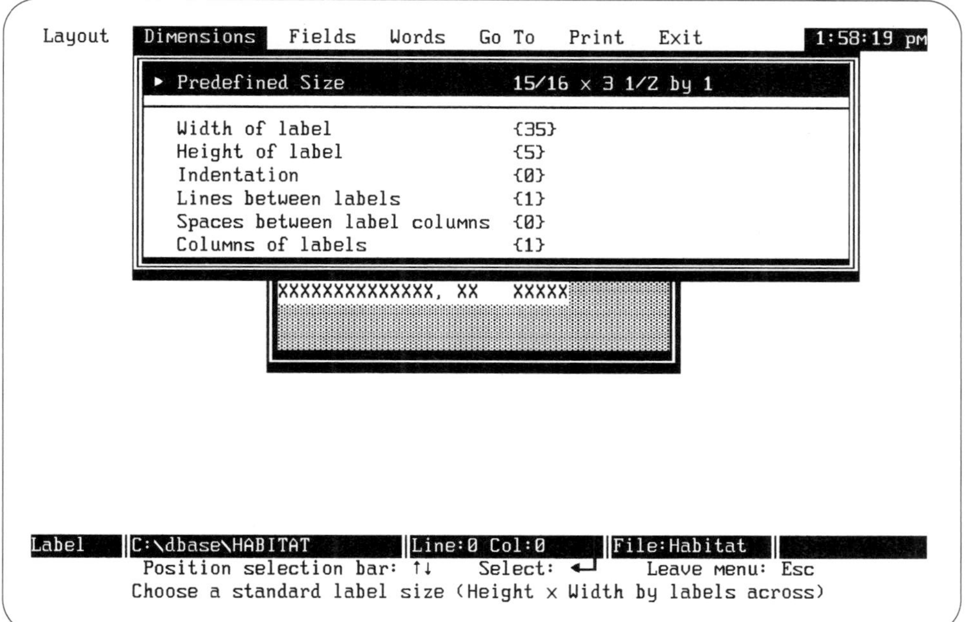

FIGURE 5-32

Dimensions Menu from Label Work Surface

size and to print up to 255 characters per line in side-by-side labels. The **Print** option on the same menu bar provides a way (through its *Control of Printer* option) to adjust the text pitch between four settings:

- Default
- Pica
- Elite
- Condensed.

The elite and condensed settings provide for 12 and 17 characters per inch, respectively, and offer a way to squeeze more information into a given label size. dBASE must be installed for your printer for these settings to work.

CHAPTER REVIEW

Preparing dBASE Reports

dBASE Reports are traditionally organized with fields spaced horizontally across the page, and records going down the page. dBASE IV introduced multiple layouts, including column, form and mailmerge layout types. Quick Reports are generated with the Shift-F9 command. Custom reports can be designed and generated within a few minutes. Custom labels can be designed similarly and printed with only a few commands.

Designing Reports and Labels

Reports and labels begin with painting the design onto the screen in a facsimile of the actual report or label layout. dBASE will place all fields on the page if you wish, and you can move them around as desired. Or you can add fields one at a time and place them precisely where they are to print. The Report design screen uses five standard areas for placing information on the page, each delineated by a report band. The Page Header band refers to information appearing at the top of each page; likewise, the Page Footer band covers material to appear at the bottom of each page. The Report Intro band contains information to be placed at the beginning of the report; the Report Summary band includes information that appears at the end of the report. The Detail band describes the template for fields that are to appear on each line of the report. You can add group bands that will print summaries for certain groups, provided the records are ordered properly, with all group member records appearing consecutively.

KEY TERMS

CALCULATED field
CD column
column layout
control-break report
Detail band
form layout report
Group Intro band
Group Summary band
label
mailmerge layout
Page Footer band
Page Header band
pick list
picture
PREDEFINED field
Quick Layout
report bands
report design
Report Intro band
Report Summary band
side-by-side labels
SUMMARY field
template

DISCUSSION QUESTIONS

1. Discuss the purpose of the seven steps in creating a dBASE IV report.
2. Compare the three types of Quick Layouts available in the Report screen. What types of reports would make use of a given type?
3. Suppose you allowed dBASE to place the fields on the report template using the Quick Layout option. How would you accomplish the following report design functions?
   a. Change the spelling of a column heading
   b. Move a database field to another location
   c. Change the width of a database field in the report
   d. Delete a database field
   e. Add a report summary total for a numeric field.
4. Explain how you would divert a copy of the report from the printer to a DOS file.
5. Suppose the report includes a memo field. How do you access that field when using a dBASE report?
6. List the name of the Report band in which each of the following items is normally placed.
   a. Report title and column headings
   b. Individual database field values
   c. Page number and report name that will go at the bottom of each page
   d. Column totals that are to print at the end of the report
   e. Totals for a group of records that share a common field value
   f. Common field value for a group of records that share that value.

7. Discuss the meaning of the following numeric and character field templates in custom dBASE reports. If possible, give an example of how a particular field value would appear. You may wish to try these out in the Report work surface.
   a. 999.99
   b. ###############
   c. A9AA9A
   d. 999-99-9999
   e. (999)999-9999
   f. 999,999
   g. *999.9
   h. !!!!!
8. List the steps necessary to create a calculated field and place it in the Detail band of a dBASE report.
9. Give the meaning of the following Predefined and Summary functions when used in a dBASE report.
   a. Pageno
   b. Recno
   c. Count
   d. Min
   e. Sum
   f. Std
10. List the steps needed to create a set of mailing labels. Assume that the database file is in order by zipcode using the ZIP tag. Also assume the labels are the one-across variety. Be explicit. You may wish to try out your steps in dBASE.
11. Explain the use of the following Report menu bar items.
    a. *Text pitch for band* line of **Bands** bar
    b. *Style* line of **Words** bar
    c. *Position* line of **Words** bar
    d. *Box* line of **Layout** bar
    e. *Modify ruler* line of **Words** bar.
12. Explain the process that dBASE uses in creating the files used to print a custom report. In particular, describe the use of the DBF, MDX, FRM, FRG and FRO file extensions. Which of these files are necessary to make changes to the report design?
13. Discuss the following **Print** menu bar options.
    a. Begin printing
    b. View report on screen
    c. Destination
    d. Output options.
14. Explain how you might direct dBASE to print a report that has already been designed.

EXERCISES

1. Open the STOCKS database that is stored on the data disk accompanying this textbook. Do not activate any of the index tags at this time. There are 25 records in the file, whose structure is shown in Figure 5-33. Prepare the custom report form described below.
   a. Create a custom report using the default Column layout and print a copy for reference. The title should be **STOCK PORTFOLIO REPORT**. List the records in natural order (no index tags activated). Name this report **STOCKS1**.
   b. Modify column headings to resemble Figure 5-34.
   c. Remove the totals templates in the Report Summary band for the YRHIGH, YRLOW and RECENT fields because they are not meaningful in that context.
   d. Print a report with the changes that you have made.
2. Again use the STOCKS database. Prepare another custom report form with the following specifications. We will name this report form **STOCKS2**.
   a. Instead of using the *Quick Layout* menu selection, we will create this report by using the *Add a field* menu selection. We will want to use the following fields, laid out in similar fashion to the previous problem. Use the default template for each field. Place the fields to the left side of the page so that an additional calculated field can be added at the end of the line.

      STOCK_NAME EXCHANGE RECENT NO_SHARES
   b. Choose meaningful column headings and an overall report title and place those in the Page Header band.
   c. Move the cursor to the end of the Detail band, after the NO_SHARES field. Press **Alt-F** to add a calculated field that would multiply **RECENT*NO_SHARES;** call this field **EQUITY.**
   d. Move the cursor beneath the calculated field in the Report Summary band and add a Summary field there that would sum the EQUITY fields.

FIGURE 5-33

Sample Data for Exercise 1

```
Structure for database: C:\DBASE\STOCKS.DBF
Number of data records:      25
Date of last update   : 11/01/89
Field Field Name  Type        Width    Dec    Index
    1  STOCK_NAME  Character     20              Y
    2  EXCHANGE    Character      6              Y
    3  YRHIGH      Numeric        7      3       N
    4  YRLOW       Numeric        7      3       N
    5  RECENT      Numeric        7      3       N
    6  NO_SHARES   Numeric        5              N
** Total **                      53
```

FIGURE 5-34

Sample Headings for Exercise 1

```
          STOCK       52-WEEK    52-WEEK    RECENT    NUMBER OF
 STOCK    EXCHANGE      HIGH       LOW      PRICE      SHARES
```

e. Save your report design as **STOCKS2** and obtain a printed copy of your report.

f. Optional: Calculate and print an expression for each stock that measures the recent price's percentile between the year's lowest and highest figures. If the stock is trading at the year's low price, the percentile would be 0. If the stock is trading at the year's highest price, the percentile is 100%. Your expression would be **(RECENT-YRLOW)/(YRHIGH-YRLOW)*100.**

3. Use the STOCKS database and create a control break report that summarizes stocks by exchange. Open the database file and order the records by the EXCHANGE index tag. You may wish to view them with the Browse screen (or with LIST at the dot prompt) to assure yourself that they appear in order by the Exchange name.

   a. Create a third custom report form which will be called **STOCKS3.** You may use the *Quick Layout* option to build the basic column layout, similar to the format in STOCKS1.

   b. Add a suitable report title in the Page Header band that will identify this exchange report. Modify any column headings as needed.

   c. Move the cursor to the Report Intro band and add a group band to represent the exchange field. You should see a Group 1 Intro band appear above the Detail band, and a Group 1 Summary band appear below the Detail band. Obtain a printed copy of this report.

   d. Further modify your group report to include the **AVG NO OF SHARES** in the Group 1 summary band. Move the cursor to that band and add the summary field that averages the NO_SHARES field beneath that column.

4. Use the CUSTOMER database file from the previous chapter and build a set of mailing labels for the five customers in this database. (Refer to problems 3–4, Chapter 3.)

   a. Assume the traditional label layout with CNAME on the first line, ADDRESS on the second line, and CITY ST ZIPCODE on the third line, similar to the example in this chapter. Save this label format as **CUST1**.

   b. Use the standard label size and print on regular printer paper one-across labels on a single sheet.

   c. Modify your one-across label format and assume that you are printing two-across labels. Print the five labels on regular printer paper. Use the **Layout** menu bar to save this label design as **CUST2**.

5. Use the SCHED database file discussed in the previous chapter. Prepare a group report showing sets of five courses together, then a blank row. Specifications appear below.

   a. The title of the report is **SYSTEMS AND DECISION SCIENCES DEPARTMENT SPRING SCHEDULE**. You will need to split the title into two rows. Use appropriate column headings to match the fields below.

   b. Fields to be printed include **PREFIX+NUMBER** (a calculated field), **SECTION**, **INSTRUCTOR**, **DAY**, **TIME** and **ROOM**. The first field should be 8 characters long.

c. The report should show five detail lines in each group. Open a group band and select the *Record count* option. Delete the Group Summary band but leave a blank Group Intro band.

d. Save the report as **SCHED1** and obtain a printed copy.

6. Again use the SCHED database to prepare a group report. In this instance first activate the INSTRUCTOR index tag so that the courses appear in instructor order.

   a. The report title will be **SDS DEPARTMENT SPRING SCHEDULE BY INSTRUCTOR.** Use appropriate column headings.

   b. Fields to be printed include **PREFIX, NUMBER, SECTION, TITLE, DAY, TIME,** and **ROOM.** Do not print the INSTRUCTOR field on the detail line.

   c. Add a Group band and use **INSTRUCTOR** as the *Field value.* Within the Group Intro band place the label Instructor: and display the name of the instructor.

   d. In the Group Summary band place the Count Summary field for each instructor's number of courses. Use the *Reset every* line to reset COUNT every time the INSTRUCTOR field changes. (This is the default.) A portion of the report is shown in Figure 5-35.

   e. Save the report as **SCHED2** and obtain a printed copy.

7. Prepare a custom report for the HABITAT database file stored on the data disk. This report will feature printing the contents of a memo field.

   a. The title for the report will be **HABITAT FOR HUMANITY VOLUNTEER REPORT.**

   b. Use appropriate column headings for the following fields: **FNAME, LNAME,** and **SKILL.**

   c. In the Detail band place the first two fields with one space between each field.

   d. Place the SKILL field at column 30 of the Detail band. Press **Ctrl-End** to accept the default template and picture for this field. When the cursor returns to the Detail band, select the SKILL field and change its size with the **Shift-F7** command. It should extend from column 30 to column 60.

   e. Save this report as **HABITAT1** and obtain a printed copy.

```
Instructor:  Fox
  SDS 350     3     Introduction to Mgt. Science     MWF 10:00
  SDS 350     4     Introduction to Mgt. Science     MWF 2:00    SB 205
  SDS 350    10     Introduction to Mgt. Science     MWF 3:00    SB 205
                      3 Courses
Instructor:  Hodges
  SDS 265     5     Business Statistics I            TTH 11:00   SB 206
  MIS 320     1     Survey of Data Base Management   TTH 2:00    SB 108
                      2 Courses
```

FIGURE 5-35

Partial Report for Exercise 5

8. In this exercise you will make use of the **Words** band *Style* features of dBASE. This may requires that your copy of dBASE IV be installed for the printer you are using. Your lab assistant can help you make this determination.
   a. Begin with the **CDGROUP.FRM** report stored on the data disk. We will modify this control-break report to add bold and underline to the fields.
   b. Select the title with the **F6** command and press **Alt-W** to activate the **Words** menu bar. Select the *Style* line and press **B** to turn Bold on.
   c. Select the **PUBLISHER** field in the Group Intro band and activate the Underline feature in the *Style* menu.
   d. Save the report and obtain a printed copy. This will replace the original copy of the CDGROUP.FRM file with the new settings. You can get another copy from the data disk.

CHAPTER 5 PROJECT
COMPUTER PRINTER COMPARISON

You are to gather data on computer printers and prepare tables and reports that compare features, performance and price. Sources of data include popular computer magazines such as *PC Magazine, PC Computing, PC World,* and *The Computer Shopper.* Each fall *PC Magazine* issues a comprehensive report on printers. There are several hundred printer models currently available for use with personal computers.

Possible printer classifications include 9-pin dot matrix, 24-pin dot matrix, 4 page per minute laser, 8 page per minute laser, and other models. Other fields include manufacturer name, model number, retail price, print speed, number of built-in fonts, paper width, input ports (parallel, serial, Apple LocalTalk), noise level, paper-handling characteristics (continuous, single sheet), and available accessories. Some data will require a memo field or a wide character field. Data should be coded in such a way as to provide meaning yet not take up large amounts of space. You may wish to maintain sales prices from several vendors for the same printer.

Design reports that are suitable for displaying the information in the printer database. You may wish to have some group reports by printer classification and others in alphabetical or price order. Careful attention should be paid to design of the Detail band lines to display the appropriate information in an attractive manner.

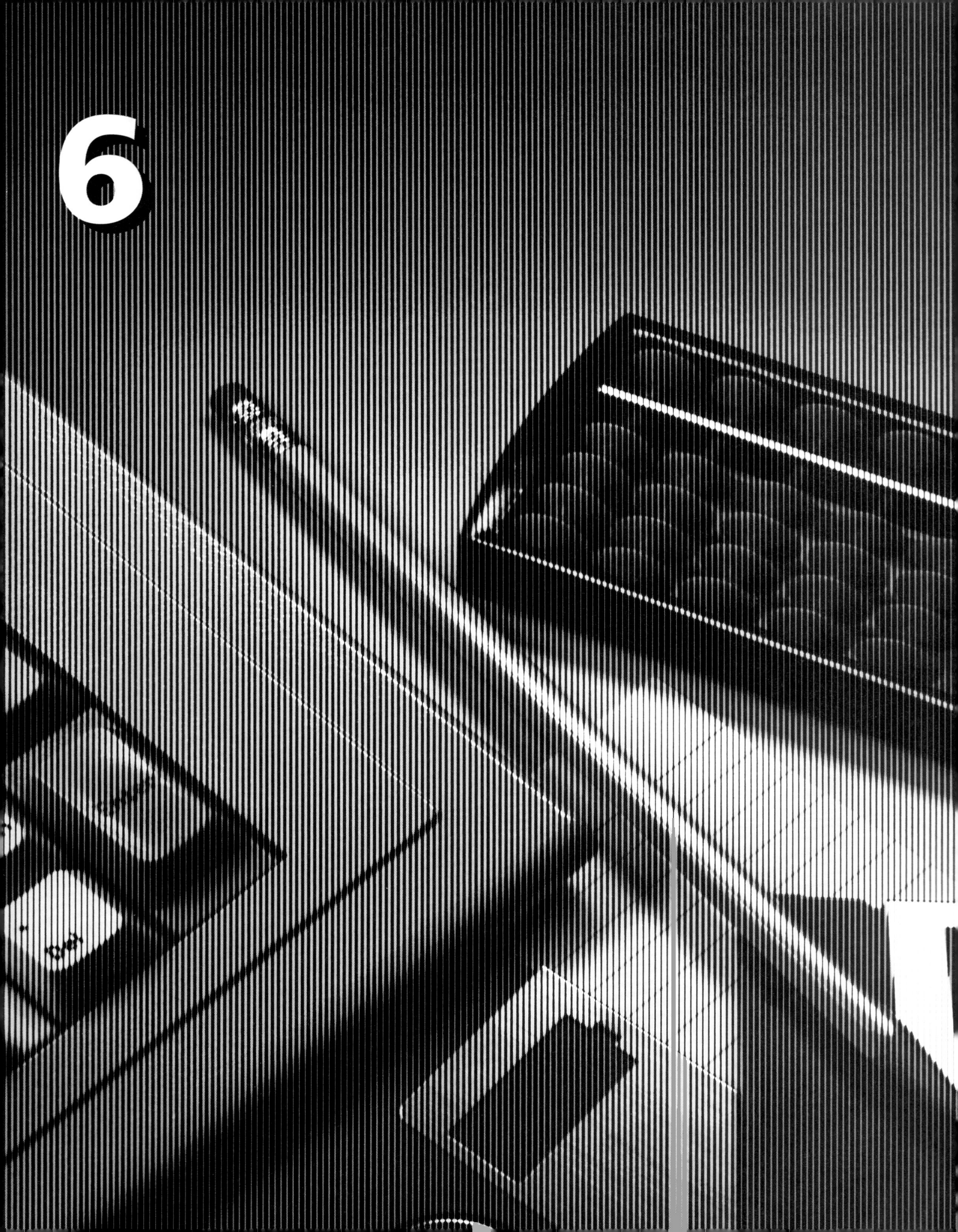
6

Using dBASE IV Dot Commands and Functions

Objectives

After completing this chapter, you should be able to:

- Compare using dBASE IV from the Control Center and from the dot prompt mode.
- Enter the dot prompt mode from and return to the Control Center screen.
- Understand and enter dBASE commands from the dot prompt.
- Describe the basic numeric dBASE operators such as +, –, *, /, and ^.
- Describe the dBASE string operators such as +, –, and $.
- List the six categories of dBASE functions.
- Provide examples of dBASE expressions using these functions.

INTRODUCTION

Each new version of dBASE has included a different menu-driven user interface. The resulting menu commands are not consistent from version to version. However, the dBASE commands issued from the dot prompt are similar in most versions. Experienced dBASE users who are not familiar with the Control Center menu commands can use the dot commands with dBASE IV.

This chapter presents a discussion of the dot prompt mode. Examples of introductory and advanced dot commands are given. The chapter introduces the concept of dBASE numeric, character, and date expressions. Many of the most common dBASE functions are illustrated, with examples of each.

ENTERING dBASE COMMANDS DIRECTLY: THE DOT PROMPT

So far we have only described accessing dBASE IV through the Control Center screens. The **dot prompt** represents another mode to use dBASE. Users of previous versions of dBASE will find that most of the commands used in those versions work in the same manner with dBASE IV. Experienced users may be able to enter commands more quickly at the dot prompt than by going through several layers of pull-down menus. All of the dBASE IV Help screens are available at the dot prompt as well as through the Control Center.

To get to the dot prompt from the Control Center, activate the Menu Bar by pressing **F10**, then move the cursor to the **Exit** bar. Execute the *Exit to dot prompt* command by pressing **Enter**. The screen will clear and you will see the dot prompt and the Status bar. The Status Bar will indicate **Command** when in the dot prompt mode, along with the name of the database file currently in use. The Status Bar maintains the record pointer's location, along with the toggle indicators and the Delete marker. Figure 6-1 shows the dot prompt screen with the CD database file in use.

Dot Command Basics

Dot commands consist of a command verb, followed by optional clauses. The square brackets around the optional clauses are *not* to be typed as part of the command. The angle brackets are *not* to be typed. The basic dBASE command format is shown below. Some commands do not use all of the clauses.

```
verb [<scope>] [expression list] [FOR <cond>] [WHILE <cond>]
     [TO PRINTER/TO FILE <file-name>]
```

- **verb** is replaced with the name of the command as explained below.
- **<scope>** is a phrase that determines which records the command will consider. Examples include **RECORD 5, NEXT 3, REST,** and **ALL.**
- **<expression list>** will depend on the particular command. Examples of commands are shown later in this chapter.
- **FOR** **<cond>** provides for a condition to be met for that record to qualify. All records are examined. For example, FOR YEAR="1983" would only allow records with 1983 in the Year field to be included.
- **WHILE <cond>** also provides for a logical condition to be met for that record to qualify. Unlike the FOR clause, as soon as records do not qualify for the WHILE condition, the command stops.
- **TO PRINTER** will cause the output from the command to be sent to the printer as well as the screen. This clause works with the DISPLAY, LIST, REPORT and LABEL commands.
- **TO FILE <file-name>** will cause the output from the command to be copied to a DOS file under the specified filename on the default disk drive. This clause works with the DISPLAY, LIST, REPORT and LABEL commands.

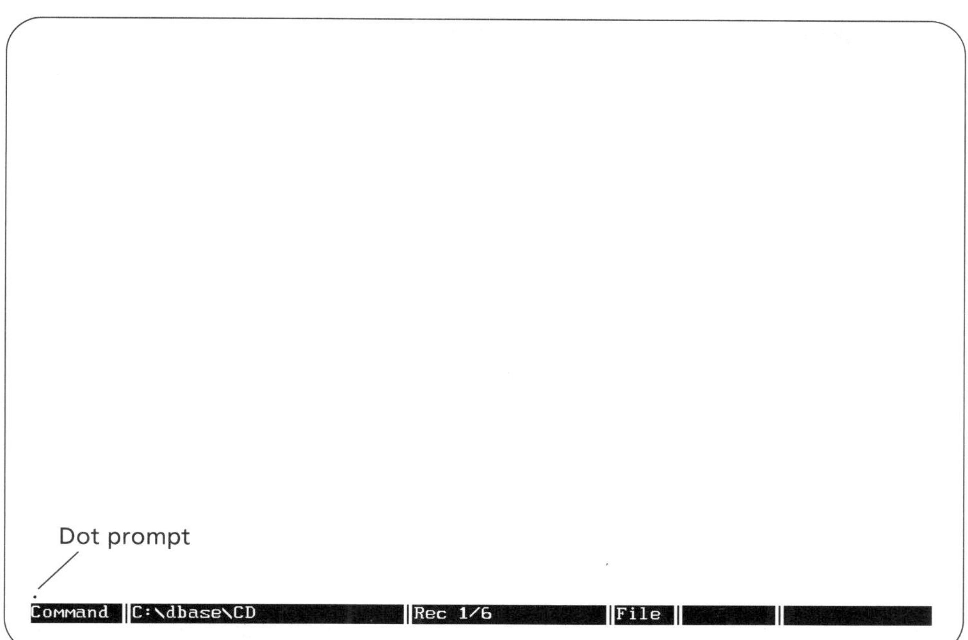

FIGURE 6-1

Command Screen for Dot Prompt Mode

Entering Dot Commands

Dot prompt commands are entered after the dot. Corrections may be made by using the backspace key; the **Ins** key can be used to toggle between Insert and Overtype modes. To execute the command, press **Enter**. You may execute the previous command by pressing the up arrow key followed by **Enter**. Each up arrow keypress brings back older commands; you can modify the commands as needed before pressing **Enter**. dBASE will maintain approximately 20 previous commands.

Spelling or other typing errors result in an error dialog box as shown in Figure 6-2. The incorrect command, **LIS**, was entered. dBASE caught the mistake and displays an error diagnostic message. It prompts the user for a Cancel, Edit or Help response.

- **Cancel** will cancel execution of the errant command and return you to the dot prompt.
- **Edit** permits you to make changes to the command line and try to execute it again.
- **Help** will bring up one or more help screens describing the error or similar commands.

In this case you would probably select **Edit**. When dBASE displays the previous command line, add the "**T**" to the end of LIS and press **Enter** to try to execute the modified LIST command.

Commands may be abbreviated by the first four letters. For example, **DISPLAY** may be abbreviated as **DISP**. You must fully spell out field names and file names.

Introductory Dot Commands

The following command verbs correspond to actions accomplished through the Control Center in the previous chapter. Command options are shown where appropriate. To receive more help on each command, at the dot prompt type **HELP <command-name>**, filling in the appropriate command name. You can

FIGURE 6-2

Error Dialog Box

also type in a portion of the command, then press the **F1** Help key; dBASE will display the Help screen that is pertinent to that command.

Creating a New Database File: CREATE

Use the **CREATE <file-name>** command to create the structure for a new database file. You will see the usual Database screen for filling in field names, types, and lengths. The Menu Bar commands at the top of the Database screen are also available by pressing **F10** as described in the previous chapter. When you have finished, press **Ctrl-End** to store the file structure. You will return to the dot prompt when the file structure has been saved. For instance, **CREATE CD** would be used to establish the database structure for the CD.DBF database file.

Using an Existing Database File: USE

To use an existing database file from the default drive, type **USE <file-name>**. The file name will appear in the Status Bar. Thus **USE CD** will open the CD database file. If you have already created a multiple index file, the index can be activated by typing **USE <file-name> ORDER <tag-name>** where <tag-name> is the name of the index tag expression. In the CD example, we created an index tag called ARTIST. Thus **USE CD ORDER ARTIST** would open the CD database file and activate the ARTIST index tag.

Editing Data Records: EDIT, BROWSE

Use the **EDIT** command to enter the Edit mode, or the **BROWSE** command to use the Browse mode. dBASE will display the current record in the Edit or Browse display mode. You can move between records in Edit with the **PgUp** and **PgDn** keys; use ↑ and ↓ in Browse. When you leave Edit or Browse by typing **Ctrl-End** (or going through the **Exit** menu bar choice), you'll return to the dot prompt. Any changes made are permanent unless you press the **Esc** key, in which case changes made to the current record are discarded, but changes to other records have already been saved.

```
. USE CD
. LIST ARTIST, YEAR, LENGTH
Record#  ARTIST              YEAR LENGTH
      1  The Canadian Brass  1983     51
      2  Wiener Philharmoni  1987     72
      3  Wynton Marsalis     1983     40
      4  Stern, Rampal       1978     44
      5  Glenn Gould         1982     51
      6  Festival Strings L  1972     62

.
Command  C:\dbase\CD          Rec EOF/6          File
```

FIGURE 6-3

Output from LIST Command

Edit and Browse can also be used with optional parameters. **EDIT 6** would move the record pointer to record 6 and display the Edit screen for that record. By adding the **FIELDS <field-list>** clause you can cause dBASE to only display the specified fields in the Edit or Browse screens; <field-list> is a list of one or more field names from the current database, separated by commas. **EDIT FIELDS ARTIST, TITLE, YEAR** would display only those three field values on each screen. By adding the **NOEDIT** clause the EDIT or BROWSE command can also be used to scroll through data records without allowing any changes to be made; adding **NODELETE** to the EDIT or BROWSE command also prohibits the user from deleting any records while in the Browse screen.

Moving the Record Pointer: GO, SKIP

The Status Bar shows the current location of the record pointer. The command **GO TOP** will move the record pointer to the top record in the database file; **GO BOTTOM** will move to the last record in the file. **GO 7** would move to record 7. The **SKIP** command is used to move the pointer forward or backward a specified number of records. For instance, **SKIP 10** will move the pointer 10 records later in the database file. **SKIP –5** will move 5 records backward. **SKIP** by itself simply moves to the next record.

Viewing Data Records: DISPLAY, LIST

The dBASE **LIST** and **DISPLAY** commands can be used to view data records on the screen, or to echo them to the printer. With no conditions specified, **LIST** will scroll through the entire database on the screen, beginning with the top record. **DISPLAY** defaults to showing just the current record. Both commands can be used to show certain fields by adding a **<field-list>** to the end of the command. With the CD database, we could enter **LIST ARTIST, YEAR, LENGTH** and see the display in Figure 6-3 on the screen.

To send the command's output to the printer, add the phrase **TO PRINTER** to the end of the LIST or DISPLAY command. In fact, most dBASE dot commands that send information to the screen can be modified with TO PRINTER so that the information is printed. Likewise, you can add **TO FILE <file-**

name> to the end of the same commands and send the output to a DOS text file with the specified name. The default file extension if none is provided is .TXT. Thus **LIST TO FILE XYZ** would produce a file called XYZ.TXT containing the output from the LIST command.

If you use a <scope>, FOR, or WHILE condition with DISPLAY, dBASE will display a screen of records, then pause at the bottom until you press any key to continue. Thus you can page through a long list of records. LIST will not pause at the bottom of the screen. For example, **DISPLAY NEXT 20** will display the next 20 records. **DISPLAY REST** will display the remaining records.

Viewing Selected Records: FOR, WHILE

It is also possible to display certain records that meet a criterion by adding the FOR condition to another command. **FOR <field-condition>** specifies a logical condition such as YEAR>"1984" or LENGTH<50. For example, **LIST FOR LENGTH<50** will display the two records whose length is less than 50 minutes, shown in Figure 6-4. The WHILE condition clause can also be used to qualify records for inclusion in a LIST or DISPLAY command.

- The FOR clause will examine *all* records that meet the condition for inclusion.
- The WHILE clause will qualify records that meet the condition until there is a record that does not meet the condition; it will not examine any additional records.

Viewing a Field or Expression: ?

The **?** (question mark) command is used to display the value of a database field, function or expression at the dot prompt. This command will not move the record pointer or examine more than a single record. For instance, typing **? ARTIST** at the dot prompt will display the Artist's name of the current record.

Adding New Records: APPEND

The **APPEND** command will cause dBASE to move the record pointer to the end of the database file and display a blank record in the Edit screen. You can then enter values into the field boxes. As each new record is filled, dBASE will display a new blank record. Terminate the APPEND operation by pressing **Ctrl-End** and the new record(s) will be saved in the database file.

You can add data from another database file to the current database file with the **APPEND FROM <file>** command. Field names must match for data to be copied from another file.

Deleting Records: DELETE, RECALL

You can mark one or more records to be deleted with the **DELETE** command. The default scope for this command is the current record. Move the record pointer to the desired record and enter **DELETE** at the dot prompt. You can delete a group of records by adding the FOR clause to the DELETE command. For example, **DELETE FOR YEAR < "1970"** would mark those records whose YEAR field was prior to 1970. You can also provide a scope such as **RECORD 5, NEXT 4, REST** or **ALL**. Records will not be actually deleted until you PACK the database, described in the next section.

The **RECALL** command will remove the **Del** deletion mark in the status bar from one or more records. The default scope for this command is the

```
. LIST FOR LENGTH<50
Record#  ARTIST              TITLE                      PUBLISHER     CATALOG_NO Y
EAR CLASS LENGTH DIGITAL
      3  Wynton Marsalis     Trumpet Concertos          CBS Master    MK37846     1
983 CL          40 .T.
      4  Stern, Rampal       Play Vivaldi & Telemann    CBS Master    MK35133     1
978 CL          44 .F.

.
Command ||C:\dbase\CD                ||Rec EOF/6           ||File ||        ||
```

FIGURE 6-4

Example of LIST FOR Command

current record. Move the record pointer to the desired record and enter **RECALL** at the dot prompt. You can also provide a scope such as **RECORD 5, NEXT 4, REST** or **ALL**. The deletion mark will be removed. RECALL has no effect on records deleted before the database file was last packed—those records were permanently erased by the PACK command.

Removing Deleted Records: PACK

The **PACK** command will permanently erase all records that have been marked for deletion. Don't issue the PACK command unless you are certain those records should be removed. There are no options to the PACK command.

Changing the Database Structure: MODIFY STRUCTURE

To make changes to the structure of the database in use, enter **MODIFY STRUCTURE** at the dot prompt. You'll see the usual Database screen and can make desired changes. When finished, press **Ctrl-End** (or go through the **Exit** Menu Bar) to save your changes. If you do not wish to save the changes, press the **Esc** key. To view the current file structure, type **DISPLAY STRUCTURE**. To print a copy of the file structure, enter **DISPLAY STRUCTURE TO PRINT**.

Creating an Index Tag: INDEX ON

The **INDEX** command is used to create a new index tag for the current database file. The command to create an index tag is **INDEX ON <key-expr> TAG <tag-name>** where <key-expr> is the name of the field you wish to index on and <tag-name> is the name of that index tag expression. For instance, in the CD database file you could enter **INDEX ON ARTIST TAG ARTIST** to create an index tag called ARTIST using the ARTIST field. Records would be displayed in ascending order by the ARTIST field. You can create a descending order index by adding the phrase **DESCENDING** to the INDEX ON command. The dot command **DISPLAY STATUS** will show the tag-names of all key expressions in the current database file.

Activating an Index Tag: SET ORDER TO

The most common way to activate an index tag is by specifying the tag-name in the USE command when the database file is opened. However, you can use the **SET ORDER TO TAG <tag-name>** command to change to a different index tag. For instance, in the CD database you could enter **SET ORDER TO TAG ARTIST** to change the master index to ARTIST. The command **SET ORDER TO** with no tag-name specified will deactivate all indexes, returning the database file to its natural order.

Finding a Specified Field Value: LOCATE, CONTINUE

The **LOCATE** command is used to find the first record having a specified field value. dBASE will search sequentially until it finds a qualifying record or reaches the bottom of the file. The dBASE function FOUND() is set to logical true (.T.) if a qualifying record is found; otherwise it is set to logical false (.F.). The command syntax is **LOCATE FOR <condition>**. For example, the command **LOCATE FOR LENGTH > 60** will determine if the LENGTH field in a record is greater than 60 minutes. Each record will be tested, in turn, until the record pointer is moved to the first record meeting the condition, or to the end-of-file location if no record matches the condition.

The **CONTINUE** command is used to move the record pointer to the *next* occurrence of the same condition. If no record matches the condition, the pointer is placed at the end of the file, and the FOUND() function is set to .F.

Locating an Indexed Record: SEEK

The **SEEK** command is similar to LOCATE except that it assumes the field in question has been indexed. If the ARTIST tag of the CD database is activated, the command **SEEK "Stern"** would look through the ARTIST index for the first record whose ARTIST field matches that expression. If found, the record pointer is moved to that record and the FOUND() function is set to .T. If not found, the record pointer is moved to EOF and the FOUND() function is set to .F. If the **SET EXACT ON** command is issued before the SEEK, dBASE requires that the two strings being compared have exactly the same length and content. The default condition (SET EXACT OFF) permits a match if the expression in the index begins with the expression in the SEEK command. For example, **SEEK "Stern"** matches the record whose ARTIST field was "Stern, Rampal". If SET EXACT ON were used, **SEEK "Stern"** would not match because the two strings do not have the same length and content.

Obtaining Help from the Dot Prompt: HELP

Type **HELP <command>** to activate the dBASE Help system from the dot prompt. Help is also available by pressing the **F1** function key. You can use the Help system in the same manner as from the Control Center.

Returning to the Control Center: ASSIST

At any time you can return to the Control Center by typing **ASSIST** and pressing the **Enter** key. (Pressing the **F2** key at the dot prompt will do the same thing.) Any file opened in the dot prompt mode remains open in the Control Center. To return to the dot prompt mode from the Control Center, press the **Esc** key. When dBASE asks if you wish to Abandon the operation, reply **Yes**. You could also press **Alt-E** and select the *Exit to dot prompt* line.

Closing the Database: USE

To close the current database, type the command **USE** (with no database file specified) at the dot prompt. This will close the current database file and return you to the dot prompt. You may also open another database file with the USE <file-name> command; the first file is closed before the new file is opened.

Leaving dBASE IV: QUIT

To leave dBASE from the dot prompt, type **QUIT**. All open files are automatically closed and you will return to the DOS prompt. You can also return to the Control Center and exit from that screen.

Example: *Using Dot Commands*

In this example we will create a financial database structure, add data to it, and perform some simple operations using dot prompt commands.

1. Begin dBASE as usual. From the Control Center, press **Alt-E** and select the *Exit to dot prompt* line. You should see the dot prompt in the lower left corner of the screen with the word Command in the status bar.
2. Issue the command **CREATE FINANCE** and press **Enter**. You will see the usual Database work surface. Enter the field information shown in Figure 6-5. When finished, save the structure by pressing **Alt-E** and selecting the *Save changes and exit* line.
3. To review the database structure, at the dot prompt type **DISPLAY STRUCTURE** and press **Enter**. dBASE will display the field information and the record size on the screen. If you have a printer attached and on line, repeat the command but add **TO PRINT** at the end; dBASE will print the structure on the printer. See Figure 6-6.
4. Next you will add the records shown in Figure 6-7 to the file. Use the **APPEND** command and add the five records.

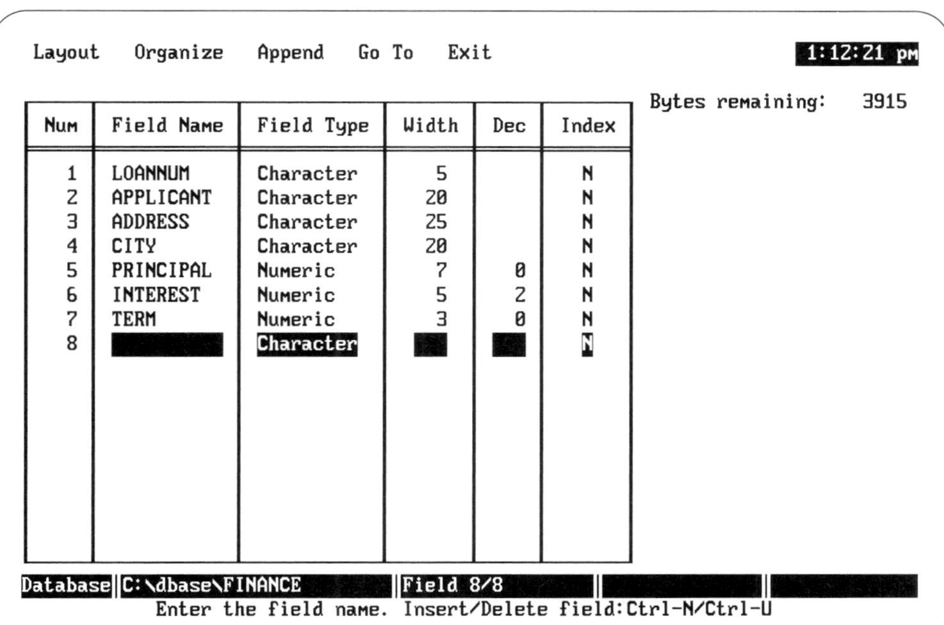

FIGURE 6-5

Field Information for the Example

FIGURE 6-6

Results of the DISPLAY STRUCTURE Command

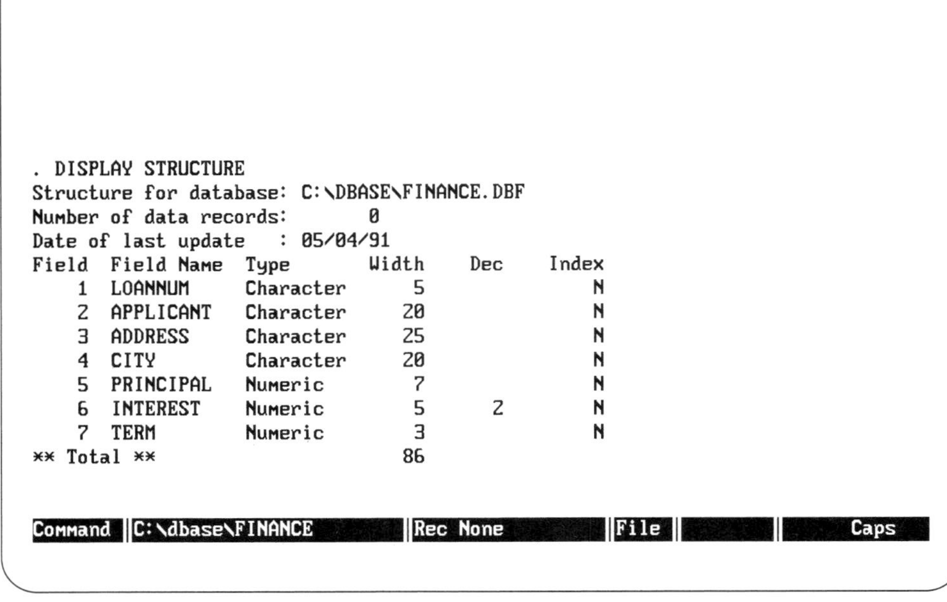

```
. DISPLAY STRUCTURE
Structure for database: C:\DBASE\FINANCE.DBF
Number of data records:       0
Date of last update   : 05/04/91
Field  Field Name  Type        Width    Dec    Index
    1  LOANNUM     Character       5               N
    2  APPLICANT   Character      20               N
    3  ADDRESS     Character      25               N
    4  CITY        Character      20               N
    5  PRINCIPAL   Numeric         7               N
    6  INTEREST    Numeric         5      2        N
    7  TERM        Numeric         3               N
** Total **                       86

Command ||C:\dbase\FINANCE     ||Rec None     ||File ||    ||    Caps
```

FIGURE 6-7

Records to be Added to the File

B2314	Smith, Sally M.	1852 1st Avenue	San Diego, CA 92133	64000	9.08	20
B2452	Wilson, William	231 Terrace Place	La Canada, CA 91011	57000	10.45	25
B3508	Perez, Jason	11820 Pendle Road	Phoenix, AZ 82410	123500	10.25	30
B6776	Lu, Lin	2407 Wyndham	Seattle, WA 98073	78000	9.35	25
B8787	Thomas, Stacy	10003 Hernadez Avenue	Indianapolis, IN 46256	80000	11.25	15

5. You will see that the CITY field is too small to contain the entire Indianapolis city and zip code for record. Issue the **MODIFY STRUCTURE** command at the dot prompt to move to the Database work surface. Move the cursor to the CITY field and change the length from 20 to 25, then use the **Alt-E** command to *Save the changes and exit.* You will be asked to confirm these changes. Press **Enter** to select Yes.

6. When the dot prompt reappears, use the **LIST** command to view the data, shown in Figure 6-8.

7. You'll note that the fifth record shows only "462" for the zipcode and there is one extra blank record at the end. Use the **GOTO 5** command to position the record pointer to the fifth record. The status bar should show "Rec 5/6" for the record pointer. Use the **EDIT** command and add **56** to the end of the CITY field in this record.

8. Next press **PgDn** to move to the sixth record. Press **Ctrl-U** to mark that record for deletion, activating the Del indicator in the status bar. Press **Alt-E** to *Exit* back to the dot prompt. [Note: You could have used the **DELETE RECORD 6** command at the dot prompt to accomplish this.]

```
. LIST
Record#  LOANNUM APPLICANT           ADDRESS                  CITY
          PRINCIPAL INTEREST TERM
      1  B2314    Smith, Sally M.    1852 1st Avenue          San Diego, CA 92
133          64000     9.08   20
      2  B2452    Wilson, William    231 Terrace Place        La Canada, CA 91
011          57000    10.45   25
      3  B3508    Perez, Jason       11820 Pendle Road        Phoenix, AZ 8241
0           123500    10.25   30
      4  B6776    Lu, Lin            2407 Wyndham             Seattle, WA 9807
3            78000     9.35   25
      5  B8787    Thomas, Stacy      10003 Hernandez Avenue   Indianapolis, IN
 462         80000    11.25   15
      6
                 0     0.00    0

.
Command ||C:\dbase\FINANCE          ||Rec EOF/6        ||File ||
```

FIGURE 6-8

Results of LIST Command

9. Enter the following dot command to display the three applicants having TERM over 20 years:

   ```
   LIST APPLICANT, PRINCIPAL, INTEREST, TERM FOR TERM>20
   ```

10. Next let's create an index tag for an alphabetical listing. Use the **INDEX ON APPLICANT TAG ALPHA** command to do so, creating a tag called ALPHA. Use the **LIST** command to confirm that the records now appear in alphabetical order.

11. Notice that record 6 appears with an asterisk following its record number. To permanently erase this record, use the **PACK** command.

12. Next we will display the monthly payment for the five records based on their loan values. We need the PAYMENT function from the next section of this chapter. This function uses the PRINCIPAL, INTEREST as a decimal, and TERM in months to calculate the monthly payment. Because INTEREST is stored in our database as a percentage, convert it to a decimal by dividing by 100. Likewise, convert TERM to months by multiplying by 12. Enter the following command whose output is shown in Figure 6-9:

   ```
   LIST APPLICANT, PAYMENT(PRINCIPAL,INTEREST/100,TERM*12)
   ```

13. Finally, we will search through this database to find specific values. At the dot prompt issue the **GO TOP** command to move to the first record. [Note: Because we have activated an index for this database, the first record is not necessarily record number 1.] We want to find the Indianapolis record, so key in **LOCATE FOR CITY="Indiana"** and press **Enter**. If it exists, dBASE will move the record pointer to that record. You do not have to key in the entire field value but must match capitalization. Type **DISPLAY** to see its fields, shown in Figure 6-10.

14. In larger databases it is much quicker to use the index lookup feature of dBASE. For this step we will search through the index for the Perez record.

FIGURE 6-9

Displaying the Monthly Payments

```
. LIST APPLICANT, PAYMENT(PRINCIPAL,INTEREST/100,TERM*12)
Record#  APPLICANT            PAYMENT(PRINCIPAL,INTEREST/100,TERM*12)
      4  Lu, Lin                                              7293.00
      3  Perez, Jason                                        12658.75
      1  Smith, Sally M.                                      5811.20
      5  Thomas, Stacy                                        9000.00
      2  Wilson, William                                      5956.50

.
Command ||C:\dbase\FINANCE        ||Rec EOF/5        ||File ||       ||
```

FIGURE 6-10

Using LOCATE to find "Indianapolis"

```
. GO TOP
FINANCE: Record No       4
. LOCATE FOR CITY="Indiana"
Record =       5
. DISPLAY
Record#  LOANNUM APPLICANT            ADDRESS                   CITY
     PRINCIPAL INTEREST TERM
      5  B8787   Thomas, Stacy        10003 Hernandez Avenue    Indianapolis, IN
 462      80000     11.25   15
.
Command ||C:\dbase\FINANCE        ||Rec 5/5          ||File ||       ||      Caps
```

Type **SEEK "Perez"** and press **Enter**. dBASE will position the record pointer to record 3. You may use the **DISPLAY** command to see its fields. See Figure 6-11.

15. To complete this dot prompt example, type **QUIT** and press **Enter**. dBASE will close the FINANCE.DBF and FINANCE.MDX files and return to the DOS prompt. When you next use dBASE the FINANCE file will appear in the Data file panel of the Control Center.

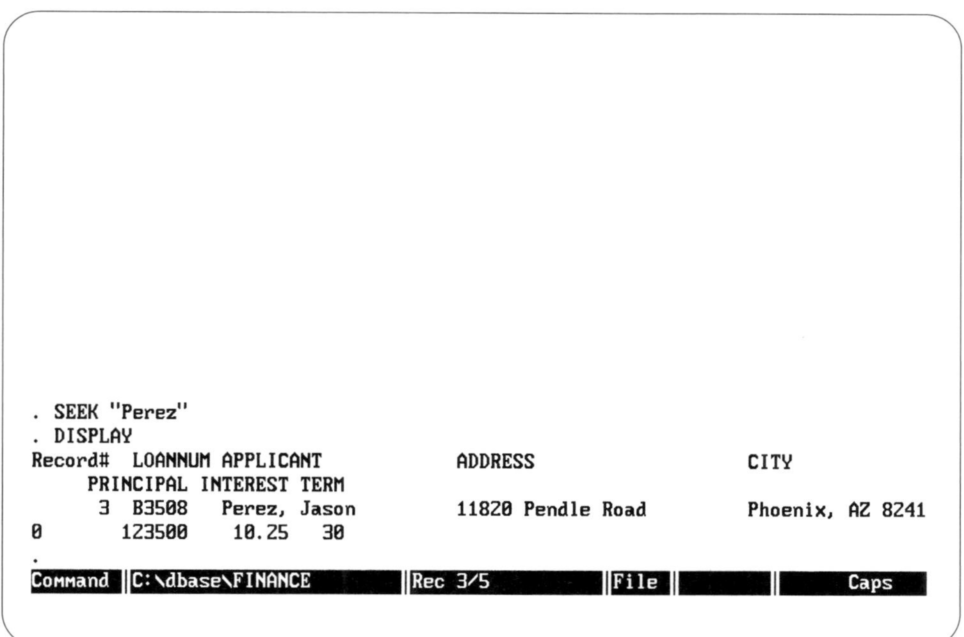

FIGURE 6-11

Using SEEK to find "Perez"

Advanced Dot Commands

The commands described in this section were explained in more detail in individual sections in the previous chapters. The REPORT, LABEL, QUERY and FORM work surfaces within dBASE may be activated from the Control Center or directly from the dot prompt. They work in the same manner from the dot prompt as when called from the Control Center. This section will illustrate how these commands are activated from the dot prompt.

Creating a Report or Label: CREATE REPORT/LABEL

The CREATE command can be used to create a new report or label design by adding the REPORT or LABEL phrase to the CREATE command. If you omit the REPORT or LABEL phrase, dBASE will think you wish to build the structure for a new database file. The usage of the command is **CREATE REPORT/LABEL <file-name>**/?. Choose between REPORT and LABEL, depending on the type of report desired. For instance, **CREATE REPORT CDTITLE** would instruct dBASE to create a new report form called CDTITLE. If the **?** is used instead of a filename, dBASE will display the names of all files of the indicated type that are stored on the default disk drive. You may select one from the list of files.

Modifying an Existing Report or Label: MODIFY REPORT/LABEL

Adding REPORT or LABEL to the MODIFY command will instruct dBASE to display the design saved under the indicated filename, and allow you to make changes to that design. The usage of the command is **MODIFY REPORT/ LABEL <file-name>**/?. Choose REPORT or LABEL according to the type of report desired. The **?** tells dBASE to display the names of all files of that type saved on the default drive; you may select a file from that list to modify.

Printing a Report or Label: REPORT/LABEL FORM

From the dot prompt you can activate a previously created REPORT FORM or LABEL FORM. The usage of the command is **REPORT/LABEL FORM**

<file-name> [TO PRINTER/TO FILE <file-name>]. Unless TO PRINTER or TO FILE is included in the command line, dBASE will display the report on the screen. The TO FILE clause will create a text file with a .PRT file extension. You may add the **FOR <condition>** or **WHILE <condition>** optional clauses to these commands.

Creating, Modifying, and Using a Query: CREATE/MODIFY QUERY, SET VIEW

The CREATE QUERY command is used to gain access to the Query screen for creating a QBE (Query-By-Example) query. The usage of the command is **CREATE QUERY <file-name>/?**. Use of the **?** will cause dBASE to display all files of that type that are stored on the default drive. The **MODIFY QUERY <file-name>** command is used to make changes to a previously created query. The dot command to activate the query is **SET VIEW TO <file-name>**. Only the records matching the conditions in that query file will be available to commands issued at the dot prompt.

Creating a Data Entry Form: CREATE SCREEN, SET FORMAT

Use the CREATE SCREEN command to open the Forms screen in preparation for building a custom data entry form. The usage of the command is **CREATE SCREEN <file-name>/?**. The **?** will display all files of the desired type that are stored on the default drive. Type **SET FORMAT TO <file-name>** to activate that screen format for the EDIT and APPEND commands.

dBASE EXPRESSIONS AND FUNCTIONS

In the previous chapter we introduced dBASE fields, the values or measurements of objects in our database. Occasionally we need to construct **expressions** involving one or more of these values or measurements. For example, if the field ANNPAY contains the annual pay of an employee of our firm, we might wish to divide that by 12 to find the monthly pay. We might want to know the year someone was hired from the hire date field. We might want the file sorted or indexed on the combination of last and first name fields. dBASE functions and expressions allow us to manipulate database fields and combine them in ways that are appropriate for the application. Expressions and functions can be used in the Query, Report and Label work surfaces wherever a database field could be used.

dBASE Expressions

Numeric Expressions

dBASE utilizes expressions that are similar to those in Lotus 1-2-3. The four arithmetic operators (**+, – ,*,/**) provide for addition, subtraction, multiplication and division for **numeric expressions.** Like Lotus, dBASE uses the ^ symbol for exponentiation, as in 2^3 or 2 to the third power. Parentheses are used to denote precedence in numeric expressions. Within the parentheses, exponentiation is done first; then multiplication and division are performed. Finally, addition and subtraction are done.

For example, the expression (1+2^3)*(4+5/2) would be evaluated as follows:

1. The first expression in parentheses, (1+2^3), is evaluated.
2. Within that expression, the exponentiation is done first. Thus 2^3 yields 8.

3. Next (1+8) is evaluated, yielding 9.
4. Then the second expression in parentheses, (4+5/2), is evaluated.
5. Within that expression, the division is done first. Thus 5/2 yields 2.5.
6. Next (4+2.5) is evaluated, yielding 6.5.
7. Finally, the two quantities are multiplied. Thus 9*6.5 yields 58.5.

Character Expressions

The + operator also works with strings of characters to **concatenate**, or join, them together. The expression **"ABC"+"DEF"** would add the two character strings together, resulting in the overall string "ABCDEF". To concatenate two database fields together, you would use **FIRST+" "+LAST** to represent one complete name, with a single space (enclosed in quotes) between the two names. In this example FIRST and LAST are field names which contain character data and are not to be enclosed in quotes. Of course, if the FIRST name value doesn't fill the complete field, there will be more than one space between the two names.

The command **INDEX ON LAST+FIRST TAG WHOLENAME** would prepare an index tag called WHOLENAME that maintains the file in alphabetical order with LAST as primary key and FIRST as secondary key. From the Control Center the equivalent *Index on expression* would be **LAST+FIRST**.

The – operator works the same way as the + operator, except that it first removes all blanks from the end of the first string. **"ABC " – "DEF"** results in "ABCDEF".

dBASE uses the **$** operator to determine whether the first string exists within the second string. Thus **"Smith"$"Smithsonian"** would return .T., but **"Jack"$"Smithsonian"** would return .F.

Date Expressions

dBASE IV provides for direct entry of dates using the {mm/dd/yy} expression. Thus **{10/22/89}** represents October 22, 1989. Dates can be compared with the relational operators <, <=, =, >=, > and <>, described below.

Logical Expressions

The relational operators in dBASE are also similar to Lotus operators, and return the logical value .T. or .F. Thus, **<, <=, =, >, >=,** and **<>** are used for less than, less than or equal to, equal to, greater than, greater than or equal to, and not equal to when comparing numeric expressions. The **<** and **>** operators can also be used to compare character strings (ASCII comparison) or dates (chronologically). Note that dBASE will *not* find that "ABC" and "abc" are equal because the capital letter ASCII codes come before the lowercase ASCII codes.

When making comparisons you may also use **.AND.**, **.OR.**, and **.NOT.** to form compound **logical expressions.** For example, the expression **STATE="IN" .OR. STATE="IL"** combines the two logical conditions so that if either is correct the overall expression is considered to be true. The **.AND.** operator requires that both conditions be true in order for the overall expression to be true.

dBASE Functions

dBASE IV has an extensive set of functions that can be used in expressions involving field values such as in Report, Label, and Query work surfaces. These functions can be grouped into the following categories:

- Date and time manipulation and conversion
- Mathematical
- Financial
- Statistical
- Character string manipulation
- Database information.

The most important functions are described here, along with examples. See the dBASE manual for a complete list of functions.

Date and Time Functions

dBASE stores dates in a special format and determines the validity of **date values** whenever they are entered. These functions provide a means of manipulating date and time values, and converting contents of data fields from or to date type fields. In the following tables "date-expr" is a dBASE date value or date expression given as {mm/dd/yy} fashion. For example, {10/22/89} represents October 22, 1989. Functions appearing without parameters must have the pair of parentheses as shown, such as **DATE()**.

CDOW(date-expr)	Displays the character name of the day of the week in a date expression. **CDOW({06/19/90})** would return "Tuesday". If a date field called XDAY contains the date 02/01/90, **CDOW(XDAY)** would return "Thursday". Also see DOW().
CMONTH(date-expr)	Displays the character name of the month in a date expression. **CMONTH({10/22/89})** would return "October". Also see MONTH().
DATE()	Returns the current system date as a character string in mm/dd/yy format.
DAY(date-expr)	Displays the numeric value for the day of the month. DAY() will be between 1 and 31. **DAY(XDAY)** would return 1.
DOW(date-expr)	Returns the numeric code for the day of the week. DOW() will be between 1 and 7. **DOW(XDAY)** would return 5, indicating Thursday.
MDY(date-expr)	Returns the character date of the date expression in Month Day, Year format. **MDY(XDAY)** would return "February 01, 90".
MONTH(date-expr)	Displays the numeric code for the month of the year. MONTH() will be between 1 and 12. **MONTH(XDAY)** would return 2.
TIME()	Returns the current system time as a character string in hh:mm:ss format.
YEAR(date-expr)	Displays the four-digit numeric year in the date expression. Thus **YEAR(XDAY)** would return 1990.

CTOD(char-expr)	Converts a character date string ("mm/dd/yy") to date format. **CTOD("02/01/90")** would create a date formatted value for that date. This function has the same effect as **{02/01/90}**.
DTOC(date-expr)	Converts a date value into a character string. Thus **DTOC(XDAY)** would return "02/01/90".

Mathematical Functions

Most of the same mathematical functions of Lotus 1-2-3 are available in dBASE IV. The most useful are described below. Trigonometric functions are available for scientific users. In the table below, "expr" refers to a valid dBASE numeric expression. The functions will return a numeric result accurate up to 18 decimal places. However, if the result is displayed on the screen, it will be rounded to the number of decimal places established with the SET DECIMALS TO command. The default value is two decimal places.

ABS(expr)	Returns the absolute value of the expression. **ABS(4–6)** would return 2.
CEILING(expr)	Returns the smallest integer greater than or equal to the expression. **CEILING(4/3)** would return 2. **CEILING (–4/3)** returns –1.
EXP(expr)	Calculates e to the power given in expr: e^{expr}. **EXP(2)** would return 7.39 if the default number of decimals were 2. The result if SET DECIMALS TO 18 was used would be 7.389056098930650407 . The value is not rounded internally, but just for display purposes.
FLOOR(expr)	Returns the largest integer that is less than or equal to the expression. **FLOOR(4/3)** would return 1. **FLOOR(–4/3)** would return –2.
INT(expr)	Converts a numeric value to an integer value by truncating the fraction. **INT(4/3)** would return 1. **INT(–4/3)** would return –1.
LOG(expr)	Calculates the natural logarithm (base e) of the expression. **LOG(2)** would return 0.69 if two decimals were the default for display purposes.
LOG10(expr)	Calculates the common logarithm (base 10) of the expression. **LOG10(1000)** would return 3.
MAX(exp1,exp2)	Returns the larger of the two expressions. The expressions may be numeric or date values. Date functions must be delimited by braces {}. **MAX(4/3,17/15)** would return 1.33 to two decimal places.
MIN(exp1,exp2)	Returns the smaller of the two expressions. The expressions may be numeric or date values, the latter delimited by braces {}. For example, **MIN(LOG(2),INT(4/3))** would return 0.69 to two decimal places.
MOD(exp1,exp2)	Returns the remainder of exp1 divided by exp2. For example, **MOD(14,3)** returns 2.
PI()	Returns the value of pi, or 3.14 to two decimal places.

ROUND(expr,n) Returns the rounded value of expr to n places. Thus **ROUND(4/3,3)** would return 1.333.

Financial Functions

The three functions in this section may be helpful when doing financial calculations relating to the time value of money. "Payment" refers to the payment per period. "Rate" refers to the interest rate per payment period, expressed as a decimal. "Term" is the number of periods for the payment or cash flows.

FV(payment,rate,term) Returns the compounded future value of **term** equal **payments** at the specified interest **rate**. For example, **FV(100,0.005,12)** would return 1233.56.

PAYMENT(prin,rate,term) Calculates the periodic payment to amortize a loan of principal amount **prin** over **term** periods at the specified interest **rate**. Thus **PAYMENT(8000,.008,36)** would yield 256.64.

PV(payment,rate,term) Calculates the present value of **term** equal **payments** at the specified interest **rate**. Thus **PV(100,.005,12)** would yield 1161.89.

Statistical Functions

The functions within this section are only available with the CALCULATE command. The syntax of the command is:

```
CALCULATE [scope] <option list> [FOR <condition>]
```

The <option list> in the CALCULATE command includes one of the following statistical functions. The FOR <condition> clause permits you to select certain records according to a criterion, similar to the Lotus @D functions. Unless the scope or a FOR condition is provided, dBASE will process all of the records. In these functions **expr** is a field name or a numeric expression.

AVG(expr) Calculates the average (mean) of the field in the specified records.

CNT() Counts the number of records that match the condition.

MAX(expr) Determines the largest value of the specified field or expression.

MIN(expr) Determines the smallest value of the specified field or expression.

STD(expr) Calculates the standard deviation of the specified field or expression.

SUM(expr) Determines the sum of the values in the specified expression.

VAR(expr) Calculates the variance of the specified field or expression.

String Functions

These advanced functions are useful for manipulating character data and preparing dBASE character expressions involving portions or combinations of character fields. Those who write dBASE programs will make use of these functions. The term "string" will refer to a string expression of text characters. Other parameters are described as needed.

AT(str,string)	Returns a value representing the starting location (in characters) of the substring "**str**" within the overall **string**. Returns 0 if the substring is not found. For example, **AT("ABC","123ABCD")** would return 4.
LEFT(string,n)	Returns the left-most **n** characters of the **string** expression. Thus **LEFT("ABCDEFG",3)** would return "ABC".
LEN(string)	Returns the length, in characters, of the **string** expression. LEN includes trailing blanks, if any. **LEN("ABCDEFG ")** would yield 8.
LOWER(string)	Converts uppercase characters in the **string** to lowercase characters. **LOWER("Smith")** would yield "smith".
LTRIM(string)	Trims leading blanks from the specified **string**. **LTRIM(" Abc")** would return "Abc".
REPLICATE(str,n)	Returns a character expression in which the "**str**" string is repeated **n** times. Thus **REPLICATE("IN",3)** would return "INININ".
RIGHT(string,n)	Returns the right-most **n** characters from the **string** expression. **RIGHT("ABCDEFG",3)** would return "EFG".
RTRIM(string)	Trims trailing blanks from **string** expression. **RTRIM ("ABC ")** would return "ABC". **TRIM(string)** is identical to RTRIM(). Thus **TRIM("ABC ")** would return "ABC". **LEN(TRIM("ABC ")** would return 3.
SPACE(n)	Returns a character string of **n** blanks. **SPACE(5)** would return " ".
STR(expr,n,pl)	Converts a numeric **expression** to a character string of width **n** and "**pl**" decimal places. Thus **STR(7/8,6,3)** yields " 0.875".
STUFF(str1,start,n,str2)	Replaces the **n** characters of string "**str1**" beginning at the **start** location with the string "**str2**". Thus **STUFF("ABCDEFG",2,3,"123")** returns "A123EFG".
SUBSTR(str,start,n)	Returns a character string from "**str**" consisting of the **n** characters beginning at the "**start**" character position. **SUBSTR("ABCDEFG",2,3)** returns "BCD".

UPPER(string)	Converts any lowercase characters in the **string** to uppercase characters. **UPPER("yes")** would yield "YES".
VAL(expr)	Converts a character **expr**ession to a numeric value. Defaults to 2 decimal places. **VAL("1.2345")** results in 1.23.

Database Functions

The functions in this group relate to the database and the record pointer's position. These functions are useful to those writing dBASE programs and those who work at the dot prompt, particularly with the Status Bar off. Logical functions return a value of True (.T.) or False (.F.). Other functions are described as needed. Functions followed by () have no parameters.

BOF()	Logical function to indicate whether the record pointer is at the beginning of the file.
DELETED()	Logical function to indicate whether the current record has been marked for deletion.
EOF()	Logical function to indicate whether the record pointer is at the end of the file.
FOUND()	Logical function to indicate whether the previous SEEK, LOCATE, or CONTINUE operation was successful.
IIF(cond,exp1,exp2)	Returns expression exp1 if the condition given in "cond" is true; otherwise returns expression exp2. The result expressions may be numeric or character type. For example, **IIF(STATE="IN",1,0)** would return the value 1 if the STATE field equals "IN", otherwise returns the value 0.
ISLOWER(expr)	Returns .T. if the first character in the string expression is a lowercase character.
ISUPPER(expr)	Returns .T. is the first character in the string expression is an uppercase character.
KEY(tagno)	Returns the index expression for the specified tag number.
LUPDATE()	Returns the date (in data type) of the last update of the database file.
MEMLINES(memo)	Returns the number of lines in the specified memo field.
MLINE(memo,n)	Retrieves line "n" of the specified memo field.
ORDER()	Provides the name of the controlling (master) index tag.
RECCOUNT()	Returns the number of records in current database file.

RECNO() Returns the record number of the record pointer.

CHAPTER REVIEW

Entering dBASE Commands Directly: The Dot Prompt

dBASE commands can be entered directly at the dot prompt or selected from the Control Center. For experienced users, the dot prompt mode provides a faster means of executing commands. The dBASE IV dot commands are almost identical to those of previous dBASE versions. Most commands follow a standard command line syntax, with several clauses or phrases that can restrict the command to certain records, or divert the command's output to the printer or a DOS text file.

Dot commands are entered at the dot prompt and are executed by dBASE as soon as the ENTER key is pressed. Pressing the ESC key will cause the command to be abandoned. The HELP command will display one or more help screens for desired commands. Previously entered commands can be re-displayed by pressing the up arrow key until the desired command appears. You can modify that command or execute it immediately by pressing Enter.

dBASE Expressions

The usual arithmetic and logical operators are available in dBASE IV. Parentheses can be used to provide levels of precedence for complicated numerical expressions. The $ operator is used to determine whether a sub-string is contained within another string of characters. Date values can be entered directly into date type fields by surrounding them with curly braces, as in {mm/dd/yy}.

dBASE Functions

Numerous functions are available to assist the user in preparing dBASE expressions involving database fields. There are functions to manipulate date and time values, to perform mathematical functions, and to do limited financial calculations. Other functions are used to manipulate character strings and to access certain database information such as location of the record pointer and status of search operations. The CALCULATE command is used to access statistical functions.

KEY TERMS

? (command)
APPEND
ASSIST (F2)
BROWSE
concatenate
CONTINUE
CREATE
CREATE REPORT/SCREEN/QUERY
date values
dBASE expressions
dBASE functions
DELETE
DISPLAY
DISPLAY STRUCTURE
dot prompt
EDIT
GO TOP/BOTTOM
HELP (F1)
INDEX ON
LABEL FORM
LEN()
LIST
LOCATE
logical expressions
MODIFY REPORT/SCREEN/QUERY
MODIFY STRUCTURE
numeric expressions
PACK
QUIT
RECALL
REPORT FORM
SEEK
SET ORDER TO
SET VIEW
SKIP
TRIM()
USE

DISCUSSION QUESTIONS

1. Write down the general syntax of a dBASE dot prompt command and explain the meaning of each phrase or clause.
2. Define the purpose and give an example of each of these dot commands.
   a. APPEND
   b. ASSIST
   c. CREATE REPORT
   d. MODIFY STRUCTURE
   e. USE
   f. INDEX ON
   g. GO TOP
   h. LIST
   i. DELETE
   j. PACK.
3. Explain the differences and similarities between the Control Center and dot prompt user modes for dBASE. What are the major advantages of each mode? Is one always preferred?
4. Give the result of each of the following dBASE expressions and functions. Also indicate the data type of the result. Be explicit.
   a. **{2/20/90}**
   b. **"MIS"$"ACCTMGTMISMKTSDS"**
   c. **12^2**
   d. **MONTH({10/29/89})**
   e. **CMONTH({10/29/89})**
   f. **TIME()**
   g. **FLOOR(13.3)**
   h. **CEILING(13.3)**
   i. **LEFT("Wednesday",4)**
   j. **UPPER("Wednesday")**
   k. **SUBSTR("JANFEBMARAPRMAYJUN",4,3)**
5. Explain how to obtain help from the dot prompt for a particular dBASE command.
6. Suppose you entered an incorrect dot command such as **USER CD**. Explain the meaning of the options in the error box in Figure 6-12.

EXERCISES

1. Begin dBASE IV as usual, but at the Control Center use the *Exit to Dot prompt* option to activate the dot prompt user mode. Use the appropriate dot commands to accomplish the following steps. Write down the complete dot commands used for each step and print output on the printer.
   a. Open the CD database file and display its structure, making an extra copy on the printer.
   b. List all of the records in the CD database file.
   c. List only the records whose YEAR field is later than 1980.
   d. List the ARTIST, YEAR, and DIGITAL fields for those records that were 100% digitally recorded.
   e. Use the Browse screen to examine the ARTIST, TITLE, CATALOG_NO, and LENGTH fields.
   f. Close the CD database file, then return to the Control Center.

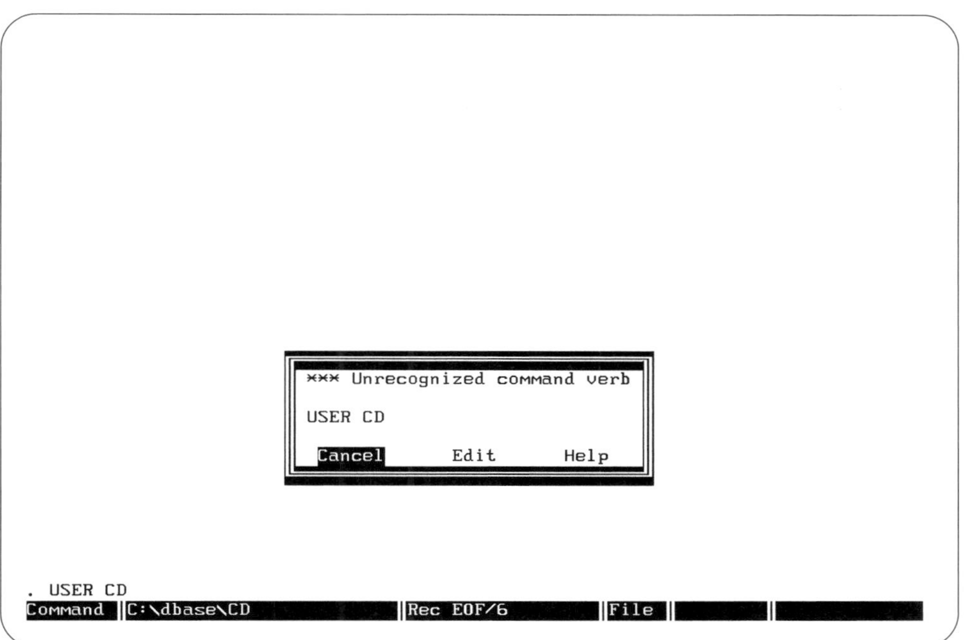

FIGURE 6-12

Dialog box for Question 6

2. From the dot prompt mode, open the SCHED.DBF database file that was introduced in the previous chapter. Prepare dot commands and dBASE functions to accomplish the following steps. Write down the complete dot commands used for each step and submit that to your instructor showing that you were able to accomplish these steps.
   a. Print a copy of the SCHED structure.
   b. Move the cursor to the first record for which the INSTRUCTOR field is “Staff”.
   c. Use the ? command to display the PREFIX, NUMBER, and TITLE for that class. Remember to separate the field names with commas.
   d. Display the full records for the classes scheduled for room SB 205. Use the command which pauses at the bottom of each screenful of data.
   e. Move the cursor to record number 16.
   f. Using the ? command, display the concatenation of PREFIX and ROOM for the course of record 16.
   g. Using the ? command, display the left-most 10 characters of the TITLE field.
   h. Use the ? command to display in uppercase the instructor’s name for record 16.
   i. List the PREFIX, NUMBER, and INSTRUCTOR for all records having a LIMIT of more than 35 students *and* being taught on TTH.
   j. List the PREFIX, NUMBER, and INSTRUCTOR for all records having a LIMIT of more than 35 students *or* being taught on TTH.

3. Use the appropriate dot commands to build the structure for the EMPLOYEE database in Figure 6-13, then add the data from Figure 6-14 to it. LIST the contents of the database to the printer.

FIGURE 6-13

Sample EMPLOYEE Database Structure for Exercise 3

Field Name	Type	Width
EMP_NAME	Char	18
DEPT	Char	10
HIRE_DATE	Date	8
SALARY	Numeric	8 (2 decimal places)
COMMENTS	Memo	

FIGURE 6-14

Sample Data for Exercise 3

EMP_NAME	DEPT	HIRE_DATE	SALARY	COMMENTS
Williams, John	Accounts	10/01/76	19500	Last assignment was carried out in exemplary fashion.
Johnson, Catherine	Personnel	12/17/81	14600	Was first in her training class and is likely to be a responsible manager.
Schmidt, James	Finance	02/01/70	33000	Handled the Limco merger negotiations exceptionally well.
Taylor, Donna	Management	08/22/86	29600	MBA, excellent record in handling problems at the Dalton strike.
Anderson, Henry	Operation	06/19/82	22450	Well-liked by colleagues, but too early to ascertain aptitude for higher management.

4. Use appropriate dot commands to accomplish the following database operations for the EMPLOYEE database of the previous problem.
   a. Create an index tag for the EMP_NAME field.
   b. List the records alphabetically on the printer.
   c. Create a second index tag for SALARY in descending order.
   d. List the EMP_NAME, DEPT, and SALARY fields on the printer.
   e. List the EMP_NAME and first four characters of the DEPT field on the printer.

f. List the name and number of years with the company on the printer. Use an appropriate time function to determine the year hired. Assume the current year.

5. Open the SCHED database. Prepare several index expressions as shown below. Document each expression and submit it along with your printed output. Clearly mark your outputs as to which index is in use for that output.
   a. Index on the INSTRUCTOR field; call the tag **INSTR**. List PREFIX, NUMBER, and INSTRUCTOR on the printer using this index tag.
   b. Index on the ROOM field; call this tag ROOM. List PREFIX, NUMBER, TIME, and ROOM on the printer using this index tag.
   c. Index on the expression **PREFIX+NUMBER** which concatenates the course prefix and number into a single character string. Call this tag **NATURAL**. List PREFIX and NUMBER to the printer using this index tag.
   d. Index on the expression **DAY+TIME**; call this tag **DAYTIME**. List PREFIX, NUMBER, SECTION, DAY, and TIME on the printer using this index tag.

6. Again using the SCHED database file, perform the following actions using the dot commands LOCATE, CONTINUE, and SEEK. For parts (a) and (b), have no index tag activated. You can do this by closing the file, then opening it again.
   a. Locate the first instance of a course taught in ROOM **SB 108**. Display that record on the printer.
   b. Next locate the *second* occurrence of a course in ROOM **SB 108**. You'll need the CONTINUE command. Display that record's contents on the printer.
   c. Activate the ROOM index tag, and repeat part (a) above for ROOM **SB 108**. Display that record on the printer. Did the SEEK command work faster than the LOCATE command?
   d. To display the next instance of ROOM **SB 108**, simply move the record pointer to the following record. Because the records are ordered by ROOM number, all the SB 108 records are together. Display the second SB 108 record on the printer.

7. Open the STOCKS database that is stored on the data disk accompanying this textbook. Do not activate any of the index tags at this time. There are 25 records in the file, whose structure is shown in Figure 6-15. Use dot commands to accomplish the following procedures.
   a. List to the printer the entire stock portfolio database.
   b. List to the printer only those stocks whose RECENT price is at least 90% of the YRHIGH price.
   c. List the records that belong to the AMEX exchange.
   d. Use the CALCULATE command to determine the total equity amount for the stock portfolio by multiplying RECENT by NO_SHARES.
   e. Activate the STOCK_NAME index tag and print an alphabetical listing of the stocks in the portfolio.

FIGURE 6-15

Sample Data for Exercise 7

```
Structure for database: C:\DBASE\STOCKS.DBF
Number of data readord:      25
Date of last update    : 11/01/89
Field  Field Name  Type        Width    Dec  Index
    1  STOCK_NAME  Character      20            Y
    2  EXCHANGE    Character       6            Y
    3  YRHIGH      Numeric         7      3     N
    4  YRLOW       Numeric         7      3     N
    5  RECENT      Numeric         7      3     N
    6  NO_SHARES   Numeric         5            N
** Total **                       53
```

CHAPTER 6 PROJECT
TEXTBOOK REFERRAL CENTER

You are to prepare a database to hold textbook information for students who wish to sell or trade textbooks at the end of the semester. The Textbook Referral Center (TRC) would serve as an alternative to the university bookstore. The TRC would act as a referral agent for students wishing to buy textbooks for a variety of courses. TRC would not buy books for later resale.

Your database should maintain information about buyers and sellers, including how to contact them. You may need to design a database file for courses or textbooks in addition to the buyer/seller database file.

The reports from TRC should display names of people who wish to sell the books for a particular class and the names of those who wish to buy the books for a particular class. Other reports might include a class list showing courses for which there are interested buyers or sellers, and a summary report showing referrals that were made through TRC. Design any other reports that seem appropriate.

7
Del

Advanced Database Management with dBASE IV

Objectives

After completing this chapter, you should be able to:

- Change the dBASE IV startup configuration.
- Add files to an existing dBASE catalog and switch to a different catalog.
- Explain the concept of a relational database.
- Discuss how dBASE can be used to access several database files in multiple work areas.
- Create a report form using fields from multiple database files.
- State the advantages of using the dBASE applications generator to create programs.
- Create a simple reporting program.
- Discuss the advantages of using the SQL mode instead of the native dBASE IV mode.
- Prepare SQL commands to create a new table, add data to the table, and retrieve records from that table.
- Discuss the differences between dBASE IV and its previous versions.
- Discuss other database management software packages.

INTRODUCTION

In earlier chapters we have illustrated the easy-to-use features of dBASE IV, including commands given from the Control Center for creating databases and reports, forms, and queries. We also introduced some of the commands from the dot prompt. In this chapter some of the more sophisticated capabilities are described for advanced users.

The startup configuration is controlled by a file called CONFIG.DB. This chapter will discuss how to make changes in this file. It also covers use of dBASE IV catalogs, including how to change catalogs and how to add a file to an existing catalog.

Relational database concepts are introduced, along with an example to illustrate use of multiple files in dBASE work areas. Multiple file queries, forms and reports are also covered, starting from the Control Center.

This chapter also includes a section on writing programs in the dBASE language, with examples. A brief discussion of the dBASE IV Applications Generator is also given.

The Structured Query Language (SQL) features of dBASE IV are covered, along with an extended example showing how SQL databases can be constructed and manipulated with dBASE.

dBASE IV is compared with earlier dBASE versions, as well as other available database management products.

CHANGING THE STARTING CONFIGURATION

This textbook assumed in previous chapters that dBASE IV had already been installed on your computer according to the default configuration settings. It is possible to customize dBASE according to individual preferences by making changes in the **Tools Menu Bar** or directly to a special file called **CONFIG.DB.** Any changes made with the **Tools** bar are not written to the CONFIG.DB file. The CONFIG.DB file that resulted from installing dBASE IV is shown in Figure 7-1. Information at the top of the file describes the colors used for various types of screen information and the type of screen display used by dBASE. In this case the screen is assumed to be a 25-line EGA color display. The CONFIG.DB file includes the line **COMMAND = ASSIST**, indicating that dBASE is to start up in the Control Center. Experienced users may wish to remove that line, preferring

FIGURE 7-1

CONFIG.DB File Listing

```
CONFIG.DB 09/15/90                                                  1


*
*       dBASE IV Configuration File
*       Tuesday August 21, 1990
*

COLOR OF NORMAL      = W+/B
COLOR OF HIGHLIGHT   = GR+/BG
COLOR OF MESSAGES    = W/N
COLOR OF TITLES      = W/B
COLOR OF BOX         = GR+/BG
COLOR OF INFORMATION = B/W
COLOR OF FIELDS      = N/BG
COMMAND              = ASSIST
DISPLAY              = EGA25
SQLDATABASE          = SAMPLES
SQLHOME              = C:\DBASE\SQLHOME
STATUS               = ON

.
Command ||C:\dbase\CD            ||Rec EOF/6      ||File ||      ||
```

dBASE to begin at the dot prompt or **SQL dot prompt**. The next two lines describe the directory for SQL databases. The final line tells dBASE to display the Status Bar whenever it displays a work panel. If your computer center has installed dBASE for specific printer models, lines containing references to those printers will also appear in the CONFIG.DB file. In most cases the settings that are already in the CONFIG.DB file should not be changed.

Using the Tools Menu Bar

The **Tools** Menu Bar appears in Figure 7-2. Press **Alt-T** to activate the **Tools** bar. The *Settings* choice is used to select and edit initial settings for dBASE. When activated, there will be two settings choices: *Options* and *Display*. *Options* choices determine how dBASE will handle various user interface items, while *Display* choices are used to tell dBASE what colors to use for parts of the screen.

Settings Options Choices

Some of the *Options* selections appear below, along with their default value, in parentheses. To make changes in these commonly used parameters, move the cursor to the desired entry and press **Enter**.

- *Bell* Enables warning beep (ON).
- *Carry* When appending new records, used to carry forward one record's values to the following record (OFF).
- *Century* Used to display all four digits of year for date fields MM/DD/YYYY; default is (OFF), indicating dates are displayed as MM/DD/YY.
- *Confirm* Requires that **Enter** be pressed when a database field has been filled; the default (OFF) means that dBASE will go on to the next field when the current field is filled.
- *Decimal places* The number of decimal places displayed when new fields are calculated or unformatted displays are shown (2).

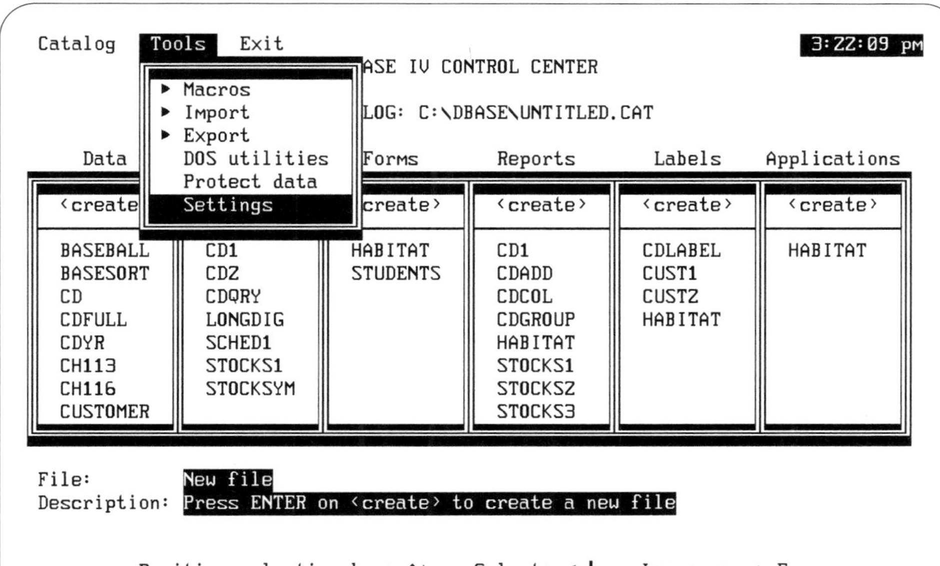

FIGURE 7-2

Tools Menu Bar (Press **Alt-T**)

- *Deleted* Tells whether to display records that have been marked for deletion; (OFF) means that deleted records are displayed. **Del** will appear in the Status Bar for deleted records.
- *Exact* Indicates whether matching strings must be the same length; (OFF) means that so long as the leading characters match, they are considered the same.
- *Memo width* The width used when memo fields are displayed. The default is (50) columns.

Settings Video Display Choices

The menu in Figure 7-3 is used to change the way dBASE shows information on the display, including colors and text attributes for various menus and screens. The first choice, **EGA25**, will depend upon the particular display of your computer and how dBASE IV was installed. EGA25 implies EGA or VGA color monitor with a 25-line display. The alternate setting for EGA or VGA color monitors is EGA43, which will display 43 lines on the screen using smaller size characters.

The colors menu shows the various colors available for the *Standard* display. To change colors you would move the cursor to the desired color for the foreground and press **Ctrl-End**. Repeat the process for the background color.

The default colors were created when dBASE was installed for your computer. The CONFIG.DB file shown earlier in this chapter contains the COLOR command lines. For instance, the COLOR OF NORMAL entry (**=W+/B**) indicates that normal text is to appear as bright white (the + indicates bright) on a blue background. Colors may also be changed from the dot prompt by use of the SET COLOR OF command. Figure 7-4 shows the color codes.

FIGURE 7-3

Display Screen from the Settings Menu Bar

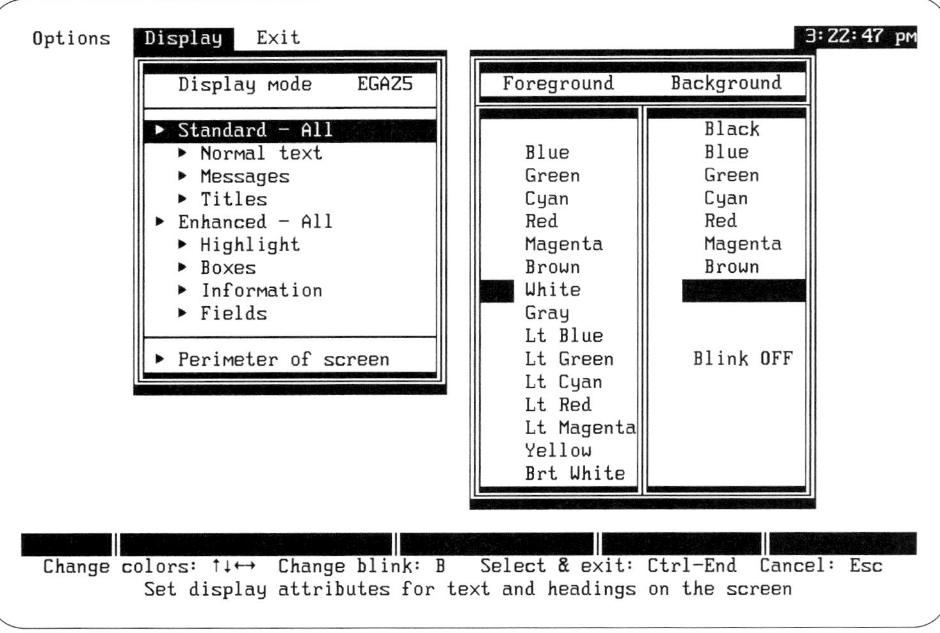

Using the Catalog Menu Bar

A dBASE IV **catalog** is a database file containing information about the various database objects (database files, reports, forms, screens, etc.) associated with a particular application. If you use the Control Center to create database, report, query, form and label files, these files are added automatically to the current catalog in use. The catalog name appears at the top of the Control Center screen, and the member files are displayed in the work panels. The catalog contains the file name and type of file, along with an optional **file description** displayed for the highlighted file. The Catalog bar appears in Figure 7-5.

Changing the Default Catalog

The start-up catalog is the one in use at the end of the previous dBASE session. You may have several catalogs within dBASE, and the default line in the Catalog bar can be used to change to a new catalog. When you activate this choice, a choice box will open at the right edge of the screen, listing all the catalogs on the default disk drive. The box at the bottom center contains the catalog description entry if one has been entered for the highlighted catalog. To create a new catalog, use the **<create>** entry at the top of the choice box. Figure 7-6 shows the change catalog screen.

Black	=	N or blank	Red	=	R
Blue	=	B	Magenta	=	RB
Green	=	G	Brown	=	GR
Cyan	=	BG	Yellow	=	GR +
Blank	=	X	White	=	W
Gray	=	N +			

FIGURE 7-4

Codes for Selecting Screen Colors

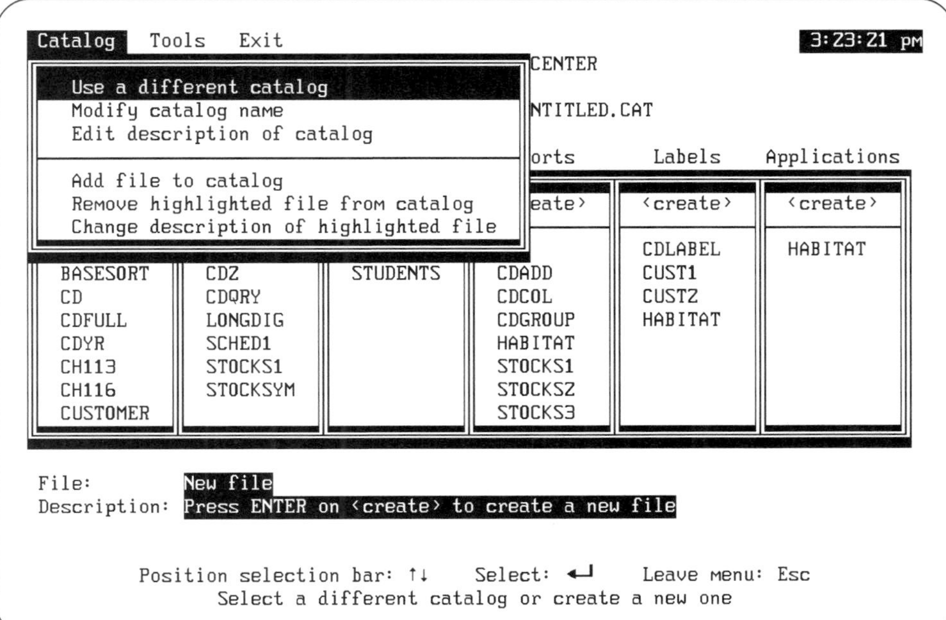

FIGURE 7-5

Catalog Menu Bar Screen (Press **Alt-C**)

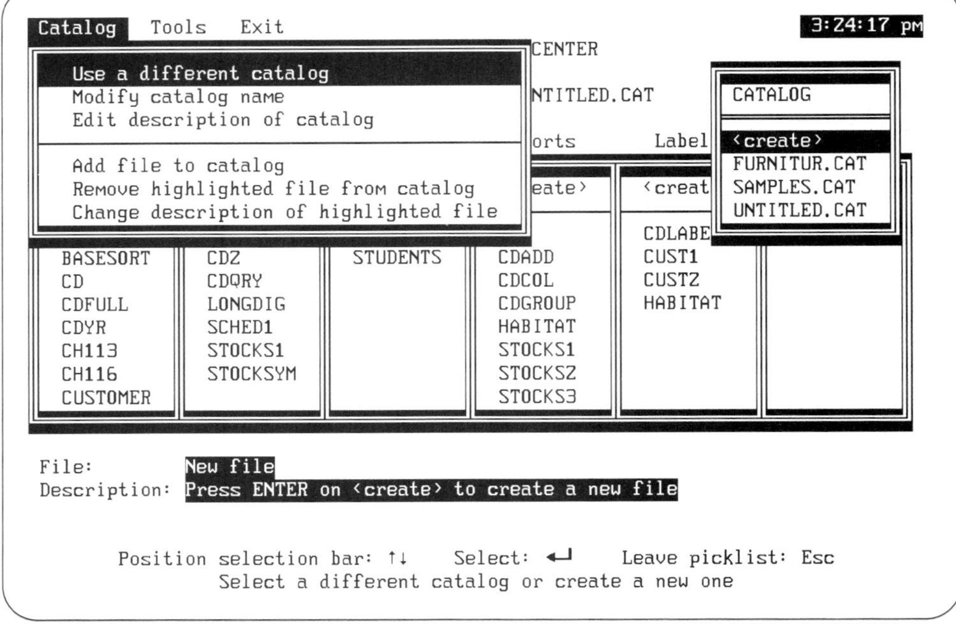

FIGURE 7-6

Control Center with Change Catalog Menu Bar Selection

Adding a File to the Catalog

Files created from the dot prompt or outside of dBASE IV are not automatically added to the current catalog when they are used. Therefore they do not appear in the file panels of the Control Center. Move the cursor to the file panel of the type of file you wish to place in the catalog. Use the *Add file to catalog* line of the **Catalog** bar to add a file to the current catalog. A list of files will appear in a file box at the right side of the screen, and you can move the cursor to the desired file and press **Enter** to select that file. If the file you choose is already in the catalog, you will get a beep and an error message. Only files of the current panel type are displayed in the box; if the cursor was in the Reports panel when you activated the add file line, only .FRM and .FRO files will be shown.

Removing a File from the Catalog

To remove a file from the catalog, first move the cursor to that file in the appropriate file panel, then activate the **Catalog** Menu Bar and select the *Remove highlighted file from catalog* option line. Unless a file has first been highlighted, the *Remove highlighted file* option line will appear dimly lit and not available as an option.

Changing the Description of a File

First move the cursor to the desired file in the proper Control Center file panel, then activate the **Catalog** Menu Bar. Choose the *Change description of highlighted file* option line. dBASE will open a dialog box for you to fill in the description. Once entered, this description appears in the bottom part of the Control Center whenever you move the cursor and highlight the file. This can be done for any file in any of the file panels. We recommend that you provide descriptions for all your database files so that they may be clearly identified.

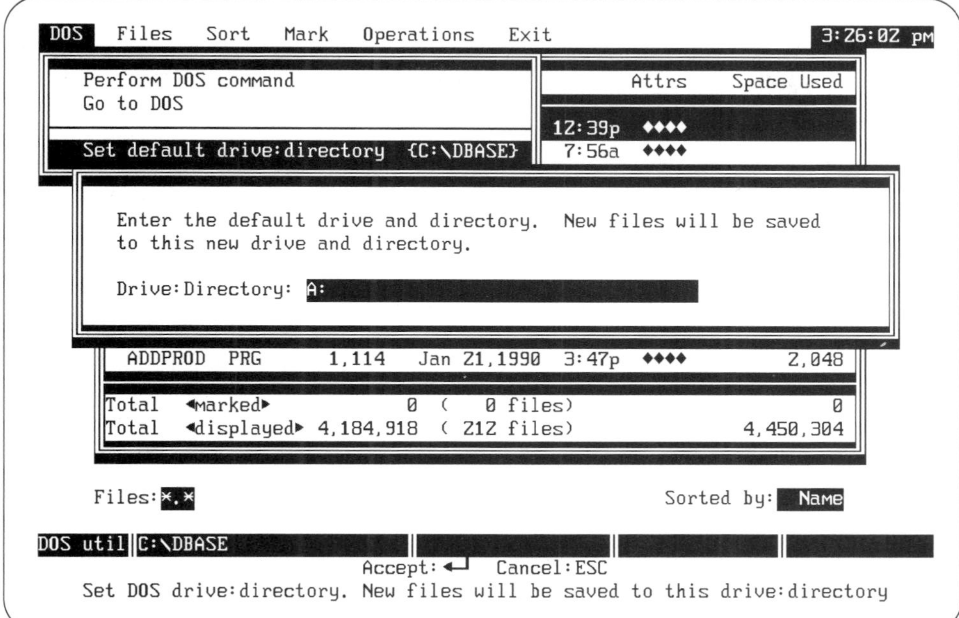

FIGURE 7-7

Set Default Directory Screen

Changing the Default Directory

To access files from a different disk directory, use the **Tools** Menu Bar and select the *DOS utilities* line. When the screen shows the directory display, move the cursor to the desired directory name and press **Enter**. When you return to the Control Center you will have access to files from the selected directory, and new files will be placed in that directory.

Example: *Changing the Default Directory to the A Drive*

For this example you will change the default directory to the A drive. All files will be saved to the new default directory during this session. The permanent settings in the CONFIG.DB file are *not* changed with this procedure.

1. From the Control Center press **Alt-T** to select the **Tools** Menu Bar. Press **D** to activate *DOS settings*.
2. At the DOS Util screen press **Alt-D** to select the **DOS** Menu Bar.
3. Press **S** to choose the *Set default drive:directory* line. Insert a formatted floppy disk into the A drive of your computer.
4. Then type **A:** (you may have to delete the current directory to leave just A: at the prompt) and press **Enter** to complete the entry. The screen should resemble Figure 7-7.
5. Press **Alt-E** and **Enter** to return to the Control Center. Notice that the default catalog near the top of the screen has the A: prefix in front, indicating that your change took effect.
6. You should change the default directory back to its original setting. Either repeat steps 1–5 for the default directory, or Quit from dBASE and begin again. The original default directory will be restored.

WORKING WITH MULTIPLE DATABASE FILES

The ability to work with several database files at the same time is one of the advantages of dBASE IV and other high-end database management software packages. Relational database management systems provide a way of linking database files containing related information. Reports containing fields from related files can be generated using the dBASE IV Reports facility. Forms can be created that collect information for several files. Views linking several files are also easily prepared from the Control Center.

Relational Database Capabilities

The **relational database** is the most popular database model used today. Information is stored in one or more **flat-file tables** where the columns represent fields and the rows represent records. (dBASE IV uses the table concept for the database file.) It is more convenient to store data in several smaller tables than to put it together in one large file. Tables are related to one another through common field values. For example, we might have a customer master file containing information about customers and an orders file containing information about specific customer orders. When information is desired from both tables, the fields are accessed from rows in which the account number field values match.

Designing the Relational Database

We'll use a furniture manufacturer order entry system to illustrate the relational database model principles. Suppose our organization keeps a list of customers and related information in a table called **CUSTOM**. The CUSTOM table contains the customer number, name, address, telephone number, last purchase date, and other permanent information about the customer. The CUSTOM table is indexed by customer number and customer name.

Our organization also keeps information about the products we sell in a table called **PRODUCTS**. This table contains the product number, name, unit price, current inventory balance, reorder quantity, and other permanent information about products. The PRODUCTS table is indexed on product number.

When a customer makes an order, a third table called **ORDERS** is created. Each row in ORDERS contains the order number, customer number, order date, delivery date, and other information relating to that order. ORDERS is indexed by order number and customer number. We can **relate** the CUSTOM and ORDERS tables together by matching the common customer number. Because names are not unique, it is preferable to use the unique customer number as the match field.

A fourth table contains line item information about the products within a specific order. This table is called **ITEMS**, and contains a row for each product in each customer order. The table includes the order number, product number, and quantity of that part ordered, and other information pertinent to that line item. This table relates the ORDERS and PRODUCTS tables: the order number can be matched with one from ORDERS and the product number can be similarly matched with one from the PRODUCTS table. The ITEMS table is indexed on the expression ORDER_NO+PRODUCT_NO, also known as a **concatenated key.**[1]

One way to represent the organization of our four-table database is to provide the name of each table and, in parentheses, the names of the fields in

---

1 We need the concatenated key because there may be several records with the same order number, and several records with the same product number. The combination of ORDER_NO+PRODUCT_NO uniquely identifies a particular row in that table.

```
   CUSTOM     (CUST_NO, CUST_NAME, ADDRESS, CITY, STATE, ZIP,
               PHONE, LAST_ORDER)
 PRODUCTS     (PROD_NO, PROD_NAME, PRICE, ON_HAND, REORDER)
   ORDERS     (ORDER_NO, CUST_NO, ORDER_DATE, DEL_DATE)
    ITEMS     (ORDER_NO, PRODUCT_NO, QTY)

     The primary index fields for each table are in italics.
```

FIGURE 7-8

Order Entry System Relational Database Design

that table. The primary index fields for each table are italicized.[2] Figure 7-8 shows the design of our relational database.

We can think of several input operations with our sample database that would require a data entry form. We could add new customers or modify the information for an existing customer. We might add or modify the product information for one of our products. When a customer places an order, we would add a record to the ORDER table plus a row in the ITEMS table for each product within that order. The first two operations each use just one table, but the third operation will use all four tables.

Several reports will be prepared using data from the tables. A customer list only requires the CUSTOM table, and a product report can be prepared from the PRODUCTS table. But filling in the order form will require data from all four tables. The order date and order number will come from the ORDERS table. The customer data will come from the CUSTOM table for the customer number that matches the one from the ORDERS record. The line items for that order come from the ITEMS table. Each line item's price and product name will be taken from the PRODUCTS table.

Example: *Sample Tables for the Order Entry System*

The order entry system described above could represent a furniture manufacturer. The tables in Figure 7-9 contain typical data for customers, orders, items, and products. For this example, and others in the chapter, we will use a new catalog called FURNITUR.

1. To create a new catalog, press **F10** from the Control Center screen and select **Catalog** on the Menu Bar. (Or press **Alt-C** from the Control Center display.)

2. Press **Enter** to choose the first line, *Use a different catalog.*

3. When the dialog box appears, select the **<create>** option and enter the name **FURNITUR**. [Note: Remember that catalog names follow DOS filename restrictions, with a maximum of eight characters.]

4. All of the file panels will be empty in your new catalog. Because we used a different database file called CUSTOMER.DBF in an earlier example, enter the name CUSTOM to represent the customer file. Create the database structure for the CUSTOM.DBF file and add the data from Figure 7-9.

---

2 These tables have been **normalized** to permit easier retrieval and data modification. Relational database theory suggests that the database be placed in normal form such as this one. Refer to a database management textbook for a thorough discussion of normalization techniques.

FIGURE 7-9

Contents of Sample Data Files for Furniture Order-Entry Example

CUSTOM Table

CUST_NO	CUST_NAME	ADDRESS	CITY	STATE	ZIP	LAST_ORDER
1004	Williams Gallery	2604 Elm Street	Terre Haute	IN	47802	10/21/89
1007	Fox Furniture	1008 Main Street	Oblong	IL	62456	02/01/88
1013	Mason Sofa	850 Kingston Pike	Knoxville	TN	39722	06/19/89
1020	Weaver's Dept. Store	801 Webster Avenue	Murray	KY	42071	01/03/90
1023	The Table Gallery	P.O. Box 17086	Baltimore	MD	21203	01/12/90
1028	The Wood Shop	124A Highland Towers	Detroit	MI	48202	11/11/89
1030	Lovejoy's Furniture	3812 Walnut Avenue	Indianapolis	IN	46226	12/06/89

ORDERS Table

ORDER_NO	CUST_NO	ORDER_DATE	DEL_DATE
1112	1004	01/15/90	03/01/90
1113	1013	01/15/90	02/24/90
1114	1020	01/16/90	01/31/90

ITEMS Table

ORDER_NO	PRODUCT_NO	QTY
1112	14352	5
1112	14453	5
1112	14552	5
1113	16253	3
1113	17352	12
1114	16253	2

PRODUCTS Table

PROD_NO	PROD_NAME	PRICE	ON_HAND	REORDER
14253	60" Bookcase	224.95	10	30
14352	48" Bookcase	199.95	14	25
14453	30" Bookcase	144.00	10	30
14552	24" Bookcase	122.35	21	50
16253	Student Desk	179.95	15	25
17352	Sm Kitchen Chair	75.50	25	60
17552	Kitchen Chair	95.50	45	90
21152	End Table	119.45	11	25

5. You should create the remaining database structures and add the data from Figure 7-9. These files are also stored on the data disk.

dBASE Work Areas

So far in our discussions of dBASE IV we have dealt with only one database file at a time. In fact, the Control Center permits only a single database file to be in use from the Data panel unless you link multiple files in a Query. But from the dot prompt (and in dBASE programs) you can have up to ten database files open at the same time, each in its own work area.

Work areas are identified in three ways: by number (1–10), by letter (A–J), or by the **alias** of the file that is open in that work area. The alias is another way of naming the database file and is usually shorter than the full file name. From the dot prompt, you can select a specific work area with the SELECT command, then open a file in that area. For example, the following dot commands will open the CUSTOM.DBF file in work area 1 and ORDERS.DBF in work area 2.

```
SELECT 1
USE CUSTOM ALIAS CU
SELECT 2
USE ORDERS ALIAS OR
```

The alias for work area 1 is CU: if you precede the field name with **CU–>** dBASE will assume that it is from the file whose alias is CU. In this case, **CU–>CUST_NO** refers to the value of the CUST_NO field from the current record in work area 1, the CUSTOM file. **OR–>CUST_NO** refers to the current value of the CUST_NO field from the current record in the file now open in work area 2, the ORDERS file. In this way you may have values from fields with the same name, but from different work areas. From the dot prompt dBASE will allow you to access data from any of the database files that are open in one of the ten work areas.

Linking Data Files with Query

You can use the Query work surface from the Control Center to create a View that accesses data from multiple database files without opening each in a separate work area. The following example links values from several tables, based on common field values, to create **linked data files.**

Example: *Linking Two Database Files with Query*

Suppose we wish to link the ITEMS and PRODUCTS files together to determine the price for each line item. The ITEMS table contains the product number and quantity ordered fields, but no price. The PRODUCTS table contains the product name and price fields. We want to print a revised table containing the information from ITEMS and PRODUCTS, including the extended price (quantity * price).

1. Begin dBASE as usual. From the Control Center select the **Catalog** Menu Bar by typing **Alt-C**.
2. Press **Enter** to select *Use a different catalog.* Move the cursor to the FURNITUR catalog and press **Enter**.
3. First open the ITEMS database file from the Control Center, then select the **<create>** line in the Query panel. The three ITEMS fields will appear in the file skeleton at the top of the query display.
4. Next we want to add the PRODUCTS file to the screen. Activate the Menu Bar with **F10**, and choose the **Layout** option. Select the *Add file to query* line, and choose the PRODUCTS file from the next box. The screen will look like Figure 7-10.
5. We next need to create the **Link** between the two tables. If not already there, press the **F3** key to move the cursor up to the PRODUCTS table, and press the **Tab** key to move the cursor over to the PROD_NO field.

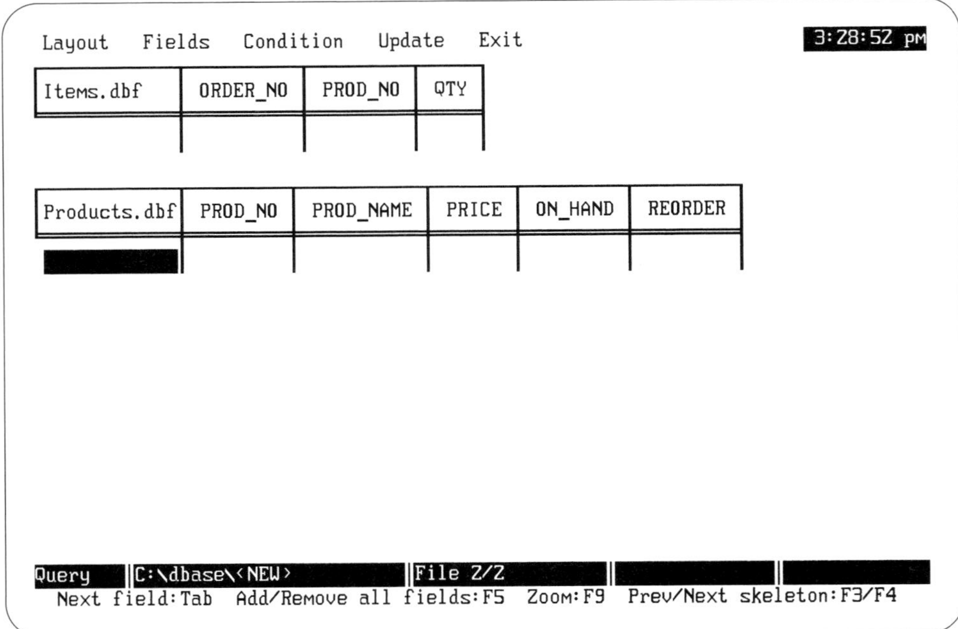

FIGURE 7-10

Query Screen with Both Files in the File Skeleton

6. Activate the Menu Bar, and select the *Create link by pointing* line from the **Layout** bar. The phrase LINK1 will appear in that box.
7. Use the **F3** key to move the cursor to the ITEMS table skeleton, and press the **Tab** key until the cursor is in the PROD_NO field of that table. Press **Enter** and the corresponding LINK1 indicator will also appear in that box. dBASE will link records from the two tables which have matching product numbers. [Note: The linked fields do *not* have to be named the same.]
8. Next we must place fields in the View skeleton. Move the cursor to the ORDER_NO field in the ITEMS file and press **F5**.
9. In a similar manner add the PROD_NO and QTY fields from the ITEMS.DBF file to the view skeleton.
10. Press **F4** to move the cursor to the PRODUCTS.DBF row. Move the cursor to the PROD_NAME field of PRODUCTS table skeleton and press **F5** to place it in the View skeleton.
11. Similarly select the PRICE field for the View skeleton. The View skeleton should resemble Figure 7-11.
12. Press **F2** to view the data from the linked view, shown in Figure 7-12.
13. Press **Alt-E** and select *Transfer to Query Design*.
14. Next activate the Menu Bar and select the *Create calculated field* line from the **Fields** bar. Type the expression for that value, **QTY*PRODUCTS–>PRICE**, followed by **Enter**.
15. Press **F5** to select the calculated field and place it in the View skeleton at the bottom of the screen. When the box opens, use the name EXT_PRICE for the calculated value. Figure 7-13 shows the View with the calculated field.

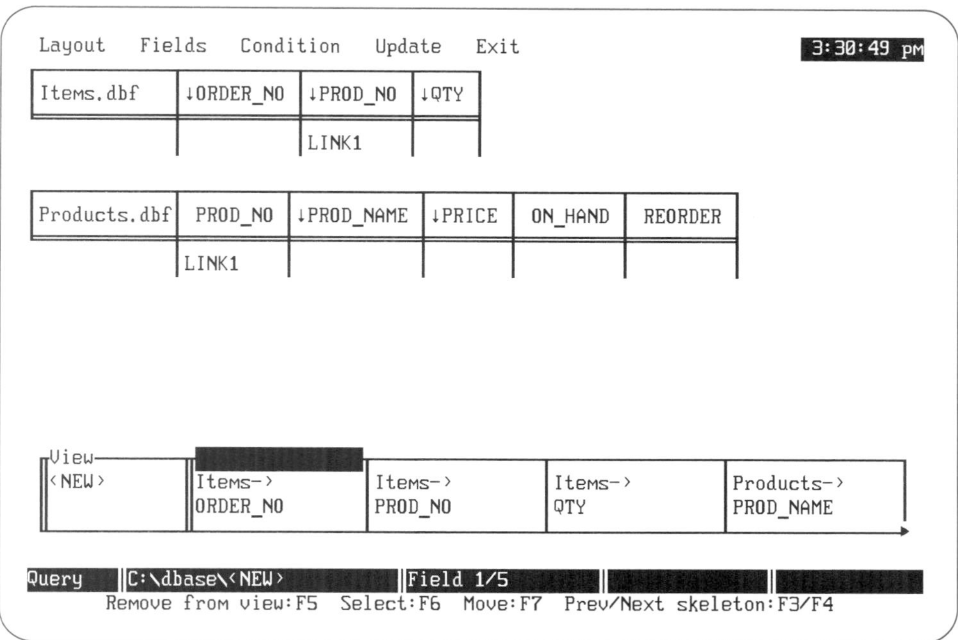

FIGURE 7-11

Query Screen with Link in Place

Records Organize Fields Go To Exit

ORDER_NO	PROD_NO	QTY	PROD_NAME	PRICE
1112	14352	5	48" Bookcase	199.95
1112	14453	5	30" Bookcase	144.00
1112	14552	5	24" Bookcase	122.35
1113	16253	3	Student Desk	179.95
1113	17352	12	Sm Kitchen Chair	75.50
1114	16253	2	Student Desk	179.95

Browse C:\dbase\<NEW> Rec 1/6 View ReadOnly

FIGURE 7-12

View of the Data from the Query (Press **F2**)

16. Save the query by typing **Ctrl-End**. Call it **EXTENDED** and dBASE will save the query as EXTENDED.QBE.

Saving Linked Data Files as a New Database File

dBASE IV is able to link the two database files upon command, as illustrated in the previous example. You can also save the view as a separate database file. The new file can be used in other applications, such as reports, or have its own indexes. Of course, it contains fields from the two linked data files that were in

FIGURE 7-13

View of the Data from the Query with the Calculated Field (Press **F2**)

```
Records   Organize   Fields   Go To   Exit

ORDER_NO PROD_NO QTY PROD_NAME          PRICE  EXT_PRICE
1112     14352     5 48" Bookcase       199.95     999.75
1112     14453     5 30" Bookcase       144.00     720.00
1112     14552     5 24" Bookcase       122.35     611.75
1113     16253     3 Student Desk       179.95     539.85
1113     17352    12 Sm Kitchen Chair    75.50     906.00
1114     16253     2 Student Desk       179.95     359.90

Browse  C:\dbase\EXTENDED   Rec 1/6   View  ReadOnly
```

existence when the view was created and saved, not their current values if you have further changed the original database files. You may wish to recreate the linked view if the data values change, or if new records are added.

Example: *Saving a Linked View as a Database File*

We'll start with the previous example's view.

1. From the Control Center select the **EXTENDED** file from the Queries file panel and return to the Query work surface.
2. Press **Alt-L** to select the **Layout** bar. Press **W** to choose the *Write view as database file* line. dBASE will save the file as EXTENDED.DBF unless you override the file name. Press **Enter** to confirm the name.
3. Type **Alt-E** to exit from the Query work surface and return to the main Control Center screen.
4. You'll now see EXTENDED listed among the files in the Data panel. Move the cursor to that file and press **Enter** to use that database file. Its structure is shown in Figure 7-14. The data values are identical to those shown in the Query example above.

Creating a Report from Linked Files

The easiest way to build a report from multiple files is to first link them with a Query like EXTENDED. Use the **EXTENDED.QBE** view then choose **<create>** from the REPORT file panel. All the fields selected for that view will be available for the report in read-only fashion. The following example of a **report program** will illustrate building a report from a view.

Example: *Building a Report from a Linked View*

This example will use the EXTENDED.QBE view to prepare a report showing the data from the linked PRODUCTS and ITEMS database file.

```
Layout  Organize  Append  Go To  Exit                                3:40:53 pm

                                                        Bytes remaining:   3940
 Num | Field Name | Field Type | Width | Dec | Index
  1  | ORDER_NO   | Character  |   4   |     |   N
  2  | PROD_NO    | Character  |   5   |     |   N
  3  | QTY        | Numeric    |   4   |  0  |   N
  4  | PROD_NAME  | Character  |  20   |     |   N
  5  | PRICE      | Numeric    |   7   |  2  |   N
  6  | EXT_PRICE  | Numeric    |  20   |  2  |   N

Database  C:\dbase\EXTENDED          Field 1/6
          Enter the field name. Insert/Delete field:Ctrl-N/Ctrl-U
Field names begin with a letter and may contain letters, digits and underscores
```

FIGURE 7-14

Database Structure for EXTENDED.DBF Database File

1. At the Control Center move the cursor to the **EXTENDED** view in the Queries file panel and press **Enter** two times to use that view.
2. From the Control Center move the cursor to the **Reports** panel and select **<create>**.
3. Next build the report as usual. If not already active, press **Alt-L** to activate the **Layout** Menu Bar and choose the *Quick layouts* option, *Column* format by pressing **Enter** two times.
4. dBASE will place the fields from the **View skeleton** on the Report work surface. You should remove the total price field in the Report Summary band because adding unit prices is not meaningful. Move the cursor to the total price field in the Report Summary band and press the **Del** key.
5. You should add a suitable title such as **FURNITURE EXTENDED PRICING**, centered above the columns in the report. Modify column headings as needed to clarify contents of the report.
6. Press **Alt-P** followed by **Enter** to begin printing the report shown in Figure 7-15.
7. Press **Ctrl-End** to save the report. Call this report **EXTENDED**.

Using Other Data Files: APPEND FROM and COPY TO

dBASE can accept data from sources other than the keyboard. The **APPEND FROM** command is used to read data from other database files—values from fields with the same name as the database file in use are added to the end of the file. You can add a FOR clause to this command that specifies which of the records are appended from the other file. The IMPORT command is able to do limited conversion from other types of database files, such as Lotus 1-2-3, pfs:FILE and Framework. The dBASE IMPORT and APPEND FROM commands are discussed in Chapter 9.

The **COPY TO** command allows the user to copy data values from the current database in use to another database or text file. The FOR clause may be added to specify which records are to be copied. The EXPORT command is

FIGURE 7-15

Report Form Generated from the EXTENDED Query

```
Page No.    1
12/13/89
                         FURNITURE EXTENDED PRICING

ORDER     PRODUCT                                                EXTENDED
NUMBER    NUMBER      QTY  PRODUCT DESCRIPTION           PRICE      PRICE

1112      14352         5  48" Bookcase                 199.95    $999.75
1112      14453         5  30" Bookcase                 144.00    $720.00
1112      14552         5  24" Bookcase                 122.35    $611.75
1113      16253         3  Student Desk                 179.95    $539.85
1113      17352        12  Sm Kitchen Chair              75.50    $906.00
1114      16253         2  Student Desk                 179.95    $359.90

   TOTALS              32                                       $4,137.25
```

used to do conversions of the dBASE database into other formats. The EXPORT and COPY TO commands are also illustrated in the final chapter.

CREATING CUSTOM COMMAND-FILE PROGRAMS

dBASE programs consist of dot prompt commands and programming statements that are stored in disk files with the .PRG extension. These **command-file programs** serve the same purpose as Lotus macros—to automate the execution of certain command steps and to provide for a more sophisticated environment for entering and retrieving data records.

Advantages of Custom Programs

Previous dBASE versions were quite limited in the kinds of reports that could be created from the Reports screen. So writing programs to improve the report's appearance was common. dBASE IV has several new features that reduce the need for writing custom report programs. There are situations where even the dBASE IV capabilities are not quite what are desired. Custom programs can place information virtually anywhere on the screen or page.

Another reason for custom programs is to automate the execution of certain commands that are frequently used. This is especially useful for new users who are unfamiliar with dBASE commands. Because dBASE is capable of far more than single-file data management, some users will develop systems of programs with custom menus and sophisticated processing steps. Thus a less-sophisticated user can work with a **turn-key system**, one that is written specifically for the application.

Although dBASE IV is able to prepare custom data entry screens, there may be some advantages to writing programs to accept data. You can check the type of data entered or assure that values fall within a specified range. Based upon certain input values, you can branch to other screens.

Working with dBASE Program Files

Rather than programming in COBOL or another business programming language, our database programs are written in the dBASE language. Developed over many years and several versions of dBASE, the language has become something of an industry standard. Programs can be created and edited from within dBASE, then executed whenever desired. dBASE automatically adds the .PRG extension to a program file when it is saved. When you run the program

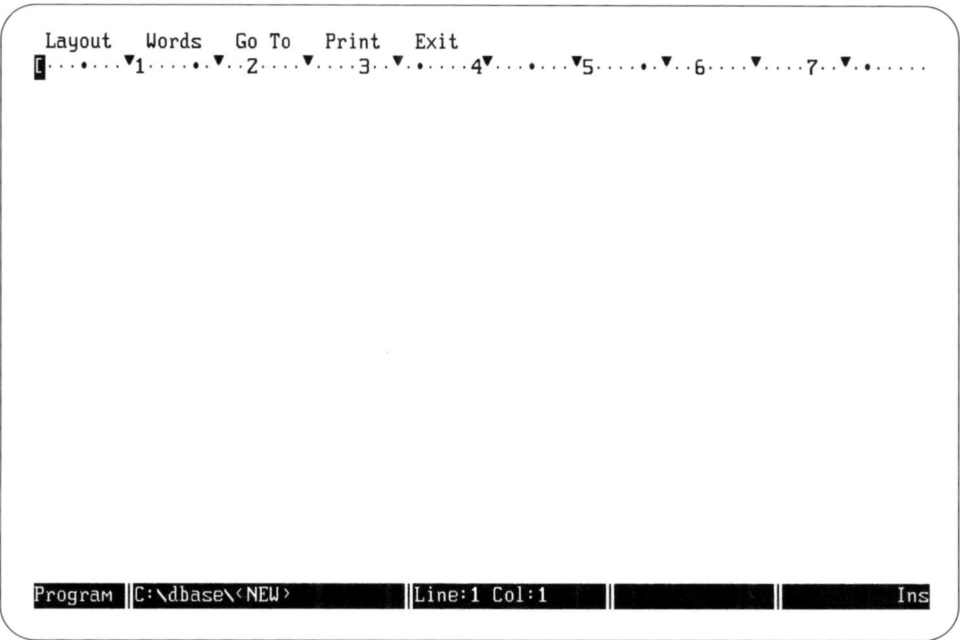

FIGURE 7-16

dBASE Program Editor Screen

for the first time or after making changes, dBASE will translate the commands into an intermediate form called object code, with the .DBO file extension. These files are stored in the default directory on the hard drive.

Creating the Program File

A dBASE program is created via the **<create>** choice in the Applications file panel from the Control Center, or by using the **MODIFY COMMAND filename** statement from the dot prompt. In either case dBASE will display the Program Editor screen where you may enter programming statements. A blank screen is shown in Figure 7-16. The ruler line shows left margin and tab settings.

You can type in program lines in a fashion similar to the Reports screen, using the arrow keys to move the cursor to the desired location. After each line, press the **Enter** key. Previously entered lines can be changed by typing over them with the correct characters. The **Ins** key will toggle from typeover to insert mode as necessary if text must be inserted at the cursor location. The default mode is Insert. The **Tab** key works as in WordPerfect.

Running the Program

dBASE allows you to run the program from within the editor if desired by selecting the **Exit** option on the Menu Bar, then choosing *Run program* from the pull-down menu. Or you can save the program, exit from the program editor, and run the program from the Applications panel of the Control Center. If you're working from the dot prompt, type the command **DO filename** and the program will execute.

Modifying the Program

The program can be modified by selecting its name from the Applications panel in the Control Center and choosing *Modify application* from the next menu. If you're working from the dot prompt type **MODIFY COMMAND filename**. In either case you will see the Program screen with the version of the program that was previously saved. Make the changes and save the new program.

Fundamental dBASE Programming Concepts

There are four general classes of dBASE programming commands.

- **Sequences** of commands or statements execute sequentially, one after another until the end of the program is reached or a transfer statement is encountered.
- **Loops** represent statements that are executed repeatedly, until a condition occurs (or stops occurring).
- **Conditions** are implemented as IF statements that cause one set of statements to be executed if a certain condition is true; otherwise another set of statements is to be executed.
- **Nonexecutable statements** represent those commands that don't actually cause anything to happen, including documentation and comments.

When writing dBASE programs, it is customary to capitalize all of the dBASE key word portions of the statements, and type the user's own phrases in lowercase letters. For example, the statement **USE Orders** indicates that the USE phrase is mandatory, and must be typed exactly as it appears, while the Orders phrase represents the name of the database file for use. dBASE does not care whether certain words are capitalized. If you wish them to appear as literals in output, enclose the words in quotes. For example, the statement **@ 10,0 SAY "ACCOUNTS RECEIVABLE"** would display the heading in capital letters at row 10, column 0. More about this command will appear in a later section.

Example: *A Sample Report Program*

To facilitate our discussion of dBASE programming concepts, we will use a sample program that displays information from the PRODUCTS table of our earlier furniture example. While this report could be created within the Reports panel of the Control Center, it will serve as an example program. The program statements are explained after the example.

1. To create this file from the Control Center, move the cursor to the **<create>** line in the Applications panel and press **Enter**.
2. Choose *dBASE program* from the next prompt box.
3. Next you will see the Program screen. Enter the program in Figure 7-17 into that screen. Press **Enter** at the end of each line.
4. When you have finished entering the program and have scanned the lines for errors, press **Alt-E** to activate the **Exit** Menu Bar.
5. Select *Run program* from the Exit menu. When dBASE prompts with the *Save As:* dialog box, reply **REPORT.PRG** and press **Enter**. dBASE will save the program, then attempt to compile (translate) the statements into a form that the computer can execute. If you have errors in any of the lines, an error box will open with a message about the kind of error. If there are no errors, the program's output will appear on the printer, as shown in Figure 7-18. Then dBASE returns to the Control Center.

FIGURE 7-17

Example REPORT.PRG Program

```
** REPORT.PRG -- Sample program to illustrate programming statements.
** Author:  B. McLaren     5/14/91

*  Prepare On-Hand Products Report

SET TALK OFF                 && Commands are not shown as they execute
USE Products                 && Use proper database file
SET DEVICE TO PRINT          && Cause @..SAY output to go to printer
SET DECIMALS TO 2
Line=56                      && Cause title, headings on first page

*  Set up print loop

DO WHILE .NOT. EOF()         && Loop until we reach end-of-file
  IF Line > 55               && Check for new page

    *  Set up report title lines and headings

    EJECT                    && Skips to next page if we've reached bottom
    @ 2,17 SAY "SAMPLE FURNITURE COMPANY"
    @ 3,17 SAY "On-Hand Products Report"
    @ 5,01 SAY "Product                           Price    Number   Total"
    @ 6,01 SAY " Number   Product Name             Each    On Hand   Value"
    @ 7,01 SAY "--------------------------------------------------------"
    Line=8                   && First detail line for table
  ENDIF
  @ Line,02 SAY Prod_no      && Customary to indent loops two spaces
  @ Line,10 SAY Prod_name
  @ Line,30 SAY Price
  @ Line,41 SAY On_hand
  Totvalue=Price*On_hand     && Calculate total value of on-hand units
  @ Line,43 SAY Totvalue
  SKIP                       && Moves record pointer to next record
  Line=Line+1                && Next record will print on next line
ENDDO
SET DEVICE TO SCREEN         && All @..SAY statements revert to screen
SET TALK ON                  && Output from commands will now appear
** End of REPORT.PRG         && A comment line to indicate end of program
```

Explanation of Commands in REPORT.PRG

* This program features many comment lines that begin with an asterisk (*). Anything following the asterisk is treated as documentation and ignored by dBASE as it executes the program. The first line is the place to name the program and give a brief explanation of its purpose. The second line comment tells who the author is and when the program was written. Modification dates should also be placed in the second line of your program, to indicate which version of the program you are examining. Other comment lines appear before major sections of the program. Blank lines are also used to subdivide sections of the program.

```
                    SAMPLE FURNITURE COMPANY
                    On-Hand Products Report

Product                               Price    Number    Total
 Number   Product Name                 Each   On Hand    Value
--------------------------------------------------------------
 14253   60" Bookcase                224.95      10    2249.50
 14352   48" Bookcase                199.95      14    2799.30
 14453   30" Bookcase                144.00      10    1440.00
 14552   24" Bookcase                122.35      21    2569.35
 16253   Student Desk                179.95      15    2699.25
 17352   Sm Kitchen Chair             75.50      25    1887.50
 17552   Kitchen Chair                95.50      45    4297.50
 21152   End Table                   119.45      11    1313.95
```

FIGURE 7-18

Output from the REPORT.PRG Program

&& The in-line comment is designated by the double ampersand (**&&**) and is used to document the statement entered at the beginning of the same line. This example program features many comments to help the beginning user. Beginning programmers would probably add in-line comments only for unusual statements. However, experienced programmers realize that more documentation in a program is generally preferred, especially for reference in the future when that program might need to be modified.

SET TALK OFF This line instructs dBASE to not display the commands as they execute. Otherwise users receive confirmation of the command's action. It is recommended that you do not use this command when running a new program, until you are convinced that it is working properly.

USE Products This command, covered earlier in the Dot Command section, will activate the PRODUCTS.DBF database file and make it available for use. Because no TAG is mentioned, the index is not activated: records will be accessed in their physical order of entry, also known as natural order.

SET DEVICE TO PRINT Ordinarily the @..SAY commands display text or data on the screen. This statement diverts the @..SAY output to the printer. The matching **SET DEVICE TO SCREEN** at the bottom of the program causes @..SAY output to revert to the screen.

SET DECIMALS TO 2 This line instructs dBASE to display two decimal places for all calculated values, such as the total value shown below.

Line=56 Line is a user variable, used here to denote the next available line for output to appear in. User variables may be used to store values in programs that are independent of the database file in use. The dBASE convention is to use lowercase letters for user variables, and uppercase letters for statement or command names. In this instance the value of 56 will cause the program to start a new page and print title and headings. See the IF Line>55 statement below.

DO WHILE .NOT. EOF() This DO statement will execute all of the lines between it and the matching ENDDO so long as the WHILE condition is true. The EOF() function tells whether we have reached the end of the database file currently in use. If the condition is initially true (as it is when we open the PRODUCTS file which has 8 records) the lines beneath the DO are executed.

IF Line > 55 This IF statement tests whether the line counter has reached line 55 on the page. If it is true, the statements following the IF are executed. If it is not true, control passes to the statement following the ENDIF statement.

EJECT This causes the printer to move the paper to the top of the next page, just as if you had pressed the FormFeed button on the printer. dBASE also generates an automatic eject if you reference a printer line in an @..SAY statement that comes *above* the current printer line position. So if you have just printed line 12, and issue the statement @ 8,2 SAY .. the printer will go to the 8th line of the next page.

@ 2,17 SAY "SAMPLE FURNITURE COMPANY" This powerful output statement tells dBASE to write the literal string "SAMPLE FURNITURE COMPANY" on the selected output device (in this case, the printer) beginning at row 2, column 17. [Because dBASE begins counting at row 0 and column 0, this string actually appears on the third row, beginning in the 18th column. Generally we do not use row 0 or column 0 for output. dBASE may use row 0 for some special messages.] On the printer, you may use rows 0 through 59, and columns 0 through 131 (for condensed print). On the screen, you may use rows 0 through 24 and columns 0 through 79 for output.

@ 5,01 SAY "Product ... Price Number Total" Rather than having a separate @..SAY statement for each item in the column headings, we save a few statements by putting the entire row in a single statement. Likewise, the next statement in the program gives the print line for the second heading row. Notice how easy it is to line up the two rows, provided the literal begins with the quotation character (") in the same column in both statements.

Line=8 We start Line at 8, the line directly beneath the column heading underline. Line will be used to control placement of output on the page with the @ .. SAY commands.

ENDIF This signifies the end of the IF statement range. IF statements may be nested within other IF statements; the first ENDIF is associated with the *last* IF entered.

@ Line,02 SAY Prod_no dBASE will substitute the current value for Line into the statement, and print the product number of the current record, beginning in column 2. The same thing is done for the product name, price, and on-hand quantity. Because the line number doesn't change, all of these fields are printed on the same line.

Totvalue=Price*On_hand This statement will calculate total value for the current record by multiplying the quantity on hand by the unit price. The user memory variable that will hold this value is Totvalue. Like the Line memory variable, its value does not automatically change when the record pointer is moved to another record; it must be recalculated.

@ Line,43 SAY Totvalue The memory variable's value can be printed like the database field values. dBASE provides special formatting characters that can be used to format the field value. Formatting is discussed in a later section (see Figure 7-21 on page 220).

SKIP Without this statement, the record pointer would remain at the first record and never pass though the rest of the file. In this program, that would result in an "infinite loop." If dBASE continues to print the same record, over and over, you can interrupt an executing program by entering **Ctrl-Break**. Although it is possible to disable the Break key in a program, this is not advisable because runaway programs cannot be interrupted.

Line=Line+1 We add one to the line counter, resulting in the next record being placed on the next line of the report.

ENDDO This statement signifies the end of the DO WHILE loop. Control is passed back to the DO WHILE where the test for the WHILE condition is made. If the condition is no longer true, control is passed to the statement following the matching ENDDO.

SET DEVICE TO SCREEN This causes the @..SAY output to revert to the screen.

SET TALK ON dBASE will now begin echoing output from the commands to the screen.

** **End of REPORT.PRG** It is a good idea to end the program with a comment statement. It signifies the last line of the program when viewing a listing of the program's lines.

Running the Report Program from the Program Screen

You can test the program from within the Program work surface. Press **Alt-E** to activate the **Exit** Menu Bar. Select the *Run program* option. dBASE will first save the program under the desired name, then attempt to execute the program. Any errors will be highlighted. You will be given the opportunity to correct the errors as described earlier.

Running the Report Program from the Control Center

To run a program from the Control Center, move the cursor to the name of that program in the Applications panel and press **Enter** two times. If the program name does not appear in the application panel of the current catalog, you may need to change to a new catalog.

Running the Report Program from the Dot Prompt

To run the REPORT program from the dot prompt, type **DO REPORT** and press **Enter**. The program will execute normally, and control will return to the dot prompt when the program is finished.

Example: *Creating a Menu Program*

This **menu program** will display a user menu on the screen, and execute different subprograms depending on the user's choice. Figure 7-19 shows the MENU.PRG program.

1. As usual, select the **<create>** box in the Applications file panel in the Control Center, and choose *dBASE program* from the next dialog box.
2. Enter the statements, and save them before exiting.
3. Statements from the program are explained on the following pages.

FIGURE 7-19

Listing of MENU.PRG Program

```
** MENU.PRG -- Sample Menu Program to illustrate programming concepts
** Author:  B. McLaren     1/18/90

* Display Menu of Screen Choices

SET TALK OFF                  && Don't show commands as they execute
SET DEVICE TO SCREEN          && Cause @..SAY to go to screen

DO WHILE .T.                  && Begins loop to display menu continuously

  CLEAR                       && Clears the screen

  @ 5,20 TO 8,60              && Draws a box from upper left to lower right
  @ 6,25 SAY "FURNITURE COMPANY APPLICATION"
  @ 7,35 SAY "OPENING MENU"

  Choice=0                    && User variable for Menu Choice (default=0)

  @ 10,28 SAY "0  Exit from Application"
  @ 11,28 SAY "1  Add a New Product"
  @ 12,28 SAY "2  Delete a Product"
  @ 13,28 SAY "3  Modify an Existing Product"
  @ 14,28 SAY "4  Print Product Report"
  @ 16,31 SAY "Enter Choice: " GET Choice PICTURE "9" RANGE 0,4
  READ

* Set up subprogram call

  DO CASE                     && Set up checking loop for user's Choice
    CASE Choice=0
        EXIT                  && If Choice is 0, leave DO loop
    CASE Choice=1
        DO Addprod            && If Choice is 1, run Addprod.PRG program
    CASE Choice=2
        DO Delprod            && If Choice is 2, run Delprod.PRG program
    CASE Choice=3
        DO Chgprod            && If Choice is 3, run Chgprod.PRG program
    CASE Choice=4
        DO Report             && If Choice is 4, run Report.PRG program
  ENDCASE                     && Signifies end of checking loop

ENDDO                         && End of DO WHILE .T. loop
RETURN                        && Return to dBASE
** End of MENU.PRG
```

Explanation of Commands in MENU.PRG

DO WHILE .T. This statement is always true, and will continue to display the menu until the user selects option 0. The ENDDO statement matches this DO statement.

CLEAR This will clear the screen. The normal dBASE Status Bar will appear at the bottom unless SET STATUS OFF is added to the program.

@ 5,20 TO 8,60 dBASE will draw a single-line box from row 5, column 20 to row 8, column 60. Adding DOUBLE to the end of the statement will draw a double-line box instead of a single-line box. It is also possible to change colors within the box.

Choice=0 Choice is a user variable that will contain the menu choice number, from 0 to 4. dBASE requires that the menu variable be predefined to some value, in this case 0, meaning the default menu choice is to leave the program and return to dBASE.

@ 16,31 SAY "Enter Choice: " GET Choice PICTURE "9" RANGE 0,4 This line provides the user prompt for the menu choice. It will get the value and store it in the Choice variable, using the picture template of "9", meaning this may contain a single numeric digit (already defined when we entered Choice=0 above) that will be one column wide. The possible range of values is from 0 to 4. Any values entered outside this range will cause dBASE to beep and wait for a proper input value.

READ This statement causes dBASE to move the cursor to the top-most GET field and wait for the user to input some values. In this example program, there is a single GET.

DO CASE This statement sets up a loop that is terminated by an ENDCASE statement. dBASE will search through the various CASE statements within this loop, and will do the action indicated by the first true condition.

CASE Choice=0 .. EXIT If the Choice memory variable is 0, dBASE will execute the statements between this CASE and the next CASE. For our example program, the statement is EXIT, the dBASE command to leave this DO loop. Thus control would pass to the line beneath the ENDDO statement, and the statement following the ENDDO (RETURN) will return to dBASE. If the statement were QUIT instead of EXIT, all files would be closed, dBASE IV would terminate, and control would return to DOS.

CASE Choice=1 .. DO Addprod This statement assumes that we would execute the program called Addprod.PRG if Choice were 1. When the Addprod program is finished, control will return to this menu program. Presumably, the Addprod.PRG program would open the appropriate files and do the necessary operations to add a new product to the Product table. The other CASE commands perform similar functions for the remaining options.

ENDCASE This statement signifies the end of the DO CASE loop. If none of the CASE statement conditions were true, no error message would be displayed. After the statements following a true CASE condition were executed, control would pass to the statement following the ENDCASE statement.

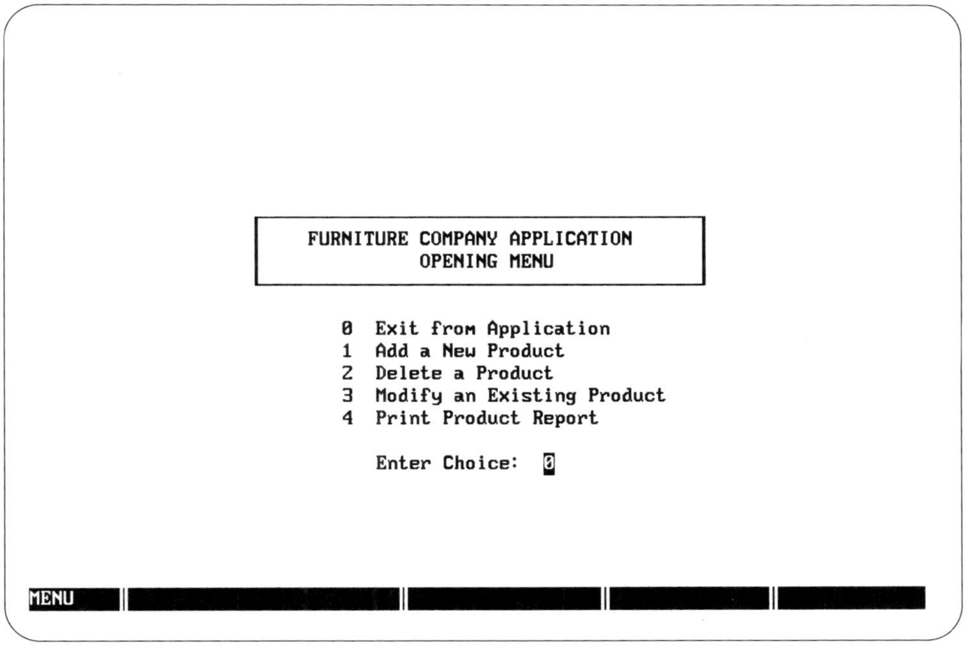

```
FURNITURE COMPANY APPLICATION
OPENING MENU

0  Exit from Application
1  Add a New Product
2  Delete a Product
3  Modify an Existing Product
4  Print Product Report

   Enter Choice: 0

MENU
```

FIGURE 7-20

Sample Menu Screen from the MENU.PRG Program

ENDDO This signifies the end of the DO WHILE loop. At this point dBASE will determine whether the looping condition is still true. If so, control passes back to the statement following the DO WHILE. If the condition is no longer true, control passes to the statement following the ENDDO statement.

RETURN This statement causes control to pass back to the program that called this program, if any. Otherwise you will go back to dBASE.

Figure 7-20 illustrates use of the MENU.PRG program. The screen shows the menu, and indicates that the computer is waiting for the user to make a selection. Notice that the Status Bar does appear in this menu—ordinarily the Status Bar display would be suppressed by **SET STATUS OFF** in programs.

Example: *Creating a Data Entry Program*

The following example program will add data for the Product table, illustrating use of additional data entry programming techniques. For this program we will use a simple data entry format, created within the program. It is also possible to use a custom data entry form that is created in the Forms screen of dBASE IV.

1. As usual, select the **<create>** box in the Applications file panel in the Control Center, and choose *dBASE program* from the next dialog box.
2. Enter the statements, and save them before exiting. See Figure 7-21.
3. Following the program are explanations of the commands.

Explanation of Commands in ADDPROD.PRG

@ 5,20 TO 8,60 dBASE will draw a single-line box from row 5, column 20 to row 8, column 60. This is the same size box as the one in the heading that appears in the MENU.PRG program.

FIGURE 7-21

ADDPROD.PRG Program for Adding New Products to Database

```
** ADDPROD.PRG -- Program to demonstrate adding a new record to PRODUCTS file
** Author:   B. McLaren     1/22/90

*  Open file, prepare for adding new data

SET TALK OFF              && Don't show output from commands
USE Products              && Opens Products database file

CLEAR                     && Clears the screen

Q 5,20 TO 8,60            && Draws a box from upper-left to lower-right
@ 6,25 SAY "FURNITURE COMPANY APPLICATION"
@ 7,35 SAY "ADD A RECORD"

Addmore=.T.               && Assumes we wish to add the first record

DO WHILE Addmore          && Loop to continue adding new records
  APPEND BLANK            && Adds a new blank record to end of file
  @ 10,25 SAY "Product Number: " GET Prod_No PICTURE "#####"
  @ 11,25 SAY " Product Descr: " GET Prod_Name
  @ 12,25 SAY "  Retail Price: " GET Price PICTURE "99999.99"
  @ 13,25 SAY " Units on Hand: " GET On_Hand PICTURE "99999"
  @ 13,50 SAY "Reorder Quantity: " GET Reorder PICTURE "99999"
  READ

  @ 18,25 SAY "Do you wish to add more records? Y/N " GET Addmore PICTURE "Y"
  READ

ENDDO                     && Marks end of the add record loop
RETURN                    && Return to calling program

** End of ADDPROD.PRG
```

Addmore=.T. Addmore is a logical type memory variable that is used to determine whether to add another record to the PRODUCTS file. It is set to true (.T.) initially so that we go through the DO WHILE loop at least once.

DO WHILE Addmore Because Addmore is a logical type variable, we can just use its name to express a true condition. We will continue to execute the loop so long as Addmore is True.

APPEND BLANK This statement adds a blank record to the end of the PRODUCTS file. The @..GET statements below are used to enter the proper values for the fields.

@ 10,25 SAY "Product Number: " GET Prod_No PICTURE "#####" This statement will display the user prompt **Product Number:** starting at row 10, column 25. Then dBASE will display a reverse video data entry box where the product number can be entered. The PICTURE "#####" template indicates that the product number can be no longer than five characters. The # sign allows any character (digit, letter, punctuation) to be placed in that position. Without a PICTURE the field will appear as it does in the database structure.

Other **@..SAY..GET** Statements The next three @..SAY..GET statements ask the user to enter the product name, retail price and number of units on hand. Notice the PICTURE for PRICE is **"99999.99"**—used to control the number of decimal places that appear on the input screen. The output values are written to begin in column 25 but have one or two spaces at the beginning so that the colons align in the same column. While each value could be written to start in a different column, the output looks better when aligned vertically.

@ 13,50 SAY "Reorder Quantity: " GET Reorder PICTURE "99999" This input prompt is short enough to be placed on the same line as the input prompt for ON_HAND. Fields may be placed in any order on any part of the screen; you do not have to follow the same field order as the file structure.

READ dBASE will display all of the input prompt characters and the field boxes on the screen as those lines are executed. The READ statement causes the cursor to be placed in the first field, and the user can enter data and move between fields as needed to make corrections. To complete the data entry for this record, the user presses **Enter** while the cursor is in the last field, or presses **Ctrl-End** while the cursor is in any field.

@ 18,25 SAY "Do .. more records? Y/N " GET Addmore PICTURE "Y" This statement will ask the user to specify if more records are to be added. dBASE will display the current True value of the Addmore memory variable. The PICTURE "Y" template directs dBASE to show the value as Y or N rather than .T. or .F. If the user changes the value to N, Addmore will be considered False.

ENDDO The ENDDO statement sends control to the matching DO WHILE loop. At that point, the value of Addmore will determine whether the loop is executed again. If the user changed Addmore to N on line 18, the loop will not be executed again and control will pass to the statement following the ENDDO. Otherwise the loop is executed again, with another blank record appended, and new values are filled in.

RETURN This statement causes this program to stop executing. Control is passed to the program that called ADDPROD, in this case MENU.PRG.

Data Entry Screen from the ADDPROD Program

The data input screen in Figure 7-22 illustrates the effects of the ADDPROD.PRG program. A new record has been entered, and the program has asked the user to indicate if more records are to be entered. Notice that the Status Bar is displayed on this screen, providing the user with information about the PRODUCTS.DBF file and the lock keys. The command SET STATUS OFF will remove that bar, if placed at the top of the ADDPROD.PRG program. To restore the Status Bar after using the SET STATUS OFF command, add the SET STATUS ON statement near the bottom of the program, before the RETURN statement.

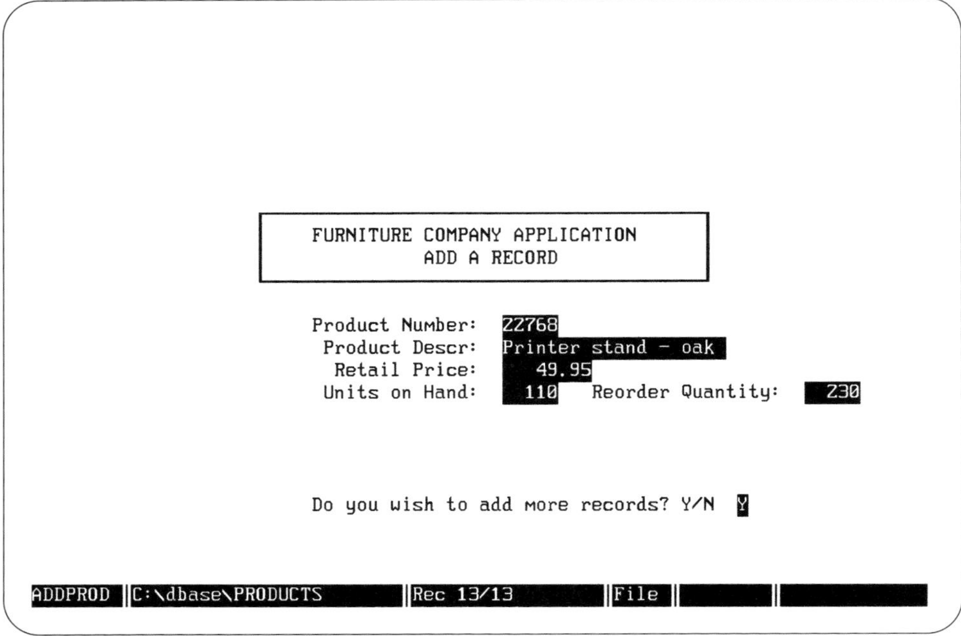

FIGURE 7-22

Sample Data Entry Screen from the ADDPROD.PRG Program

The dBASE IV Applications Generator

Thus far we have illustrated the traditional way of creating custom programs in dBASE. In previous versions this was the only way of writing such programs. dBASE IV introduced a new way of building custom programs. The **Applications Generator** is able to build sophisticated systems of menus and programs without requiring that the user learn any programming commands. You can build a single application, or develop a much bigger system of related applications.

Database Objects

The Applications Generator writes dBASE programs that link the user-created database system objects. It is an example of a **CASE** (computer-assisted software engineering) **tool.** These **database objects** include:

- Database files and associated indexes
- Queries and associated views, including those that link related files
- Screen Forms for custom data entry
- Report Forms for custom reports
- Label Forms for custom label applications
- Other .PRG programs.

Advantages of the Applications Generator

There are several advantages for using the Applications Generator instead of writing programs by hand.

- Programs can be created by non-programming users.
- There are fewer errors in the programs, thus the development cycle is shorter.

- Programs can be quickly re-generated if changes occur in the problem specification.
- Programs can generally be finished in half the time of previous methods.
- Professional developers can rapidly develop **prototype systems** for users to evaluate.

Disadvantages of the Applications Generator

There are a few disadvantages in using the Applications Generator rather than manually coding the programs.

- The user must learn how to use the Applications Generator feature of dBASE IV.
- The generated programs are much longer and may not be as efficient as hand-written versions.
- It is more difficult to make small changes in the generated programs due to the style of programming statements used.
- The generated programs are considerably larger than hand-written ones, requiring more disk space for storage.

Applications Generator Design Objects

This module permits you to build user menus, prepare lists of items to choose from, and establish batch processes. The design objects include:

- Horizontal bar menu (similar to the dBASE IV Menu Bar)
- Pop-up menu (a vertical menu associated with a Menu Bar selection)
- Files list (users can select from a list of database files)
- Structure list (users can select a field from a database or view)
- Batch process (a series of commands to accomplish some task out of sight of the user).

Types of Actions

The Applications Generator provides for manipulating most dBASE functions. Types of actions include:

- Create/edit text (no action)
- Open a menu
- Browse (add, delete, edit records from Browse work surface)
- Edit (add, delete, edit records from Edit work surface)
- Display or print (Report or Label form, Display or List)
- Perform file operations (file copy, add records from file, copy to file, mark/unmark deleted records, generate index and reindex, sort database, import/export foreign file)
- Run a .PRG program.

Developing Applications with dBASE IV

Because the training necessary for the Applications Generator is beyond the scope of this textbook, further coverage is not included. The *Applications Generator* manual packaged with dBASE IV gives complete coverage, including a detailed example problem.

SQL—STRUCTURED QUERY LANGUAGE

SQL is the concise query language used widely in industry in relational database systems. It was originally developed by IBM in 1970 as a part of a relational database management package used on IBM mainframe computers. In the early 1980s IBM's SQL database package called DB2 became very popular. The Oracle and Ingres relational database packages also used SQL. dBASE IV has a built-in SQL command set that gives it many SQL capabilities.

SQL Terminology

SQL and dBASE share many data hierarchy characteristics. The **SQL database** corresponds roughly to a dBASE catalog and consists of the set of related database files in an application. A **table** in SQL is equivalent to a dBASE .DBF file. An SQL **row** is the same thing as a dBASE record. The **column** of a SQL table corresponds to a dBASE field. An SQL **view** is a subset of the rows and columns of one or more tables, and has more options than the corresponding dBASE view created in QBE.

SQL	dBASE
database	catalog
table	database (.DBF) file
row	record
column	field
view	view

Basic SQL Commands

The SQL commands follow a standard syntax. A command may be entered in upper- or lowercase letters, and each command must be terminated by a semicolon (;). Let's use the CUSTOM database file from the furniture example earlier in this chapter. The sample data for the equivalent SQL CUSTOMER table is shown in Figure 7-23. Suppose we wanted to display the customer number, customer name, and last order date from this table for customers in Indiana. The SQL query would be:

```
SELECT Cust_no, Cust_name, Last_order
FROM Customer
WHERE State = "IN";
```

The SELECT verb will retrieve the rows from the Customer table that match the WHERE condition. The FROM qualifier specifies from which table the records are to come. The three column names specify which fields are to be retrieved. The SQL query is shown in Figure 7-24.

Creating an SQL Database

The SQL commands for creating a database are shown below. The steps are:

- CREATE the database that will hold the tables
- START the database
- CREATE a table within the database.

FIGURE 7-23

Sample Data for the SQL CUSTOMER Table

CUSTOMER Table

CUST_NO	CUST_NAME	ADDRESS	CITY	STATE	ZIP	LAST_ORDER
1004	Williams Gallery	2604 Elm Street	Terre Haute	IN	47802	10/21/89
1007	Fox Furniture	1008 Main Street	Oblong	IL	62456	02/01/88
1013	Mason Sofa	850 Kingston Pike	Knoxville	TN	39722	06/19/89
1020	Weaver's Dept. Store	801 Webster Avenue	Murray	KY	42071	01/03/90
1023	The Table Gallery	P.O. Box 17086	Baltimore	MD	21203	01/12/90
1028	The Wood Shop	124A Highland Towers	Detroit	MI	48202	11/11/89
1030	Lovejoy's Furniture	3812 Walnut Avenue	Indianapolis	IN	46226	12/06/89

```
SQL. START DATABASE Furnitur;
SQL. SELECT Cust_no, Cust_name, Last_order FROM Customer WHERE State = "IN";
 CUST_NO CUST_NAME            LAST_ORDER
 1004    Williams Gallery     10/21/89
 1030    Lovejoy's Furniture  12/06/89


SQL.
SQL      C:\dbase\furnitur\                    DB:FURNITUR
```

FIGURE 7-24

SQL SELECT Query to Retrieve Indiana Customers

The first step is to name the overall database. The SQL database corresponds roughly to the dBASE catalog. dBASE SQL allows names up to eight characters long following the same rules as database file names. dBASE SQL will create a separate disk subdirectory with the name of your database. **CREATE DATABASE name;** is the command for this.

After creating the database, it can be activated by starting that database. This step is equivalent to changing to the proper dBASE catalog. **START DATABASE name;** is the syntax for this command.

Once the database has been started, you have access to all the SQL tables within that database. There is no need to open a table in a separate step. SQL uses the regular .DBF file format for SQL tables. You create new tables with the CREATE command, whose syntax is

```
CREATE TABLE tablename (colname datatype [,colname datatype ...]);
```

You may specify up to 255 columns with a total width of 4000 characters, the same as for other dBASE database files. dBASE SQL supports seven data types:

- SMALLINT — Holds integers from –99,999 to 999,999.
- INTEGER — Holds integers up to 11 digits, from –9,999,999,999 to 99,999,999,999.
- NUMERIC(x,y) — This type holds decimal numbers with *y* decimal places and overall width of *x* places. The maximum width is 20 places, including the sign.
- FLOAT(x,y) — Holds a floating point number in what is called scientific notation. For example, 6.02E+23 is Avogadro's number shown in floating point notation. This is used for scientific values. The number can have *x* total digits and *y* digits to the right of the decimal point. The exponent range is –307 to 308.
- CHAR(n) — Holds character data with a maximum length of *n* characters; *n* may be any value up to 254.
- DATE — Holds a date in the usual dBASE date format. The default format is mm/dd/yy.
- LOGICAL — Holds logical true or false values, represented by .T. or .F.

Example: *Creating the CUSTOMER Table*

Before creating the CUSTOMER table, we need to create the FURNITUR SQL database.

1. Begin dBASE IV as usual. When you get to the Control Center work surface, press **Alt-E** to activate the **Exit** Menu Bar and select *Exit to dot prompt.*
2. At the dot prompt type **SET SQL ON**. You will see the new prompt, SQL. At this prompt you may begin entering SQL commands. Commands may be entered in upper- or lowercase letters, and each command must be terminated by a semicolon (;). Required SQL keywords will be shown in uppercase letters in this example. If you make a typing mistake, use the left arrow to move the cursor to the incorrect character(s) and make the corrections. The **Ins** key will toggle between Insert and Overtype modes; INS appears in the Status Bar during Insert mode. dBASE SQL has a special full screen edit mode that allows you to make changes more easily. Press **Ctrl-Home** to enter the editor, and **Ctrl-End** to leave the editor and execute the command.
3. To create the new database, enter the command

   ```
   CREATE DATABASE Furnitur;
   ```
4. To activate the Furnitur database, enter the command

   ```
   START DATABASE Furnitur;
   ```
5. Next we will create the first table, which will be called Customer. It will have the same data columns (fields) as the previous CUSTOMER example. Because the command will be much longer than the previous ones, we will

build it in the full screen editor. Press **Ctrl-Home** to enter the editor, then build the command as shown in Figure 7-25.

6. When you have finished building the command, press **Ctrl-End** to return to the SQL prompt. Press **Enter** to execute the command.
7. The SQL screen should resemble Figure 7-26 below. dBASE will submit the CREATE TABLE command to the SQL processor. It may combine several commands on a single line, ending with the semicolon.

```
 Layout   Words   Go To   Print   Exit
[···•···▼1····•·▼··2····▼····3··▼·•····4▼···•█··▼5····•·▼··6····▼····7··▼·•····]
CREATE TABLE CUSTOMER
(Cust_no CHAR(4), Cust_name CHAR(20), Address CHAR(20), City CHAR(20),
State CHAR(2), Zip CHAR(5), Last_order DATE);

SQL      ||C:\dbase\furnitur\        ||Line:3 Col:46     ||DB:FURNITUR   ||          Ins
```

FIGURE 7-25

SQL Full-Screen Editor with CREATE TABLE Command (Press **Ctrl-Home**)

```
. SET SQL ON
SQL. CREATE DATABASE FURNITUR;
SQL. START DATABASE FURNITUR;
SQL. CREATE TABLE CUSTOMER (Cust_no CHAR(4), Cust_name CHAR(20), Address CHAR(20
), City CHAR(20), State CHAR(2), Zip CHAR(5), Last_order DATE);
SQL.
SQL      ||C:\dbase\Furnitur\        ||                  ||DB:FURNITUR   ||          Ins
```

FIGURE 7-26

SQL Commands to Create a New Table Within the FURNITUR Database

Inserting Data into a Table

The structure of the table will be stored in a regular dBASE .DBF file, and dBASE SQL is able to access the table. There are two methods to add rows to the table. The **INSERT INTO** command allows the user to add a row of data by entering it at the SQL prompt. The syntax is

```
INSERT INTO table [columns-list] VALUES (value list);
```

The value list consists of individual column values, separated by commas. Character data should be enclosed in quotes; dates should follow the {mm/dd/yy} convention found in dBASE. If the optional columns-list is used, you specify which columns are to receive data from the INSERT. If the columns-list is omitted, SQL expects the user to provide values for all fields in the table.

The **LOAD** command represents the other method of adding data by loading it from another data file. This command's usage is

```
LOAD DATA FROM filename INTO TABLE tablename;
```

The default file type is dBASE (III, III PLUS, IV versions). An optional TYPE clause permits you to specify other database file types such as SDF, DIF, WKS, FW2 and delimited files. Data is copied from fields having the same name as columns in the specified table.

Example: *Adding Data to the CUSTOMER Table*

In this example we will first insert data into the table, then copy additional records from the already-existing CUSTOM.DBF dBASE file used in the earlier example. [Note: The CUSTOMER.DBF file used in SQL is stored in a different subdirectory. Even if they shared the same name, both can exist at the same time in separate directories.]

1. From the SQL prompt, enter the command

   ```
   INSERT INTO CUSTOMER VALUES("1031", "Hillside Furniture", "9234
   N. 116th Street", "Indianapolis", "IN", "46245", {01/02/90});
   ```

   SQL will display "1 row(s) inserted."

2. Next from the SQL prompt, enter the command

   ```
   LOAD DATA FROM CUSTOM INTO TABLE CUSTOMER;
   ```

   SQL will display a message indicating how many rows were added.

3. Issue the command below to display all data.

   ```
   SELECT * FROM CUSTOMER;
   ```

   The table in Figure 7-27 shows the results table from the SELECT query. Note that the columns are wider than 80 characters, and spill over onto the next line.

Other SQL Commands

The SELECT Command

The **SELECT** command is the most powerful in SQL, and warrants a more thorough understanding. This command will gather data from one or more tables, placing the results in a results table. The results table is usually displayed on the screen, but may be temporarily saved for further operations.

The full syntax of the dBASE SELECT command is shown below. An explanation of each part follows.

```
SQL. SELECT * FROM Customer;
 CUST_NO CUST_NAME          ADDRESS             CITY                 STATE ZI
P   LAST_ORDER
 1004    Williams Gallery   2604 Elm Street     Terre Haute          IN    47
802 10/21/89
 1007    Fox Furniture      1008 Main Street    Oblong               IL    62
456 02/01/88
 1013    Mason Sofa         850 Kingston Pike   Knoxville            TN    39
722 06/19/89
 1020    Weaver's Dept. Store 801 Webster Avenue Murray              KY    42
071 01/03/90
 1023    The Table Gallery  P.O. Box 17086      Baltimore            MD    21
203 01/12/90
 1028    The Wood Shop      124A Highland Towers Detroit             MI    48
202 11/11/89
 1030    Lovejoy's Furniture 3812 Walnut Avenue Indianapolis         IN    46
226 12/06/89
 1031    Hillside Furniture 9234 N. 116th Street Indianapolis        IN    46
245 01/02/90

SQL.
SQL      ||C:\dbase\furnitur\       ||                 ||DB:FURNITUR ||         Ins
```

FIGURE 7-27

SELECT SQL Query Results

```
SELECT [ALL/DISTINCT] <column list>
   [FROM <table list>]
   [WHERE <condition>]
   [GROUP BY <column list>]
   [UNION <additional SELECT>]
   [ORDER BY <column list>]
   [SAVE TO TEMP <table> [KEEP]];
```

ALL/DISTINCT <column list> The column list names all of the columns you wish to retrieve from this table. Placing an asterisk (*) in the column list specifies all columns. ALL will select all the rows that meet the WHERE condition whereas DISTINCT will remove duplicate records from the results table.

FROM <table list> This clause indicates the tables from which the specified columns are to be obtained.

WHERE <condition> The condition(s) in this clause specify which rows should be retrieved, based upon values in the condition. You can use AND and OR to form compound conditions.

GROUP BY <column list> SQL will group all of the rows with a common value in the results table.

UNION <additional SELECT> This clause enables you to build several SELECT commands into a single results table. The SELECT tables must meet certain compatibility criteria such as having the same number of columns and the same data types in each column. Column widths must also be the same in corresponding columns between tables.

ORDER BY <column list> This clause directs SQL to sort the records in the result table by the specified column. You may specify an additional column as a secondary key.

SAVE TO TEMP <table> [KEEP] This clause will save the current result table temporarily in memory. The next SELECT command will not replace the previous result table.

Some SELECT Examples

SELECT * FROM CUSTOMER WHERE STATE = "IN"; This command will retrieve all the rows from the CUSTOMER table whose STATE fields are "IN".

SELECT CUST_NO, CUST_NAME, LAST_ORDER FROM CUSTOMER ORDER BY CUST_NAME This command will retrieve the customer number and name and date of last order from the CUSTOMER table and sort the records alphabetically by customer name.

SQL Command Summary

The table in Figure 7-28 shows a summary of many of the dBASE IV SQL commands. They are shown in order of their usage during a SQL session.

Leaving SQL

Before leaving SQL you should first close the database in use with the **STOP DATABASE**; command. There are two ways to leave SQL:

- From the SQL prompt you may return to dBASE by typing **SET SQL OFF**.
- You may also go directly to the DOS prompt by typing **QUIT**. All database files are closed and dBASE IV is terminated.

OTHER dBASE VERSIONS

dBASE is one of the oldest products available for personal computers, beginning as a minicomputer database package called Vulcan. The first version was **dBASE II**, developed for computers with the 8080 and Z80 microprocessor using the CP/M operating system, precursor to DOS. dBASE II was quite popular at that time and was converted for use on the fledgling IBM PC in 1982. A few new features were available in the IBM version, but dBASE II was primarily a file management product rather than a full database management system. dBASE II could handle up to 65,535 records per file, with up to 1000 characters per record.

dBASE III

In 1984 the more powerful **dBASE III** was released. Touted as a relational database management system, dBASE III featured much-improved help screens, more programming capabilities, and greater data storage capabilities. dBASE III could handle up to 10 open database files at once, with one billion records per file. The memo field type was introduced with dBASE III. With dBASE III came the Assist menu system, allowing inexperienced users to build files and reports, and to organize and retrieve data more easily.

dBASE III PLUS

Released in 1986, **dBASE III PLUS** introduced local area network capabilities for multi-user file access. The Plus version's pull-down Assist menu was much enhanced. Menus for certain commands became easier to read. Additional programming commands and functions were added to this version. Query capability was added to this version, along with the concepts of catalogs and views. Custom screen data entry forms were added to the Plus version of dBASE.

FIGURE 7-28

SQL Command Summary

Command	Explanation
SHOW DATABASE;	List names of all SQL databases.
CREATE DATABASE <dname>;	Create a new database called <dname>. <dname> must be unique.
START DATABASE <dname>;	Activate or open the database called <dname>. Only one database may be active at a time.
CREATE TABLE <tname> (..) ;	Create a table within the active database and provide the structure.
ALTER TABLE <tname> ADD .. ;	Add a column to the specified table.
INSERT INTO <tname> VALUES .. ;	Insert values into new row in specified table. Values must match columns in data type and length.
INSERT INTO <tname> SELECT .. FROM <tname2>;	Copy values from <tname2> into first table. Can also specify a WHERE condition.
LOAD DATA FROM <file> INTO TABLE <tname>;	Copy data from an existing dBASE file into the specified SQL table. SQL can copy from other file types.
SELECT <columns> FROM <tname>;	Select specified columns from the indicated table. May add WHERE clause to specify conditions for rows to be retrieved.
UPDATE <tname> SET <col>=<expr> WHERE .. ;	Replace column value in the row(s) specified by the WHERE clause.
DELETE FROM <tname> WHERE .. ;	Delete row from specified table according to condition in the WHERE clause.
DROP TABLE <tname>;	Delete specified table from current database. This is a permanent change—all data will be lost.
STOP DATABASE;	Close (deactivate) current database.
DROP DATABASE <dname>;	Delete specified database permanently.

The report generator's formatting capability was not flexible enough for some applications. Thus dBASE III PLUS users frequently wrote programs to create acceptable reports. Not all of the regular dot prompt command features were available through the Assist menu, requiring some users to learn the dot prompt commands.

dBASE IV

The first version of dBASE IV was released in late 1988. It completely replaced the Assist interface with the Control Center, allowing easy access to most of the capabilities of dBASE without requiring programming expertise. Also new to dBASE IV are query-by-example (QBE) capability, and the ability to link records selected via QBE to reports and labels. The QBE capability is discussed in Chapter 4.

The report and label generator modules of dBASE IV are much more sophisticated than those of previous versions. The screen paint feature allows you to place fields and text labels where they belong. The applications generator allows you to create .PRG files by answering questions to screen prompts, building application menus and execution modules.

Version 1.1 of dBASE IV was released in August 1990 and shipped free of charge to all registered 1.0 users. It fixed errors in the 1.0 version and required less memory. Although some new features were added to the 1.1 version, most screens are the same as the 1.0 screen. [Note: All users should be upgraded to version 1.1 or higher.]

OTHER DATABASE MANAGEMENT PRODUCTS

Although dBASE has been the most popular database management software package for IBM-compatible microcomputers, other vendors have developed add-on utilities that made earlier versions of dBASE easier to use. These packages include report writers, applications generators, statistical utilities and graphics software that are designed to work with dBASE data files. dBASE IV represents a significant breakthrough by combining many of these functions as a standard part of dBASE.

Report Writers

Several vendors developed and marketed add-on programs called **report writers** that would let the user specify the report format, then automatically create the dBASE III PLUS commands necessary to print that report. Some of these packages could access data from several work areas in the same output. These were called relational report writers. Perhaps the best known of these is the **R&R Relational Report Writer,** with versions available for dBASE III and dBASE IV. This package enables you to quickly create customized reports with choice of fonts and other print enhancements.

Prior to dBASE IV the only way to create more sophisticated reports was to write a custom program in the dBASE language. With the various report bands of dBASE IV, the end user is able to develop custom reports without programming. However, the ability of dBASE IV to work with multiple files is somewhat clumsy because you must first create a Query linking the files.

Applications Generators

The applications generator within dBASE IV is able to prepare the dBASE commands necessary to perform certain standardized functions within a database system. Earlier dBASE versions did not have this capability, so the user had to resort to writing custom programs. An **applications generator** is able to prepare the program commands based upon the user's responses to a series of questions. The dBASE IV manual describes how to make use of this feature.

Other applications generating programs are available that are superior to the one provided with dBASE IV. **Genifer** is probably the best-known example of these.

Statistical and Graphical Add-ins

Because dBASE includes neither statistical nor graphical output capabilities, third-party vendors have marketed packages that will accomplish these tasks. **DBSTAT** is one such statistical program.

dBASE-Compatible Database Packages

Just as with Lotus 1-2-3, there are several database products that are compatible with dBASE. Some utilize the same commands, while others create and read dBASE data files. Most of these products are less expensive than dBASE and some offer new features that improve upon dBASE. Two types of products are available: **database interpreters** such as dBASE III PLUS and IV execute commands immediately, in an interactive fashion. Interpreters are useful for development and testing of custom programs. **Database compilers** are used to convert finished command programs into a machine-executable format.

Database Interpreters

An interpreter will execute command programs line by line. As each line is executed, it is scanned and translated into the machine language of the microprocessor. A program loop must be translated each time the lines in that section are executed. Thus interpreters are slower than compilers at running a given program. However, because the compilation process takes several minutes it is not convenient when minor changes are made to the program. The database interpreter package is typically used for non-programming applications and during the development process.

Other than dBASE IV, dBASE III PLUS is the best known dBASE-compatible interpreter. Other popular products include **dBXL** and **FoxBase**. Each is faster than dBASE III PLUS and is nearly 100% compatible with dBASE commands. Both will read all dBASE files. Because such "clone" products must offer something extra to lure buyers from the original package, dBXL and FoxBase feature enhancements and extensions to the dBASE standard. The latest version of FoxBase is called **FoxPro**, and is compatible with dBASE IV.

Database Compilers

Compilers are used to speed up the execution of command programs, and permit use of the system without the original database program. In fact, once the programs have been developed and tested with an interpreter product such as dBASE or FoxPro, they can be translated into an executable format for future use. There is a pseudo-compiler in dBASE IV that will partially translate command programs. However, you must still have dBASE IV to run these programs. A true compiler will produce files that can be executed by themselves without needing the database software. Of course, no changes can be made to the programs, but all of the features in the programs are available. A subtle advantage of using compiled programs is that the programs themselves cannot be seen or changed when in compiled form. A system consisting of 20 or more .PRG files that runs under dBASE or dBXL can be compiled to a single executable .EXE file of 250 KB.

The two best-known compilers are **QuickSilver** and **Clipper**. Each has features that extend dBASE capabilities, and will accept all standard dBASE III PLUS and many dBASE IV commands. As new versions are released, these packages add more dBASE IV compatibility.

A database compiler will scan all the commands in a program for possible errors, whereas the interpreter will only flag errors when the line containing that error is executed. Thus potential errors are pinpointed during the development process, rather than at some point in the future.

Relational Database Packages Not Compatible with dBASE

Perhaps the best known of this group of relational database packages not compatible with dBASE is the **R:Base** family of products. Long locked in a features war with dBASE, each new R:Base product surpassed the then-current dBASE version. The current products include R:Base for DOS and R:Base for OS/2. The R:Base products are based upon SQL data queries with enhancements for easier data entry and reporting. R:Base also comes with an applications generator for creating database systems without programming. Older versions include R:Base System V, R:Base 5000 and R:Base 4000.

Paradox is another powerful product that is highly rated. While particularly easy to use for beginners, Paradox is also well suited for developers creating new application systems. Paradox queries are SQL-based, with a simple-to-use query-by-example module as well.

Oracle is a SQL-based relational database product that is able to run on many different types of computers, including mainframes, minicomputers and microcomputers. For the organization with data on more than one type of computer, Oracle allows common database commands to work across the machines. Oracle runs on DOS provided you have at least 1 megabyte of extended memory beyond 640 KB. Oracle is user-friendly and is easy to use through menu-driven screens.

Another similar multi-platform product is **Ingres**. Originally designed for minicomputers, Ingres has been implemented on mainframe and microcomputers. Its features are similar to Oracle's, with SQL-based queries and menu driven interface.

Other Non-Relational Database Packages

There are a number of easy-to-use file management packages that are able to build, retrieve and report records from single files. Usually much less expensive than the relational databases, these programs are generally easier to use as well. Professional File is an excellent product for manipulating single database files. Other flat file management packages include Reflex, Q&A, and PC:File.

CHAPTER REVIEW

Changing the Starting Configuration

The CONFIG.DB file contains the dBASE startup configuration settings. You can edit this file as necessary to make permanent changes, or use the **Tools** Menu Bar to make temporary changes to the configuration.

Using the Catalog Menu Bar

The dBASE catalog is a database file that maintains information about all the database objects associated with a particular application. As you add files from the Control Center, they are automatically placed in the current catalog. dBASE starts up with the catalog that was in use at the end of the previous session. From the **Tools** Menu Bar you can change to a different catalog, and add files to, or remove files from the current catalog.

Relational Database Capabilities

dBASE IV is a relational database management system. It can work with up to ten database files at a time, linking files together via common field values. The dBASE IV Query work surface provides a means of linking such files together through the Control Center. The linked view can be displayed as a normal database file would be, used in a report, or saved as a separate database file.

Using Other Data Files: APPEND FROM and COPY TO

dBASE IV database files can accept data from other dBASE files with the APPEND FROM command, or copy data to other dBASE files with the COPY TO command. The IMPORT and EXPORT commands are used to exchange data with non-dBASE files.

Creating Custom Command-File Programs

To produce reports and custom forms in the desired format, previous dBASE versions required that users write custom programs, similar to Lotus macros. dBASE IV gives the user significantly more control over placement of items on the screen and on printed reports with the Control Center functions. Some users will still wish to write programs with dBASE IV that go beyond the built-in capabilities.

Working with dBASE Program Files

dBASE programs consist of dot prompt commands that are entered from the keyboard in a full-screen editor work surface. You can create or modify programs from the Control Center or from the dot prompt. When you exit from the editor work surface, programs are translated by dBASE into an executable form called object code. Programs may be executed from the Control Center by moving the cursor to the name of the program in the Applications panel and pressing **Enter.**

The dBASE IV Applications Generator

The Applications Generator lets you link database objects such as database files, queries and associated views, screen forms, reports, and labels into a system. The Applications Generator can build menus and perform file operations on these database objects without requiring that the user write dBASE programs.

SQL-Structured Query Language

The standard query language used in many relational database systems is SQL, or Structured Query Language. SQL is especially well suited for relational operations that link two or more files. dBASE IV contains a subset of SQL that may be used to create and manipulate SQL databases. SQL commands resemble dBASE dot prompt commands, and are entered at the SQL prompt.

Other dBASE Versions

dBASE IV is the latest in a long line of dBASE versions. dBASE II was originally designed for CP/M computers in 1980, but was translated into an IBM-compatible version for DOS computers. dBASE III introduced many new features, including much greater storage capacity. dBASE III PLUS offered multi-user and network access, and a menu-driven user interface called Assist. dBASE IV is radically different from earlier versions. The Control Center interface offers easy and consistent access to virtually all of the features. Other new features include query-by-example queries and sophisticated screen and report generators, along with the applications generator.

dBASE-Compatible Database Packages

dBXL, FoxBase and FoxPro are work-alike database management software packages that provide compatibility with many dBASE commands. QuickSilver and Clipper are compilers that will translate systems of dBASE programs into stand-alone .EXE files that will execute without a database program. R:Base, Paradox, Oracle and Ingres are powerful SQL-based database management systems products.

KEY TERMS

@..SAY..GET
@..SAY
alias
APPEND BLANK
APPEND FROM command
Applications Generator
calculated field
CASE tool
catalog
CLEAR
Clipper
command-file programs
concatenated key
CONFIG.DB
COPY TO command
CREATE DATABASE (SQL)
CREATE TABLE (SQL)
database compiler
database interpreter
database objects
dBASE II
dBASE III
dBASE III PLUS
DBSTAT
dBXL
DO CASE .. ENDCASE
DO Program
DO WHILE .. ENDDO
file description
flat-file table
FoxBase, FoxPro
Genifer
IF .. ENDIF
Ingres
INSERT INTO (SQL)
linked data files
LOAD (SQL)
menu program
MODIFY COMMAND
normalized tables
Oracle
Paradox
prototype systems
QuickSilver
R&R Relational Report Writer
R:Base
relational database
report program
report writer
RETURN
SELECT (SQL)
SET SQL ON/OFF
Settings option
SKIP
SQL
SQL column
SQL database
SQL dot prompt
SQL row
SQL table
SQL view
START DATABASE (SQL)
STOP DATABASE (SQL)
Tools Menu Bar
turn-key system
View skeleton
work areas

DISCUSSION QUESTIONS

1. Discuss the purpose of the CONFIG.DB file. Are there any ways to change the configuration other than by modifying the CONFIG.DB file? Explain.
2. Explain the meaning of the default values of the following Settings options from the **Tools** Menu Bar.
   a. Carry (OFF)
   b. Confirm (OFF)
   c. Deleted (OFF)
   d. Exact (OFF)
   e. Memo width (50).
3. Explain the purpose of the dBASE IV catalog, and list the information it contains.
4. Suppose you have created a new database file at the dot prompt, but cannot find it in the file panels of the Control Center. Explain how you could add this file to the catalog.
5. What is the purpose of the file description shown on the Control Center screen? How would you create or modify a file's description?
6. Explain what is meant by the term "relational database." How is a relational database different from the database files we developed in earlier chapters?
7. What is a concatenated key? Why was one necessary in the ITEMS table of the Furniture example?

8. Discuss the use of an alias in relational database applications using multiple database files.
9. Explain how one might link two database files through the Query work surface. Why would we want to link these files?
10. Discuss reasons for saving a linked view as a separate database file. Are there other options for retrieving the linked files? Explain.
11. Discuss the meaning of the following database commands.
    a. **APPEND FROM**
    b. **IMPORT**
    c. **COPY TO**
    d. **EXPORT**.
12. List at least three reasons for writing custom command-file programs in dBASE. Are the same reasons still valid for dBASE IV? Explain.
13. Briefly define the purpose of the following dBASE program statements.
    a. **SET TALK OFF**
    b. **@ 2,17 SAY "SAMPLE FURNITURE COMPANY"**
    c. **DO WHILE .NOT. EOF()**
    d. **SKIP**
    e. **EJECT**
    f. **CASE Choice=5**
    g. **Line=Line+1**
    h. **APPEND BLANK**
    i. **@ 13,25 SAY "Units on Hand: " GET On_Hand PICTURE "99999"**
    j. **SET TALK ON**.
14. What is the Applications Generator designed to do? Explain.
15. Define the following SQL terms. What are their dBASE IV counterparts?
    a. Database
    b. Table
    c. Row
    d. Column
    e. View.
16. Briefly define the purpose of the following SQL commands.
    a. **CREATE TABLE**
    b. **INSERT INTO**
    c. **SELECT * FROM**
    d. **ALTER TABLE**
    e. **STOP DATABASE**.
17. Describe the improvements that dBASE IV offers over earlier versions. Be explicit.
18. List other database products that are compatible with dBASE.
19. What are the advantages of using a database compiler instead of an interpreter. Are there any disadvantages with using a compiler? Explain.

```
Structure for database: C:\DBASE\STOCKS.DBF
Number of data records:       25
Date of last update   : 11/01/89
Field  Field Name  Type       Width    Dec    Index
    1  STOCK_NAME  Character     20              Y
    2  EXCHANGE    Character      6              Y
    3  YRHIGH      Numeric        7      3       N
    4  YRLOW       Numeric        7      3       N
    5  RECENT      Numeric        7      3       N
    6  NO_SHARES   Numeric        5              N
** Total **                      53
```

FIGURE 7-29

STOCKS.DBF Structure to Accompany Exercise 3

EXERCISES

1. At the dBASE IV Control Center screen, activate the Menu Bar and select the **Tools** menu. Change the **Confirm** setting from OFF to ON. What effect does this change represent?

2. Make a list of the database catalogs available in your version of dBASE IV. If you find a catalog named SAMPLES.CAT, make it the default catalog. This catalog contains the sample files packaged with dBASE IV. What files are maintained in this catalog?

3. Open the **STOCKS.DBF** database that is stored on the data disk accompanying this textbook. There are 25 records in this file, whose structure is shown in Figure 7-29.
   a. Create a QBE query for this file in the Queries work surface. Only STOCK_NAME, RECENT and NO_SHARES should be placed in the View skeleton.
   b. Next add the **SYMBOLS.DBF** file (also on the data disk) to the query using the *Add file to query* line of the **Layout** menu.
   c. Use the *Create link by pointing* line of the **Layout** menu to link the two files together by the STOCK_NAME fields.
   d. Add the SYMBOL field to the View skeleton and view the data.
   e. Obtain a quick report of the linked files.
   f. Save the linked view under the name **STOCKSYM**.

4. Use the **STOCKSYM** linked view from the previous problem and do the following.
   a. Add a calculated field to the View skeleton to calculate the total equity amount in each stock, multiplying RECENT by NO_SHARES.
   b. Build a report using the modified STOCKSYM view. Your report title should be centered over the columns and should read **STOCK PORTFOLIO REPORT**. The column headings should reflect the names of the fields as shown in Figure 7-30.
   c. Your report should total the equity column.
   d. Print a copy of your report.
   e. Save the report under the name of your choice.

```
                 STOCK        NUMBER OF       RECENT      TOTAL
STOCK NAME       SYMBOL         SHARES        PRICE       EQUITY
```

FIGURE 7-30

Sample Column Headings for Exercise 4

```
          STOCK        52-WEEK    52-WEEK       RECENT       NO. OF
STOCK     EXCHANGE       HIGH        LOW        PRICE        SHARES
-----     --------     -----------------        ------       ------
```

FIGURE 7-31

Sample Column Headings for Exercise 6

5. Again start with the **STOCKSYM** view from the previous problem, and modify the view as noted.
   a. Add a condition that will include only the NYSE stocks in the view. Do not include the exchange name in the view skeleton. Print a quick report of the records that qualify for this condition.
   b. For this problem print only those stocks which are *not* from the NYSE. Print a quick report of the records that match this condition.

6. Create a command-file program that will print a simple report showing the information contained in the **STOCKS.DBF** database.
   a. Use the centered title **ANNUAL PORTFOLIO REPORT**.
   b. Use the column headings shown in Figure 7-31.
   c. Print a copy of your report.
   d. Save the report program using the name **REPORT1** in the Applications file panel.

7. Modify the report program from the previous problem to calculate and print the Equity for each stock, found by multiplying the number of shares by the recent price. Modify the column headings to account for the new column, and recenter the title. Save the report program using the name **REPORT2**, and obtain a printed report.

8. Write a menu program that would offer the following choices:

   ```
   0 Exit from Application
   1 Add a New Stock
   2 Change an Existing Stock
   3 Delete an Existing Stock
   4 Print Reports
   ```

   Use a DO CASE statement to determine appropriate action in each case. Assume that you will call (DO program-name) the following programs, according to the menu selection.

   ```
   ADDSTK (1)
   CHGSTK (2)
   DELSTK (3)
   REPRTS (4)
   ```

   Save your program under the name **MENU1**. Print a copy of your menu program's statements.

FIGURE 7-32

Sample Data for Exercise 9

```
Williams, Gary      2231     MIS      812-555-7194
Gilbert, Anne       1899     ACCT     317-234-6754
Blythe, Shirley     1752     MKTG     812-217-9229
McDaniel, Mike      7234     MGT      000-000-0000
Turner, Devon       3151     FIN      219-231-1876
```

9. In this exercise you will create an SQL database for a new student information system. The database will be called **SIS** (Student Information System).

   a. From the Control Center, **Exit** to the dot prompt. Issue the **SET SQL ON** command to activate the SQL prompt.

   b. Create the SIS SQL database. dBASE IV will create a subdirectory on the default drive with the same name as your SQL subdirectory. All SQL objects will be placed within this subdirectory.

   c. Create the **STUDENT** table within the SIS database. Its columns include:

```
NAME      char(20)
SID       char(4)
MAJOR     char(4)
PHONE     char(12)
GPA       decimal(5,2)
```

   d. Insert the Figure 7-32 data into the STUDENT table. We will insert the GPA data later.

   e. Select and print all of the columns.

10. Create the following tables within the SIS database and follow the instructions.

   a. The table **CLASSES** contains these columns:

```
SID       char(4)
COURSE    char(6)
GRADE     char(2)
```

   b. Insert the Figure 7-33 data into the CLASSES table.

   c. Select rows from the CLASSES table for students earning the grade of B+ or A.

11. This exercise will illustrate SQL operations within the **SIS** database.

   a. Use the SQL SELECT command to print only those rows belonging to students who are taking the MIS276 or MIS280 courses.

   b. Select and print the rows in which student number 2231 is taking classes.

   c. Select and print a table which is ordered by the grade column in descending order.

   d. Using the LIKE clause, print a table of all students taking MIS courses.

   e. Print a table of all students taking courses numbered 300 or higher.

1752	MIS276	B+
1752	ACC202	B
1752	SDS350	C+
1752	BLA363	A
1899	MGT300	C+
1899	MKT305	B+
1899	FIN300	B
2231	MIS280	A
2231	MIS300	B
2231	MIS430	C+
2231	ENG305	B+
3151	FIN433	A
3151	FIN460	B+
3151	MGT452	C+
7234	SDS265	D+
7234	MIS276	C

FIGURE 7-33

Sample Data for Exercise 10

CHAPTER 7 PROJECT
SAMPLE FURNITURE COMPANY

This project will use the four tables from the furniture order entry example developed in this chapter. Create a separate dBASE catalog (*not* SQL) for this application called FURNORD. Create the four tables (CUSTOM, ORDERS, ITEMS, PRODUCTS) and add them to this catalog. Use the built-in dBASE IV query, form, and report generators to develop the following database modules. Don't write dBASE programs for this project.

1. Build a custom data entry screen that would add new customers to the CUSTOM table. Call this form ADDCUST.
2. Build a QBE view linking the ORDERS and CUSTOM tables that will combine permanent customer information with information about the order. Make ORDERS the primary file, placing it first in the view. Call this view ORDCUST.
3. Using the ORDCUST view and the Report work surface, build a custom report that would display the order information, including the necessary customer data. Call this report ORDPRT.
4. Build a QBE view linking the ITEMS and PRODUCTS tables similar to the one called EXTENDED in the chapter example.
5. Add a new numeric field to the ORDERS table called AMOUNT that will be the total amount of the order. Next use the EXTENDED QBE view. From the dot prompt use the SUM command to calculate the total EXTENDED amount for each order number. Then replace the blank AMOUNT value in ORDERS with this calculated sum.
6. Modify the ORDRPT report to accommodate the AMOUNT field.
7. Prepare a list and brief explanation of additional database modules that ought to be developed for the FURORD application.

8

Introduction to dBASE III PLUS

Objectives

After completing this chapter, you should be able to:

- Explain how to use the dBASE III PLUS Assist menu.
- Compare using dBASE III PLUS from the dot prompt mode and from the Assist menu.
- Understand and enter dBASE commands from the dot prompt.
- Create a database file structure and append data to the structure.
- Demonstrate how to move the record pointer through the database.
- Use the EDIT and BROWSE commands to examine and make changes to the database.
- Organize the records in a specific order using the SORT and INDEX commands.
- Build a custom report with the dBASE III PLUS CREATE REPORT command.
- Design a group report.
- Create and print mailing labels using dBASE III PLUS.
- Create a query to retrieve desired records.
- List the features of dBASE IV that are not present or not as well developed in dBASE III PLUS.

INTRODUCTION

dBASE III PLUS, released in 1986, was the predecessor database package to the current release, dBASE IV, and is still marketed by Ashton-Tate for smaller applications. It requires only 384KB RAM and will run from a two–floppy disk drive computer; however, it requires some disk swapping on a 360KB floppy drive.

dBASE III PLUS provides the same four **user modes** as dBASE IV. It has a simpler menu with access to a report writer, form builder, and basic data retrieval features. The query feature is more difficult to use and less powerful than dBASE IV's.

Because there are fewer built-in capabilities, users must do more programming to create sophisticated reports, labels, and custom screen forms. The dot commands used in dBASE III PLUS programs are nearly identical to those in dBASE IV. In fact, the programming examples in Chapter 7 use only statements common to both versions so they will run in dBASE III PLUS without changes.

dBASE III PLUS QUICKSTART

dBASE III PLUS uses a simple menu system called ASSIST to enter commands, rather than the Control Center, which was introduced with dBASE IV.

Starting dBASE III PLUS

dBASE III PLUS can be used on either a two–floppy drive or a hard–drive personal computer. You may store your data files on either floppy disks or on the hard drive, if you have one.

Starting from a Floppy Disk Computer

If you are using a floppy disk personal computer, place a formatted data disk in the B drive. Then place dBASE Disk 1 in the A drive, type **DBASE** and press **Enter.** After dBASE loads the files from Disk 1 you will be prompted to place Disk 2 in the A drive and press **Enter**. Do *not* remove your data disk from the B drive until you have quit from dBASE and returned to the DOS prompt.

Starting from a Hard Disk Computer

If you are using a personal computer with a hard disk, use the DOS **CD** command to change to the directory on the C drive where dBASE III PLUS is stored. At the C> prompt, type **DBASE** and press **Enter.** Database files will be stored in the same directory as the dBASE program files are stored.

After a few seconds you will see a startup screen that asks you to confirm that you have read the license agreement. Press **Enter** to go to the next screen. Unless your version of dBASE has been configured differently, the next screen will be the Assist menu. If your version of dBASE comes up with the dot prompt mode, type **ASSIST** and press **Enter** (or press **F2**) to activate the main menu.

Using the Assist Menu

Figure 8-1 shows the **Assist menu** when dBASE starts up. Your screen will show the starting drive location where the database files are stored, either the B drive or the C drive. The Assist menu consists of several elements common to many dBASE screens.

- The top row holds the **Menu Bar,** consisting of the main menu options available.
- The submenu of the highlighted main menu option, **Set Up,** is pulled down.
- System time is displayed in the top row right corner.

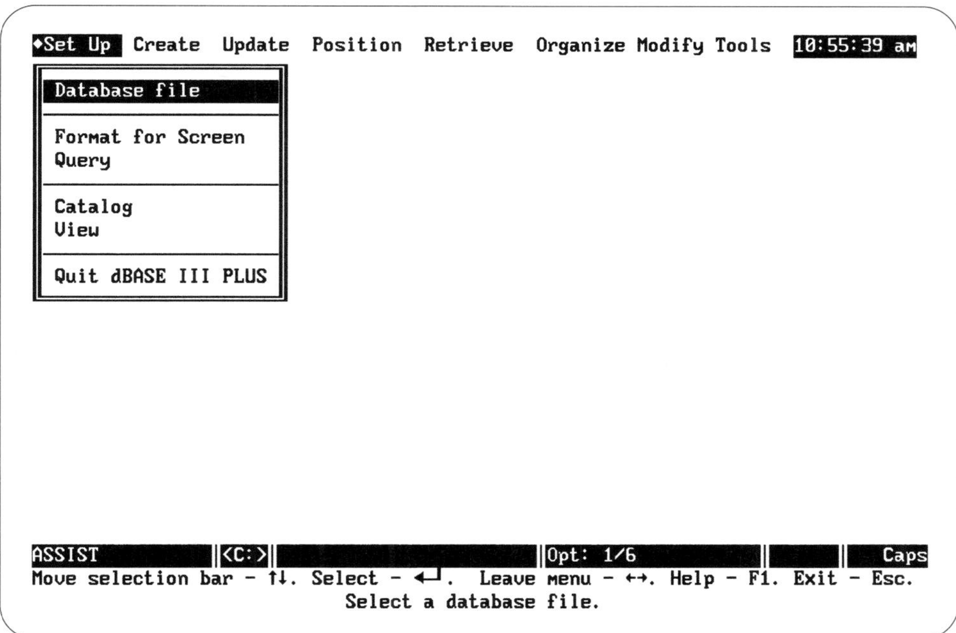

FIGURE 8-1

Main dBASE III PLUS Assist Menu

- The **action line** shows the dBASE command being prepared by the Assist menu processor.
- Near the bottom of the screen is the **Status Bar,** which provides information about the current screen, database file in use, record pointer location, and toggle settings.
- Immediately below the status line is the **navigation line,** which explains how to accomplish activities relevant to the current screen.
- The **message line** provides information about the command currently selected or the area of the work surface that is highlighted.

Selecting Commands from the Assist Menu

To select a command from the main menu, use the right and left arrow keys to move the cursor to the desired option. Then use the up and down arrow keys to move the cursor to the proper line in the pull-down menu beneath that option. Available choices in the pull-down menu appear in bright text. Dim or gray menu choices are not currently available. The message line at the bottom of the screen provides a brief explanation of the highlighted choice. Press **Enter** to select that line.

Main Menu Choices

The choices in the Assist menu are arranged by type of function rather than by type of file as with dBASE IV. The most commonly used choices appear at the left of the menu.

- **Set Up** allows you to select an already-existing database file, screen form, or query. This option is also used to exit from dBASE back to DOS.
- **Create** is used to create a new database file, screen format, query, report, or label.

- **Update** provides ways to change the database by adding new records, editing existing records, and deleting records.
- **Position** allows you to move the record pointer to a specific record or search for the next record that matches a certain condition.
- **Retrieve** is used to print a report or label and to list fields from one or more records on the screen.
- **Organize** is used to index, sort, or copy records from one database file to another.
- **Modify** can be used to make changes in an existing database object such as a database file, screen format, query, report, or label.
- **Tools** choices are used to perform such operations as changing the default disk drive, copying, and renaming files, displaying a disk directory, listing the structure of a database file, and erasing files.

Dot Prompt Commands

Once they become familiar with dBASE III PLUS, users often switch from the Assist menu to the **dot prompt** interface in which they key in commands instead of picking them from menus. The dot prompt interface in dBASE III PLUS is almost identical to that in dBASE IV. Most of the dot commands described in Chapter 6 work similarly in both database packages.

Unlike the Control Center of dBASE IV, the dBASE III PLUS Assist menu does not provide full functionality. Some commands and functions cannot be entered through the Assist menu. It is possible to switch back and forth between the two modes with no loss of data. To switch from the Assist menu to the dot prompt, press **Esc.** To switch from the dot prompt mode to the Assist menu, press the **F2** function key.

For the remainder of this chapter we will use dot commands to illustrate various dBASE III PLUS database concepts.

Dot Command Basics

Dot commands consist of a **command verb,** followed by optional clauses. The square brackets around the optional clauses are *not* to be typed as part of the command. The angle brackets are *not* to be typed. The basic dBASE command syntax is shown below. Some commands do not use all of the clauses.

```
verb  [<scope>] [expression list] [FOR <cond>] [WHILE <cond>]
      [OFF] [TO PRINT] [TO FILE <filename>]
```

- **verb** is replaced with the name of the command, as explained later.
- **<scope>** is a phrase that determines which records the command will consider. Examples include **RECORD 5, NEXT 3, REST,** and **ALL.**
- **<expression list>** depends on the particular command. Examples of commands are shown later in this chapter.
- **FOR <cond>** provides a condition to be met for that record to qualify. All records that meet the <scope> are examined. For example, FOR YEAR="1983" would only allow records with "1983" in the YEAR field to be included.
- **WHILE <cond>** also provides for a logical condition to be met for that record to qualify. Unlike the FOR clause, as soon as records do not qualify for the WHILE condition, the command stops.

- **TO PRINT** causes output from the command to be sent to the printer as well as the screen. This clause works with the DISPLAY, LIST, REPORT, and LABEL commands.
- **TO FILE <filename>** causes the output from the command to be copied to a DOS file under the specified file name on the default disk drive. This clause works with the REPORT and LABEL commands.

Entering Dot Commands

Dot commands are entered after the dot prompt. Corrections may be made by using the backspace key; the **Ins** key can be used to toggle between Insert and Overtype modes. The word "Ins" will appear in the Status Bar when you are in Insert mode. To execute the dot command, press **Enter.** You may execute a previous command by pressing the up arrow key followed by **Enter.** Each up arrow keypress brings back older commands; you can modify the commands as needed before pressing **Enter.** dBASE maintains as many as 20 previous commands; this number can be changed with the **SET HISTORY TO** command.

Spelling or other typing errors result in an error message. If you would like a Help screen for the command in question, type **HELP <command>** and press **Enter.** Figure 8-2 shows the Help screen for the LIST command. For more general help, type **HELP** (or press **F1**). The Help main menu screen is shown in Figure 8-3. Unlike dBASE IV, the help system in dBASE III PLUS is not context-specific. In other words, if you press **F1** while performing a certain command or procedure, you will get the Help main menu screen.

Commands may be abbreviated by their first four letters. For example, **DISPLAY** may be abbreviated as **DISP.** You must fully spell out field names and file names.

Using an Existing Database File

To use an existing database file from the dot prompt, issue the **USE <filename>** command. If there is another database file in use, it will first be closed, then the new file will be opened. If you give the **USE** command without specifying

```
♦
                                                              LIST

                                LIST
                                ════

 Syntax      :  LIST [<scope>] [<expression list>] [FOR <condition>]
                     [WHILE <condition>] [OFF] [TO PRINT]

 Description :  Displays the contents of a database file.
                Used alone, it displays all records.  Use the scope and
                FOR/WHILE clauses to list selectively.  The expression
                list can be included to select fields or a combination
                of fields, such as Cost * Rate.  OFF suppresses the record
                numbers.



HELP          ||<C:>||                  ||                ||    ||  Caps
 Previous screen - PgUp. Previous menu - F10. Exit with Esc or enter a command.
                     ENTER >
```

FIGURE 8-2

Screen Output from **HELP LIST** Dot Command

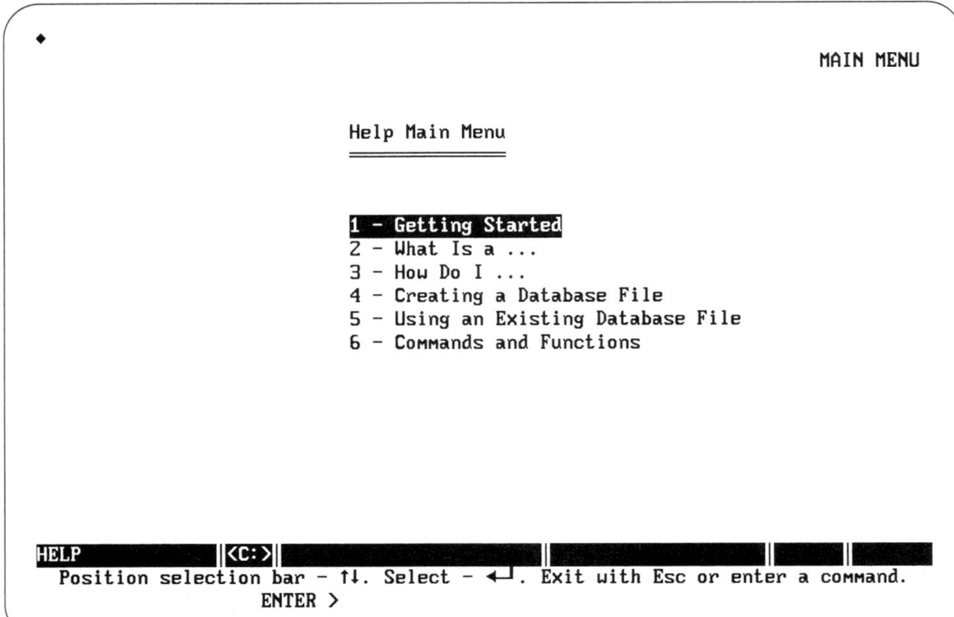

FIGURE 8-3

Main Menu for HELP, Accessed with **F1**

another database file, the current file will be closed. At this point it is safe to remove your floppy data disk from the disk drive. Never remove a floppy disk while any files are open—you could lose all the data on that disk.

Creating a New Database File

There are two steps in creating a database file. First you must design the **structure** of a record—that is, determine the appropriate data fields, then for each field choose a meaningful name, a type, and the proper width. The second step involves populating the database file by *appending data* to it.

Create the Record Structure

The Create screen in Figure 8-4 results from typing **CREATE CD.** The table in the screen will be filled with field specifications for the current database. dBASE field names must begin with a letter, and may be up to ten characters (letters and digits) long. The underscore is the only special character allowed in field names. dBASE III PLUS allows 128 fields per record. You can define up to 4000 characters in a record's width; dBASE displays the number of remaining bytes (characters) as you add new fields.

Types of Database Fields

dBASE III PLUS uses all of the dBASE IV data types except the **float** type. The field types are listed below and described in Chapter 3.

- **Character fields** contain text characters and digits in a fixed width.
- **Numeric fields** hold numbers that are used in mathematical operations.
- **Date fields** contain dates in a special format.
- Results of conditions—true or false—are stored in **logical fields**.
- **Memo fields** hold large amounts of textual data and can vary in width. Memo fields are stored in a separate .DBT file.

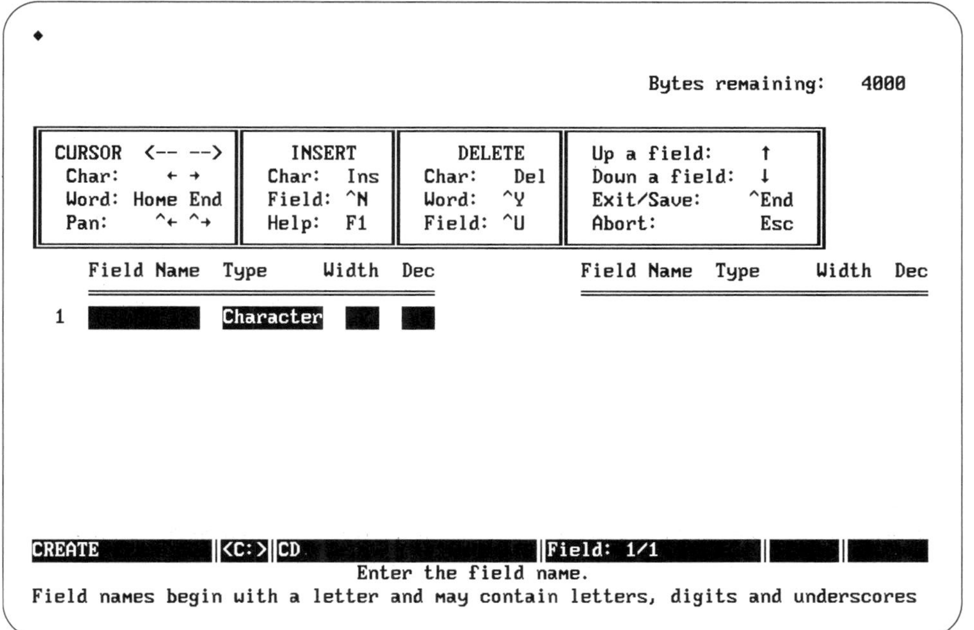

FIGURE 8-4

Create Database Screen

Making Changes to the Structure

If you have made a mistake or wish to make changes to the structure, use the cursor keys to move the cursor to the proper box and enter the correction. Pressing **Ins** once will put you into the Insert mode, indicated in the Status Bar at the far right. Pressing **Ins** again will turn off Insert mode. If you need to insert a field between two others, move the cursor to the second field and press **Ctrl-N** to open a new field line. To delete a field, move the cursor to that field and press **Ctrl-U.**

Example: *Working with the CD Sample Database*

This example is the same one covered earlier in the dBASE IV section. A compact disk database is used to illustrate the procedure of creating a database file. For each compact disk there will be several fields:

ARTIST	Name of the performer or group
TITLE	Title of the performance
PUBLISHER	Name of the disk publisher
CATALOG	The catalog number
YEAR	Year of issue
CLASS	Music category (jazz, rock, classical)
LENGTH	Total recording time in minutes
DIGITAL	Whether this is a digital recording

1. First start dBASE and wait until the main Assist menu screen appears. Press **Esc** to activate the dot prompt mode. You will see a dot prompt in the lower left corner of the screen.
2. Type in the command **CREATE CD** and press **Enter.** This example assumes the C drive will be the default drive. You'll next see the Create

screen of Figure 8-4. Note that the file name and drive location appear in the Status Bar at the lower left of the Create screen.

3. The cursor is on field name line for field 1. You must enter the field name, type, and width of the eight fields in the current file. Type the name of the first field, **ARTIST.** Press **Enter** to go to the Type box.
4. The field type defaults to Character, but the other choices are accessed by pressing the first letter of that choice. In this case press **Enter** to select Character type. The cursor will move to the Width box.
5. You'll next be asked to supply the width of the field, in characters. Width refers to the overall width of the field, including decimal places for numeric fields. The Dec box indicates the number of decimal places. Fill in the ARTIST field's width of **18** and press **Enter.** dBASE will skip over Dec for nonnumeric fields.
6. Fill in the rest of the Database work surface for the remaining fields. Figure 8-5 shows the table filled in with a description of the fields. All of these specifications form what is known as the *structure* of the database file.
7. To save the structure, press **Ctrl-End.** The explanation of this command is given below.

Saving the Structure

When you have finished creating the structure, press **Ctrl-End.** dBASE will ask you to press **Enter** to confirm the save operation. (Pressing any other key will stop the save and leave you in the Create screen.) When you have confirmed the save, dBASE will create a file called CD.DBF on the selected disk drive. When asked if you want to append data now, reply **N** for No.

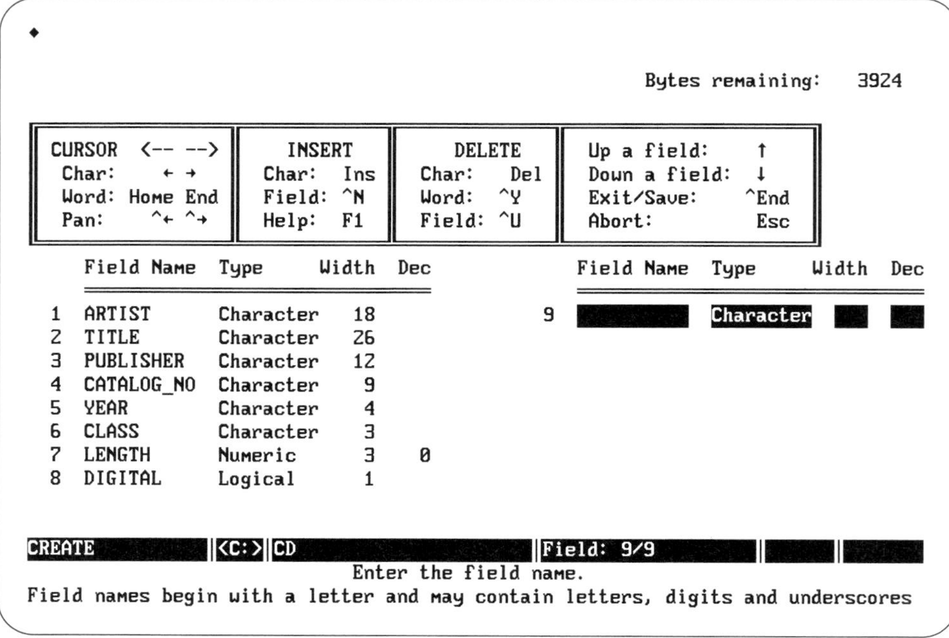

FIGURE 8-5

Create Structure Screen with Filled-in Values

Adding Data to the Database Structure

The dBASE III PLUS .DBF database file format is very similar to that used by dBASE IV. We will create the same database used in the dBASE IV chapters, but we could also read the CD.DBF file we created earlier in dBASE III PLUS.

Example: *Appending Data to the Structure*

In this example you will add data to the CD.DBF file using the **APPEND** command from the dot prompt. We will assume you have already created the database structure in the previous example.

1. Start dBASE as usual. If CD is not the current database file, enter the command **USE CD** and press **Enter.** You will see CD in the third box of the Status Bar to confirm that this file is in use.

2. Type **DISP STRU** from the dot prompt. Remember that dBASE permits you to abbreviate commands and key words by their first four characters. You will see the output shown below:

```
.DISP STRU
Structure for database: C:cd.dbf
Number of data records:       0
Date of last update   : 05/21/91
Field  Field Name  Type       Width     Dec
    1  ARTIST      Character     18
    2  TITLE       Character     26
    3  PUBLISHER   Character     12
    4  CATALOG_NO  Character      9
    5  YEAR        Character      4
    6  CLASS       Character      3
    7  LENGTH      Numeric        3
    8  DIGITAL     Logical        1
** Total **                      77
.
```

3. Next type **APPEND** and press **Enter.** dBASE displays the Append screen, allowing you to key in values for the current record. See Figure 8-6.

4. Enter the following field values into the eight fields. At the end of each field, press **Enter** to go to the next field. [Note: Some labs may have installed dBASE to *automatically* go on to the next field when the current field is filled. Watch the screen as you fill up a full field.]

```
The Canadian Brass
High, Bright, Light and Cl
RCA
RCD14574
1983
CL
51
Y
```

5. When you press **Enter** after the last field, dBASE will save that record and present you with a new blank screen for record 2. The record pointer in the Status Bar shows Rec: EOF/1, meaning that we're at the end of the file with a total of 1 record.

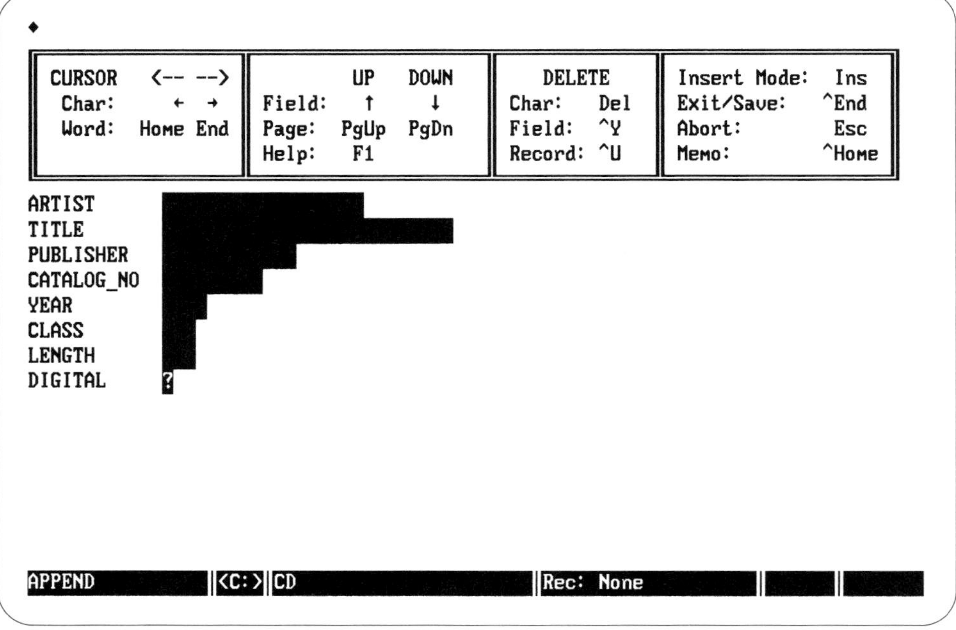

FIGURE 8-6

Append Screen for Adding Data

6. Next enter the remaining five records as shown in Figure 8-7. After all six records have been added, press **Ctrl-End** to terminate the APPEND process. Some of the fields have been truncated because the database fields are not wide enough to contain their entire contents.

7. To display the data in our database, type **LIST** at the dot prompt. You should see values for all six records as shown in Figure 8-8. Because the display is wider than the 80 characters on the screen, part of the record will wrap around to the next line.

8. To better display the data without wrapping to the next line, enter the command **LIST ARTIST, TITLE, YEAR, LENGTH.** Only those four fields will be displayed. You'll see the output shown below.

```
. LIST ARTIST, TITLE, YEAR, LENGTH
Record# ARTIST             TITLE                   YEAR LENGTH
      1 The Canadian Brass High, Bright, Light and Cl 1983     51
      2 Wiener Philharmoni Beethoven: Symphony No. 9  1987     72
      3 Wynton Marsalis    Trumpet Concertos          1983     40
      4 Stern, Rampal      Play Vivaldi & Telemann    1978     44
      5 Glenn Gould        Bach Goldberg Variations   1982     51
      6 Festival Strings L Adagio Albioni,Pachelbel,B 1972     62
.
```

Moving the Record Pointer

The Status Bar shows the current location of the **record pointer.** To move the pointer to another record, use the **GOTO** or **SKIP** commands.

FIGURE 8-7

Contents of CD.DBF Database

Wiener Philharmoni	Beethoven: Symphony No. 9	Deutsche Gr.	419598-2	1987	CL	72	Y
Wynton Marsalis	Trumpet Concertos	CBS Master	MK37846	1983	CL	40	Y
Stern, Rampal	Play Vivaldi & Telemann	CBS Master	MK35133	1978	CL	44	N
Glenn Gould	Back Goldberg Variations	CBS Master	MK3777	1982	CL	51	Y
Festival Strings L	Adagio Albioni,Pachelbel,B	Deutsche Gr.	4132248-2	1972	CL	62	N

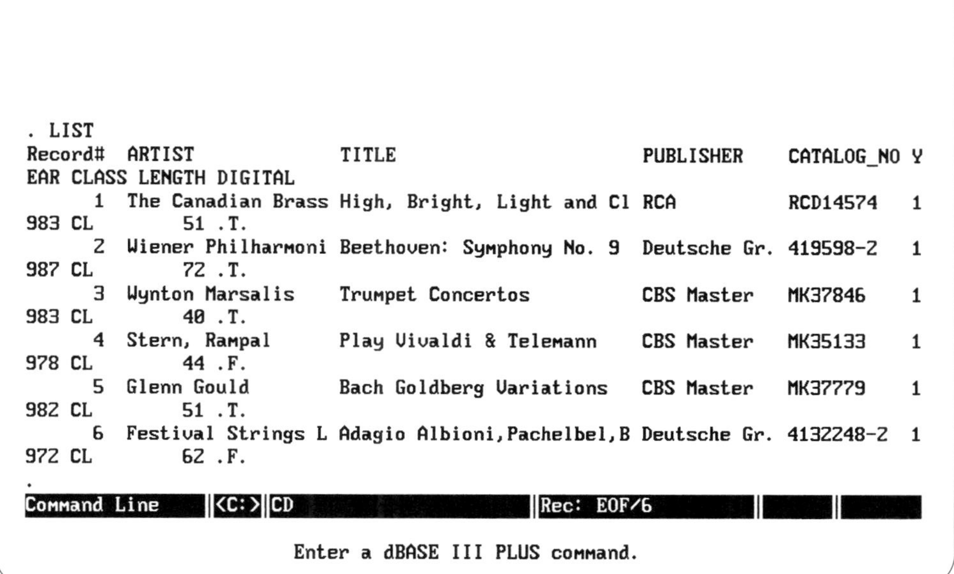

```
. LIST
Record#  ARTIST             TITLE                      PUBLISHER     CATALOG_NO Y
EAR CLASS LENGTH DIGITAL
      1  The Canadian Brass High, Bright, Light and Cl RCA           RCD14574   1
983 CL        51 .T.
      2  Wiener Philharmoni Beethoven: Symphony No. 9  Deutsche Gr.  419598-2   1
987 CL        72 .T.
      3  Wynton Marsalis    Trumpet Concertos          CBS Master    MK37846    1
983 CL        40 .T.
      4  Stern, Rampal      Play Vivaldi & Telemann    CBS Master    MK35133    1
978 CL        44 .F.
      5  Glenn Gould        Bach Goldberg Variations   CBS Master    MK37779    1
982 CL        51 .T.
      6  Festival Strings L Adagio Albioni,Pachelbel,B Deutsche Gr.  4132248-2  1
972 CL        62 .F.
.
Command Line    ||<C:>||CD               ||Rec: EOF/6      ||    ||
                     Enter a dBASE III PLUS command.
```

FIGURE 8-8

LIST Display for CD Database

- **GOTO** moves the pointer to a specified record number, such as **GOTO 4. GOTO TOP** positions the pointer at the first record. **GOTO BOTTOM** positions the pointer at the last record.

- **SKIP** moves the record pointer forward or backward a specified number of records. **SKIP 3** moves ahead three records. **SKIP -1** moves backward one record. **SKIP** is the same command as **SKIP 1.**

You can also move the pointer to a record that matches a certain condition with the **LOCATE FOR <cond>** command. The <cond> is a logical expression, such as **YEAR>"1983", PUBLISHER="CBS"** or **DIGITAL.** [Note: The last expression is complete as written, without an operator, because DIGITAL is a logical field having the value of True or False.]

Displaying Fields from One Record

DISPLAY is used in conjunction with the GOTO and SKIP commands. The **DISPLAY** command displays the values of the field in the current record. **LIST** displays *all* records, regardless of the record pointer's location. The **FOR** clause can be used to show records that match a condition.

Example: ***Moving the Record Pointer***

1. Start dBASE as usual. If it is not already in use, issue the command **USE CD** to make CD.DBF the default database.
2. Issue the command **GOTO 4** and press **Enter.** The Status Bar should show Rec: 4/6. Type **DISPLAY** to see the field values for record 4.

```
. DISP
Record#  ARTIST              TITLE                      PUBLISHER    CATALOG_NO Y
EAR CLASS LENGTH DIGITAL
      4  Stern, Rampal       Play Vivaldi & Telemann    CBS Master   MK35133    1
978 CL        44 .F.
.
```

3. The ? command can be used as shorthand to display certain fields. Issue the command **? ARTIST,DIGITAL** to show just those two fields for the current record.

```
. ? ARTIST,DIGITAL
Stern, Rampal      .F.
.
```

4. For this step we will examine the ARTIST and PUBLISHER fields for CBS Masterworks recordings. Issue the command **LIST ARTIST,PUBLISHER FOR PUBLISHER="CBS".** You should see the following output. Note that dBASE allows you to specify just enough leading characters in the PUBLISHER field to identify the condition. Any value in that field that begins with CBS would qualify for the LIST.

```
. LIST ARTIST,PUBLISHER FOR PUBLISHER="CBS"
Record#  ARTIST              PUBLISHER
      3  Wynton Marsalis     CBS Master
      4  Stern, Rampal       CBS Master
      5  Glenn Gould         CBS Master
.
```

Modifying Data

As with dBASE IV, you can use the Edit and Browse screens to display and change data values.

Using the Edit Screen

The field display in the APPEND command is also available with the **EDIT**command. This command brings up a display showing the fields of the current record arranged vertically on the screen. You can position the record pointer at the desired record before issuing the EDIT command. Use the arrow keys to position the cursor at the field to be changed and enter the corrections. Use the **PgUp** and **PgDn** keys to move to other records. When you are finished, press **Ctrl-End** to save the changes. To abort the changes made to the *current*

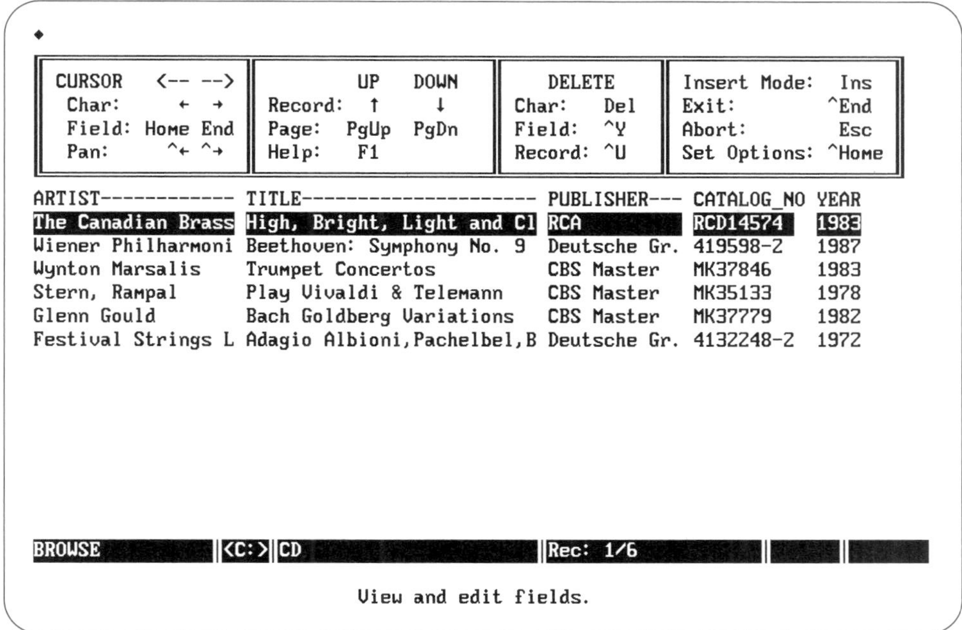

FIGURE 8-9

Typical Browse Screen

record, press **Esc;** changes made to previous records are saved permanently when you move the record pointer to a new record.

Using the BROWSE Command

dBASE III PLUS provides a way of "browsing" through multiple records on the screen. The **BROWSE** command brings up a full screen similar to that of dBASE IV with the fields stretching horizontally across the screen and the records stretching vertically. You can use the ↑ and ↓ keys to move between records and the **End** and **Home** keys to move between fields. The → and ← arrow keys move from character to character within a field. A typical Browse screen is shown in Figure 8-9.

The Browse screen shows the first five fields in the CD.DBF database. Pressing the **End** key repeatedly moves the cursor to the right. To pan the screen to the right, press **Ctrl-→**; likewise, to pan the display back to the left-most fields, press **Ctrl-←**. To edit or replace values in the fields, move the cursor to the desired location and begin typing the correct characters. The **Ins** key can toggle between the Insert and Overtype modes.

Sorting with dBASE III PLUS

The **SORT** command in dBASE III PLUS is similar to that command in dBASE IV. Its syntax appears below:

```
SORT TO <filename> ON <fieldname> [/A] [/D]] [/C]
     [,<field2> [/A] [/C] [/D]...] [<scope>]
     [FOR <condition>] [WHILE <condition>]
```

The first field listed is the **primary key.** Any following fields are **secondary keys.** The / options that follow refer to:

/A Ascending order (default)

/D Descending order

/C Ignore upper-/lowercase differences

Thus we could use the command **SORT TO CDPUB ON PUBLISHER** to create another database file called CDPUB.DBF that is in order by the PUBLISHER field.

Indexing with dBASE III PLUS

Indexing is usually preferred to sorting, particularly when we wish to view the database in more than one order. Indexes take up less room than the separate database file that results from sorting. Indexes can be used to quickly locate a desired record by looking up its value in the index table. The syntax for the **INDEX ON** command is shown below:

```
INDEX ON <key expression> TO <index file> [UNIQUE]
```

The <index file> will have an .NDX file extension. The UNIQUE parameter will cause all records to have unique key expressions; any record having the same key expression as one already in the index will not be added to the index.

Thus we could use the command **INDEX ON PUBLISHER TO CDPUB** to create an index. Results from that command and a listing of the records in indexed order are shown below:

```
. INDEX ON PUBLISHER TO CDPUB
  100% indexed          6 Records indexed
. LIST ARTIST, TITLE, PUBLISHER
Record#  ARTIST              TITLE                        PUBLISHER
      3  Wynton Marsalis     Trumpet Concertos            CBS Master
      4  Stern, Rampal       Play Vivaldi & Telemann      CBS Master
      5  Glenn Gould         Bach Goldberg Variations     CBS Master
      2  Wiener Philharmoni  Beethoven: Symphony No. 9    Deutsche Gr.
      6  Festival Strings L  Adagio Albioni,Pachelbel,B   Deutsche Gr.
      1  The Canadian Brass  High, Bright, Light and Cl   RCA
```

Using an Existing Index File

If the database file has been previously indexed, you can specify that the index be activated when you open the file. **USE CD INDEX CDPUB** opens the CD.DBF database file and makes CDPUB the primary index. If the database file is already in use, the command **SET INDEX TO CDPUB** activates the index.

Finding Records in the Index

Use the **SEEK <expr>** command to find the first record in the index that matches the expression. Thus **SEEK "CBS"** could be used to find the first record in the CDPUB index that begins with "CBS". To find the next record, if any, use the **CONTINUE** command.

Deleting Records

As with dBASE IV, you can mark records for deletion in dBASE III PLUS with the **DELETE** command. The default scope for this command is just the current record. If you wish to delete several records, you must add a range to the end of the command. Examples of DELETE scope include:

- **ALL** deletes all records.
- **REST** deletes all remaining records from the current record pointer position on, including the current record.
- **NEXT n** deletes the next *n* records where *n* is an integer number.
- **RECORD n** deletes record number *n*.

To unerase records that are marked for deletion, use the **RECALL** command. It shares the same scope as DELETE. To permanently erase records that have been marked for deletion, use the **PACK** command. It has no parameters. PACK should only be used occasionally, because it is very time-consuming with large databases.

Leaving dBASE III PLUS

To leave dBASE III PLUS type **QUIT** at the dot prompt. dBASE will close all files and return to the DOS prompt. As with dBASE IV, the user does not have to issue any file save commands before exiting. Changes made to a database file are automatically saved when the user quits dBASE.

BUILDING dBASE III PLUS REPORTS

The dBASE III PLUS Report facility is similar to the Quick Report feature of dBASE IV. Although it is quite limited in formatting and location of fields, it permits you to design custom reports up to the width of the paper used. There are no report bands with this version of dBASE and a single detail line. You may design a report title that is up to four lines long; each column heading may be up to four lines long. There is a group facility for producing **control-break group reports** with two group levels.

The Report Screen

Whether you create a report from the dot prompt with the **CREATE REPORT** command or from the Assist menu, the Create Report screen is the same, shown in Figure 8-10.

The Menu Bar choices are shown at the top of the screen with the first one highlighted. These choices are explained below. To select a menu choice use the right and left arrow keys to highlight its Menu Bar. Unlike dBASE IV, in dBASE III PLUS the Menu Bar is always activated in the Report screen.

Options This choice lets you specify the title and page margins for the report. You can select single or double spacing through this menu and control whether the printer should do a page eject before or after the report.

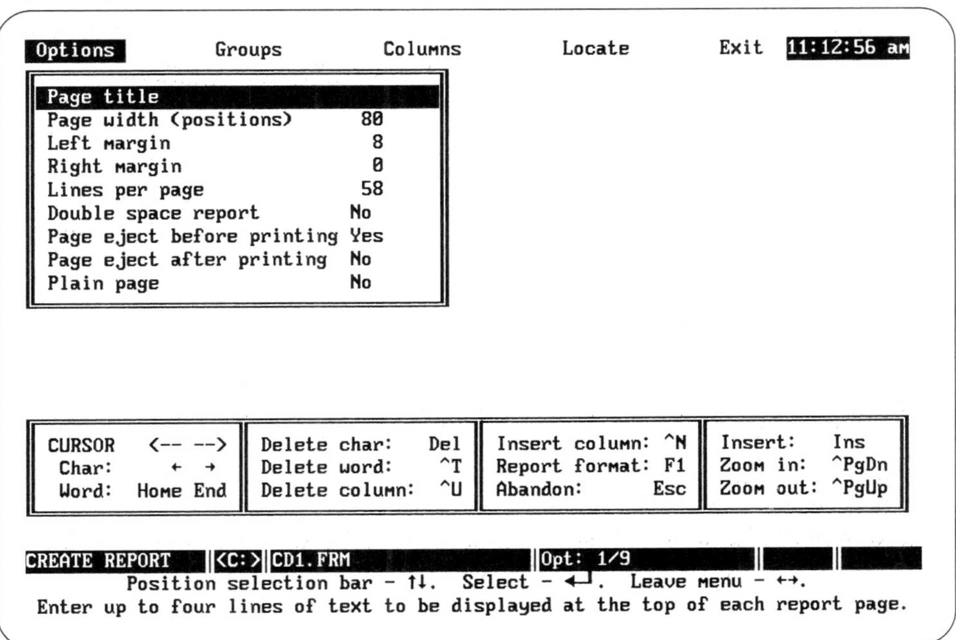

FIGURE 8-10

Opening Create Report Screen

Groups This menu allows you to indicate whether a group report is to be generated. You can specify the group expression and a heading for the group.

Columns This is the primary menu choice when building a report. For each field (column) in the report, you specify the field or expression to be printed, the column heading, and the field width. For numeric fields, you can choose whether to total the field at the bottom of the report.

Locate This shortcut option lets you move the cursor to the report column by picking it from a pick list. The other way is to use the **PgUp** and **PgDn** keys to move from column to column.

Exit This choice is used to save or abandon the current report and return to the dot prompt or the Assist menu.

Creating a Report

The steps in creating a dBASE III PLUS report are similar to those for dBASE IV:

- Design the report on paper.
- Select a database file and issue the **USE** command.
- Issue the **CREATE REPORT** command, giving the report name.
- Select report options including title, margins, and line spacing.
- For each column in the report choose the field, column heading, and column width.
- Save the report and return to the dot prompt.
- Print the report.

Design the Report

Unlike dBASE IV, dBASE III PLUS has no report bands. Because there is only a single detail band, you must be careful to select the proper fields and their column widths to make everything fit on one line. Unless you use a compressed print font or wide paper, the line width is 80 characters minus the left and right margin space.

As you build the report, dBASE displays a report format template in the bottom portion of the screen that shows a view of the detail line. dBASE uses special characters to represent the fields in each column. The width of each field is depicted visually by the number of special characters in the template.

>	Shows character positions in the left margin.
X	Shows a character field position.
#	Shows the position of a numeric field digit. The decimal point (if any) is also shown within the field.
.L.	Shows the location of a logical field.
mm/dd/yy	Shows the location of a date field.
–	Shows unused character positions in the right margin area.

The Options Menu Bar

The first line in the **Options** Menu Bar is *Page title.* dBASE will automatically center this title using the current page width. If your report is narrower than 80 characters, the title will not center properly. Do not put spaces in front of the title or they will be considered as part of the title when it is centered.

Example: *Create a Simple Report*

In this example you will create a simple custom report called CD1.FRM using the CD database file, which is available on the data disk.

1. Start dBASE normally. If CD is not already in use, issue the command **USE CD.**
2. To start the report creation process, give the command **CREATE REPORT CD1** and press **Enter.** dBASE will present the opening Create Report screen shown in Figure 8-10.
3. With the cursor on the *Page title* line press **Enter** to open the page title box shown in Figure 8-11. Enter the title **COMPACT DISK COLLECTION** and press **Ctrl-End** to save the title.
4. Press the right arrow key to move the cursor to the **Columns** Menu Bar. In this Menu Bar you will type the field name and a column heading, and determine the field width.
5. Figure 8-12 shows the **Columns** Menu Bar choices. Press **Enter** to select the *Contents* line. When the right triangle appears on the line, type in **ARTIST** and press **Enter** to place the ARTIST field in the first column. Note that dBASE has used the current field width, 18 characters, as the width for this column.
6. Press the down arrow key to move to the *Heading* line. Press **Enter** to open the Heading box. On the first line of the Heading box, type **ARTIST** and press **Ctrl-End** to save this column heading. Figure 8-13 shows this screen just before the column heading is saved.
7. Press **PgDn** to move to the next column. This column will hold the TITLE field. Press **Enter** to open the *Contents* line, but instead of typing in the

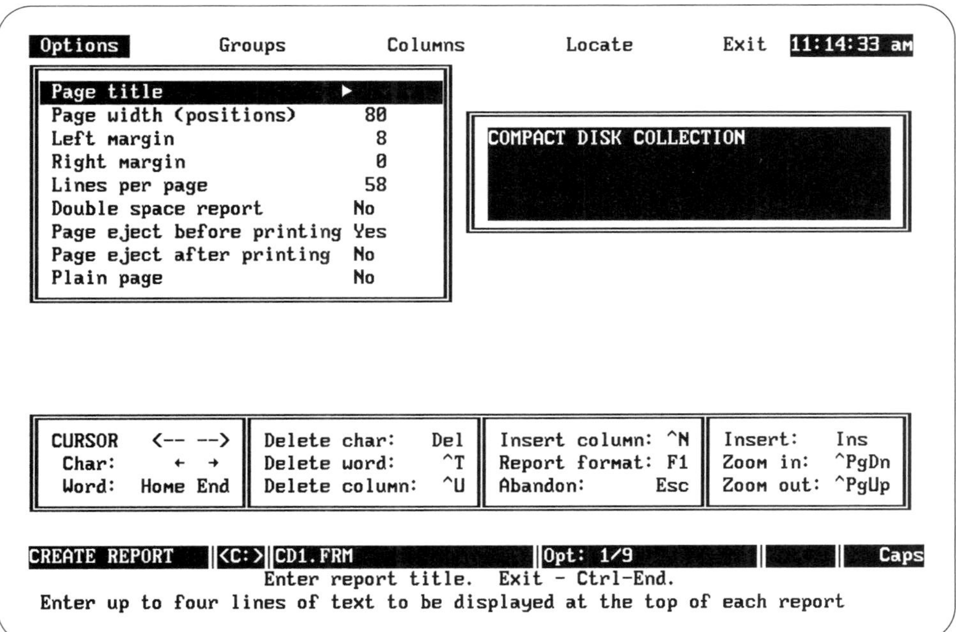

FIGURE 8-11

Page Title Option Screen

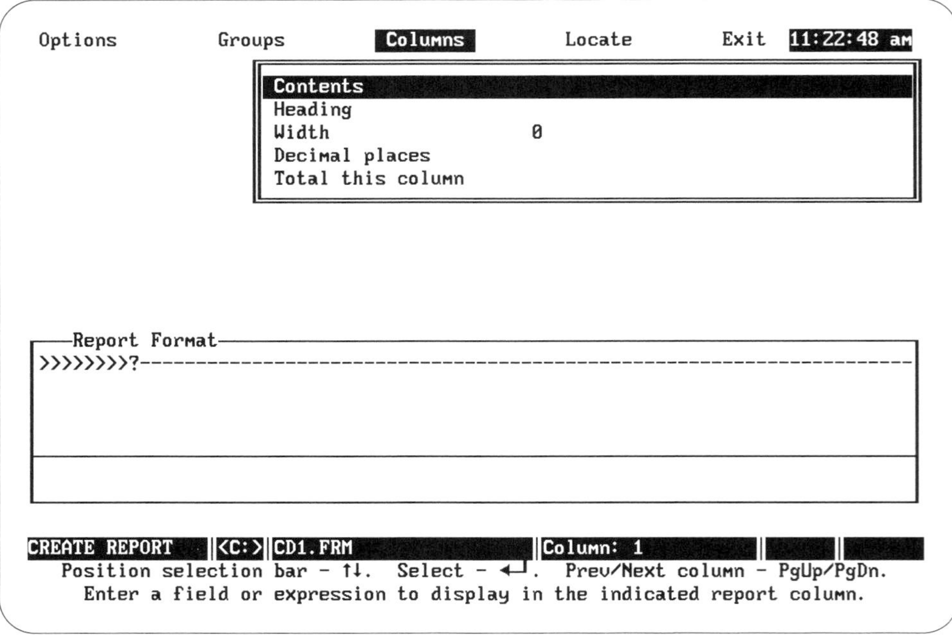

FIGURE 8-12

Blank Columns Screen

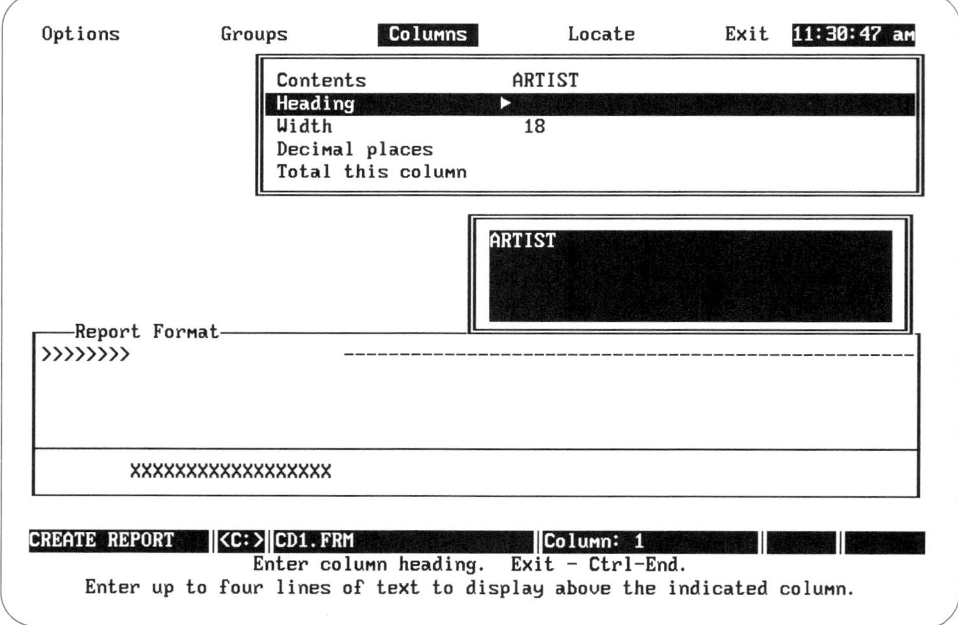

FIGURE 8-13

Create Heading in Columns Menu Bar

field name, press **F10** to open a field list menu. From this list, move the cursor to the **TITLE** field and press **Enter** to select this field. Many dBASE III PLUS menus use the F10 key to activate a pick list. Figure 8-14 shows the field pick list.

8. For the second column, type **DISK TITLE** as the heading. For now, change the column width from 26 to 15 characters. dBASE will put any "extra" characters past position 15 on the line just beneath the first line.

9. Press **PgDn** to move to the third column for our report. Place the **CATALOG_NO** field in the *Contents* line of this column. For the *heading,*

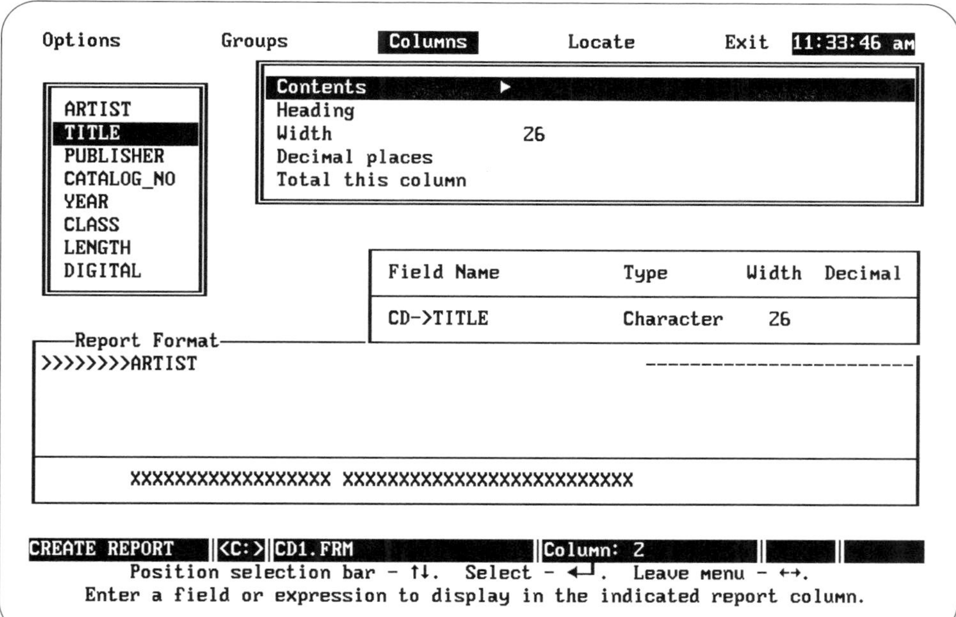

FIGURE 8-14

Field Pick List Display

```
Options          Groups        Columns          Locate        Exit  02:55:48 pm

                        Contents                  CATALOG_NO
                        Heading                   ►
                        Width                       9
                        Decimal places
                        Total this column

                                              CATALOG
                                              NO.

Report Format
>>>>>>>>ARTIST              DISK TITLE               ------------------------

        XXXXXXXXXXXXXXXXXX XXXXXXXXXXXXXXX XXXXXXXXX

CREATE REPORT  <C:> CD1.FRM                 Column: 3
                  Enter column heading.  Exit - Ctrl-End.
     Enter up to four lines of text to display above the indicated column.
```

FIGURE 8-15

Two-Line Column Heading

place **CATALOG** on the first line and **NO.** on the second line. Figure 8-15 shows this arrangement. dBASE will automatically center each line of the heading over the report. Press **Ctrl-End** to save the heading.

10. Let's save the report now by pressing the right arrow to highlight the **Exit** Menu Bar. Choose the *Save* line and press **Enter.** The report will be saved in a file called CD1.FRM.

11. To execute the report, type **REPORT FORM CD1** and press **Enter.** The report is shown on the following page. Add **TO PRINT** to send the report to the printer.

```
. REPORT FORM CD1
       Page No.     1
       05/23/91
                              COMPACT DISK COLLECTION

       ARTIST              DISK TITLE      CATALOG
                                           NO.

       The Canadian Brass High, Bright,    RCD14574
                          Light and Cl
       Wiener Philharmoni Beethoven:       419598-2
                          Symphony No. 9
       Wynton Marsalis    Trumpet          MK37846
                          Concertos
       Stern, Rampal      Play Vivaldi &   MK35133
                          Telemann
       Glenn Gould        Bach Goldberg    MK37779
                          Variations
       Festival Strings L Adagio           4132248-2
                          Albioni,Pachelb
                          el,B
.
```

Example: *Modifying a Report*

In this example we will modify the CD1 report to include more fields and to make sure the report title is centered above the report.

1. If you have not already started dBASE III PLUS, do so now. Issue the command **USE CD** to open the compact disk database.

2. For this example we will modify an existing report, so issue the command **MODIFY REPORT CD1.** dBASE will load the report file and show you the **Options** Menu Bar.

3. Press the right arrow key two times to move the cursor to the **Columns** Menu Bar. Press **PgDn** three times to move to a new column with a blank *Contents* line. In the new column, place the expression **YEAR+CLASS,** a concatenation of the two character fields. [Note: The string concatenation operator requires that both fields be the same type—you cannot concatenate a character and a numeric field.]

4. For the *Heading* of the new column, put **YEAR** on the first heading line and **CL** on the second heading line. Make the column width **4** characters. Press **PgDn** to go to the next new column.

5. Place the **LENGTH** field in the next column. Use the two-line heading with **DISK** on line 1 and **LENGTH** on the second line. Press **PgDn** to go on to the next column.

6. Place the **DIGITAL** field in the final column on the *Contents* line. The heading will be **DIGI-** on the first line and **TAL?** on the second line. Figure 8-16 shows the last column and a portion of the report template. Notice that there are several hyphens in the report template to the right of the last field. They indicate that there are unused character positions that will cause the report title to be off-center.

7. Our last adjustment of this report will be to move the cursor to the **Options** Menu Bar and reduce the *Page width* by eight characters to 72.

```
Options          Groups          Columns          Locate          Exit  04:04:28 pm

                    Contents               digital
                    Heading                DIGI-;TAL?
                    Width                    5
                    Decimal places
                    Total this column

-Report Format-
    DISK TITLE       CATALOG   YEAR  DISK    DIGI- --------
                     NO.       CL    LENGTH  TAL?

XXXXX XXXXXXXXXXXXXXX XXXXXXXXX XXXX      ### .L.

MODIFY REPORT  ||<C:>||CD1.FRM                ||Column: 6
  Position selection bar - ↑↓.  Select - ←┘.  Prev/Next column - PgUp/PgDn.
    Enter up to four lines of text to display above the indicated column.
```

FIGURE 8-16

Modified CD1.FRM Report Form

8. Move the cursor to the **Exit** Menu Bar and *Save* the report form. When you return to the dot prompt, issue the command **REPORT FORM CD1.** The revised report appears below:

```
Page No.      1
05/23/91
                    COMPACT DISK COLLECTION

ARTIST               DISK TITLE       CATALOG    YEAR    DISK DIGI-
                                      NO.        CL    LENGTH TAL?

The Canadian Brass High, Bright,      RCD14574   1983      51 .T.
                   Light and Cl                  CL
Wiener Philharmoni Beethoven:         419598-2   1987      72 .T.
                   Symphony No. 9                CL
Wynton Marsalis    Trumpet            MK37846    1983      40 .T.
                   Concertos                     CL
Stern, Rampal      Play Vivaldi &     MK35133    1978      44 .F.
                   Telemann                      CL
Glenn Gould        Bach Goldberg      MK37779    1982      51 .T.
                   Variations                    CL
Festival Strings L Adagio             4132248-2  1972      62 .F.
                   Albioni,Pachelb               CL
                   el,B
*** Total ***
                                                          320
```

Creating a Group Report

As with dBASE IV, dBASE III PLUS is able to prepare reports that group together records that share a common characteristic. These reports are also known as control-break reports. Before we can print the group report form, we need to reorder the records by the group field, in this case by PUBLISHER, so that all records sharing that group value will be together. Otherwise, whenever the group field's value changes, a new group will be printed.

Example: *Preparing a Group Report on an Indexed Database*

In this example we will create the index by PUBLISHER and prepare a custom report that is grouped by the PUBLISHER field.

1. Start dBASE as usual and make CD.DBF the database file in use.
2. Issue the command **INDEX ON PUBLISHER TO CDPUB** and press **Enter.** dBASE will create the index file CDPUB.NDX and will activate it.
3. We will start with a new report form, so issue the command **CREATE REPORT CDGR.**
4. Activate the *Page title* line of the **Options** Menu Bar and give the following two-line title. When finished, press **Ctrl-End** to save the title.

```
COMPACT DISK COLLECTION
REPORT BY PUBLISHER
```

5. Press the right arrow key to move to the **Groups** Menu Bar. On the *Group on expression* line, place **PUBLISHER**. On the *Group heading* line, place **Publisher:** . Be sure to put one space after the colon.
6. Press the right arrow key to move to the **Columns** Menu Bar. In the first column, place **ARTIST** with the heading of **Artist.** Press **PgDn** to move to the second column.
7. In the next three columns place the **TITLE, CATALOG_NO,** and **LENGTH** fields. You may use the **F10** Field List command to enter the field contents. Headings for these fields are **Disk Title, Catalog,** and **Time,** respectively.
8. Save the report in the **Exit** Menu Bar. From the dot prompt type **REPORT FORM CDGR** to see the report, shown below. Note that subtotals and totals for the TIME field are displayed in the report. dBASE will automatically total all numeric fields unless you instruct it not to do so in the **Columns** Menu Bar.

```
 Page No.     1
 05/24/91
                         COMPACT DISK COLLECTION
                           REPORT BY PUBLISHER

 Artist              Disk Title                 Catalog    Time

** Publisher: CBS Master
 Wynton Marsalis     Trumpet Concertos          MK37846      40
 Stern, Rampal       Play Vivaldi & Telemann    MK35133      44
 Glenn Gould         Bach Goldberg Variations   MK37779      51
** Subtotal **
                                                            135
** Publisher: Deutsche Gr.
 Wiener Philharmoni Beethoven: Symphony No. 9  419598-2     72
 Festival Strings L Adagio Albioni,Pachelbel,B 4132248-2    62
** Subtotal **
                                                            134
** Publisher: RCA
 The Canadian Brass High, Bright, Light and Cl RCD14574     51
** Subtotal **
                                                             51
*** Total ***
                                                            320
```

CREATING dBASE III PLUS LABELS

The Create Label screen shown in Figure 8-17 is somewhat similar to the Create Report screen. The **Options** Menu Bar allows you to select the size and number of labels on each page. The default size is 3.5 inches wide by 1 inch high, allowing five lines of 35 characters each with one blank line between labels. You can specify up to three labels across the page and change margins as needed. There are five different predefined label sizes available, which are accessed by pressing **Enter** when the cursor highlights the *Predefined size* line.

Creating a Label Design

The first step is to open the desired database file, then issue the command **CREATE LABEL** from the dot prompt. When prompted, give the file name for this label design to be saved. Then select the desired label size and modify any of the parameters in the **Options** Menu Bar as needed. When finished, press the right arrow key to move to the **Contents** Menu Bar.

The display will show the number of lines per label that you specified in the **Options** Menu Bar. Press **Enter** to open the first label line and enter a field name or expression for that line. When finished, press **Enter** to close that line and press the down arrow key to move to another line. Continue entering the fields in the label template until all are entered, then press the right arrow key to move the cursor to the **Exit** Menu Bar, where you can *Save* the label design. dBASE will add .LBL as a file extension to your label file.

Printing Labels

Once you have opened the desired database file, enter the command **LABEL FORM <filename> TO PRINT,** where <filename> is the name of the label design file. If you add **SAMPLE** to the end of the command, dBASE will give you a chance to print a sample label to align the label form in the printer. When ready for printing, reply **N** and dBASE will begin printing labels. If you omit the **TO PRINT** clause, the labels will appear on the screen.

Example: *Creating Labels in dBASE III PLUS*

In this example we will prepare a set of labels that could be applied to a catalog of compact disk titles.

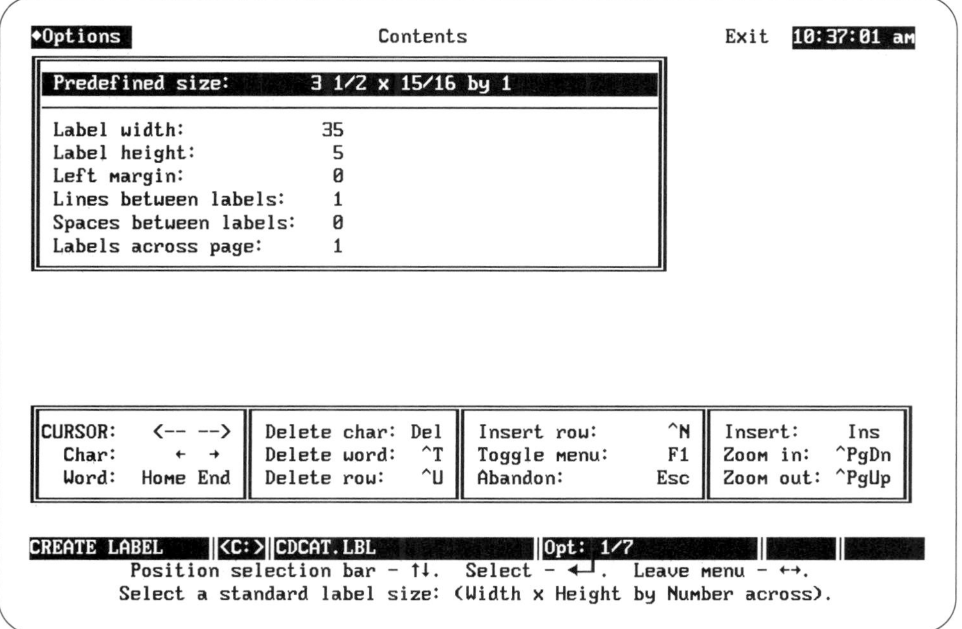

FIGURE 8-17

Opening Create Label Screen

1. Start dBASE as usual and open the CD.DBF database file with the command **USE CD.**
2. Type **CREATE LABEL CDCAT** and press **Enter.** You should see the opening Label screen shown in Figure 8-17. We will use the predefined size of 3 1/2 × 15/16 by 2, so press **Enter** one time with the cursor on the first line of the **Options** Menu Bar. This will allow us to display two labels per line.
3. Press the right arrow key to move to the **Contents** Menu Bar. The label will consist of the following fields and expressions as shown in Figure 8-18:

   Line 1: **ARTIST**

   Line 2: **TITLE**

   Line 3: **PUBLISHER+" "+CATALOG_NO**

   Line 4: **YEAR,LENGTH**

   The line 3 expression concatenates the publisher and catalog number together with one space in between. Line 4 shows both the YEAR and LENGTH fields with one blank space between them.
4. Press the right arrow key and then **Enter** to *Save* the label design in a file called CDCAT.LBL.
5. At the dot prompt type **LABEL FORM CDCAT** and press **Enter.** The labels will immediately display on the screen as shown below:

```
. LABEL FORM CDCAT
The Canadian Brass                      Wiener Philharmoni
High, Bright, Light and Cl              Beethoven: Symphony No. 9
RCA          RCD14574                   Deutsche Gr. 419598-2
1983  51                                1987  72

Wynton Marsalis                         Stern, Rampal
Trumpet Concertos                       Play Vivaldi & Telemann
CBS Master   MK37846                    CBS Master   MK35133
1983  40                                1978  44
```

FIGURE 8-18

Contents of Label

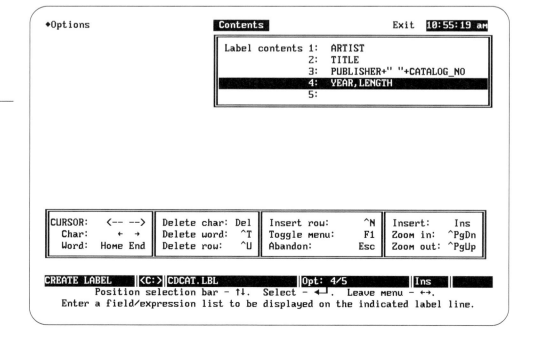

```
•Options                       Contents                    Exit  10:55:19 am
                              Label contents 1:  ARTIST
                                             2:  TITLE
                                             3:  PUBLISHER+" "+CATALOG_NO
                                             4:  YEAR,LENGTH
                                             5:

CURSOR:   <-- -->  | Delete char: Del | Insert row:    ^N | Insert:    Ins
 Char:      ←  →   | Delete word:  ^T | Toggle menu:   F1 | Zoom in:  ^PgDn
 Word:   Home End  | Delete row:   ^U | Abandon:      Esc | Zoom out: ^PgUp

CREATE LABEL  |<C:>|CDCAT.LBL          |Opt: 4/5          |Ins |
        Position selection bar - ↑↓.  Select - ↵.  Leave menu - ←→.
   Enter a field/expression list to be displayed on the indicated label line.
```

```
Glenn Gould                          Festival Strings L
Bach Goldberg Variations             Adagio Albioni,Pachelbel,B
CBS Master   MK37779                 Deutsche Gr. 4132248-2
1982  51                             1972  62
```

Modifying an Existing Label Design

Use the **MODIFY LABEL <filename>** command to make changes to an existing label design. You will see the same Label screen and can make changes in the **Options** or **Contents** Menu Bars. When you use the **Exit** command, the changes will be saved in the named file. Note that you cannot save the changes under a *different* file name. To do this, you must first copy the label design file to a new name and then modify the new file.

CREATING A dBASE III PLUS QUERY

Query is used to select records from the database that match certain conditions specified in the query. The Query feature in dBASE III PLUS is much less powerful than its counterpart in dBASE IV. The command **CREATE QUERY <filename>** is used to create a new query. The command **MODIFY QUERY <filename>** can be used to make changes to an existing query. To use a query, issue the command **SET FILTER TO FILE <filename>** where <filename> is the name of the query file. Then subsequent **LIST** or **DISPLAY** commands will show only those records that qualify according to the conditions in the query. There is also a facility within the Query screen to display the contents of qualifying records.

The main Create Query screen is shown in Figure 8-19. You can specify up to seven filter conditions with one query. Each line represents one filter condition and the lines are linked with the *Connect* line to represent either of the two **connect types,** AND or OR.

- An **AND** connection means that both lines must be true in order for the query to be true.
- An **OR** connection means that if either line is true then the query will be true.

```
♦Set Filter              Nest              Display              Exit  11:24:14 am

 Field Name
 Operator
 Constant/Expression
 Connect

 Line Number        1

| Line | Field | Operator | Constant/Expression | Connect |
| 1    |       |          |                     |         |
| 2    |       |          |                     |         |
| 3    |       |          |                     |         |
| 4    |       |          |                     |         |
| 5    |       |          |                     |         |
| 6    |       |          |                     |         |
| 7    |       |          |                     |         |

CREATE QUERY   |<C:>|CD1.QRY              |Opt: 1/2        |Ins |
      Position selection bar - ↑↓.  Select - ◄┘.  Leave menu - ←→.
              Select a field name for the filter condition.
```

FIGURE 8-19

Create Query Opening Screen

The Set Filter Menu Bar

The **Set Filter Menu Bar** is used to create each line in the query. Choices are explained below:

- *Field Name* is the field whose value is to be compared against a constant or expression. When you press **Enter** on this line, a field list appears; move the cursor to the desired field and press **Enter** to place it on that line.
- *Operator* lets you specify the conditional **operator** that is appropriate for the field type selected for this line. Typical choices for a numeric field include =, >, >=, <, <=, and <> (not equal to). Other field types have different operator choices.
- *Constant/Expression* is the matching value to complete the condition line. You can specify a constant value or a dBASE expression.
- *Connect* lets you connect this line with other condition lines as explained above. This is used only if you have a compound condition in the query.

Using a Query from the Dot Prompt

To use a query from the dot prompt, issue the command **SET FILTER TO FILE <filename>.** Only records that qualify according to the query file named will be processed by further dot commands such as LIST and REPORT FORM. To cancel the query, issue the **SET FILTER TO** command without a file name; all records will once again be processed by dot commands.

Example: *Creating a Simple Query*

In this example we will create a query to examine just the CBS Masterworks disks using the CD.DBF database file.

1. Start dBASE as usual. Open the CD.DBF database file with the **USE CD** command.
2. Start the query with the command **CREATE QUERY CD1.** You will see the Query screen shown in Figure 8-19. Press **Enter** on the *Field Name* line, move the cursor to **PUBLISHER** and press **Enter** to select it for Line 1.
3. Next, press the down arrow key to move to the *Operator* line. When you press **Enter,** you'll see the list of operators shown in Figure 8-20. Select *Begins with* and press **Enter.**
4. With the cursor in the *Constant/Expression* line, press **Enter.** At the right triangle prompt, type **"CBS Master"** (including the quote characters) and press **Enter.** Any PUBLISHER field that begins with "CBS Master" will qualify for the query. Note that we could have just used "CBS" as the constant in this case.
5. Press the right arrow key two times to activate the **Display** Menu Bar. Press **Enter** to display the first matching record as shown in Figure 8-21. To see the other matching records press **PgDn** or **PgUp.** There should be three matching records to this query.
6. To save the query, press the right arrow key once more to **Exit** and select the *Save* line. dBASE will save this query as a file called CD1.QRY and you will return to the dot prompt.
7. Use the **LIST** command to see if the query is still in effect. How many records appear? Next issue the **SET FILTER TO** command without specifying a query file. Issue the **LIST** command to see that all six records now appear.

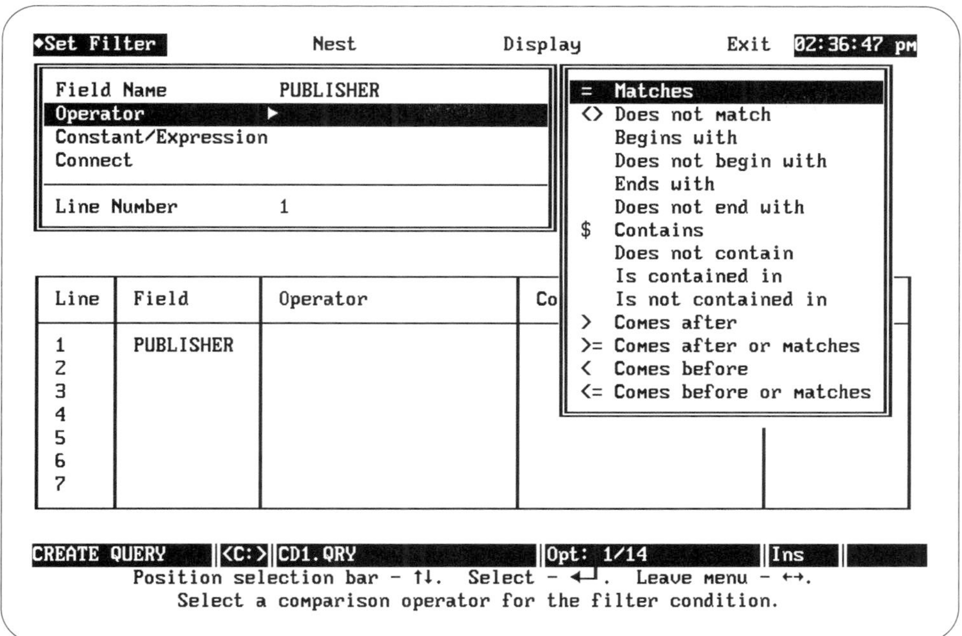

FIGURE 8-20

Operators for Character Field in Query

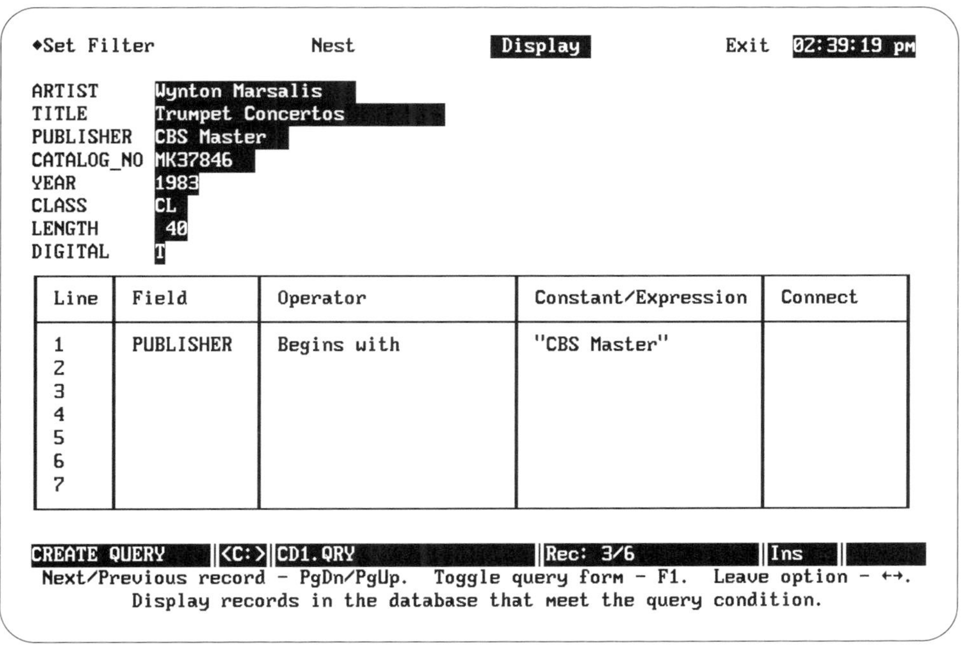

FIGURE 8-21

First Matching Record for CD1 Query

8. Finally, issue the command **SET FILTER TO FILE CD1** and try the **LIST** command. Only those records that match the CD1 query should appear.

Example: *Creating a Compound Query*

In this example we will create a compound query that will show all the digital disks that exceed 45 minutes in length.

1. Start dBASE as usual. Issue the **USE CD** command to open the compact disk database.

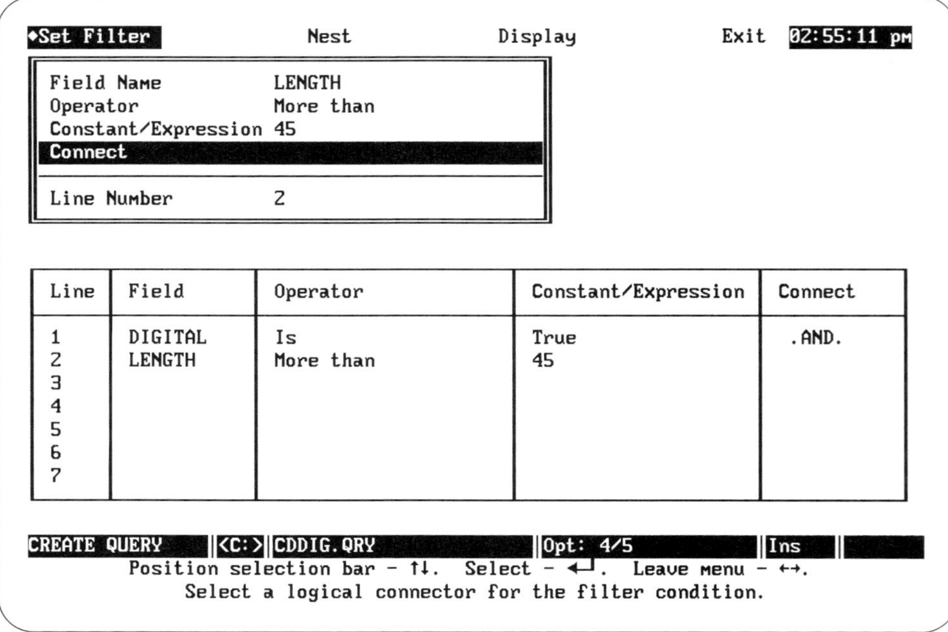

FIGURE 8-22

Compound Query Example

2. Next give the **CREATE QUERY CDDIG** command to create a new query called CDDIG.
3. At the **Set Filter** Menu Bar use **DIGITAL** as the *Field Name.* The operator will be **Is True.** dBASE will place Is in the *Operator* line and True in the *Constant/Expression* line.
4. Move to the *Connect* line with the down arrow key and press **Enter.** From the list select *Combine with .AND.* and press **Enter.** dBASE will open up the second line for the last part of the query.
5. The *Field Name* for the second line will be **LENGTH.** The *Operator* will be **More than.** The *Constant/Expression* line will be **45.** Figure 8-22 shows the complete query.
6. Move the cursor to the **Exit** Menu Bar and *Save* the query.
7. When you return to the dot prompt give the command **LIST ARTIST, LENGTH, DIGITAL** to show which records qualify for this compound query. Its output is shown below:

```
. LIST ARTIST, LENGTH, DIGITAL
Record#  ARTIST               LENGTH DIGITAL
      1  The Canadian Brass       51 .T.
      2  Wiener Philharmoni       72 .T.
      5  Glenn Gould              51 .T.
.
```

OTHER dBASE III PLUS ADVANCED TOPICS

dBASE III PLUS introduced many advanced capabilities previously unavailable to dBASE users. For example, local area network support was added to permit multi-user file access. The Assist menu was much enhanced, including menus for commands not previously available through Assist. Other advanced capabilities were not fully developed until dBASE IV. This section outlines the availability of special features in dBASE III PLUS.

Custom Screen Forms

dBASE III PLUS has a screen form facility in which you can design a custom input form for adding data to the database. To build a new screen form use the **CREATE SCREEN <filename>** command. The screen form is stored with the .SCR file extension. The screen form is activated with the **SET FORMAT TO <filename>** command. The screen form facility is more difficult to use than the dBASE IV version but does have some formatting control other than width of fields.

dBASE III PLUS Functions

Most of the dBASE IV functions work the same way in dBASE III PLUS. dBASE III PLUS does not provide for direct entry of dates in the {mm/dd/yy} format, however. You must use the CTOD(date) function to convert the character date to the dBASE date type. dBASE III PLUS does not contain any of the financial function types of dBASE IV.

Programming in dBASE III PLUS

The programs that appeared in Chapter 7 were written exclusively with dBASE III PLUS commands, which will work in either dBASE version. dBASE IV adds some specialized programming features such as pop-up windows and moving bar menus. Because the built-in report facility in dBASE III PLUS lacks formatting capability, more users turn to writing custom programs to create acceptable reports in that version.

Compatibility with dBASE IV

In most cases you will be able to read a dBASE III PLUS database file in dBASE IV and vice versa. The biggest difference is the multiple-tag index (.MDX) files used in dBASE IV, which are not available in dBASE III PLUS. The older dBASE III PLUS index (.NDX) files have been implemented in dBASE IV, should you wish to move them from dBASE III PLUS.

Most of the other dBASE IV database design objects such as report and label forms, queries, and screen input forms will *not* work properly in the dBASE III PLUS version and will have to be recreated. However, dBASE IV is able to translate most dBASE III PLUS design objects as it converts them to the dBASE IV format. dBASE III PLUS has no support for SQL.

CHAPTER REVIEW

Starting dBASE

Type **DBASE** at the DOS prompt to begin dBASE. Data files will be saved and retrieved from whatever drive or subdirectory you began in when you started dBASE. dBASE III PLUS can be run from either a hard drive or from a two–floppy drive computer. The initial screen contains a menu at the top and a status area at the bottom of the screen that is similar to that of dBASE IV.

The dBASE III PLUS Assist Menu

The Assist menu provides pull-down menu access to some of the dBASE III PLUS features. Menu bar choices may be selected by moving the cursor with the left and right arrow keys or by typing the first letter of the desired Menu Bar. Highlight a line from the current Menu Bar by using the up and down arrow keys and press **Enter** to execute the highlighted line.

The Dot Prompt Mode

Most users will press **Esc** to switch to the dot prompt mode. To return to the Assist menu, press the **F2** function key. dBASE III PLUS dot commands are very similar to dBASE IV dot commands. You may abbreviate dBASE commands by their first four letters to save typing time; all field names and file names must be spelled out completely.

Obtaining Help in dBASE III PLUS

You can press **F1** to receive general help and to access the Help index. Or you can type **HELP** followed by the name of the command you want help for and dBASE will display help screens specific to that topic. Unlike dBASE IV, the **F1** Help key does *not* bring up context-specific help screens when pressed in a specific menu or screen.

Creating a New Database File

The first step in creating a new database file is to design the structure. You need to determine the appropriate data fields, enter names for these fields, and select the type and width of each field in characters. There are five field types in dBASE III PLUS: character, numeric, date, logical, and memo. You may have up to 128 fields in a single record, which may be up to 4000 characters long.

Building the Database

To enter the file structure, type **CREATE <filename>** from the dot prompt. At the Create screen you can enter the field name, field type, and field width. To save the structure, press **Ctrl-End** and a database file will be created on the default drive. To make changes in a database structure that has already been saved, use the **MODIFY STRUCTURE** command. **Ctrl-N** inserts a new field above the highlighted field; **Ctrl-U** deletes the highlighted field. Simply type over the field width if you need to make changes.

Adding Data to the File

From the dot prompt, issue the **APPEND** command to add data. You will see the Edit screen with the fields appearing vertically from the top of the screen. A reverse-video box to the right of the field name visually shows the width of the field. When you have filled a field, press **Enter** or the ↓ key to go to the next field. When you have filled the last field in a record, dBASE will automatically go on to a new blank record. When you have finished adding data, press **Ctrl-End** to return to the dot prompt. To correct typing mistakes, use the arrow keys to place the cursor in the desired location, then type over the incorrect characters. The **Ins** key can be used to toggle between the Insert and Overtype modes; the Status Bar will display "Ins" when you are in Insert mode.

Opening an Existing Database

Issue the command **USE <filename>** to open an existing database file. dBASE uses the .DBF file extension for database files. The name and drive location of the file will appear in the Status Bar at the bottom of the screen. To see the structure of the current database file, type **DISPLAY STRUCTURE.**

Moving the Record Pointer

The record pointer, abbreviated as "Rec:", shows the number of records in the database and the current record number. Thus 14/255 indicates that the pointer is on record 14 of a total of 255 records in the current database file.

To move the record pointer, use the **GOTO** command and specify a record number, TOP or BOTTOM as the location. The **SKIP** command can be used to move forward or backward a specified number of records.

Displaying Field Values

The **LIST** command displays the field values for all of the records in the database. You can specify fields to be listed by placing their names after the LIST verb. The **FOR <condition>** clause can be added to restrict listed records to those that meet a logical condition. **DISPLAY** shows fields from one record.

Changing the Record Order

You can use the **SORT** and **INDEX** commands to change the order of the records. Normally in natural order (in original entry order), the records can be sorted and placed in a new database file. Indexing allows fast retrieval of records and provides for accessing the database in more than one order. When you open a database file that has been previously indexed, use the command **USE <filename> INDEX <indexname>.** To change to a different index, use the command **SET INDEX TO <indexname>. SET INDEX TO** without specifying an index file name will remove the index and revert to natural order. dBASE III PLUS indexes use the .NDX file type.

Creating a Report

The **CREATE REPORT** command is used to design a custom report in dBASE III PLUS. While not as sophisticated as dBASE IV's report design capability, the dBASE III PLUS Report facility provides for four page title lines, four column heading lines, and a single detail line with totals. Two levels of groups can be designated for control-break group reports. dBASE displays a report format template as the report is being built. The **REPORT FORM** command is used to display and optionally send the report to printer and/or a disk file. To change an existing report form, use the **MODIFY REPORT** command.

Creating Labels

Creating labels is very similar to creating a report. The **CREATE LABEL** command is used to design the label form and the **LABEL FORM** command will display and/or print the labels. There are five predefined label sizes with up to three labels across the page. To change an existing label form, use the **MODIFY LABEL** command.

dBASE III PLUS Queries

The Query feature in dBASE III PLUS is not as easy to use as that in dBASE IV. It does permit you to build up to seven filter expressions that can be linked together with connecting phrases such as AND and OR. To create a query, you must specify at least one field name, an operator, and a constant or expression against which the field is to be compared. Only records that match the filter condition in the query will qualify for further dBASE commands. To make the query, use the **CREATE QUERY** command. From the dot prompt, issue **SET FILTER TO FILE <filename>** to activate the query. To cancel the query, use **SET FILTER TO** without a file name. To change an existing query, issue the **MODIFY QUERY** command.

Other dBASE III PLUS Advanced Features

There is a custom screen form facility in this version of dBASE. It provides a means of changing the default Append and Edit screens to a more pleasing way to enter or change data values. To create a screen form use the **CREATE SCREEN** command. To use the screen, issue the command **SET FORM TO <filename>,** where the name of the screen file is given.

Programming in dBASE III PLUS is very similar to dBASE IV. In fact, the programming examples shown in Chapter 7 will run in either dBASE version without changes.

dBASE III PLUS File Types

There are six dBASE III **file types:** Database files use the .DBF file extension; memo fields are stored in the .DBT file type. Indexes use the .NDX file type. Report designs are stored as .FRM files, while label designs are maintained in .LBL files. Query files use the .QRY extension.

dBASE IV Compatibility

The major difference between the two versions is the introduction of the comprehensive Control Center in dBASE IV. The Assist menu in dBASE III PLUS is primarily employed by new users, and not all features are available through it. The dot prompt modes are nearly identical. Both packages support the four user modes: turnkey custom menu-driven system, standard dBASE menu system, dot prompt commands, and writing programs.

Nearly all dBASE III PLUS database objects such as database files, indexes, reports, labels, and screen forms will work in dBASE IV much as they do in the older version. dBASE III PLUS is able to read *most* dBASE IV database files, but it cannot handle the multiple tag (.MDX) index files. There are some differences between the versions in the way memo field data files are implemented. dBASE III PLUS has no SQL database support.

Leaving dBASE III PLUS

From the dot prompt, issue the **QUIT** command to return to the DOS prompt. From the Assist menu, use the **Set Up** Menu Bar and select the *Quit dBASE III PLUS* line. All files will be closed. When the DOS prompt appears, it is safe to remove floppy disks.

KEY TERMS

?
action line
APPEND
ASSIST (F2)
Assist menu
BROWSE
character field
Columns Menu Bar
command verb
connect type
Contents Menu Bar
CONTINUE
control-break group report
CREATE
CREATE/MODIFY LABEL
CREATE/MODIFY QUERY
CREATE/MODIFY REPORT
CREATE/MODIFY SCREEN
date field
DELETE
DISPLAY
DISPLAY STRUCTURE
dot prompt **(Esc)**
EDIT
EXIT
file type
FOR condition
GOTO [TOP] [BOTTOM]
Groups Menu Bar
HELP (F1)
INDEX ON
LIST
LOCATE FOR <cond>
Locate Menu Bar
logical field

memo field
Menu Bar
message line
MODIFY STRUCTURE
navigation line
numeric field
operator
Options Menu Bar
PACK
primary key
QUIT
RECALL
record pointer
secondary key
SEEK <expr>
Set Filter Menu Bar
SET HISTORY TO
SET INDEX TO <filename>
SET FILTER TO FILE <filename>
SET FORMAT TO
SKIP
SORT TO <filename> ON ..
Status Bar
structure
USE <filename>
user mode
WHILE condition

DISCUSSION QUESTIONS

1. Discuss the limitations in the file structure for a single dBASE III PLUS database file.
   a. Number of fields per record
   b. Maximum width of a field name
   c. Total record length, in characters
   d. Maximum width of each field type
   e. Maximum length of the database file name.
2. Discuss the reasons for using the Assist menu and for using the dot prompt mode in dBASE III PLUS. Which is preferred and why?
3. Describe the use of the following commands when issued from the dot prompt.
   a. **F1**
   b. **F2**
   c. **USE CDPUB**
   d. **MODIFY STRUCTURE**
   e. **? ARTIST,TITLE,YEAR**
4. Discuss the differences between dBASE III PLUS and dBASE IV. Are there instances in which the former would be preferred to the latter?
5. Define the purpose and give an example of each of these dot commands.
   a. **APPEND**
   b. **ASSIST**
   c. **CREATE REPORT**
   d. **MODIFY LABEL**
   e. **USE**
   f. **INDEX ON .. UNIQUE**
   g. **GO BOTTOM**
   h. **DISPLAY**
   i. **DELETE**
   j. **RECALL**
6. Discuss the steps for preparing a dBASE III PLUS report. How are these steps different from those in dBASE IV?
7. Describe the information that normally appears in the status area of the screen at the dot prompt. If necessary go to the computer and experiment with some of the commands from this chapter to see their effects.
8. Suppose you were given a database file containing a field called ADDRESS of character type and with a length of 20. When you add a record, you diskover that the field is too short and ought to be at least 30 characters

long. How would you rectify this situation? Assume that there are now 500 records in the database file. Will these records have to be re-entered?

9. Explain the purpose of the following dBASE III PLUS database objects.
   a. Label
   b. Query
   c. Screen Form
   d. Index
   e. Program.
10. Discuss how records are deleted in dBASE. What can you do if a record was accidentally marked for deletion?
11. How do you leave dBASE? Explain the caution about removing a data diskette before closing all files.

EXERCISES

1. Using dBASE III PLUS build a structure for the following database file called CUSTOMER.DBF. Fields are shown below. After you have saved the file, use the command **DISPLAY STRUCTURE TO PRINT** to print a copy of the structure.

Field Name	**Type**	**Width**
CNAME	Char	15
ADDRESS	Char	20
CITY	Char	14
STATE	Char	2
ZIPCODE	Char	5
LASTORDER	Date	8
TAXABLE	Logical	1

2. Using the data in Figure 8-23, append records to the CUSTOMER file. Use the command **LIST TO PRINT** to print a complete copy of the database file.

3. At the dot prompt, open the SCHED.DBF file that is packaged with the data disk accompanying this textbook. Prepare dot commands to accomplish the following steps. Write down the complete dot command used for each step and submit that with output (if any).
   a. Print a copy of the SCHED.DBF database structure.
   b. Move the cursor to the first record for which the INSTRUCTOR field is "Staff".
   c. Use the **?** command to display just the PREFIX, NUMBER, and TITLE fields for the record from part b.
   d. Display the full records for the classes that meet in room SB 205.
   e. Create an index on the INSTRUCTOR field and name it INSTR. List the fields in order by this index.
   f. Using the index, find and display the first record taught by Woodworth.
   g. Display the *second* record taught by Woodworth.

FIGURE 8-23

Sample Data for Exercise 2

Record#	CNAME	ADDRESS	CITY	STATE	ZIPCODE	LASTORDER	TAXABLE
1	Jones, B.	244 19th St.	Wabash	IN	47521	06/21/89	.T.
2	Hollar, W.	1804 Thames	Richmond	IN	46154	10/15/89	.F.
3	Anderson, M.	Box 128	Vincennes	IN	48231	02/01/88	.T.
4	Snow, B.	605 Ohio St.	Terre Haute	IN	47807	09/13/89	.T.
5	O'Reilly, W.	1332 Western	Cory	IN	47823	09/30/89	.F.
6	Mains, W.	2199 West Lawrin	Princeton	IN	47233	06/12/72	.T.

h. List the PREFIX, NUMBER, LIMIT, and INSTRUCTOR for all records having a LIMIT of more than 35 students.

i. List the PREFIX, NUMBER, SECTION, LIMIT, and DAY for all records having a LIMIT of more than 35 students *and* that are taught on TTH.

j. List the PREFIX, NUMBER, SECTION, LIMIT, and DAY for all records having a LIMIT of more than 35 students *or* that are taught on TTH.

4. Create a custom report called STOCKS using the STOCKS.DBF database file. Specifications appear below:

   a. The report title should be **STOCK PORTFOLIO REPORT** and should be centered over the columns in the report.

   b. Include all fields as columns in the report. Suggested column headings are shown below. Adjust spacing as needed.

```
          STOCK      52-WEEK  52-WEEK    RECENT    NUMBER OF
STOCK   EXCHANGE      HIGH      LOW      PRICE       SHARES
```

   c. Remove the totals for all of the numeric fields by answering No to the *Total this column* line in the numeric columns.

   d. Print the report as single spaced.

   e. Print the report with double spacing.

5. Create a new STOCKS report as a group report based on the stock exchange for the company. The records already appear in order by the EXCHANGE field. Call this report **STOCKEX.**

   a. The report should be single spaced.

   b. The Group heading should be **EXCHANGE:**, and the EXCHANGE field should *not* appear on the detail line as a separate column.

   c. The title of this report is shown below:

```
STOCK PORTFOLIO REPORT
LISTED BY EXCHANGE
```

6. Using the SCHED database file, create a query and list the records that match the following conditions:
   a. List the records whose departmental PREFIX is **SDS,** and
   b. Only courses taught by doctorally qualified persons are to be included, and
   c. Only classes taught on MWF are to be included.
7. Use the **COPY** command to copy all of the records from the STOCKS.DBF file to a file called NEWSTOCK.DBF.
   a. **USE** this new database file, then modify its structure to create a new field called **EQUITY.** It will be a numeric type with width 10 and no decimal places.
   b. Use the **REPLACE** command to **REPLACE ALL EQUITY WITH RECENT*NO_SHARES.** This will multiply the recent share price by the number of shares and place the result in the new EQUITY field for all records.
   c. List those records whose EQUITY is greater than 10000.
   d. List those records whose EQUITY is at least 1000 but less than 5000 dollars.

CHAPTER 8 PROJECT
RESALE BOUTIQUE

The proprietor of the Resale Boutique has finally decided to purchase a computer to keep track of customers and sales. The Resale Boutique was founded five years ago as a place where individuals could take good used clothing for resale. The boutique prices the clothing at one-third of its original price. The original owner gets 40% of the resale value, with the boutique keeping 60% as commission for selling the goods. If the clothing does not sell within three months of its arrival, the price is reduced.

The boutique wants to assemble sample data representing original owners, new customers, and clothing items with various arrival dates. You have been asked to develop database files for these three entities, including record structure, field names, and sample values. Create indexes as needed to produce the outputs below. Each data file should have at least ten records whose values represent most of the categories. Print file structures to show the organization of your database.

From this data, develop a set of mailing labels for original owners and another for new customers. To save on mailing costs, the labels should be printed in zip code order. Produce a group report that shows the clothing items in order by their original owners. Another report should show for each clothing item its original price, Resale Boutique price, amount of commission, and the proceeds going to the customer. In this report, include a column to indicate whether the article has not sold within three months of its arrival at the boutique.

9

Integrating the Tools

Objectives

After completing this chapter, you should be able to:

- Understand how data can be shared between the three software packages.
- Move print files between Lotus and WordPerfect.
- Transfer data records from dBASE to WordPerfect.
- Translate dBASE data to Lotus 1-2-3 format.
- Merge print in WordPerfect using data from Lotus or dBASE.

INTRODUCTION

This textbook has illustrated dBASE III PLUS and dBASE IV version 1.1, the most popular database software packages. This chapter presents ways in which we can benefit by transferring data between dBASE and two other popular software programs, WordPerfect 5.1 and Lotus 1-2-3. Each package is able to manipulate data in certain ways that other packages cannot. WordPerfect is a word processing package while Lotus is an electronic spreadsheet program, maintaining data in a rectangular grid.

dBASE comes with data conversion commands to translate data from one file format to another. WordPerfect and Lotus each have their own translation features. In addition, each is able to read data directly under certain conditions.

Although Lotus 1-2-3 will print tables in hardcopy format, we can print the report to a disk file which can be retrieved into a WordPerfect document. The same is true with dBASE IV reports. We may also wish to do merge printing in WordPerfect with data transferred from Lotus or dBASE.

The Lotus Translate utility is able to read files in several other formats and convert them to the .WK1 spreadsheet file type. With the /File Combine and /File Import commands we can read data from other spreadsheet files and from plain text (ASCII) files. dBASE is able to import and export data directly from several file types, including the Lotus .WK1 format and plain text files.

This chapter will present examples showing how to exchange data between all three packages; we assume you already know how to use them.

Exchanging Data Between Software Packages

It is not uncommon to transfer data from one package to another. Each package stores data in a different native format, and native format files usually cannot be directly read by another package. Most of the software packages provide a **translate** or **conversion program** to assist in this process. The originating package may also have an optional file format menu so it may save data in an appropriate format. All of the packages covered in this text will also save data in plain text or ASCII files. Most of the formatting information found in the file is usually deleted when the data file is saved as a text file.

Types of Data Transfers

We have already discussed some kinds of data transfers in earlier chapters. Lotus 1-2-3 reports may be saved as a .PRN file for later Retrieval into a WordPerfect document. We can do the same with dBASE reports and WordPerfect. It is possible to Import text data into a Lotus worksheet. dBASE will allow records to be Appended from text files. We can list six different types of transfers using just these three packages. The first three transfers are perhaps the most common, but all are used.

- Lotus to WordPerfect
- dBASE to WordPerfect
- dBASE to Lotus
- WordPerfect to Lotus
- WordPerfect to dBASE
- Lotus to dBASE.

We may also wish to transfer data to other kinds of packages, such as desktop publishing or graphics programs. The rest of this section will describe transfers *from* Lotus, dBASE, and WordPerfect, as well as transfers *to* each package, beginning with WordPerfect.

TRANSFERRING DATA FROM WORDPERFECT

WordPerfect has two internal Save modes. The regular or **native format** is prepared with the **F10** Save or **F7** Exit/Save commands; the text format is prepared with the **Ctrl-F5** Text In/Out command. For those who need backward compatibility, WordPerfect 5.1 can also convert files directly to WordPerfect 4.2 and 5.0 formats with the **Ctrl-F5** command.[1] [Note: WordPerfect 5.0 and 5.1 will automatically convert a WordPerfect 4.2 document when it is retrieved with the **Shift-F10** Retrieve command.]

Some programs are capable of reading WordPerfect files directly. The Grammatik IV grammar checker package not only can read this format directly, but it can also insert changes directly into the original file. Ventura Publisher 2.0 and PageMaker will also read WordPerfect files directly. To keep the original file safe, you should only use a *copy* of the original file for such applications.

Saving Documents in Text (ASCII) Format

Neither Lotus nor dBASE can directly read or translate WordPerfect native files, so the text format is typically used to transfer data to these programs. Any tabs, indents, center or flush right codes are replaced by an equivalent number of spaces in the text file version of the document. Other formatting codes such as bold, underline, fonts, and merge codes are stripped out of the text file. None of the graphics boxes are saved in the text file, even if they contain text lines. The text within the graphics box is not saved in the text file. Footnotes and endnotes are not included in the text file.

Example: *Creating a Text File with WordPerfect*

Suppose you have created a table of names and addresses and wish to convert these to text or ASCII format. That table looks like the box in Figure 9-1. Suppose you wish to send these names to Lotus or dBASE, and intend to save the data as an ASCII file.

1. Make sure you have saved the data file as a regular WordPerfect document. We'll assume you used the name **MEMBERS.WP**. The .WP file extension will help to remind us that this is a WordPerfect format file.
2. From within WordPerfect, enter the **Ctrl-F5** command and select option **1** DOS Text.
3. From the next menu select option **1** Save, and WordPerfect will ask for the file name to save the document as. Reply **MEMBERS.TXT** and press **Enter**.
4. WordPerfect will save your membership list as a plain text file on the default drive; the .TXT extension will remind you that this is the ASCII version. [Note: Do *not* use the same file name and extension for both versions of the file.]

WordPerfect CONVERT Program

An auxiliary program called CONVERT.EXE accompanies WordPerfect and will convert between several file types. While CONVERT will not translate directly to Lotus 1-2-3 or dBASE IV, it will translate to an intermediate file type

1 WordPerfect 5.0 can convert to version 4.2 file formats with the **Ctrl-F5** command.

FIGURE 9-1

Sample Data for Text Transfer Example

```
Williams, Carolyn     1883 Huron Way          Spencer         IN 47460
Smith, Robert         Box 220, RR 51          Otterbein       IN 47970
Muraska, Eric         155 Keane Lane          Terre Haute     IN 47803
Osmon, Randy          899 N. 9th Street       Terre Haute     IN 47807
Green, Janet          2307 Highland Drive     Clinton         IN 47842
McCune, Michael       3404 Marquette          Terre Haute     IN 47804
Todd, Bernard         1246 Lafayette Ave      Pimento         IN 47822
Whitlock, Jane        543 Nancy Lane          Indianapolis    IN 46226
Joslin, Wallace       2956 S. 8th Street      Seelyville      IN 47878
Moore, Edith          RR 53                   Greencastle     IN 46135
Gauer, Harold         2214 Lakeview           Sullivan        IN 47591
Hughes, Samuel        410 E. Tennessee        Zionsville      IN 46077
Josephs, Cameron      8745 Newsom Drive       South Bend      IN 46522
```

which can be imported by Lotus or dBASE. The CONVERT program will convert *from* WordPerfect 5.1 to the following file formats:

- IBM DCA format (revisable form and final form)
- Navy DIF (private Navy format)
- WordStar 3.3 and 4.0 format
- MultiMate Advantage II
- Seven-bit transfer format (to send WP file with modem)
- ASCII text file (duplicates Text In/Out function)
- Spreadsheet DIF format (from WP secondary merge format).

CONVERT will also convert the following file formats *into* WordPerfect 5.1 format:

- IBM DCA
- Navy DIF (private Navy format)
- WordStar 3.3 and 4.0
- MultiMate Advantage II
- Seven-bit transfer format (WP files received by modem)
- WordPerfect 4.1 format

```
Mr. William Hassler{END FIELD}
Starcraft Industries, Inc.{END FIELD}
2804 East 19th Street{END FIELD}
Jonesville, IN 45678{END FIELD}
Budget Planner{END FIELD}
{END RECORD}
================================================================================
Ms. Sally Hansen{END FIELD}
French Public Accounting{END FIELD}
188 Poplar Street{END FIELD}
Sheybogan, WI 56234{END FIELD}
Accounting Trainee{END FIELD}
{END RECORD}
================================================================================

Field: 1                                                    Doc 1 Pg 1 Ln 1" Pos 1"
```

FIGURE 9-2

WordPerfect Merge Format File for CONVERT Example

- Mailmerge (to WP secondary merge format)
- Spreadsheet DIF (to WP secondary merge format)
- Microsoft Word 4.0 (only with WordPerfect 5.1)
- DisplayWrite (only with WordPerfect 5.1).

For transfers to Lotus 1-2-3, the ASCII and Spreadsheet DIF formats are recommended. The example below discusses how the **DIF format** can be created from the WordPerfect CONVERT program.

Example: *Converting a WordPerfect Merge File to DIF Format*

The CONVERT.EXE program is a separate program that is run from the DOS prompt. You must have first created the WordPerfect document in secondary merge file format and saved it.

1. From DOS, change to the directory where the CONVERT program is stored (usually the directory where WordPerfect is stored). Type **CONVERT** at the DOS prompt and press **Enter**.
2. We'll assume the file to be converted is called EMPLOY.SEC and stored on the A: drive. When DOS asks for the name of the Input File, provide the pathname of the file: **A:EMPLOY.SEC** and press **Enter**. This file is shown in Figure 9-2.
3. You'll next be asked for the Output File, so enter a name and the drive you wish it to be stored in. Call the new file **A:EMPLOY.DIF**.
4. Next you'll see the Convert menu as shown in Figure 9-3A. Select **1** (WordPerfect to Another Format), then choose **8** (WordPerfect Secondary Merge to Spreadsheet DIF) in Figure 9-3B and press **Enter**.
5. After a few seconds, WordPerfect will inform you that the conversion has been completed.

```
Name of Input File? EMPLOY.SEC
Name of Output File? EMPLOY.DIF


0 EXIT
1 WordPerfect to another format
2 Revisable-Form-Text (IBM DCA Format) to WordPerfect
3 Final-Form-Text (IBM DCA Format) to WordPerfect
4 Navy DIF Standard to WordPerfect
5 WordStar 3.3 to WordPerfect
6 MultiMate Advantage II to WordPerfect
7 Seven-Bit Transfer Format to WordPerfect
8 WordPerfect 4.2 to WordPerfect 5.1
9 Mail Merge to WordPerfect Secondary Merge
A Spreadsheet DIF to WordPerfect Secondary Merge
B Word 4.0 to WordPerfect
C DisplayWrite to WordPerfect

Enter number of Conversion desired 1
```

FIGURE 9-3A

CONVERT Screen for DIF Conversion Example

```
Name of Input File? EMPLOY.SEC
Name of Output File? EMPLOY.DIF


0 EXIT
1 Revisable-Form-Text (IBM DCA Format)
2 Final-Form-Text (IBM DCA Format)
3 Navy DIF Standard
4 WordStar 3.3
5 MultiMate Advantage II
6 Seven-Bit Transfer Format
7 ASCII Text File
8 WordPerfect Secondary Merge to Spreadsheet DIF

Enter number of output file format desired 8
```

FIGURE 9-3B

CONVERT Screen for DIF Conversion Example After Selecting option 1

Example: *Create a WordPerfect Secondary Merge File from a Mail Merge File*

Many software packages create a merge data file in the **mailmerge** format. While not directly usable by WordPerfect, the Mailmerge format can be converted to Secondary merge format with the WordPerfect CONVERT program.

1. From the DOS prompt, enter **CONVERT** to begin the conversion. The input file name will be **HABITAT.TXT** while the output file will be named **HABITAT.SEC** to reflect its use as a secondary merge file.
2. At the first CONVERT menu select CHOICE **9**, Mailmerge to WordPerfect Secondary Merge File.

```
Name of Input File? C:\DBASE\HABITAT.TXT
Name of Output File? HABITAT.SEC

1 WordPerfect to another format
2 Revisable-Form-Text (IBM DCA Format) to WordPerfect
3 Final-Form-Text (IBM DCA Format) to WordPerfect
4 Navy DIF Standard to WordPerfect
5 WordStar 3.3 to WordPerfect
6 MultiMate Advantage II to WordPerfect
7 Seven-Bit Transfer Format to WordPerfect
8 WordPerfect 4.2 to WordPerfect 5.1
9 Mail Merge to WordPerfect Secondary Merge
A Spreadsheet DIF to WordPerfect Secondary Merge
B Word 4.0 to WordPerfect
C DisplayWrite to WordPerfect

Enter number of Conversion desired 9
Enter Field delimiter characters or decimal ASCII values enclosed in {}
,  <Enter>
Enter Record delimiter characters or decimal ASCII values enclosed in {}
{13}{10}  <Enter>
Enter Characters to be stripped from file or press Enter if none
"  <Enter>
C:\DBASE\HABITAT.TXT Converted to HABITAT.SEC
```

FIGURE 9-4

CONVERT Screen for Mailmerge Conversion Illustration

3. The CONVERT program will prompt you to provide the field delimiter character (that separates fields); type a comma and press **Enter**.
4. You'll next be asked to provide the character that ends a record. Type **{13}{10}** to signify the carriage return and line feed that end each line of the text file, and press **Enter**. (Type the { } brace characters *and* the numbers inside the braces.)
5. The next prompt asks which characters are to be stripped from the file. Type in the double quote character, **"**, and press **Enter**.
6. When CONVERT is finished, you'll be told that the conversion is complete. Figure 9-4 illustrates the sequence of steps in this example.

TRANSFERRING DATA TO WORDPERFECT

If another package is capable of creating a document in the WordPerfect 4.2, 5.0, or 5.1 formats, WordPerfect can read it automatically[2] when the file is retrieved with the **Shift-F10** command. Text format files can be read with the **Ctrl-F5** Text In/Out command. Any other file format must first be converted before it is usable.

Reading a Text File with WordPerfect

The **Ctrl-F5** Text In/Out command is used to read text files as well as to save files in text format. From the main WordPerfect screen press **Ctrl-F5**. You'll see the following menu.

```
1 DOS Text; 2 Password; 3 Save As; 4 Comment; 5 Spreadsheet: 0
```

Choice **1** will take you to the DOS Text menu where files can be saved or retrieved in text format.

```
1 Save; 2 Retrieve (CR/LF to [Hrt]); 3 Retrieve (CR/LF to [SRt] in HZone): 0
```

2 WordPerfect 5.0 is able to Retrieve and convert version 5.1 files provided they do not use any of the word processing features unique to version 5.1.

Depending upon the type of text file, you may wish to retrieve it with choice 2 or 3. Choice **2** will convert any carriage return/line feed combination it encounters to a hard return, signifying the end of a paragraph to WordPerfect. Lines that must retain their format, such as Lotus .PRN files, will use choice 2. Choice **3** will convert the end-of-line carriage return/line feed characters to *soft* returns. With choice 3 you can later adjust margins or modify the text, and WordPerfect will automatically wrap the lines as needed. With the latter choice you will have to manually insert end of paragraph hard returns.

Example: *Reading a Lotus Text File*

Suppose we have already created a Lotus .PRN file called SMITH.PRN, and wish to insert it into the middle of an existing WordPerfect document.

1. Start WordPerfect. Before retrieving the text file, move the cursor to the document location where the Lotus .PRN file is to be placed.
2. Then press **Ctrl-F5** to bring up the Text In/Out menu. Press **1** to bring up the DOS Text menu, then **2** to retrieve the file.
3. When WordPerfect prompts for the filename, enter the complete pathname, including the drive and directory where the document is stored. On hard-disk computers this might be **C:\123\SMITH.PRN**; on a floppy disk computer this might be **A:SMITH.PRN** on the data disk.
4. The resulting integrated text is shown on this page. WordPerfect will insert the print file as if you had typed the text in from the keyboard, but will place a hard return after each line. [You might wish to use the **Alt-F3** Reveal Codes command to see the HRt codes at the end of each line.] If the report is too wide for your current margins you might wish to temporarily adjust the margins as needed. If the table falls across a page boundary, you might wish to insert a hard page break above the report, or use the **Alt-F4** Block command to define the report as a block, then use the **Shift-F8** command to protect the block.

```
SMITH -- B. McLaren 6/27/89

            SMITHTON RECREATIONAL VEHICLE SALES, INC.
                            1987         1988          1989
                       ----------------------------------
SALES                       1405         1205          1150
EXPENSES
  Cost of Vehicles         786.8        674.8           644
  Salaries                   120        130.8       142.572
  Administrative             175          175           175
  Marketing/Adv.             180          220           250
                       ----------------------------------
    Total Expenses        1261.8       1200.6      1211.572

GROSS PROFIT               143.2          4.4       -61.572
```

Example: *Reading a Text File with Soft Returns*

For this example we will read a text file into WordPerfect and convert the hard returns to soft returns. We know that the file is called ACME.TXT, stored on the data disk.

```
Dear Irwin:

     Congratulations on signing the contract with Acme
Systems for your computer-based inventory/order entry
system. I am impressed by your dedicated efforts to learn
as much as possible about distributor systems in a short
period of time. In fact, the references you obtained from
other distributors and from manufacturer representatives
made the decision process much more straight-forward.

     I plan to be available in the future should you require
more assistance, but expect to be somewhat less involved
now that the purchase decision has been made. Good luck
with your data planning efforts and the July 11-12 course.

Sincerely,

Larry Gardner
Consultant

LG
```

FIGURE 9-5

Sample Text for Soft Return Retrieval

1. Start WordPerfect as usual, and with the cursor in the desired location for the new text, press the **Ctrl-F5** Text In/Out command.
2. At the next menu press **1** to enter the DOS Text menu. Because we wish to have the document inserted with soft returns, press **3**. WordPerfect will prompt you for the file name. Enter **ACME.TXT** and press **Enter**. (Also give the drive letter and directory if this file is not on the default directory.)
3. The sample text is shown in Figure 9-5. WordPerfect uses the **hyphenation zone** area to determine whether a line should have a hard return or a soft return at the end. If the line ends within the current hyphenation zone, it will have a soft return at the end. Otherwise there will be a hard return code. The default hyphenation zone is 10% of the line length, and may be changed with the **Shift-F8 1** Format Line command. If you make changes in the text retrieved with this method, any lines ending in a soft return will be automatically reformatted to fit the current line margins.

Importing a Lotus Worksheet File Directly

WordPerfect 5.1 is able to import a Lotus worksheet (.WK1) file directly, without going through convert or having Lotus output to a .PRN file. WordPerfect will import it into a WordPerfect table or directly into the document without the table grid lines. To use this feature, press **Ctrl-F5** (Text In/Out) and select **5** to indicate spreadsheet. Press **1** to Import and and you will see the menu shown in Figure 9-6. At the Spreadsheet Import screen press **1** to name the file. Choice **3** is used to determine whether a WordPerfect table or plain text is to be used to receive the spreadsheet. Choice **4** is used to perform the import.

```
Spreadsheet: Import

    1 - Filename

    2 - Range

    3 - Type                      Table

    4 - Perform Import
```

FIGURE 9-6

WordPerfect Spreadsheet Import Screen (Press **Ctrl-F5 F 1**)

Example: *Importing a Spreadsheet Into a WordPerfect Table*

We will import a Lotus spreadsheet file called SMITH.WK1, stored on the data disk, into a WordPerfect table.

1. Start WordPerfect as usual and move the cursor to the desired location in the WordPerfect document to receive the spreadsheet.
2. Activate the Text/In command by pressing **Ctrl-F5**. Select Spreadsheet by pressing **5**, then Import by pressing **1**. Refer to the menu in Figure 9-6.
3. We'll assume the spreadsheet file is stored on the A drive. Press **1** and fill in the file name **A:SMITH.WK1** and press **Enter**. We will import the entire file range so leave the Range option unchanged.
4. Press **4** to Perform the import. You should see the same text as in the previous example, this time in a WordPerfect table. The table is shown in Figure 9-7.

Inserting a Lotus Graph Image into a Graphics Box

WordPerfect is able to directly read a number of graph image file types, including the Lotus .PIC file format. For those graph types that cannot be read directly, there is a graph file conversion program that comes with the WordPerfect 5.1 package. This text will not cover the graph conversion program, but more information is available in the WordPerfect Reference Manual.

The basic steps in importing a graphic image into WordPerfect include creating a graphic box, then providing the name of the file to be inserted into the box.

Example: *Importing a Lotus Graph into WordPerfect*

Suppose that we have a Lotus graph (see Figure 9-8) image stored in a file called EMMY41.PIC, and wish to insert it into a document called Emmy.

SMITH -- B. McLaren 6/27/89				
	SMITHTON RECREATIONAL VEHICLE SALES, INC.			
		1987	1988	1989
		---------	---------	---------
SALES		1405	1205	1150
EXPENSES				
Cost of Vehicles		786.8	674.8	644
Salaries		120	130.8	142.572
Administrative		175	175	175
Marketing/Adv.		180	220	250
		---------	---------	---------
Total Expenses		1261.8	1200.6	1211.572
GROSS PROFIT		143.2	4.4	-61.572

FIGURE 9-7

Table Created by WordPerfect

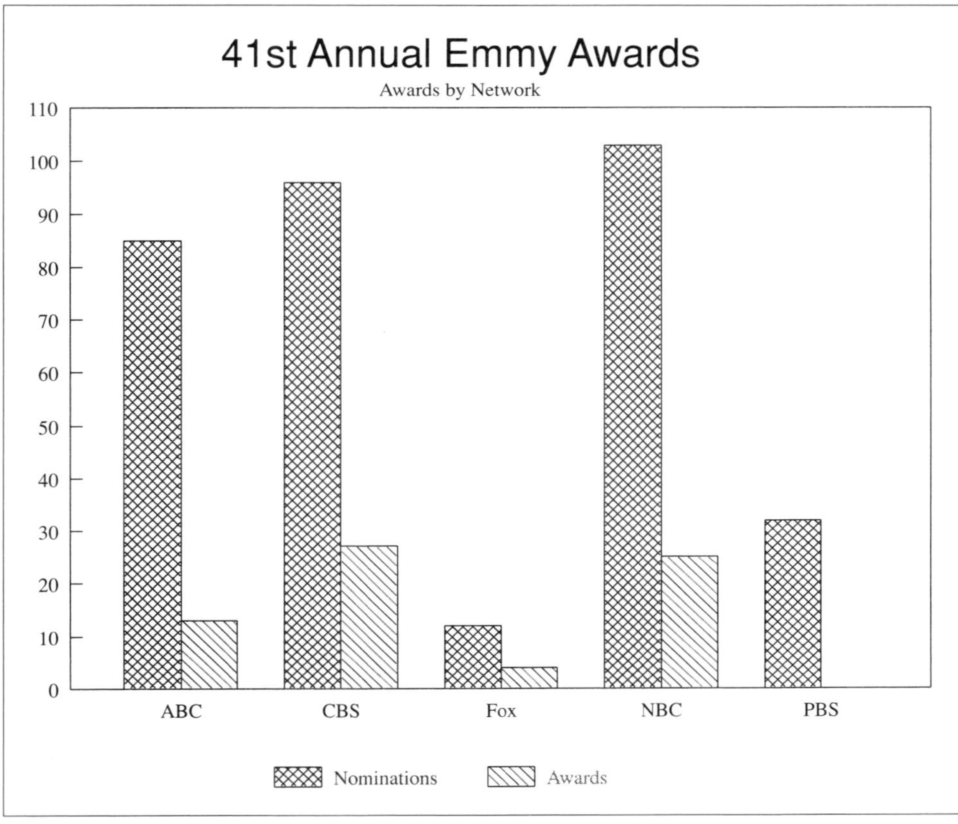

FIGURE 9-8

Sample Lotus .PIC File in Graphics Box

1. In WordPerfect, retrieve the EMMY document and move the cursor to the end. Press **Alt-F9** to view the Graphics menu.
2. Choose **1** to select Figure type and **1** to Create the graphic box.
3. From the Graph screen select **1** to enter the filename. Specify **EMMY41.PIC** (along with its location) and press **Enter**. Press **Enter** to leave Graphics.
4. WordPerfect will choose the size according to the image and the Horizontal Position selected, and place the graph on the page. The resulting graph is displayed below. Remember that WordPerfect supports three levels of print resolution (Draft, Medium, High), which will affect how the image is ultimately printed. Use View Document to see the page.

TRANSFERRING DATA FROM LOTUS 1-2-3

Lotus 1-2-3 will save data in several internal formats. The native format is the .WK1 file, and the text format is a .PRN file. Graph images are stored in a .PIC file which can be read by WordPerfect and some other packages such as Harvard Graphics and Ventura Publisher.

Creating a Lotus Text (.PRN) File

To create a text file from 1-2-3, issue the /**Print File** command (/**PF**) and provide the proper range to be printed. Lotus will use the current margins when printing to the printer or a file, so be sure the margins are wide enough to fit the lines on the page. Many users will wish to change the margins to zero within 1-2-3 and allow the destination package (usually the word processor) to do the line formatting.

Any other Print Options that are set, such as borders, headers and footers, will also be added to the .PRN file. Turn them off if they are not desired. You can use the **Unformatted** option (/**PFOOU**) to suspend printing of headers, footers and page breaks.

Example: *Printing to a Disk File*

In this example we will create the SMITH.PRN file that was discussed earlier.

1. First start 1-2-3 and retrieve the SMITH.WK1 file with /**FR.**
2. To print the worksheet to a file, issue the /**PF** command. When prompted for the name, reply with **SMITH** and press **Enter**; Lotus will fill in the .PRN file extension when the file is created. [Note: You can use a different file extension if desired—fill it in with the file name before you press **Enter**.]
3. Next Lotus will present the setting sheet for the print screen, as shown in Figure 9-9.
4. Select the **Range** option, and enter the print range as usual, in this case **A1..G17**.
5. Clear the margins by pressing the Options command (**O**) then **M** for Margins. In the Margins menu press **N** for None—this resets the left margin to 0, and the right margin to 240. Press **Q** to return to the main print menu.
6. To change the print type to unformatted, press **OOU** from the main print menu, then press **Q** to return to the main print menu.
7. Finally, press **G** (Go) to send the worksheet to the print file. This will only take a few seconds.

```
A1: 'SMITH -- B. McLaren  6/27/89                                  MENU
Range  Line  Page  Options  Clear  Align  Go  Quit
Specify a range to print
                              Print Settings
   Destination:  D:\123\SMITH

   Range:

   Header:
   Footer:

   Margins:
     Left 4    Right 76   Top 2   Bottom 2

   Borders:
     Columns
     Rows

   Setup string:

   Page length:  66

   Output:       As-Displayed (Formatted)

28-Sep-90  09:20 PM
```

FIGURE 9-9

Lotus /Print File Screen (Press **/PF**)

8. You can **Quit** from the Print menu and return to the READY mode. If you save the worksheet at this point, the modified print settings will also be saved. Generally it is better to save the worksheet before you print to a file.

Using the Lotus Translate Module

Like WordPerfect, Lotus has a translation module that will convert between several file formats. The Translate module is accessed from the Lotus Access menu, not from 1-2-3. You must first save the worksheet file from 1-2-3, then Quit from 1-2-3. The Lotus Access menu is displayed in Figure 9-10.

The Translate module can convert a Lotus spreadsheet file to the following spreadsheet file formats:

- Lotus 1-2-3 Release 1a
- Lotus 1-2-3 Release 2, 2.01, and 2.2
- Lotus 1-2-3 Release 3.0
- dBASE II
- dBASE III, III PLUS, and IV
- Spreadsheet DIF format
- Symphony 1.0
- Symphony 1.1, 1.2, and 2.0.

Release 2.2 files use the same format as Release 2 and 2.01. The following formats can be translated to the Lotus format:

- Lotus 1-2-3 Release 1a
- Lotus 1-2-3 Release 2, 2.01, and 2.2
- dBASE II

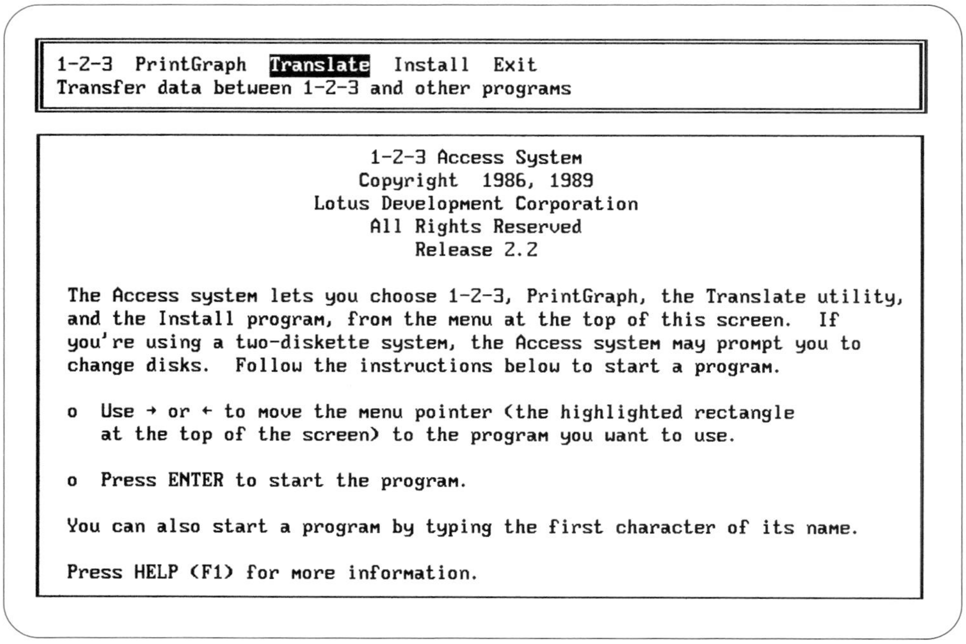

```
1-2-3  PrintGraph  Translate  Install  Exit
Transfer data between 1-2-3 and other programs

                         1-2-3 Access System
                         Copyright  1986, 1989
                     Lotus Development Corporation
                          All Rights Reserved
                             Release 2.2

The Access system lets you choose 1-2-3, PrintGraph, the Translate utility,
and the Install program, from the menu at the top of this screen.  If
you're using a two-diskette system, the Access system may prompt you to
change disks.  Follow the instructions below to start a program.

o  Use → or ← to move the menu pointer (the highlighted rectangle
   at the top of the screen) to the program you want to use.

o  Press ENTER to start the program.

You can also start a program by typing the first character of its name.

Press HELP (F1) for more information.
```

FIGURE 9-10

Lotus Access Menu (Translate Module)

- dBASE III, III PLUS, and IV
- Spreadsheet DIF format
- Multiplan
- Symphony 1.0
- Symphony 1.1, 1.2, and 2.0
- VisiCalc.

Example: *Translating from DIF to WK1 Format*

For this example we will take the EMPLOY.DIF file created in an earlier WordPerfect example and convert it to .WK1 format for Lotus Release 2.2.

1. Begin Lotus normally but do not go into 1-2-3. To use the Translate module, press **T** from the Access menu.
2. You will see the TRANSLATE FROM screen, shown in Figure 9-11, where Lotus asks you to name the type of file you wish to translate. Select the **DIF** file type by moving the cursor to that line and pressing **Enter**.
3. After you make the FROM selection, Lotus will present the TRANSLATE TO screen, shown in Figure 9-12, where you can select the type of file to translate to. Not all TO formats are available, depending upon which FROM format is chosen. From the TO screen select Release 2.2 as the desired format.
4. You will next see a screen asking for the name of the .DIF file. If the **EMPLOY.DIF** file is already shown on the screen, move the cursor to the file and press **Enter**. Otherwise follow the instructions on the screen to change to the directory where the .DIF file is stored.
5. Next you will provide a name for the new .WK1 file. Use **EMPLOY.WK1** as the name. Use the **Columnwise** version, indicating that the cells were stored in the .DIF file by column. Refer to Figure 9-13

```
Lotus  1-2-3  Release 2.2 Translate Utility
Copr. 1985, 1989  Lotus Development Corporation  All Rights Reserved

What do you want to translate FROM?

      1-2-3  1A
      1-2-3  2, 2.01 or 2.2
      dBase II
      dBase III
      DIF
      Multiplan (SYLK)
      Symphony  1.0
      Symphony  1.1, 1.2 or 2.0
      VisiCalc

            Highlight your selection and press ENTER
             Press ESC to end the Translate utility
              Press HELP (F1) for more information
```

FIGURE 9-11

Translate FROM Menu

```
Lotus  1-2-3  Release 2.2 Translate Utility
Copr. 1985, 1989  Lotus Development Corporation  All Rights Reserved

Translate FROM: DIF                What do you want to translate TO?

                                          1-2-3  1A
                                          1-2-3  2, 2.01 or 2.2
                                          Symphony  1.0
                                          Symphony  1.1, 1.2 or 2.0

            Highlight your selection and press ENTER
         Press ESC to return to the source product menu
              Press HELP (F1) for more information
```

FIGURE 9-12

Translate TO Menu

6. Press **Y** to perform the translation. Lotus will report that the conversion is completed. Press the **Esc** key two times to return to the Access menu.

7. To be sure that the original .DIF file is readable as a .WK1 file, go into the **1-2-3** module and retrieve the newly created EMPLOY.WK1 file. The EMPLOY.WK1 file is shown in Figure 9-14. Wider columns would show the complete data values. We could do further analysis on this data with Lotus, if desired.

```
Lotus  1-2-3  Release 2.2 Translate Utility
Copr. 1985, 1989  Lotus Development Corporation  All Rights Reserved

Translate FROM: DIF                    Translate TO: 1-2-3 2.2

Source file: D:\WP51\EMPLOY.DIF

Target file: D:\WP51\EMPLOY.WK1

Edit the target file specification if necessary and press ENTER
Press ESC to select a different source file
Press HELP (F1) for more information
```

FIGURE 9-13

Lotus Translate Screen for DIF Translation

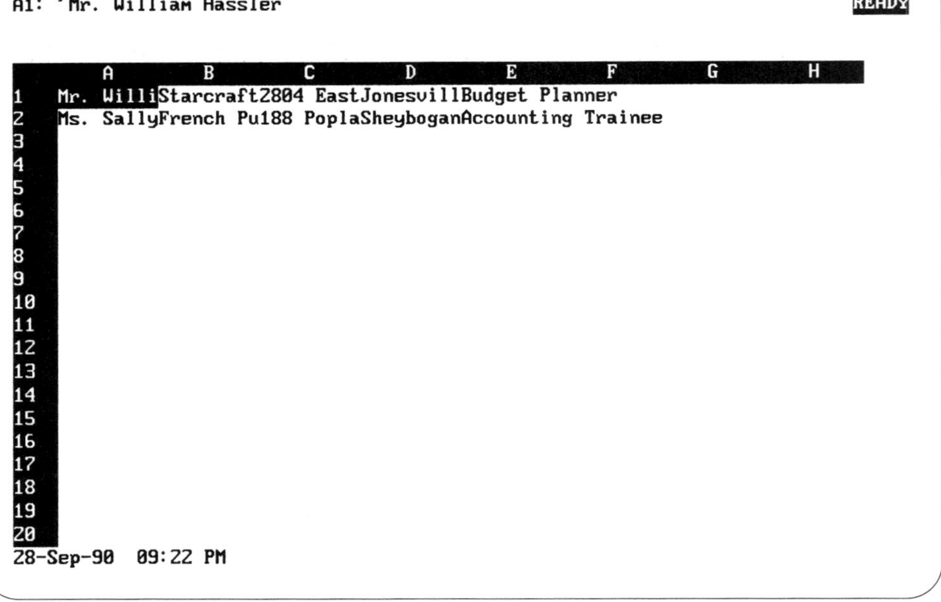

FIGURE 9-14

Converted EMPLOY.WK1 File

Example: *Translating from WK1 to DBF Format*

This example will illustrate the process of converting a Lotus .WK1 worksheet file to the dBASE .DBF format. We will use a veterinarian database file, WABASH.WK1. A portion of that file is shown in Figure 9-15.

For .WK1 to .DBF translations, the Translate program requires that the first row of the file (or a named data range) contains valid dBASE-like field names, and the second row contains data values.

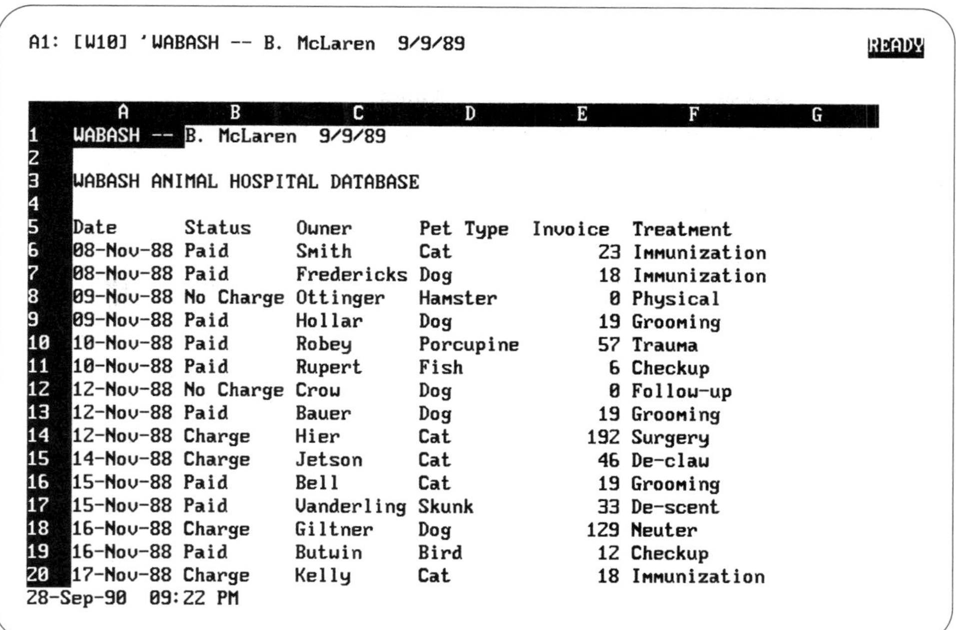

```
A1: [W10] 'WABASH -- B. McLaren  9/9/89                                  READY

      A         B           C          D          E          F          G
1   WABASH -- B. McLaren  9/9/89
2
3   WABASH ANIMAL HOSPITAL DATABASE
4
5   Date      Status    Owner       Pet Type   Invoice  Treatment
6   08-Nov-88 Paid      Smith       Cat             23  Immunization
7   08-Nov-88 Paid      Fredericks  Dog             18  Immunization
8   09-Nov-88 No Charge Ottinger    Hamster          0  Physical
9   09-Nov-88 Paid      Hollar      Dog             19  Grooming
10  10-Nov-88 Paid      Robey       Porcupine       57  Trauma
11  10-Nov-88 Paid      Rupert      Fish             6  Checkup
12  12-Nov-88 No Charge Crow        Dog              0  Follow-up
13  12-Nov-88 Paid      Bauer       Dog             19  Grooming
14  12-Nov-88 Charge    Hier        Cat            192  Surgery
15  14-Nov-88 Charge    Jetson      Cat             46  De-claw
16  15-Nov-88 Paid      Bell        Cat             19  Grooming
17  15-Nov-88 Paid      Vanderling  Skunk           33  De-scent
18  16-Nov-88 Charge    Giltner     Dog            129  Neuter
19  16-Nov-88 Paid      Butwin      Bird            12  Checkup
20  17-Nov-88 Charge    Kelly       Cat             18  Immunization
28-Sep-90  09:22 PM
```

FIGURE 9-15

WABASH.WK1 Database Spreadsheet

1. In 1-2-3, retrieve the **WABASH.WK1** file. Create a range name to represent the database portion of the worksheet. Press **/Range Name Create** to create the named range. The range name is **DATA,** which represents the data in cells A1..F31. Change the width of column F to 12 characters. Save the WABASH worksheet file as usual with the **/FS** command.
2. After 1-2-3 has saved the data in the new file, **Quit** from 1-2-3. From the Lotus Access menu press **T** to enter the Translate module.
3. In Translate, select the **1-2-3 2, 2.01, 2.2** FROM option, and the **dBASE III** TO option. The FROM filename is **WABASH.WK1** and we'll choose **WABASH.DBF** for the TO name. You will see a help screen of instructions. Press **Esc** to continue.
4. Next you'll be asked to choose either the entire worksheet or a named range to translate. Select **Range**. When prompted for the range name, reply **DATA** and press **Enter**.
5. Lotus will create the WABASH.DBF file, displaying a chart showing percentage of completion. Press **Esc** two times to leave the Translate module.

TRANSFERRING DATA TO LOTUS 1-2-3

Combining Information into a Lotus 1-2-3 Worksheet

The data transfer commands of the Lotus 1-2-3 /File menu are briefly summarized below:

- **Retrieve** Replace the current worksheet in memory with a .WK1 file retrieved from the disk.
- **Save** Saves the entire worksheet as a .WK1 file.
- **Combine** Merge another .WK1 file into the current worksheet at the cursor location. Options are to **Copy**, **Add**, or **Subtract** merged cell values.
- **Xtract** Copy a portion of the worksheet to a new .WK1 file.

- **Import** Merge a text file into the current worksheet at the cursor location. Options are to enter each row as **Text**, or break **Numbers** into separate columns. If the Text option is used, the /**Data Parse** command can be used to break the text into individual fields.

Release 2.2 also allows cell values from other worksheets to be **linked** to the current worksheet by using the **+<<filename.WK1>>celladdress** expression. The latter method requires no steps by the user to obtain the cell value from the worksheet stored on disk—the cell value is automatically fetched when the worksheet containing the link expression is retrieved, or when the /**File Admin Link** command is issued.

Importing Text Information into a Lotus 1-2-3 Worksheet

The /**File Import** command is able to bring text data into a 1-2-3 worksheet at the cursor location. You can select the **Text** option where each line of the text file (terminated by a carriage return and line feed) is placed into the first cell of a row in the worksheet. This is appropriate where the merged data is primarily text data. The /**Data Parse** command can be used to break a long label into separate columns, as shown in the example below.

Example: *Importing a Text File into 1-2-3*

This example will bring the EMPLOYEE.TXT database file into Lotus 1-2-3. You can assume that the original EMPLOYEE.DBF file was copied to a text file, as explained in the dBASE sections of this chapter. The EMPLOYEE.TXT file contains all fields for the full database of 18 records.

1. To merge the data from this file, open up a 1-2-3 worksheet and position the cursor at the location where the merged data is to be placed. In this case we'll place the data at the A1 cell.
2. Then issue the /**File Import** command. Next 1-2-3 will ask you to select between Text and Numbers. Pick **Text** for this example.
3. When prompted, enter the name of the merge file; in this case, type **EMPLOYEE.TXT** and press **Enter**. The first part of the spreadsheet will look like that shown in Figure 9-16.

Example: *Parsing Data with 1-2-3*

The spreadsheet looks just fine, but if you move the cursor to cell A3 you will see that the entire row of values has been placed into that cell. Adjacent columns are empty. To break the data into individual columns, you must use the /**Data Parse** command.

1. Move the cursor to cell A3, then press /**DP**.
2. Press **Enter** on the **Format-Line** menu choice, then select **Create**.
3. Based upon the format of the values in the first data row (where the cursor was placed initially), 1-2-3 will create a tentative format line that will be used to divide the information in the input column into separate fields. That format line may need to be edited, especially if there are spaces within any of the field values. The initial format line is shown in Figure 9-17. You can press the **F6** Window key in 1-2-3 to temporarily remove the settings sheet and see the underlying worksheet.

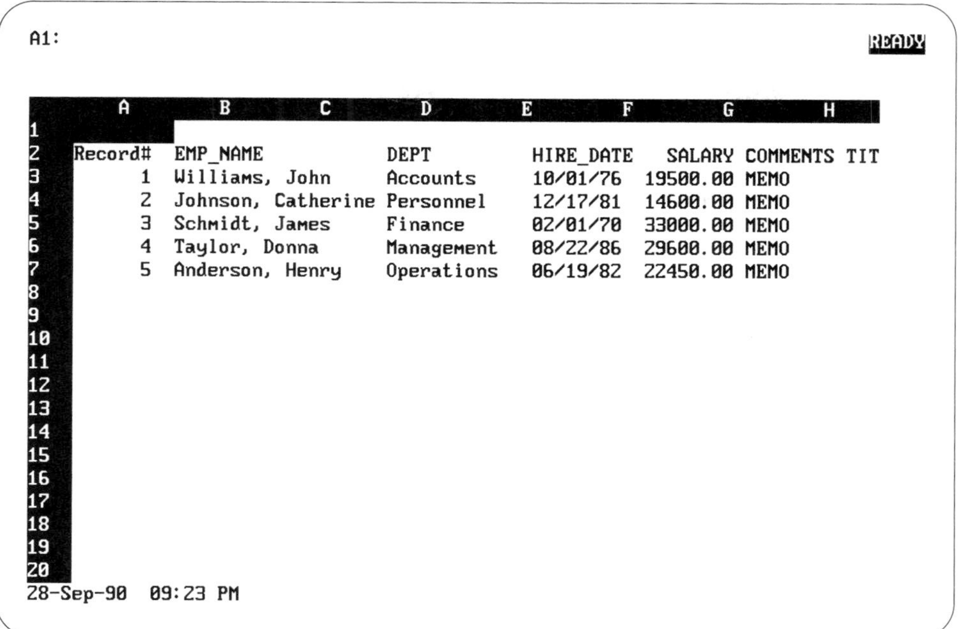

FIGURE 9-16

Spreadsheet Imported from Text File

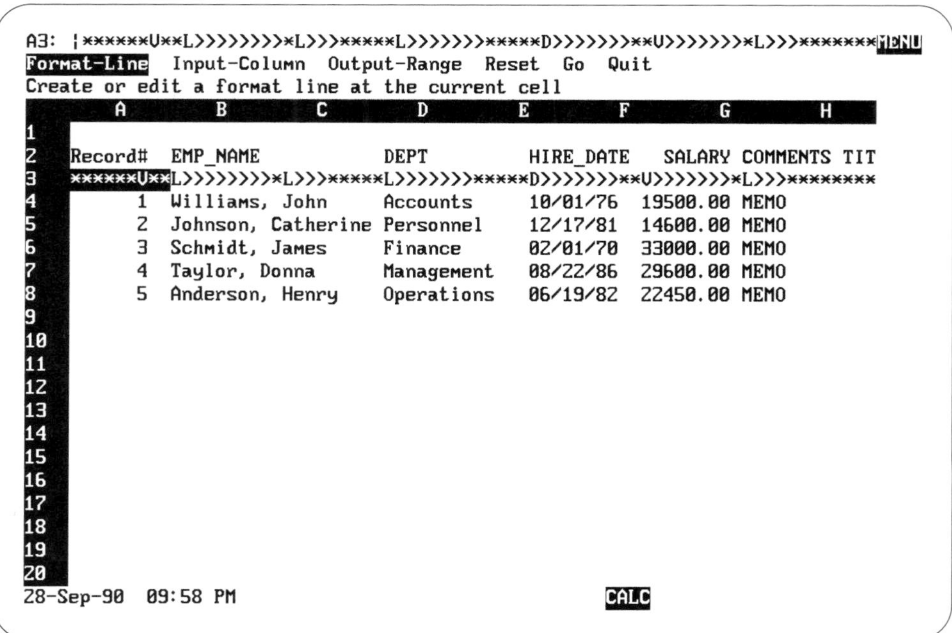

FIGURE 9-17

Parse Format Line Created by 1-2-3

4. A complete discussion of format line symbols is given in the Lotus Reference Manual. The format line begins with the special character, |. The **V** represents a value item, and the **L** a label item. The > symbol is used to denote the extent of the field. The **D** shows a possible date field, and the * means to use that extra space (if needed) when breaking data into individual fields. We need to make several corrections to the format line.

5. While still in the /Data Parse menu, select **Format-Line** again, this time choosing **Edit**. Move the cursor to the desired spot with the arrow keys and

make the corrections. Press the **Ins** key as needed to switch between Insert and Overtype modes. The record number field is not needed, so we'll fill that field with **S** characters to skip it altogether.

6. The employee name field is broken at the comma between last and first names, so we'll replace the ***L** with two > symbols to make it one field.
7. Finally, the MEMO field did not copy from the dBASE file so replace that field with all **S** characters.
8. When finished editing, press **Enter** to leave EDIT mode. The new format line is shown in Figure 9-18.

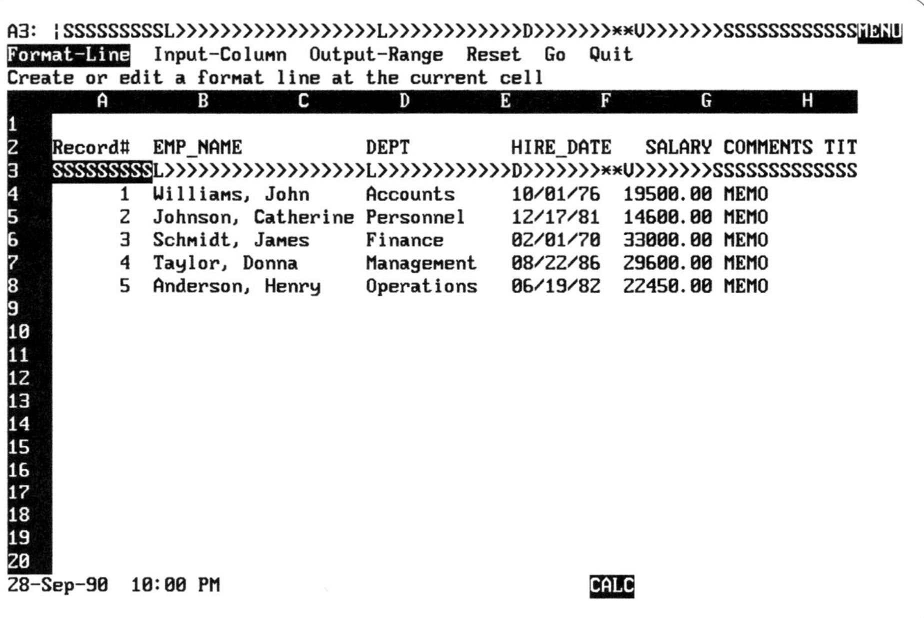

FIGURE 9-18

Revised Format Line (Row 3) for /Data Parse Example

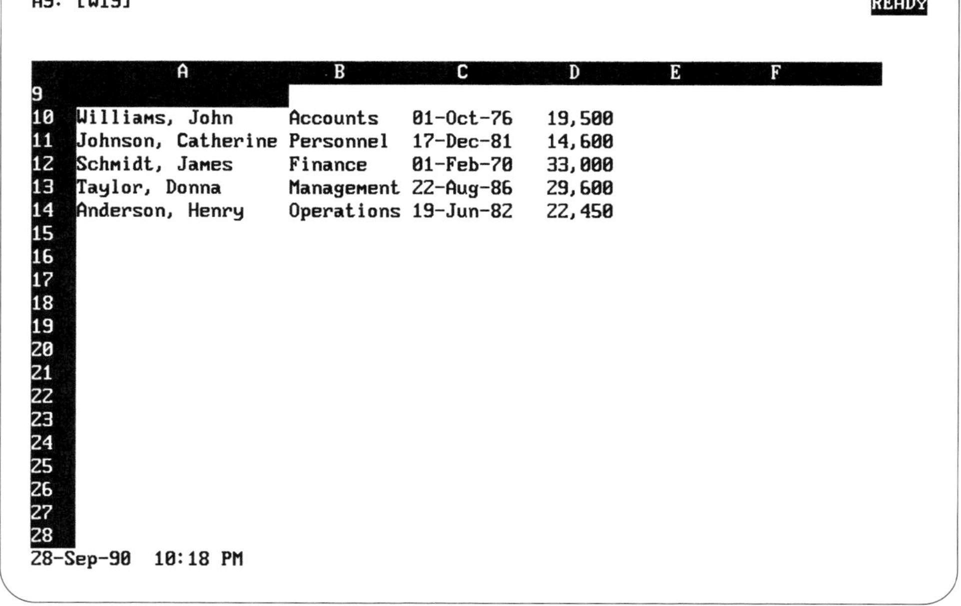

FIGURE 9-19

Parsed Data for Example

9. Finally we are ready to actually parse the data. You must specify the **Input-Column** range, in this case **A3..A8**. The **Output-Range** can be given as **A10..F14**.
10. Press **Go** and the data will be copied to the output range as specified by the format line.
11. After widening columns A and B, and formatting the date and salary fields, the data will look like Figure 9-19.

TRANSFERRING DATA FROM dBASE IV

Because the dBASE III/IV file format is well known,[3] many other packages are able to read or convert those formats directly. The Lotus Translate program can convert from dBASE to any of the 1-2-3 file formats. Although WordPerfect cannot convert the .DBF file format directly, other forms such as Spreadsheet .DIF are common to both packages.

Using the COPY TO Command to Export Data

The dBASE **COPY TO** command can be used to copy information from one file to another. The syntax of this command is

```
COPY TO <filename> [[TYPE] <filetype>]
```

The <filetype> is taken from the following table (file types *not* available in dBASE III PLUS are marked):

Filetype	**Meaning**
(Omitted)	Uses dBASE IV .DBF format.
DBASEII	The dBASE II .DB2 file format (not in III PLUS).
DELIMITED	Each field is right-trimmed and the values are enclosed in quotations. Uses .TXT extension.
DIF	Spreadsheet .DIF format.
FW2	Framework II file format (not in III PLUS).
RPD	RapidFile file format (not in III PLUS).
SDF	Standard data format where fields are fixed-length and run together with no space between. Uses .TXT extension.
SYLK	Multiplan SYLK file format.
WKS	Lotus 1-2-3 Release 1a file format.

From the dot prompt you should open a database file as usual. If an index is in use the records will be ordered according to the controlling key field. Then issue the **COPY TO** command, specifying the destination file name and the type of destination file. The word **TYPE** is optional, as indicated by the square brackets in the syntax expression above. If no filetype is specified, the destination file will have the dBASE IV .DBF format.

---

3 There are minor differences between the file formats of dBASE III and IV, but for most purposes they are interchangeable. dBASE III+ is able to read dBASE IV data files provided no features specific to dBASE IV are used..

Example: *Create an SDF Text File with the COPY TO Command*

For this example we will create a text file using the COPY TO command from the dBASE dot prompt. We need to use the **EMPLOYEE.DBF** file from the data disk.

1. From the dot prompt, issue the command **USE EMPLOYEE**. dBASE will open the database file and position the record pointer at the top of the file.
2. Then issue the command **COPY TO EMP1 SDF** and press **Enter**. dBASE will report the number of records copied and display the next dot prompt. The text file EMP1.TXT will be created on the default drive.
3. You can display the file by using the dBASE **TYPE EMP1.TXT** command. Note that with the SDF filetype the fields are packed together with no spaces between field values. The date field is converted to YYYYMMDD format with this copy option. Figure 9-20 shows these commands.

Example: *Create a WKS File with the COPY TO Command*

This example creates a Lotus 1-2-3 (Release 1a) worksheet file using the COPY TO command.

1. As in the previous example, give the **USE EMPLOYEE** command from the dot prompt to open the database file.
2. Then give the **COPY TO EMP2 WKS** command. dBASE will copy the records, creating a new file called EMP2.WKS on the default drive. You cannot TYPE a worksheet file, but it can be read directly into Lotus 1-2-3 with the 1-2-3 /**File Retrieve** command. The memo field is not copied to the .WKS file, but the dates are correctly converted to the Lotus date format.
3. The Lotus worksheet is shown in Figure 9-21 after columns are widened to show the data.

Creating a Text File with the dBASE IV LIST TO FILE Command

It is also possible to use the dBASE IV **LIST TO FILE** command to create a text file. The LIST command will copy the fields and field names for all records to the text file unless otherwise specified. All of the usual LIST options are available including the **FOR** and **WHERE** clauses, and a field list to indicate the fields and their order in the new file. If the TO FILE option is not included, the records will be listed only on the display. The LIST TO FILE command results in a file that is quite similar to the COPY TO SDF command, except that there is a space between field values and the field names are printed first. The record number is also placed in the file unless the keyword **OFF** is placed at the end of the **LIST** command line. This command is not available in dBASE III PLUS.

Example: *Create a Text File with the LIST TO FILE Command*

This example will create the EMPLOYEE.TXT text file that was used in the Lotus /File Import example.

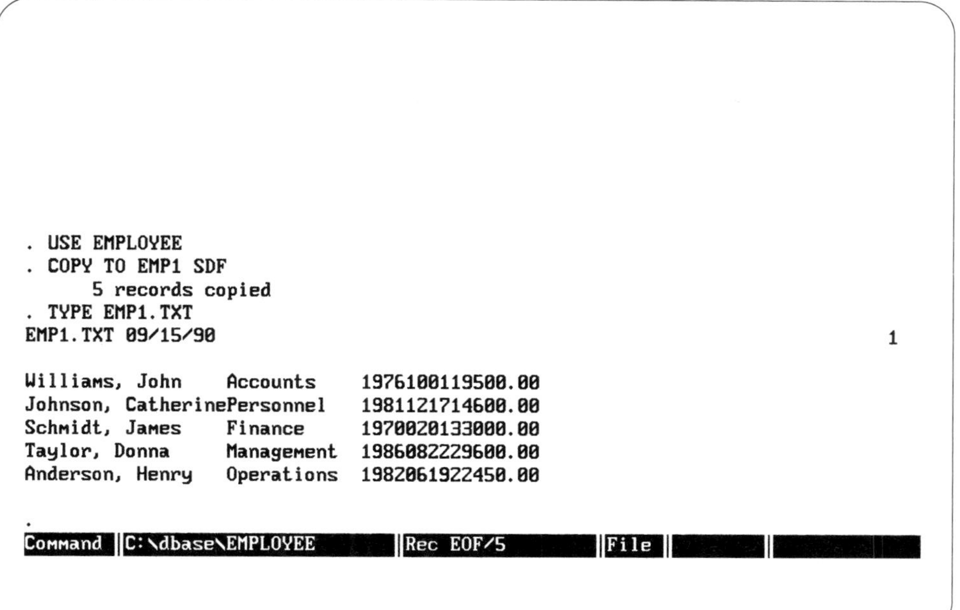

FIGURE 9-20

Illustration of Creating an SDF File from dBASE

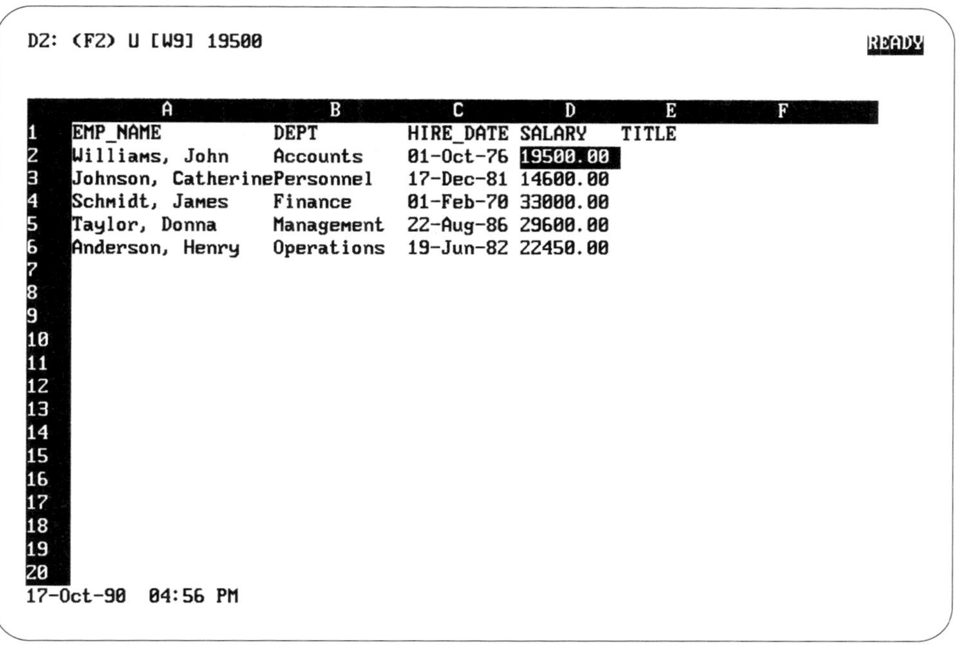

FIGURE 9-21

EMP2.WKS File Converted from EMPLOYEE.DBF

1. As before, issue the **USE EMPLOYEE** command from the dot prompt.
2. Then give the **LIST TO FILE EMPLOYEE** command. dBASE will list the records on the screen and will copy them to a text file called EMPLOYEE.TXT.
3. You can issue the **TYPE EMPLOYEE.TXT** command to display the text file as shown in Figure 9-22.

```
. LIST TO FILE EMPLOYEE
Record#  EMP_NAME            DEPT         HIRE_DATE    SALARY COMMENTS TITLE
      1  Williams, John      Accounts     10/01/76   19500.00 MEMO
      2  Johnson, Catherine  Personnel    12/17/81   14600.00 MEMO
      3  Schmidt, James      Finance      02/01/70   33000.00 MEMO
      4  Taylor, Donna       Management   08/22/86   29600.00 MEMO
      5  Anderson, Henry     Operations   06/19/82   22450.00 MEMO

. TYPE EMPLOYEE.TXT
EMPLOYEE.TXT 09/15/90                                                          1

Record#  EMP_NAME            DEPT         HIRE_DATE    SALARY COMMENTS TITLE
      1  Williams, John      Accounts     10/01/76   19500.00 MEMO
      2  Johnson, Catherine  Personnel    12/17/81   14600.00 MEMO
      3  Schmidt, James      Finance      02/01/70   33000.00 MEMO
      4  Taylor, Donna       Management   08/22/86   29600.00 MEMO
      5  Anderson, Henry     Operations   06/19/82   22450.00 MEMO

.
Command ||C:\dbase\EMPLOYEE        ||Rec EOF/5        ||File ||        ||
```

FIGURE 9-22

Illustration of LIST TO FILE Example

Exporting Data from the dBASE IV Control Center

The same data export options are available with the Control Center Menu Bar. From the main Control Center screen press the **F10** key to activate the Menu Bar. Move the cursor to the **Tools** bar and select the *Export* line. The menu shows each of the file types available from the COPY TO command, along with the resulting file extension. The *Text fixed-length fields* choice is the SDF file type discussed earlier. That display is shown in Figure 9-23. To select a choice, use the arrow keys to move the cursor to the desired line and press **Enter**.

Next dBASE will prompt for the name of the file you wish to copy. A new file with the same name but the appropriate extension will be created, and all records from the first file are copied. Note that you cannot create a file with a new name from the Control Center Export command. The destination file must be listed in the file name prompt box that appears next. In this context the COPY TO command issued from the dot prompt offers more flexibility.

Example: *Create a Delimited (MailMerge) File*

Suppose we wish to create a mailmerge format file for export to a word processor that will merge print customized letters.

1. For this file we will use the HABITAT.DBF file, so from the dBASE Control Center select **HABITAT** from the Data panel.

2. Then activate the Menu Bar with the **F10** key, and select the *Export* line of the **Tools** pull-down menu.

3. Move the cursor to the *Character delimited {"}* line and press **Enter**. Press **Enter** again at the next menu when dBASE shows you the possible delimiting characters—this selects the double quotation symbol to surround each data field.

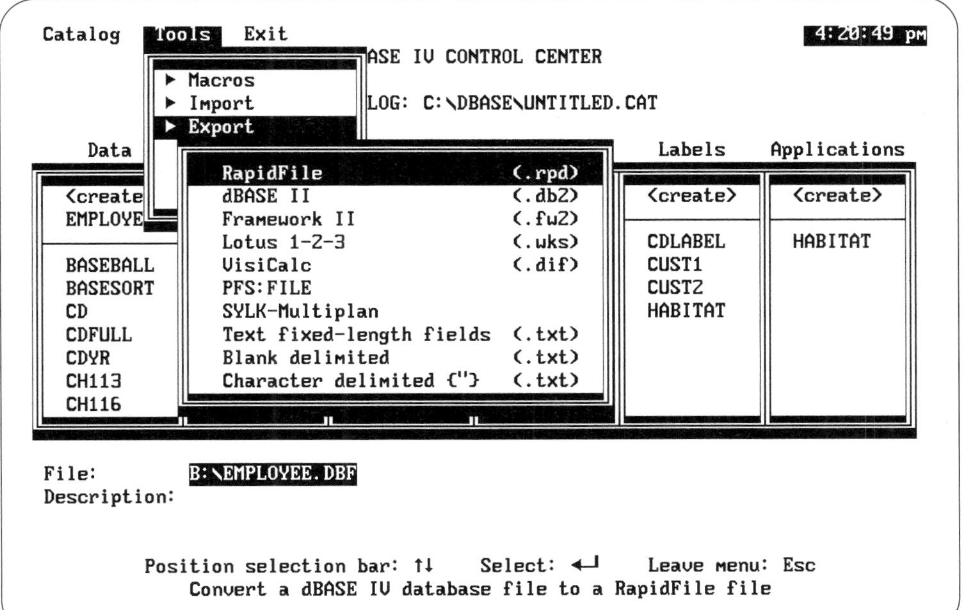

FIGURE 9-23

dBASE IV Export Menu

FIGURE 9-24

Contents of Delimited (MailMerge Format) File

4. Select **HABITAT** from the filename list. dBASE will create a new file called HABITAT.TXT that will contain the records. Each field is enclosed in quotations, and fields are separated with a comma. Each record is terminated with a carriage return and line feed. The contents of that file are shown in Figure 9-24.

TRANSFERRING DATA TO dBASE IV

There are several ways to add data to dBASE IV database files. The direct method is to issue the **APPEND** command and type the data in at the keyboard. Of course, if the data already exist in another file, it would seem desirable to **APPEND FROM** that file. In fact, dBASE supports several file import protocols, in addition to importing data from other dBASE IV .DBF files.

Using the APPEND FROM Command with Other Files

The **APPEND FROM** command will add data to the end of the current data file from the named file in the command line. You must already have a file structure in use before using APPEND FROM. The syntax of this command is:

```
APPEND FROM <filename> [[TYPE] <filetype>]
```

The <filetype> is taken from the following table (file types not available in dBASE III PLUS are marked):

Filetype	Meaning
(Omitted)	Uses dBASE IV .DBF format.
DBASEII	The dBASE II .DB2 file format (not in III PLUS).
DELIMITED	Each field is right-trimmed and the values are enclosed in quotations. Uses .TXT extension.
DIF	Spreadsheet .DIF format.
FW2	Framework II file format (not in III PLUS).
RPD	RapidFile file format (not in III PLUS).
SDF	Standard data format where fields are fixed-length and run together with no space between. Uses .TXT extension.
SYLK	Multiplan SYLK file format.
WKS	Lotus 1-2-3 Release 1a file format (not Release 2.x files).

Importing Data from Other Files

The dBASE **IMPORT FROM** command is used to translate from various file types, including Lotus Release 2.x .WK1 files. No structure need be created before issuing the command. It will create a database file with the same name as the original file, using the .DBF extension. The field names will be A, B, C, etc. You can change the field names using the MODIFY STRUCTURE command after importing the data values. The syntax of the command is:

```
IMPORT FROM <filename> [[TYPE] <filetype>]
```

The <filetype> is taken from the following table (dBASE III PLUS supports only the PFS type):

Filetype	Meaning
(Omitted)	Uses dBASE IV .DBF format.
PFS	PFS:File format.
DBASEII	dBASE II .DBF format.
FW2	Framework II file format.
RPD	RapidFile file format.
WK1	Lotus 1-2-3 Release 2.x format.

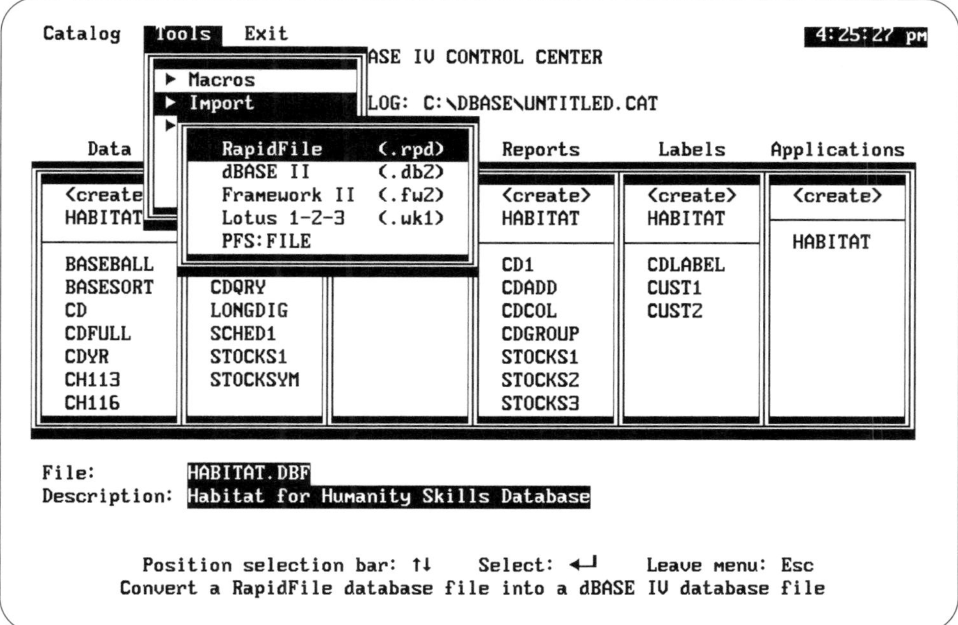

FIGURE 9-25

dBASE IV Import Menu

The previous command is issued from the dot prompt. You can achieve the same results from the Control Center. To activate the Control Center import facility, press **F10**, then select the *Import* line from the **Tools** bar. The Import menu is shown in Figure 9-25. The Control Center offers conversion from the following file types:

Filetype	**Meaning**
RPD	RapidFile file format.
DB2	dBASE II format.
FW2	FrameWork II format.
WK1	Lotus 1-2-3 Release 2, 2.01, 2.2 format.
PFS	PFS:File file format.

The Import procedure is similar to Export, except that you are given a list of files from which to choose a source of data. You may need to change to the directory where the data file of the specified type is stored. With 1-2-3 files be sure to save the worksheet with column widths sufficient to display all the data in a cell, otherwise dBASE will import only the data that fits within the column width.

There is another way to add data to a file. From the Database Design screen (**Shift-F2** from the main Control Center screen) activate the Menu Bar with **F10** and move to the **Append** bar. The three choices there are:

- Enter records from keyboard
- Append records from dBASE file
- Copy records from non-dBASE file.

The last choice allows input from the same kinds of files that were available for export in the previous section. The full screen is shown in Figure 9-26. Note that the only Lotus 1-2-3 files that may be appended from this screen are .WKS files. The **Import** Menu Bar command can also import .WK1 files.

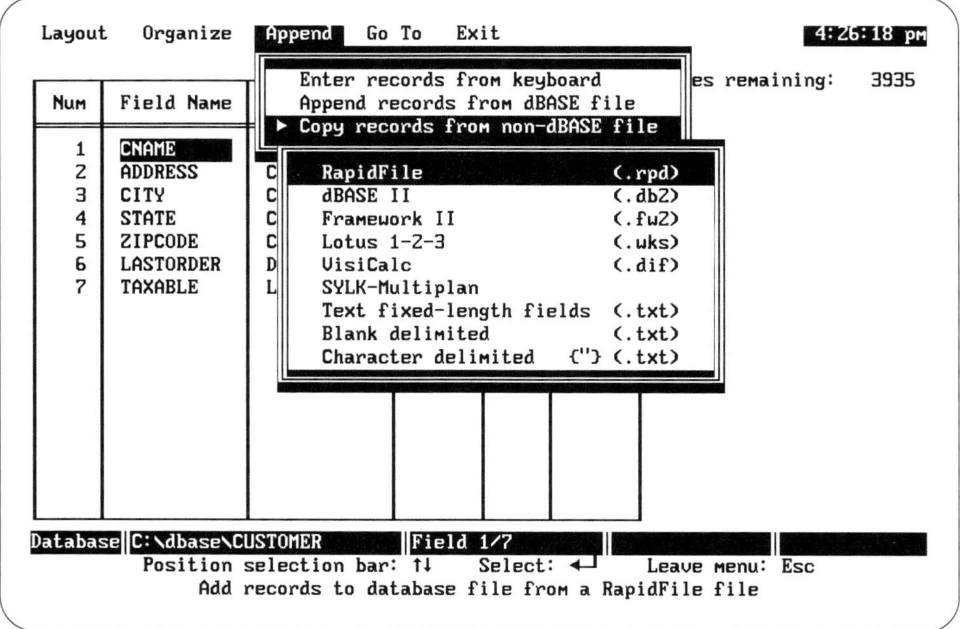

FIGURE 9-26

dBASE Append Menu–Copy Records

Example: *Adding Records from Another dBASE File*

It is possible to add records from another dBASE III PLUS or IV database file. Data will be copied from fields with the same names. No data is copied from fields that don't have the same names. For this example we will add records to a CUSTOMER database from another database file called PROSPECT.DBF, merging the two together into a single database. The contents of PROSPECT.DBF are shown in Figure 9-27. Note that the last field does not exist in the CUSTOMER database, and that several of the fields are of different lengths.

1. To merge the two files together, first open the **CUSTOMER** file from the dBASE Control Center.

2. Then press **Shift-F2** to open the Database Design screen. Activate the Menu Bar with **F10** and select the *Append records from dBASE file* line of the **Append** pull-down menu.

3. Next dBASE will display a list of all the .DBF files in the current directory; move the cursor to **PROSPECT.DBF** and press **Enter** to select it. Its four records will be appended to the end of the CUSTOMER file.

4. The CUSTOMER file will look like Figure 9-28. The final four records (those without last order dates) came from the PROSPECT file.

When adding records from an SDF text file, you must be aware of the structure of the target database file. The fields must be arranged in the same order in the target database file and in the text file. Fields are filled according to the number of characters in the field width. If the first field is 15 characters wide, the first 15 characters in the text file will be placed in the first field. With a

Records Organize Fields Go To Exit

CNAME	ADDRESS	CITY	STATE	ZIPCODE	REFERENCE
Mostichello, B,	226 Woodside Drive	Chicago	IL	60606	SP22
Frederick, R.	2444 Ashton Street	Urbana	IL	63204	SM07
Kellerman, F.	40 Wall St.,Suite 18	New York	NY	10012	BA09
Jenkins, S.	4509 Pendleton Lane	Anderson	IN	46588	IS001

Browse C:\dbase\PROSPECT Rec 1/4 File

FIGURE 9-27

Contents of PROSPECT Database

Records Organize Fields Go To Exit

CNAME	ADDRESS	CITY	STATE	ZIPCODE	LASTORDER	TA
Jones, B.	244 19th St.	Wabash	IN	47521	06/21/89	Y
Hollar, W.	1804 Thames	Richmond	IN	46154	10/15/89	N
Anderson, M.	Box 128	Vincennes	IN	48231	02/01/88	Y
Snow, B.	605 Ohio St.	Terre Haute	IN	47807	09/13/89	Y
O'Reilly, W.	1332 Western	Cory	IN	47823	09/30/89	N
Mains, W.	2199 West Lawrin	Princeton	IN	47233	06/12/72	Y
Mostichello, B,	226 Woodside Drive	Chicago	IL	60606	/ /	
Frederick, R.	2444 Ashton Street	Urbana	IL	63204	/ /	
Kellerman, F.	40 Wall St.,Suite 18	New York	NY	10012	/ /	
Jenkins, S.	4509 Pendleton Lane	Anderson	IN	46588	/ /	

Browse C:\dbase\CUSTOMER Rec 1/10 File

FIGURE 9-28

Results of Append Operation

delimited data text file, each field receives the next delimited value from the text file.

A better way to handle text transfers into dBASE is to first determine the structure implied by the fields as they appear in the text file, then create that structure in a temporary dBASE database file. Next import the data into the temporary database file. The database file can then be appended to the designated target database file using the *Append records from dBASE file* option.

FIGURE 9-29

Contents of ACCOUNTS.TXT and Structure of TEMPCUST.DBF

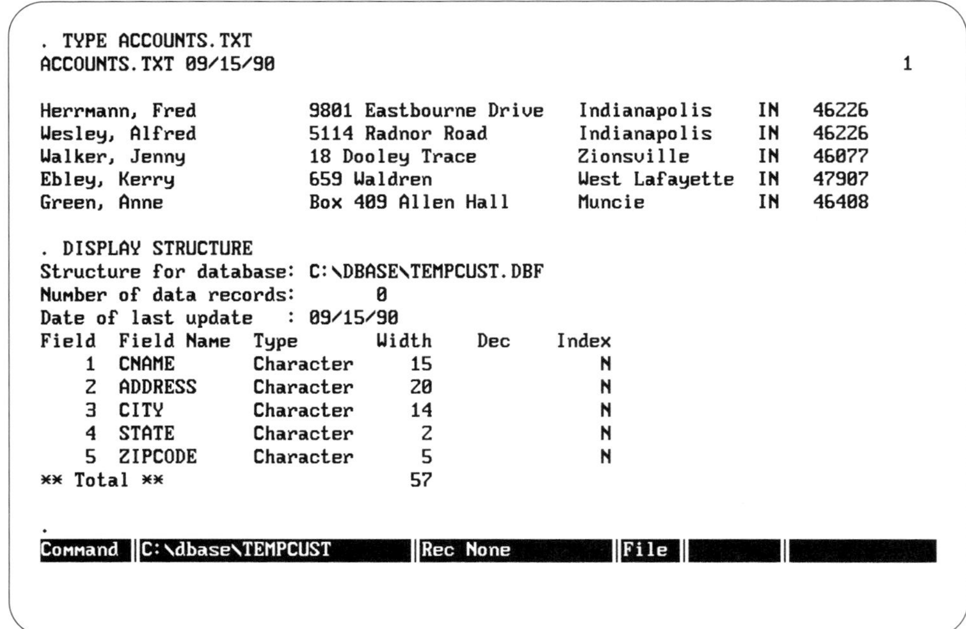

```
. TYPE ACCOUNTS.TXT
ACCOUNTS.TXT 09/15/90                                                        1

Herrmann, Fred        9801 Eastbourne Drive  Indianapolis    IN   46226
Wesley, Alfred        5114 Radnor Road       Indianapolis    IN   46226
Walker, Jenny         18 Dooley Trace        Zionsville      IN   46077
Ebley, Kerry          659 Waldren            West Lafayette  IN   47907
Green, Anne           Box 409 Allen Hall     Muncie          IN   46408

. DISPLAY STRUCTURE
Structure for database: C:\DBASE\TEMPCUST.DBF
Number of data records:       0
Date of last update   : 09/15/90
Field  Field Name  Type        Width    Dec    Index
    1  CNAME       Character      15               N
    2  ADDRESS     Character      20               N
    3  CITY        Character      14               N
    4  STATE       Character       2               N
    5  ZIPCODE     Character       5               N
** Total **                       57

.
Command ||C:\dbase\TEMPCUST        ||Rec None          ||File ||
```

Example: *Adding Records from a Text File*

Suppose we have the following text data stored in a file called ACCOUNTS.TXT. That file is shown in Figure 9-29 with a tentative file structure for the temporary file which is called **TEMPCUST**. Note that the field names are the same as those in the CUSTOMER.DBF file, in anticipation of merging the ACCOUNTS data into that file. But the field widths were chosen to match the text data as it appears in the ACCOUNTS.TXT file.

1. To merge the two files together, change to the Database Design screen in dBASE (**Shift-F2** from the Control Center) and activate the *Copy records from non-dBASE file* line of the **Append** pull-down menu.

2. Then select *Text fixed-length records* and press **Enter**.

3. The text file that contains our data is **ACCOUNTS.TXT**. Move the cursor to that file and press **Enter**. The data will be merged into the TEMPCUST file.

4. Next, select the **CUSTOMER** file from the Data panel in the Control Center, then switch to the Database Design screen.

5. Activate the Menu Bar, then choose the *Append records from dBASE file* line of the **Append** option of that menu.

6. Select the **TEMPCUST** file from the list of files, and press **Enter**. The fields from the TEMPCUST file will be appended to the end of the CUSTOMER file. Of course, there will be blank values for those fields that were not present in the TEMPCUST file.

CHAPTER REVIEW

Exchanging Data Between Software Packages

The three software packages studied in this book are able to exchange information in many ways. Each is able to save and retrieve data in the plain text, or ASCII format. But to retain formatting and other special characteristics, the native file format of the package should be used. WordPerfect is able to save documents in the native 5.1, 5.0, and 4.2 file formats. Lotus 1-2-3 uses the .WK1 format, and dBASE IV saves data to .DBF files.

Transferring Data form WordPerfect

WordPerfect will save to a text file or WP 4.2 file with the Ctrl-F5 Text In/Out command. The same command permits importation of a text file. If the usual F10 Save or F7 Exit commands are used to save the document, the WP 5.1 format is chosen.

WordPerfect Convert Program

Each package is equipped with a conversion or translation program that can accommodate numerous file formats. The WordPerfect CONVERT.EXE program handles eight formats, including .DIF, WordStar, MultiMate II, and Mailmerge. WordPerfect will import graphic images in several formats, including Lotus .PIC files and the popular .TIF and .PCX graphic formats.

Transferring Data from Lotus 1-2-3

The Lotus Translate module handles 10 formats, including other 1-2-3 and Symphony formats, dBASE, .DIF, and Multiplan files. The /Print File command is used to create a text file, and the /File Import will read a text file into the current worksheet. Unusually formatted text lines can be broken into individual columns by use of the /Data Parse command.

Transferring Data from dBASE IV

dBASE IV will export and import using ten different file types, including several text-type formats. The COPY TO and APPEND FROM commands are used from the dot prompt, while the **Tools** menu of the Menu Bar is use from the Control Center.

KEY TERMS

1-2-3 .PRN format
1-2-3 .WK1 format
1-2-3 .WKS format
APPEND FROM command
ASCII (text) file
conversion (translate) program
COPY TO
/Data Parse
dBASE .DBF format
dBASE .TXT format
delimited file
.DIF format
Exit (**F7**)
export
/File Combine
/File Import
/File Xtract
fixed-length fields
hyphenation zone
IMPORT FROM
link expression
Lotus Translate module
mailmerge format
native format
/Print File command
Save (**F10**)
SDF format
soft return
Text In/Out (**Ctrl-F5**)
unformatted option
WordPerfect CONVERT program
WP 4.2 format
WP 5.1 format
WP secondary merge format

DISCUSSION QUESTIONS

1. Discuss reasons for transferring data between the following modules. Give an example of the kind of data that might be transferred in each case.
   a. Lotus 1-2-3 to WordPerfect
   b. dBASE to 1-2-3
   c. dBASE to WordPerfect
   d. WordPerfect to dBASE
   e. dBASE to WordPerfect secondary merge.
2. Explain the meaning of the term **text (ASCII) file**. Why is it important for file transfers?
3. Describe the use of the CONVERT program packaged with WordPerfect. What file formats are supported by this program?
4. Suppose you had a program that would proofread and edit word processing documents, but did not support the WordPerfect 5.1 format. Discuss options that you might have in exporting the document to this software.
5. List the steps involved in placing a Lotus .PIC file inside a WordPerfect graphics box. Be explicit.
6. Suppose you have a colleague who is using a database program such as dBASE and you wish to use some of the data in a Lotus 1-2-3 worksheet. Discuss options that you might have in transferring that data to your worksheet.
7. Discuss the procedure to transfer data records from dBASE to WordPerfect for merge printing purposes. Be explicit.
8. WordPerfect offers two options when importing text files into a document. Define these options, and discuss the differences between them.
9. Compare the following 1-2-3 /File commands:
   a. **Retrieve**
   b. **Combine**
   c. **Import**
   d. **Save**
   e. **Xtract**.
10. Explain the differences between the 1-2-3 Text and Numbers /File Combine options.
11. Discuss the purposes of the /**Data Parse** command in 1-2-3. Describe a situation in which it would be useful.
12. Describe the Lotus 1-2-3 Release 2.2 link expression, and how it is useful in transferring data between worksheets.
13. List the file format types available with the dBASE IV Export and Import commands.

EXERCISES

1. Using WordPerfect, prepare the text in Figure 9-30 as a document.
   a. Save the document normally using the name **QUOTE.WP**.
   b. Save the document as a DOS text file named **QUOTE.TXT**.

```
                    Spectrum Computer Sales
                     3269 Westbourne Drive
                    Indianapolis, IN 46245
                        (555) 555-4321
                                  (insert current date here)


TO:       Boyer Machine Tool Company
          2278 Statesman Road
          Charlotte, VT 02316

RE:       RFQ #18234-90

We are submitting the following bid for the CAD workstation
specified in the above-named Request for Quotation. The
hardware model selected is based upon a close examination of
your needs and represents, in our opinion, an excellent
choice. The warranty period for this equipment is one year
from date of delivery, FOB Indianapolis. We will, at our
option, repair or replace defective hardware.

     1 CompuVal 386/20 Personal Computer with 4 MB RAM
     1 CADMaster Video Adapter with Full Page Display
     1 150 MB Landway Hard Drive with SCSI Interface
     1 HP Series III Laser Printer

The total bid, including delivery and setup at your premises,
is $14,844.00. This bid will expire 30 days from the date at
the top of this form.
```

FIGURE 9-30

Text for Exercise 1

2. Use Lotus 1-2-3 to prepare a financing plan for the quotation of the previous problem. Assume that the buyer must pay 20% as a down payment, financing the rest over four years at 11.2%. Your 1-2-3 report should include an explanation of all assumptions used, the monthly payment over that time period, the total amount of all payments, and the cumulative interest paid over the life of the loan.
   a. Save the worksheet normally as **FINQUOTE.WK1**.
   b. Print to a text file, using the name **FINQUOTE.PRN**.
   c. Insert the Lotus report at the end of the WordPerfect **QUOTE.WP** document created in the previous problem, and print the merged document.
3. Make a copy of the file called **SAMPLE.DIF** from the demo disk accompanying this text, and use the Lotus Translate module to convert it to the .WK1 format. Retrieve it into a Lotus worksheet and print the contents. You may need to adjust column widths and change cell formats before printing the final copy.

FIGURE 9-31

Suggested Structure for Exercise 6

NAME	Character	20
TITLE	Character	18
SALARY	Numeric	6
DEPARTMENT	Character	18
HIRE_DATE	Date	8

4. Make a copy of the file called **SAMPLE.DIF** from the demo disk accompanying this text, and convert it to WordPerfect secondary merge format. Use the name **SAMPLE.WP**. Print a copy of the SAMPLE.WP file as it appeared after it was converted. The numeric fields may appear in scientific notation, such as 2.850000000000000E+04. Written in normal format, this is 28500 and represents the salary. 3.242200000000000E+04 is the Lotus version of the hire date, or 32422. Is there a way to maintain the date in its usual format, such as October 6, 1988, when doing the conversion?

5. Use the **SAMPLE.WK1** file created in Exercise 3 to build a bar graph showing salaries for the employees. Select appropriate titles. Save the graph settings in a file called **SAMPLE.PIC**. Then create a one-page WordPerfect document that describes the graph, and insert the graph into a graphic box in the document, similar to the example of this chapter. Print the document in the highest graph resolution possible with your printer.

6. From dBASE import the data from the **SAMPLE.WK1** file you created in exercise 3. Because the first row of the spreadsheet contains the field names, you will need to delete the first record of the new database, or remove it from the .WK1 file. A possible structure for the database file is shown in Figure 9-31.

7. Use the **SCHED.DBF** file from the data disk accompanying this text to Export data to Lotus 1-2-3. For this exercise you should prepare a text fixed-length fields (SDF) file in dBASE, then use the /File Import command within 1-2-3. Use the 1-2-3 Text option, and save the file as **SCHED.WK1**. Print a copy of this database file.

8. Using the **SCHED.WK1** file from the previous problem, create a parse format that will break the values in column A into separate fields. Print this portion of the worksheet. Then use the /Data commands to do the following. Print the results for each part of the problem.

   a. Sort the rows by instructor name.

   b. Extract only the classes meeting on MW or MWF.

   c. Extract the MIS classes and sort those by time of day.

   d. List all classes meeting in room SB 106 or SB 108.

   The dBASE structure for this file is shown in Figure 9-32.

9. Use the Lotus Translate facility to convert the **SCHED.DBF** file into a 1-2-3 Release 2.2 file called **SCHED2.WK1**. Use dBASE III as the input file format. Retrieve that file in 1-2-3 and print its contents. Note that the column widths have been modified to fit the field widths.

```
Structure for database: C:\DBASE\SCHED.DBF
Number of data records:       39
Date of last update   : 10/30/89
Field  Field Name  Type        Width    Dec    Index
    1  PREFIX      Character       3               N
    2  NUMBER      Character       3               N
    3  SECTION     Numeric         2               N
    4  LIMIT       Numeric         3               N
    5  INSTRUCTOR  Character      15               N
    6  TIME        Character       5               N
    7  DAY         Character       3               N
    8  ROOM        Character       7               Y
    9  TITLE       Character      30               N
   10  DOCTORATE   Logical         1               N
** Total **                       73
```

FIGURE 9-32

Sample Structure for Exercise 8

```
Structure for database: C:\DBASE\CUSTOMER.DBF
Number of data records:       14
Date of last update   : 11/20/89
Field  Field Name  Type        Width    Dec    Index
    1  CNAME       Character      15               N
    2  ADDRESS     Character      20               N
    3  CITY        Character      14               N
    4  STATE       Character       2               N
    5  ZIPCODE     Character       5               N
    6  LASTORDER   Date            8               N
    7  TAXABLE     Logical         1               N
** Total **                       66
```

FIGURE 9-33

Sample Structure for Exercise 10

10. In this exercise we will use the **CUSTOMER.DBF** file to create a mail merge file that will be imported into WordPerfect secondary merge format. From dBASE Export the data using the Character delimited format; use the default double quote {"} character as the delimiter. From the DOS prompt run the CONVERT program to create a new file called **CUSTOMER.WP** in secondary merge format. Remember that the CONVERT program will ask for the field delimiter character, which is the comma. The record delimiter characters are **{13}{10}**. The character to be stripped out is the double quote, or **"**. Print the resulting WordPerfect file. The structure of the CUSTOMER.DBF file is shown in Figure 9-33.

11. Use WordPerfect to create a letter to be sent to each customer in the **CUSTOMER.WP** file. The letter may be of your choosing, but should include all of the fields from the file. Merge the letters, and print the first six letters. Each should be on a separate page. You may need to review the coverage of merge printing with WordPerfect.

CHAPTER 9 PROJECT
STUDENT VOLUNTEER AGENCY

Prepare a dBASE IV database containing information about students interested in doing volunteer work for the college community. Use the following job categories: tutoring, homebound visitation, park cleanup, small business assistance, hospital assistant, recreation instructor, and general help. Be sure to capture complete mailing information for each volunteer. Other personal data might include previous service, hours available per week, college major, and special skills. The database should be split into several tables. Suggestions include a table to hold mailing information about students, another table to hold job categories, and perhaps a table to store information about student skills.

Discuss the various kinds of reports and letters that can be prepared from this database. Describe situations in which the data might be transferred to other microcomputer software packages. Are there situations in which a spreadsheet might be useful?

Appendices

Appendix A
A PC Buyer's Guide

COMPONENTS OF THE DECISION

There are many alternatives for buying personal computer hardware and software today. While prices and features are constantly changing, there are certain issues to consider in addition to the current model selection. The purchasing process can be broken down into five phases:

1. Determine what applications you want to do with the microcomputer.
2. Decide the kinds and brands of the software you need.
3. Choose the most appropriate hardware that runs the software chosen.
4. Interview vendors about support, price, and product availability.
5. Make the purchase and install the equipment.

Many people are more concerned with steps 3 and 5, without giving the other three enough thought. This textbook focuses on IBM and compatible computer applications, but the steps above apply to all kinds of computers.

SOFTWARE SELECTION

Most people want to do word processing with their computer, and there are more word-processing-software applications than any other kind. Spreadsheet and database applications are also very popular. Telecommunications applications using a modem are common. Some users may wish to do programming, in BASIC, Pascal, or another programming language. This text has introduced the most popular software packages used with IBM-compatible personal computers. The final chapter in each application section compared other popular competing products with the covered software.

Many popular software packages require a hard disk. Some require a graphics video adapter. Because most vendors will not accept a software package for return after it has been opened, read the "fine print" before breaking the seal. Some vendors have a demonstration copy you can try before buying. Be sure to examine carefully the memory and operating system version required for the package. For IBM users the minimal hardware configuration would include 512 KB RAM and DOS 3.2 or higher. Macintosh users would want at least one megabyte of RAM. Additional RAM may be needed to run certain programs.

One consideration for choosing software is the availability of training, user support, and other reference materials. If your school has standardized on a particular product, it is usually desirable to choose that product unless it doesn't fulfill your needs. Another issue consists of transferring data from one application to another. Most of the popular packages can exchange data freely—be certain your chosen brands can do so if this is expected. There is a chapter in this book about exchanging data between applications.

Word Processing Packages

The most popular full-featured word processing packages are WordPerfect, WordStar, Microsoft Word, XYWrite, and Multimate Advantage. This textbook features WordPerfect 5.1, the top-selling word processing package. There are many packages with fewer features. They require less hardware and may be easier to learn. pfs-Write is an easy-to-learn package. **Integrated software** packages such as First Choice, Framework, and Enable have embedded word processing capabilities. Integrated software packages typically combine word processing, spreadsheet, database, graphics, and telecommunications features into a single program with common menus.

Spreadsheets

Spreadsheet packages have less variety than word processors. Lotus 1-2-3 has a large market share, more than 65%. This textbook demonstrates spreadsheet concepts using release 2.2 of Lotus 1-2-3. It is the dominant brand in use today. But there are several excellent alternatives, most of which are compatible with Lotus files and with most Lotus commands. SuperCalc 5, Quattro, Twin, and VP Planner are full-featured programs that go beyond Lotus Release 2.2. Microsoft's Excel runs only on an 80286 or 80386 microprocessor, and offers many new spreadsheet capabilities.

Database Software

Database management programs range from inexpensive file managers like PC-FILE or File Express to multi-user relational database systems like dBASE, Paradox and R:Base. dBASE is the best selling package, but doesn't dominate the database market as Lotus 1-2-3 does the spreadsheet market. Database management software is quite versatile, ranging from simple mailing list applications to complete, menu-driven systems. Each application should be carefully examined before deciding what to purchase. There are several dBASE imitators ("clones") available, including dBXL and Foxbase, for those who want a comparable package for less money.

Shareware and Public Domain Software

Occasionally "free" software is bundled along with certain computer brands. Such software may not be a bargain, particularly if it differs from the standard brands supported on campus or elsewhere. Be sure this software satisfies the needs you established earlier. Shareware is another inexpensive source of software, available from vendors like Public Brand Software or from local computer clubs or libraries. Catalogs describing this software are available free. Some of the software is in the **public domain,** contributed by other users without expectations of payment for the programs. Some of the software is distributed on the **shareware** basis: copy it freely, but make a nominal payment to the program's author if it is used after the trial period. There is some remarkable software available on this basis, including ProComm, an excellent intelligent terminal program. Good educational programs are also available through this distribution method.

Educational Versions

Educational, or student, versions of software are available at very low cost (often included in the price of a textbook) and serve a purpose in learning how to use a package. These versions may not be useful in regular applications, either due to license restrictions or because of size and feature limitations. Usually only limited documentation accompanies the disk. Once the learning period is over, a full working copy should be purchased. Upgrades are sometimes available—check the fine print accompanying the educational disk.

Copyrights and Software Piracy

Most software available today is licensed to a single user. Copying it for another user is a violation of the Federal copyright law. The term **software piracy** is used to describe the act of copying software illegally. Most universities have significant penalties for those who make illegal copies of software. Ethical use of software is the responsibility of each user.

CHOOSING HARDWARE

Once the software choices are made, you can consider hardware. Most users will know early in the process whether they want an IBM compatible machine, an Apple Macintosh, or some other family of microcomputers. Business users have traditionally chosen the IBM line, while elementary education users have focused on Apple II products. The Macintosh became popular with the advent of desktop publishing, but all computers can be used with virtually all applications with proper software. Of course, there are some fundamental differences between IBM compatibles and the Macintosh.

The Mac made an important contribution with its user interface, based upon graphical images (icons) that represent functions in graphical menus. The user can maneuver a mouse to move the cursor to the desired function icon, and depress the mouse button ("click") on it. Most Macintosh software is designed with the same architecture; that is, once you've learned one Mac package, others are very similar. Some people dislike having to move their hand from the keyboard to manipulate the mouse, but many appreciate the ease of communicating with a program. In fact, many software designers have used Mac features in IBM compatible software. Microsoft's Windows and DESQview utilize the graphical approach. PageMaker, a desktop-publishing program, works the same way in the Mac and the IBM versions. With the OS/2 Presentation Manager following closely the Macintosh interface, icon/graphical presentations can be achieved in the IBM world. This textbook focuses on IBM-compatible computers and related buying issues.

Microcomputer magazines are an excellent source of information on available products and vendors. *PC Magazine* regularly offers detailed reviews on products. Their printer review issues are exceptional. Other good IBM-related magazines include *Personal Computing, InfoWorld, PC World,* and *Byte.* The top two Macintosh magazines are *Mac User* and *Mac World.* There are many specialty magazines dealing with specific markets or kinds of products, and even magazines dealing with a single product like *WordPerfect The Magazine.* Another good source of information is a local computer users' group. Many communities have such groups, organized locally to help members learn more about computing. You might check with the local library or school for information about meeting times and membership.

Hardware buying decisions include type of drives (hard, floppy, storage capacity, speed), type of display adapter and monitor, central processing unit CPU type and speed, amount of RAM (conventional, expanded), desktop or portable/laptop, cabinet style and number of expansion slots, and number of I/O ports. Many users will buy a mouse, which requires either a spare serial port or a bus card.

A complete system includes the computer itself with sufficient memory (minimum 512 KB but preferably 640 KB or more), 1 or 2 disk storage devices (floppy or hard drive), serial and parallel ports for mouse and printer, video adapter, display monitor (monochrome or color, but matching the video adapter), printer cable and printer (dot matrix, ink jet, or laser), and perhaps a surge protector or modem. Since the entire system is rarely packaged together in one bundle, you will have to make some choices. Keep in mind that the software chosen will dictate certain hardware requirements. It is recommended that a hard disk be part of the configuration if budget allows the extra $200-$400 cost. A perplexing issue involves 3.5-inch versus 5.25-inch floppy disk drives. Most newer machines come with the 3.5-inch size but older machines probably have the larger drive. Software is available in both sizes, and some publishers include both size diskettes in the box. This decision depends in part on those with whom you will be exchanging information. One solution is to install both sizes of floppy drives in the same computer; the second floppy drive costs about $100.

Hardware Manufacturers

There are many manufacturers of IBM-compatible personal computers, most priced competitively. IBM offers a complete selection of personal computers. Other well-known companies such as Hewlett-Packard, AT&T, Unisys, and NCR offer similar personal computers, but there are numerous new companies with good products. Compaq is one of the fastest growing companies in U.S. history, reaching the $1 billion sales level faster than any other firm. Zenith Data Systems has a complete line of personal computers and has extensive sales agreements with the federal government and with educational institutions. Tandy sells excellent personal computers and has a well-developed hardware support network. Several mail-order vendors, including CompuAdd and Dell Computers, offer good equipment at attractive prices. Most of these machines advertise complete IBM compatibility and will run virtually all software designed for IBM personal computers.

Selecting the System Unit

With the IBM PC family nearly a decade old, there are many compatible models available. The original IBM PC and XT used the 8088 microprocessor, and have been discontinued for several years. But many clone vendors still sell 8088 machines. This processor is capable of running most applications software, but some newer packages like Microsoft's Excel spreadsheet require an 80286 processor. The 8088 will handle routine chores like word processing well, although certain tasks such as spell checking or global search-and-replace will work more slowly on an 8088 machine. In some cases a faster hard drive can make up for a slower processor. But computation-intensive applications, such as large spreadsheets, will be considerably slower on an 8088 machine. An 8087 numeric co-processor chip can speed up the calculations if the software is written to recognize the presence of the chip. The 8088 is an 8/16 processor; it uses an 8-bit data bus for data transfers between memory and the CPU, and accomplishes 16-bit internal calculations. When purchasing expansion boards for an 8088 computer, choose the 8-bit variety. The 8088 can access up to 1 MB of memory, but cannot run the OS/2 operating system.

A faster replacement was introduced in 1985. The IBM AT featured an 80286 processor and a 16-bit data bus. It also can handle some 32-bit internal calculations and is significantly faster than the PC and XT. While 8-bit expansion boards can be used with an AT, critical components such as disk controller and expansion memory should be the 16-bit variety. Another change with the AT was inclusion of high-density, 1.2-MB, 5.25-inch disk drives, making backups of larger hard-disk drives easier. This machine will run spreadsheet software up to 4 times faster than an XT, but word processing will not be speeded up comparably. The 80287 numeric co-processor can be added to these machines to speed up numeric calculations. Most experts believe that 8088 machines will eventually disappear, and the AT-class 286 machines will become the low end of the market. There are many AT clone products available.

IBM introduced its PS/2 line of microcomputers in 1987. Bundled with 3.5-inch disk drives, they are much smaller in size than previous models. The line-up consists of XT-like 8086 models (similar in performance and capabilities to 8088 models), several 80286 machines, and several 80386 and 80386SX machines. New high-end models support the 80486 microprocessor. Designed for easy customer configuration and with an advanced data bus, these machines represent IBM's current offerings. Unlike earlier models, expansion cards for older models will not work in the PS/2 line. However, more options were made standard on these machines and fewer expansion boards are needed.

Portable Computing: Laptops

Most vendors offer a complete line of computers, including portable and laptop computers. Virtually as powerful as the desktop models, the portables come with full 640 KB memory, 3.5-inch floppy drive, graphics video adapter, and a monochrome liquid crystal display (LCD), and can be ordered with hard-disk drive and modem. Expansion room is limited, but some models permit you to add more EMS memory or hook up an expansion cabinet for additional boards. Laptop computers come with a rechargeable nicad battery good for 2 to 4 hours of computing. The battery can be recharged overnight. Laptops range in weight from 6 pounds to 15 pounds, and can be used anywhere. Some ultra-light units are small enough to fit inside a briefcase. The portable computers, usually larger than the laptops, typically require AC power and may have a better resolution screen. Portables can weigh up to 20 pounds and are ill-designed for extensive carrying.

Floppy-Disk Drives

Most users should purchase the drive size (3.5- or 5.25-inch) that is used at their school or organization. The previous standard 5.25-inch drive is still popular, but today's smaller computers usually come with the 3.5-inch size. Some may wish to have both size drives in their computer, as shown in Figure A-1. Those users who need to exchange information between computers with incompatible drives can use file transfer software such as LapLink and send data between the computers' serial or parallel ports.

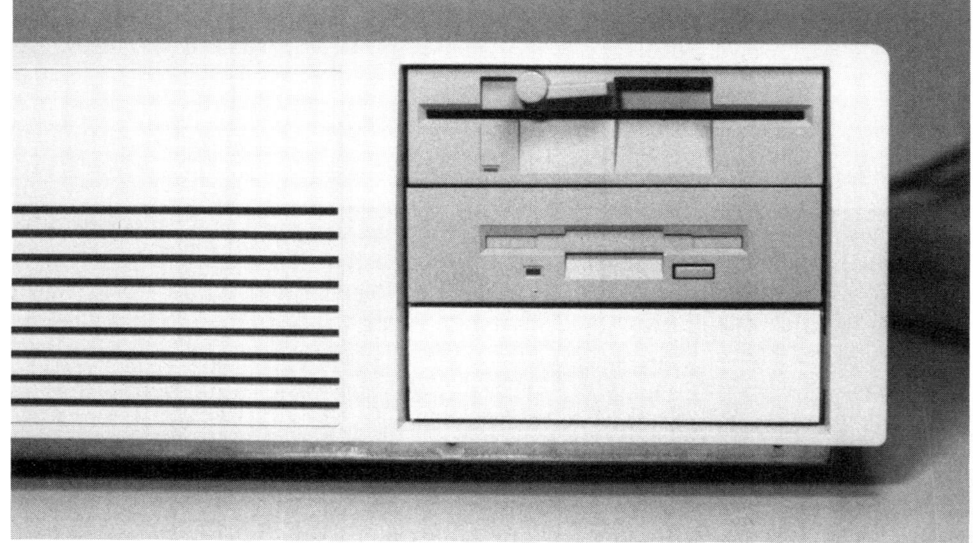

FIGURE A-1

Personal Computer with Both 3.5" and 5.25" Drives.

Hard-Disk Drives

Hard disk drives come in two physical sizes, 5.25-inch or 3.5-inch width. The system unit will dictate whether the larger size will fit in the drive bay. The capacity of the disk is given in megabytes, typically 20, 30, 40, 60, or more. Capacity of the drive depends on the number of disk surfaces, number of tracks, and recording density. The newer RLL (run length limited) drives can store 50% more bits in the same space by using magnetic recording more efficiently. Hard drives require a controller card and cables to connect the two units. The controller card installs in an expansion slot in the system unit, or may be built into the motherboard, or main circuit board. Some hard drives require a special type of controller card—it is best to purchase a matched set (hard-disk, controller card, cable) to insure compatibility between drive and controller. Larger disk drives may use the newer ESDI or SCSI interfaces, providing for much faster data transfer between the drive and the CPU. Again, special controller adapters are needed to use these drive types. ESDI and SCSI drives are somewhat more expensive than the standard drives.

The speed of a hard drive depends on two factors: number of bits transferred by the disk controller and track access time. The 286 and 386 computers come with a 16-bit disk controller and data transfers are much faster. The 8088 and 8086 computers use the slower 8-bit controller. Track access time, given in milliseconds, tells how long the disk read heads take to move halfway across the drive. XT-class drives are more than 60 milliseconds, while AT drives are 30-40 milliseconds. Newer drives offer track access times of less than 20 milliseconds.

Dot Matrix Printers

Dot matrix printers begin at under $200 and are the bargain of the microcomputing world. Items to consider when buying a dot matrix printer are number of pins in the print head (9 or 24), rated print speed (in both draft and near-letter quality modes), paper-handling abilities (paper width, continuous-form tractor feed, ability to print envelopes, sheet feed capability, and printer emulations). To take advantage of all the printer's features, your software must either have an installation option for that specific printer model, or the printer must emulate another standard printer type that is available with your software. Ribbon cost and number of characters per ribbon are also important—some printers will automatically re-ink the ribbon while it is used, allowing the ribbon to print darker for a longer time. Another consideration is the ease of selecting print styles (fonts) from the front panel. Epson and Panasonic printers have easy-to-use controls. While 9-pin printers are typically $150 less than 24-pin models, they are much slower in near-letter quality (NLQ) modes because they must make two or more passes to create characters. The 24-pin models slow down when in NLQ mode but typically print at half of the draft speed; 9-pin models print at less than one-fourth of draft speed. Compare the output samples shown in Figure A-2.

Virtually all printers come with a parallel interface, connecting to the parallel port on the computer. Some models can be ordered with an optional serial interface. The parallel method is much faster—an important consideration when printing graphics. A sizable printer buffer can speed printing by storing print characters from the computer and allowing the printer to print while the computer is doing something else. While most dot matrix printers can print multi-part forms (several sheets of paper with carbon paper between), only heavy-duty printers do a credible job of printing more than two copies at once. In fact, before purchasing a printer you should carefully estimate the print load expected of the printer: some printers are rated for occasional use, typically no more than 25% duty cycle. This means the printer should be

FIGURE A-2

Standard, 9-pin NLQ, and 24-pin NLQ Printer Output.

```
This is an example of draft quality on a 9-pin Panasonic dot
matrix printer. ABCDEFGHIJKLMNOPQRSTUVWXYZ 1234567890
abcdefghijklmnopqrstuvwxyz !#$%&*()


This is an example of near-letter quality on a 9-pin Panasonic
dot matrix printer. ABCDEFGHIJKLMNOPQRSTUVWXYZ 1234567890
abcdefghijklmnopqrstuvwxyz !#$%&*()


This is an example of a near-letter quality with an Epson 24-pin
dot matrix printer. ABCDEFGHIJKLMNOPQRSTUVWXYZ 1234567890
abcdefghijklmnopqrstuvwxyz !#$%&*()
```

FIGURE A-3

Hewlett-Packard ink jet printer output.

```
This is a sample sentence printed on an ink jet printer at highest
quality. ABCDEFGHIJKLMNOPQRSTUVWXYZ 1234567890 abcdefghijklmnopqrs
tuvwxyz#$^&%*()
```

expected to be printing only two hours out of each eight hours, and not for two hours in a row. Fortunately, most printers have a built-in thermal sensing device that slows down or turns off the printer if it senses the print head is becoming overloaded and too hot.

Ink Jet Printers

Ink jet and laser printers provide 300 by 300 dots-per-inch print resolution, with near-typeset print quality (see Figure A-3). As non-impact printers, neither is able to print multi-part forms. Ink jet printers are priced at much less than lasers, and print more slowly. The best-known manufacturer of ink jet and laser printers is Hewlett-Packard. Most applications software can be installed for use with either kind of printer. The HP ink jet emulates some of the HP laser printer's commands, but some print capabilities cannot be done by the ink jet printer due to limitations in the technology. The ink jet printer offers better print quality than either dot matrix or daisy wheel, at faster speeds. It may not have the durability for high-volume use that other printers might have.

FIGURE A-4

Laser printer sample ouptut.

```
This is an example of a Hewlett-Packard laser printer.
ABCDEFGHIJKLMNOPQRSTUVWXYZ 1234567890 abcdefghijklmnopqrstuvwxyz
!#$%&*()
```

Laser Printers

The HP Laserjet family of laser printers has become the world standard. In 1988 HP sold more than one billion dollars worth of these printers. Laser printers excel at providing high quality printing at high speeds. Although the price is beginning to fall, both for the printer and for supplies, laser printers are more expensive than other types. Many people underestimate the per-page cost of using a laser printer. However, its ability to turn out desktop publishing documents has placed it high on the want list at many organizations. The laser printer is able to print normally across the page, called **portrait mode.** It is also able to print sideways, along the long side of a page, called **landscape mode.**

Laser printers come with several print fonts built in, and additional fonts can be added either by purchasing a font cartridge or by installing downloadable soft fonts. Soft fonts are stored on the host computer's hard disk, then are sent through the printer cable and stored in the memory of the laser printer as long as it is turned on. The applications software can be programmed to change fonts quickly. Like the dot matrix printer, the laser printer can automatically change fonts and type sizes on the same page without user intervention. Laser printers do an excellent job of printing forms with different type sizes. Figure A-4 is an example of laser printer output.

Laser printer buying decisions include type of printer emulation, print speed, amount of printer memory, and additional font capability. **PostScript printers** use the high-level PostScript language to represent print information, requiring much less data be transmitted through the printer cable but relying more upon the printer itself to do formatting. PostScript printers accept more powerful editing commands and usually come with many built-in print fonts. Although non-PostScript-compatible printers are less expensive, they tie up the host computer longer to do image formatting and translation. You can purchase PostScript adapters for some non-PostScript printers. Print speed is generally given in pages per minute, with 6 or 8 being the most common speed. Some printers will print both sides of the paper at the same time, but are more expensive. Another feature is the number of paper trays in the printer: most printers have a single tray with only a single kind of paper loaded. This makes printing two-page correspondence (with letterhead as page one and plain paper for later pages) more difficult. Printer memory is generally given as 512 KB or 1 MB. Additional memory is necessary to hold additional soft fonts or to print full-page graphics. The minimum practical memory size for desktop publishing is 1.5 MB for non-PostScript laser printers, and more with PostScript printers. Font cartridges typically cost about $200 and offer a dozen print fonts. Soft fonts are a little less costly but are less convenient because they must be downloaded each time the printer is turned on. Font cartridges are instantly available at printer power-up and take up no printer memory.

Most laser printers have a replaceable print/toner cartridge containing a new light-sensitive print drum, black toner, and other critical components necessary to maintain good quality print. The cartridge lasts 3000-4000 pages, depending on type of printing and amount of toner used. The printer will signal when it is time to replace the cartridge. Per-page cost with a laser printer is 4 to 5 cents, including the cost of paper.

SELECTING A VENDOR

The next step is choosing a vendor. Caution is in order because not all vendors are able to provide necessary support. Mail order prices are generally 20-30% lower than local computer store prices, although this is not always the case. Some mail order vendors can provide installation support and ongoing assistance, but not many have extensive customer assistance. For mail order purchases, who pays the shipping and insurance charges? Is there a surcharge for using a credit card? Is the company well-known and in business for some time? Will they accept COD deliveries, or do they require pre-payment? What is the typical delivery time? Another nagging issue is the availability of local service and support for equipment purchased by mail order—some computer stores are unwilling to service equipment they did not sell.

Local computer stores are able to explore your needs and determine the proper equipment for you. Avoid the store that immediately shows you rows of hardware—if you purchase locally expect individual assistance. Local vendors should be willing to discuss complete system needs first. Expect to have your computer set up, with all optional equipment installed and tested, before accepting delivery. Mail order vendors rarely offer this service. Also expect some instruction on how to start up the computer and do routine tasks. Most vendors do so willingly, if asked, although some also offer fee-based training classes for more elaborate instruction.

Warranty Considerations

Explore the warranty options with your vendor. Do they have a no-questions-asked return policy for the first 30 days? This is especially useful for mail-order purchases. How long is the manufacturer's warranty period? Does it cover parts and labor, or just parts? Does the vendor have on-site repair technicians? Do they offer a loaner machine while your equipment is in the shop? Do they stock an adequate supply of replacement parts, or will your machine need to be shipped elsewhere for repair? Is the brand a well-known one, likely to exist in the future? Will they continue to stock accessory parts, even if they discontinue the computer line? For mail order vendors, do they have a technical support telephone line? Is it free?

Trouble-shooting problems can be a difficult task. Most hardware problems turn out to be operator problems, some of which can be fixed over the phone. For those who are afraid to "roll up their sleeves" and work with the computer's innards, local support and hand-holding may be in order. Because many local computer stores cannot provide substantial software assistance, and because software does not require "repair" like hardware does, mail order software purchases are very popular. Some mail order vendors even provide next-day deliveries. (For example, PC Connection, a mail order company located in New Hampshire, offers next-business-day air freight deliveries for just a few dollars per order.)

Software Purchases

Software is available locally and from mail order outlets, but local vendors may not have the software expertise needed to justify the higher local price. Regrettably, most computer stores sell hardware first, and include software afterwards.

Perhaps you can negotiate a system price to include software from a local vendor. Be sure the vendor sells the most current release of the software you have chosen. Ask whether the store's personnel can help in using the software. Do they offer more than one brand in a given category? Mail order suppliers sell more software than do local outlets, and offer a larger selection.

MAKING THE PURCHASE

The final step is to make the purchase and install the system. Have your vendor connect all equipment and test the computer before it leaves the store. Some computer problems may occur shortly after the item is installed, and the vendor can repair or exchange the defective part before you take it home. Your vendor may agree to **burn-in** the computer, running it for a day or two in the shop to assure all is working properly. Keep all receipts and packing materials; should equipment have to be returned, the original box is the best means of protection.

Information about setting up a new computer may be found in Chapter 2 of this textbook, and in the sections about applications software. Most the software packages have special "Getting Started" instructions that make installing the software relatively easy.

AFTER THE PURCHASE: GETTING HELP

The primary source of help with your computer will probably be the documentation that comes with the computer. A careful reading of the manuals may pinpoint problems with the system. Another good source of information about your system is the vendor who sold it to you. Local computer stores sometimes offer courses for new owners. Check with your vendor about seminars and other group activities. Mail order computer companies often have a support group available via toll-free telephone. Most prefer that you call while sitting at the computer so that diagnostic procedures can be tried immediately. Take notes when you talk to the support department, whether it be in person or by telephone.

The documentation accompanying software packages you have purchased is another excellent source of information. Many packages have a Getting Started section for new users, and some offer tutorials on paper or through the computer. Before calling the software vendor's technical support group, read the manual carefully. Some packages have a troubleshooting section that may answer your questions.

A good way to find out what other people are doing is to join a user group. Check with a local computer store for the names of local groups. Specialized groups supporting different hardware families exist in many towns. Contacts made via user groups can bring individuals together with common interests. Some groups offer informal classes and seminars.

Books and magazines are an important source of information. Magazines are more current but don't have the depth that a book can offer. Many libraries subscribe to the more popular computer publications. Otherwise, check your bookstore for magazines and books.

CARING FOR THE MICROCOMPUTER SYSTEM

There are some good practices to follow when setting up the computer system. Be careful to not block any of the ventilation ports in the system unit. Keep the computer away from heat sources or high humidity. Avoid dust and smoke around the computer area. The desk or table it sits upon should be sturdy enough to support the computer and all its devices.

Make sure there are an adequate number of electrical outlets for plugging in components. Most computers will have power cords for the system unit, monitor, and printer. Other devices like external modems may also need to be plugged in. You may wish to purchase a power strip with multiple outlets that would allow the components to be plugged into a single wall outlet. Better power adapters have filtering circuits that remove some of the electrical noise that may appear on the power line. More filtering is obtained with higher-cost power strips. Some power adapters offer **surge protection** for lightning and other power surges that may occur during storms. The best practice is to unplug computer and other electronics equipment during electrical storms. Don't forget to unplug the modem from the telephone line.

The computer needs little or no regular maintenance. Avoid eating and drinking around the computer so that spills on the keyboard or system unit don't occur. The monitor's screen will attract dust because of a static electricity charge on its surface. Turn off the monitor before cleaning the surface with a damp cloth. Avoid touching the surface of the monitor while in contact with any diskettes or the inside of the system unit. These components are particularly sensitive to static discharges.

Your printer manual will give suggestions for printer maintenance. The ribbon should be changed at the suggested interval or whenever it appears worn or frayed. You might wish to write the date on the ribbon cartridge when it is installed as a reminder of the ribbon's age. Vacuum the paper dust inside the printer and clean the case with a soft damp cloth. Periodical cleaning of the carriage shaft may also be needed.

Floppy disks should be stored in a safe place. Use the boxes that blank diskettes came in or a plastic disk storage box. 5.25-inch floppy diskettes should be stored vertically; 3.5-inch diskettes may be stacked because their rigid plastic shell gives better protection to the disk inside. Keep floppy disks away from magnetic fields and extreme heat or cold. Avoid spilling liquids on a diskette, or on any other part of the computer.

Avoid using the original disks after making a backup copy. For greater protection, hard-disk backup disks should be stored in a different location than the computer. That way an accident such as fire or water damage would not harm both the hard drive and the backup disks.

You should examine insurance policies to assure that the new equipment is properly covered. Regular homeowner's policies offer limited coverage, depending on usage. Inexpensive riders can be added for complete coverage, even away from home. It's wise to check before theft or storm damage occurs.

KEY TERMS

burn-in
integrated software
landscape mode
portrait mode
PostScript printers
public domain
shareware
software piracy
surge protection

Appendix B
DOS Commands

INTERNAL DOS COMMAND SUMMARY

Command	**Purpose**
BREAK	Allows or disables Ctrl-C interrupt of program
CHDIR (CD)	Change default directory
CLS	Clears the display screen
COPY	Copy specified file(s)
d:	Change default drive to specified letter
DATE	Display and set the current date
DEL (ERASE)	Delete specified file(s)
DIR	List files in a directory
EXIT	Exit the command processor
MKDIR (MD)	Create a new subdirectory
PATH	Set command file search path
PROMPT	Change DOS command prompt
RENAME (REN)	Rename a file
RMDIR (RD)	Remove a subdirectory
SET	Set environment variable
TIME	Display and set the current time
TYPE	Display contents of a file on the screen
VER	Show the DOS version number
VOL	Displays the disk's volume label

EXTERNAL DOS COMMAND SUMMARY

Command	Purpose
APPEND	Set a search path for data files
ASSIGN	Assign a drive letter to a different drive
ATTRIB	Set or display file attributes
BACKUP	Back up files from one disk to another
CHKDSK	Check directory for errors, also display free RAM and disk space remaining
COMMAND	Start the DOS command processor
COMP	Compare the contents of two files
DISKCOMP	Compare the contents of two disks
DISKCOPY	Copy contents of one disk
EXE2BIN	Convert .EXE files to binary format
FC	Compare files, display differences
FDISK	Configure and initialize hard disk
FIND	Locate a specific text string
FORMAT	Prepare a new disk for storing data
GRAFTABL	Load a table of graphics characters
GRAPHICS	Prepare DOS to print graphics screens
JOIN	Join a disk drive to a path
LABEL	Display and change disk volume label
MODE	Set operating characteristics for devices such as monitor and I/O ports
MORE	Display screen of output at a time
PRINT	Print contents of file
RECOVER	Recover from errors in file
REPLACE	Replace previous version of file with new version of same name
RESTORE	Restores files that were previously backed up
SORT	Sorts data in ascending or descending order
SUBST	Substitute a string for a path
TREE	Display subdirectory structure and file names
XCOPY	Copies files and subdirectories

Appendix C
dBASE IV Commands

GENERAL dBASE IV FUNCTION KEY ASSIGNMENTS

Key	Function	Meaning
F1	Help	Activate dBASE Help System
F2	Data	Display data values in Edit or Browse screen
F3	Previous	Moves to previous field or page
F4	Next	Moves to next field or page
F5	Field	Add or modify field on current layout surface
F6	Select	Select field or text on current layout surface
F7	Move	Move selected field or text
F8	Copy	Copy selected field or text
F9	Zoom	Open/close memo field or other object
F10	Menus	Activate Menu Bar
Shift-F1	Pick	Display list of choices for current operation
Shift-F2	Design	Activate the design screen of current file type (data, query, form, report, label)
Shift-F8	Ditto	Fills in current field with data from same field of previous record
Shift-F9	Quick Report	Print quick report of data

dBASE IV EDIT SCREEN COMMANDS

Command	Meaning
↑	Move up one row on screen
↓	Move down one row on screen
←	Move left one character in current field
→	Move right one character in current field
PgUp	Display previous screen
PgDn	Display next screen
Home	Move to beginning of current field
End	Move to end of current field
Tab	Move to next field
Shift-Tab	Move to previous field
Enter	Move to next field
Esc	Leave Edit screen without saving changes to current record
Ctrl-←	Move to beginning of previous word in field
Ctrl-→	Move to beginning of next word in field
Del	Delete character beneath cursor
Backspace	Delete character to left of cursor
Ins	Toggle between overtype and insert modes
Ctrl-T	Delete from cursor position to beginning of next word
Ctrl-Y	Delete from cursor position to end of current field
Ctrl-End	Save changes and leave Edit screen

dBASE IV SPECIAL NUMERIC FIELD TEMPLATE CHARACTERS

Character	Meaning
9	Allows only digits and sign
#	Allows digits, spaces and sign
.	Insert decimal point
,	Display comma if number is large enough
*	Display leading zeros as asterisks
$	Display leading zeros as dollar signs
any other	Insert that character into template

dBASE IV SPECIAL CHARACTER FIELD TEMPLATE CHARACTERS

Character	Meaning
9	Allows only digits and sign
#	Allows only digits, spaces and sign
A	Allows only alphabetic characters
N	Allows alphabetic, digits and underscore
!	Converts character to uppercase
X	Any character
any other	Any other character is inserted into the template
Y	Only Y or N allowed for logical fields
L	T, F, Y or N allowed for logical fields

dBASE IV CODES FOR SELECTING SCREEN COLORS

Black	=	N or blank	Red	=	R
Blue	=	B	Magenta	=	RB
Green	=	G	Brown	=	GR
Cyan	=	BG	Yellow	=	GR +
Blank	=	X	White	=	W
Gray	=	N +			

dBASE IV SQL COMMAND SUMMARY

Command	**Explanation**
SHOW DATABASE;	List names of all SQL databases.
CREATE DATABASE <dname>;	Create a new database called <dname>. <dname> must be unique.
START DATABASE <dname>;	Activate or open the database called <dname>. Only one database may be active at a time.
CREATE TABLE <tname> (..) ;	Create a table within the active database and provide the structure.
ALTER TABLE <tname> ADD .. ;	Adds a column to the specified table.
INSERT INTO <tname> VALUES .. ;	Insert values into new row in specified table. Values must match columns in data type and length.
INSERT INTO <tname> SELECT .. FROM <tname2>;	Copies values from <tname2> into first table. Can also specify a WHERE condition.
LOAD DATA FROM <file> INTO TABLE <tname>;	Copies data from an existing dBASE file into the specified SQL table. SQL can copy from other file types.
SELECT <columns> FROM <tname>;	Select specified columns from the indicated table. May add WHERE clause to specify conditions for rows to be retrieved.
UPDATE <tname> SET <col>=<expr> WHERE .. ;	Replaces column value in the row(s) specified by the WHERE clause.
DELETE FROM <tname> WHERE .. ;	Deletes row from specified table according to condition in the WHERE clause.
DROP TABLE <tname>;	Deletes specified table from current database. This is a permanent change—all data will be lost.
STOP DATABASE;	Close (de-activate) current database.
DROP DATABASE <dname>;	Deletes specified database permanently.

dBASE IV DOT AND PROGRAMMING COMMANDS

Command	Explanation
@..GET	Programming command for formatted input at specified screen location.
@..SAY	Programming command for formatted output at designated location.
&&	Double ampersand indicates in-line programming comment.
APPEND	Add records to database.
APPEND BLANK	Add a blank record to database.
APPEND FROM	Add record to database from another file.
ASSIST	Activate Control Center menu from dot prompt.
*	Programming command to indicate comment line.
BROWSE	Activate Browse screen with fields displayed across screen.
CALCULATE	Calculate statistical function.
CASE..ENDCASE	Programming command to provide for multiple branching on specified value or condition.
CLEAR	Erase screen.
CONTINUE	Move pointer to next record that matches LOCATE condition.
CREATE	Create a new database file structure.
CREATE FORM	Create a new screen input form.
CREATE REPORT/LABEL	Create a new report or label form.
CREATE QUERY	Create a new QBE query.
DELETE	Mark specified records for deletion.
DISPLAY	Display specified fields from current record.
DO	Programming command to begin execution of a .PRG program.
DO CASE..ENDDO	Programming command that marks the beginning and end of multiple branch loop.
DO WHILE..ENDDO	Programming command that the marks beginning and end of iterative loop of statements.
EDIT	Activate Edit screen with fields from one record displayed down the screen.
EJECT	Cause a form feed to be sent to the printer.
EXPORT TO	Save records in a foreign file format.
GOTO TOP/BOTTOM	Move record pointer to top or bottom of database.
HELP	Activate dBASE IV Help system.

Command	Explanation
IF..ENDIF	Specify condition and statements to be executed if condition is true.
IMPORT FROM	Append records from foreign database or spreadsheet file.
INDEX ON	Create new index tag.
LABEL FORM	Cause specified label form to be printed.
LIST	Display specified fields from records beginning at beginning of file.
LOCATE	Move record pointer to first record that matches specified condition.
MODIFY COMMAND	Edit existing .PRG command file.
MODIFY FORM	Make changes to screen form.
MODIFY QUERY	Make changes to QBE query.
MODIFY REPORT/LABEL	Make changes in report or label form.
MODIFY STRUCTURE	Make changes in the database file structure.
PACK	Permanently erases records marked for deletion.
?	Display contents of named fields from current record.
QUIT	Terminate dBASE IV and return to DOS prompt.
READ	Programming command to read data values from @..IF statements.
RECALL	Removes deletion mark from specified records.
REPORT FORM	Cause specified report form to be printed.
RETURN	Programming command to transfer execution back to calling program.
SEEK	Moves record pointer to first record in index that matches specified condition.
SET ORDER TO	Select a different primary index for current database file.
SET DEVICE	Programming command to select screen or printer for @..SAY output.
SET FILTER	Programming command to activate a specified query condition.
SET FORMAT	Programming command to activate a particular screen form.
SET TALK	Programming command to suppress output from routine (non-printing) commands.
SET VIEW	Programming command to select a QBE query.
SKIP	Move record pointer to another record.
USE	Open new database file with optional index tag as primary index.

Index

Figure Credits

Page 7	Courtesy of Software Publishing
Page 8	Courtesy of Mark Powell, Wordscapes
Page 9 (top)	Courtesy of International Business Machines Corporation
Page 9 (bottom)	Courtesy of Apple Computer, Inc.
Page 10	Courtesy of International Business Machines Corporation
Page 11	Courtesy of INTEL Corporation
Page 12	Courtesy of AST Corporation
Page 13	Courtesy of Paul Hightower
Page 14	Courtesy of Mark Powell, Wordscapes
Page 15	Courtesy of International Business Machines Corporation
Page 16	Courtesy of Maxell Corporation of America
Page 17	Courtesy of Apple Computer, Inc.
Page 18	Courtesy of Paul Hightower
Page 19	Courtesy of International Business Machines Corporation
Page 20	Courtesy of Hewlett-Packard Company
Page 21	Courtesy of Houston Instruments
Page 22	Courtesy of Hayes Microcomputer Products, Inc.
Page 31	Courtesy of Mark Powell, Wordscapes
Page 34	Courtesy of Mark Powell, Wordscapes
Page 322	Courtesy of Paul Hightower

Trademark Credits

PostScript is a registered trademark of Adobe Systems, Inc. Aldus and PageMaker are registered trademarks of the Aldus Corporation. Apple and Apple Macintosh are registered trademarks of Apple Computer, Inc. dBASE II, dBASE III, dBASE IV, MultiMate Advantage, MultiPlan, and Framework are registered trademarks of Ashton-Tate Corporation. Quattro, Paradox, and Quattro Pro are registered trademarks of Borland International, Inc. PCTools is a registered trademark of Central Point Software, Inc. TurboTax is a registered trademark of ChipSoft, Inc. COMPAQ is a registered trademark of COMPAQ Computer Corporation. Procomm and Procomm Plus are registered trademarks of DataStorm Technologies, Inc. Epson is a registered trademark of Epson America, Inc. Allways and Sideways are registered trademarks of Funk Software, Inc. Hayes is a registered trademark of the Hayes Microcomputer Products, Inc. Deskjet, HP, and Laserjet are trademarks of Hewlett-Packard Company. IBM, DisplayWrite, MCA, PC, XT, AT, PM, PS/2, and OS/2 are registered trademarks of International Business Machines, Inc. Lotus, 1-2-3, DIF, Freelance, Symphony, and VisiCalc are registered trademarks of Lotus Development Corporation. Allways and Impress are trademarks of Lotus Development Corporation. Managing Your Money and Managing the Market are registered trademarks of MECA Software, Inc. Excel, Xenix, Word, Works, Windows, and Flight Simulator are trademarks of Microsoft Corporation. @Risk is a registered trademark of Palisade Corporation. VP-Planner is a trademark of Paperback Software International. @Base is a registered trademark of Personics. QEMM and DESQview are registered trademarks of Quarterdeck Office Systems. Harvard Graphics, PFS:First Choice, PFS:Write, Professional Write, Professional File are trademarks of Software Publishing Corporation. Norton Utilities and 4-Word are registered trademarks of Symantec Corporation. WordPerfect, WordPerfect Library, WordPerfect Office, PlanPerfect, and DrawPerfect are registered trademarks of WordPerfect Corporation. WordStar is a registered trademark of the WordStar International Corporation. QuickSilver and dBXL are registered trademarks of WordTech Systems, Inc. Zenith is a registered trademark of Zenith Electronics Corporation.